BYZANTINE PHILOSOPHY
AND ITS ANCIENT SOURCES

Byzantine Philosophy and its Ancient Sources

edited by

KATERINA IERODIAKONOU

CLARENDON PRESS · OXFORD

OXFORD

UNIVERSITY PRESS

Great Clarendon Street, Oxford OX2 6DP
Oxford University Press is a department of the University of Oxford.
It furthers the University's objective of excellence in research, scholarship,
and education by publishing worldwide in

Oxford New York

Auckland Bangkok Buenos Aires Cape Town Chennai
Dar es Salaam Delhi Hong Kong Istanbul Karachi Kolkata
Kuala Lumpur Madrid Melbourne Mexico City Mumbai Nairobi
São Paulo Shanghai Singapore Taipei Tokyo Toronto

with associated company in Berlin

Oxford is a registered trade mark of Oxford University Press
in the UK and in certain other countries

Published in the United States
By Oxford University Press Inc., New York

© the several contributors 2002

The moral rights of the author have been asserted
Database right Oxford University Press (maker)

First published 2002

British Library Cataloguing in Publication Data

Data available

Library of Congress Cataloging in Publication Data
Byzantine philosophy and its ancient sources / edited by Katerina Ierodiakonou.
p. cm.
Includes indexes.
1. Philosophy–Byzantine Empire. I. Ierodiakonou, Katerina.
B722.B97 B98 2002   189–dc21   2001055166
ISBN 0–19–924613–0

1 3 5 7 9 10 8 6 4 2

Typeset by Kolam Information Services Pvt Ltd, Pondicherry, India.
Printed in Great Britain by
T.J. International Ltd., Padstow, Cornwall

CONTENTS

LIST OF CONTRIBUTORS

POLYMNIA ATHANASSIADI, Professor of Ancient History, University of Athens.

JONATHAN BARNES, Professor of Ancient Philosophy, University of Geneva.

LINOS BENAKIS, Director of the series *Corpus Philosophorum Medii Aevi: Philosophi Byzantini*, The Academy of Athens.

BÖRJE BYDÉN, Dr phil., University of Göteborg.

JOHN DUFFY, Professor of Classics, Harvard University.

STEN EBBESEN, Professor of Classics, University of Copenhagen.

MICHAEL FREDE, Professor of the History of Philosophy, University of Oxford.

KATERINA IERODIAKONOU, Assistant Professor of Ancient Philosophy, National Technical University of Athens, and Tutorial Fellow in Philosophy, St Hugh's College, University of Oxford.

PAUL KALLIGAS, Assistant Professor of Ancient Philosophy, University of Athens.

GEORGE KARAMANOLIS, D.Phil., University of Oxford.

DOMINIC O'MEARA, Professor of Philosophy, University of Fribourg.

INTRODUCTION

The title of this volume leaves no doubt as to its main objective; the articles here are meant to shed light on Byzantine philosophy against the background of ancient philosophical thought. The question is whether and in which ways the Byzantines were able to appropriate and to develop the philosophical tradition they had inherited from antiquity. But though ancient philosophy is a rather well-defined area which has been, and still is, extensively studied, it is not clear, at least not to everyone, what 'Byzantine philosophy' refers to, or, indeed, whether there is such a thing. The main aim of my introduction, therefore, is twofold: (i) to discuss briefly what is to be counted as Byzantine philosophy, and (ii) to explain further the purpose as well as the contents of this volume.

I

Byzantine philosophy remains an unknown field. Being regarded either as mere scholars or as religious thinkers, Byzantine philosophers, for the most part, have not been studied on their own merit, and their works have hardly been scrutinized as works of philosophy. Hence, although it is the case that distinguished scholars have in the past tried to reconstruct the intellectual life of the Byzantine period, there is no question that we still lack even the beginnings of a thorough and systematic understanding of the philosophical works produced in Byzantium.

This introduction could not even attempt to remedy the problem and offer a comprehensive overview of Byzantine thought. It does, however, try to introduce some basic features of Byzantine philosophy and to address some of the as yet open, but quite important, issues involved in its study. It should thus also become easier to place in context the specific topics which are discussed in the articles of this volume.

Is there philosophical thinking in Byzantium? Isn't it all theology?

Since theological concerns undoubtedly occupy a prominent place in the works of Byzantine thinkers, the obvious question to ask, and often asked, is hence whether there really is such a thing as Byzantine philosophy in the first place, and whether it makes any sense to talk about the development of philosophical thought in Byzantium. The general tendency among modern scholars is to believe that philosophy in Byzantium did manage to preserve its autonomy, that the borders between philosophy and theology were reasonably clearly defined, and that the view expressed by some Church Fathers (e.g. Clement, Origen) that philosophy is the handmaiden of theology (*philosophia theologiae ancilla*) was not the dominant position in Byzantium, as it was in the medieval West.

To settle the issue, however, more research needs to be done in the following three directions. First, we need to investigate further what the Byzantine scholars themselves have to say about their understanding of philosophy as a discipline and its relation to theology. Second, we need to clarify that it is not peculiar to Byzantine philosophy to have been so closely connected with theology, since philosophers in other periods of the history of philosophy were also strongly focused on theological subjects; after all, in pagan antiquity theology after Aristotle was a philosophical discipline, and in late antiquity it came to be regarded as the most imporant, and most philosophical, part of philosophy. And, third, we need to analyse systematically the writings of Byzantine thinkers to show that their reasoning and argumentation was no less philosophical than the philosophical work of any other period in the history of philosophy.

The contributors to this volume follow, in general, the third direction. Their analysis of a small, but rather representative, selection of Byzantine texts strongly indicates that, although many of the problems with which Byzantine thinkers were concerned did arise in the context of a Christian theological tradition, these problems none the less constitute genuine philosophical issues which could or would be of interest to any philosopher, even if she or he did not believe in Christian dogma. Let me list, as examples, some of the philosophical questions which have caught the attention of Byzantine philosophers and for prolonged periods in the history of Byzantine thought generated intense disputes: the creation or origin of the world, the existence of God, the character of the perceptible world, the problem of evil and human free will, the relation between soul and body, the ontological status of universals, the connection between faith and reason, the sceptical challenge to knowledge, logical fallacies, the necessary requirements for a good life, the possibility of a just state.

These are all recognizably philosophical problems still discussed by modern philosophers. But if we really want to understand and appreciate the philosophical literature in Byzantium, it is important to refrain from just pursuing the questions which we ourselves find philosophically interesting. Instead it would rather be more productive to try to find out which issues exactly were addressed at the time, or in which general frame of reference these issues were examined. This is the only way, I think, to avoid misleading anachronistic interpretations, to adequately determine the relation of Byzantine philosophy to its theological and more generally cultural background, to realize the possible philosophical interest of nowadays neglected issues, and, finally, to acquire a better insight into the development and changes in Byzantine philosophical discourse itself.

Who are the Byzantine philosophers?

Let us suppose, then, that philosophy in Byzantium is an autonomous discipline, and that it is worth our study what the Byzantines achieved in this discipline. The next issue which needs to be considered is how to compile a catalogue of Byzantine philosophers who particularly deserve our attention. To adequately fulfil this task, though, some preliminary questions have to be raised and answered.

When does Byzantine philosophy actually begin?

This is a question familiar to everyone who has, at some point, tried to specify the beginning, or for that matter the end, of any period in the history of philosophy. That is to say, it is not much easier, nor more difficult, to decide when exactly Byzantine philosophy starts, than to agree, for instance, on a particular date for the beginning of Hellenistic philosophy. The criteria which are standardly used to draw such chronological divisions do vary, and hence, not surprisingly, the answers vary too:

1. If one adopted a political hallmark, and let Byzantine history, as many Byzantinists do, start with the foundation of Constantinople, this would mean that Byzantine philosophy starts early in the fourth century.

2. If, on the other hand, one adhered to the view that Justinian's closing of the Neoplatonist Academy in 529 roughly marks the end of ancient philosophy, the beginning of Byzantine philosophy would move from the fourth to the sixth century.

3. Last but not least, if one underlined the significance of the autonomous character of philosophical thought, but also on the basis of a variety of general historical considerations, the starting-point of Byzantine philosophy could move even further down, for example, into the ninth and tenth centuries. This is when Byzantine 'humanists' such as Photios and Arethas start again studiously to read, edit, and comment on the works of ancient philosophers, but also to form their own views on the matters discussed. Photios, for instance, follows neither Plato nor Aristotle in their views on universals, for all the importance he attributes to these authors and the preservation and discussion of their works.

Some of the articles included in this volume focus on philosophically interesting texts from the early period between the fourth and the ninth century. The main reason for this is that, whatever decision one takes as to the beginning of Byzantine philosophy, there is no doubt that the distinctive character of philosophical work after Photios and Arethas owes a lot to the influence of this early period, which undeniably is dominated by the thought of the Church Fathers.

Finally, a brief remark about the end of Byzantine philosophy. It is common practice to think that Byzantine philosophy, and in general Byzantine culture, ends with the fall of Constantinople in 1453. It should be noted, however, that even after this date some Byzantine thinkers, for instance George Scholarios or Bessarion, continued their philosophical work, either having moved to the West or staying in the East under the Ottomans. We also have to remember that, in the East, though often under difficult circumstances, the Byzantine philosophical tradition lived on well into the seventeenth century, if we think, for instance, of Theophilos Korydaleus.

Who counts as a philosopher in Byzantium?

There were in Byzantium no institutions of higher education in which philosophers could be trained as philosophers. The main purpose of institutional higher studies was to train civil servants. Philosophical instruction was mainly private, but it sometimes received support from the Emperor and the Church, as in the case of the so-called 'University of Constantinople' which was founded in 1045 by Constantine Monomachos. Such support, however, also meant occasional intervention by the secular or ecclesiastical authorities, as when John Italos was put on trial and condemned for advocating the systematic use of philosophical analysis in clarifying theological issues. In general, the philosophical curriculum would start with Aristotle's logic and ethics, and advance through physics and the *quadrivium* (arithmetic, geometry, astronomy, and harmonics) to Plato's, or more precisely to Neoplatonic, metaphysics.

Thus, the figure of the Byzantine philosopher emerges as often somewhat of a polymath and an erudite scholar, who, moreover, might make use of his knowledge and rhetorical skill to play an active role in the political life of the times. This portrayal, of course, is not free of oversimplifications. For we do find among Byzantine philosophers the most diverse personalities, with different educational backgrounds and, most importantly, with completely different conceptions of their role as philosophers. In fact, it is, I think, impossible to draw a realistic picture of the figure of the Byzantine philosopher, until we have studied in detail many more texts which provide us with the necessary evidence concerning the philosopher's life and aims in Byzantine times—including, for instance, autobiographies, biographies, letters, orations, and sporadic relevant remarks in the philosophical works themselves.

Some Byzantine philosophers

The following list of Byzantine philosophers includes only some of the major figures in Byzantine philosophy. To be more precise, it includes those Byzantine philosophers whose work up till now has drawn the attention of modern scholars and, especially, those whose work is discussed in the articles of this volume. There are, of course, many Byzantine philosophers who are not included in this list, either because their writings have not been adequately studied, or because they have yet not been identified at all. In this catalogue the names of Byzantine philosophers are given in chronological order. There are no schools of philosophy in Byzantium, at least in the strict sense of the term in which we can distinguish different schools in antiquity and categorize philosophers accordingly. Surely there are groupings of philosophers in Byzantium, too, but our knowledge of Byzantine philosophy so far is not good enough for us to be able to recognize them. Therefore, Byzantine thinkers here are grouped together just on the basis of broad divisions either in the political or in the intellectual history of the Byzantine Empire. I begin with a group of authors usually categorized as Christian Fathers, not because they are Church Fathers, but because at least some of their work is distinctly philosophical.

A. Christian Fathers (4th–8th century)

> Basil the Great (329–79)
> Gregory of Nyssa (335–94)
> Nemesius (4th–5th century)
> Pseudo-Dionysius (end 5th century)
> Procopius of Gaza (460–530)
> Maximus the Confessor (580–662)
> John of Damascus (*c*.650–*c*.749)

B. Byzantine humanism (9th–10th century)

> Leo the Philosopher (the Mathematician) (*c*.790–after 869)
> Photios (820–91)
> Arethas (*c*.850–944)

C. The period of the Comneni (11th–12th century)

> Michael Psellos (1018–78)
> John Italos (*c*.1025–82)
> Theodore of Smyrna (end 11th century)
> Eustratios of Nicaea (*c*.1050–1120)
> Michael of Ephesus (*c*.1050–1129)
> Nicholas of Methone (d. 1165)

D. The empire in Nicaea

Nikephoros Blemmydes (1197–1272)
Theodore II Laskaris (1233–58)
Manuel Holobolos (fl. 1267)

E. The Palaeologan period (13th–15th century)

George Pachymeres (1242–1310)
Maximos Planoudes (*c*.1255–*c*.1305)
Leo Magentinos (13th century)
Theodore Metochites (1270–1332)
John Pediasimos (d. 1341)
Joseph Philagrios (end 14th century)
John Chortasmenos (1370–1436)
Barlaam of Calabria (*c*.1290–1348)
Nikephoros Gregoras (1290/3–1358/61)
Gregory Palamas (*c*.1296–1359)
Gregory Akindynos (*c*.1300–48)
Nicholas Kabasilas (d. 1371)
Demetrios Kydones (*c*.1324–97/8)
Prochoros Kydones (*c*.1333–69/70)
George Gemistos Plethon (*c*.1360–*c*.1453)
George Trapezountios (1395–1472)
Theodore Gazes (1400–76/8)
Andronikos Kallistos (1400–86)
George Scholarios Gennadios (*c*.1400–72/4)
Bessarion (1403–72)
Michael Apostoles (1420–80)

How could one study the works of Byzantine philosophers?

The genres of philosophical writing in Byzantium are quite diverse. For teaching purposes the Byzantine scholars produced marginal notes and explanatory paraphrases on ancient philosophical works, but also extended commentaries, sometimes in question-and-answer form, small handbooks, and more detailed companions. They also wrote small treatises on specific topics, or longer works, occasionally in dialogue form, with the aim to rebut the views of their opponents and to explain or defend their own theories. To all these, we should further add their letters and orations which frequently have philosophical content.

Most of the writings of Byzantine philosophers are still unpublished or are available only in old and often quite imperfect editions. But even when we do have reliable editions of the philosophical works of Byzantine thinkers, their philosophical contribution for the most part still needs to be critically assessed. For although eminent scholars of the nineteenth and early twentieth century worked with great care on some Byzantine philosophical texts, their interest was not primarily philosophical; they rather were trying to preserve every aspect of the Byzantine intellectual heritage and, at the most, to grasp, in historical terms, how the work of Byzantine philosophers reflected the society in which they lived. On the other hand, the philosophers of the nineteenth and early twentieth century understandably were discouraged both by the rhetorical style of the Byzantine writings and by the theological interests displayed in much of Byzantine philosophy. In addition to all this, the strong general prejudice that the Middle Ages, especially in the early period and in the Byzantine East, were the dark ages of human civilization, makes it even easier to understand why Byzantine philosophy was neglected.

After the Second World War, however, there is a significant change in the study of Byzantine philosophy, clearly connected with the rediscovery and the startling changes in the appraisal of the Western medieval philosophical tradition as well as of certain areas in ancient philosophy, for instance the philosophy of Hellenistic times and of late antiquity. During the second part of the twentieth century, in general, the study of the early history of philosophy was transformed in two respects: (i) new ways of interpreting the works of ancient and medieval philosophers were introduced, and (ii) certain areas in ancient and medieval philosophy which before had been completely neglected or marginalized were brought to the centre of scholarly attention. The philosophers and scholars who studied ancient and medieval philosophy made an attempt gradually to free themselves from earlier preconceptions and prejudices. To begin with, they insisted on taking the theories and arguments of ancient and medieval philosophers philosophically seriously; their writings were no longer simply studied as works of the past of mainly antiquarian or historical interest, but rather were studied as philosophical works on their own merit.

This new approach to the early stages of the history of philosophy has opened, I think, the path to a reassessment also of the writings of Byzantine thinkers. In fact, during the last decades of the twentieth century some of the treatises of Byzantine philosophers were published for the first time, or came out in better, critical, editions; several books and numerous articles began to be written concerning particular topics in Byzantine philosophy; interdisciplinary workshops and symposia were organized to discuss the general intellectual development in Byzantium and, as part of this, also touched on Byzantine philosophy. One gets some idea of this more recent development, if one looks at the following sample (in chronological order) of some general surveys and bibliographies which were produced in this period:

Tatakis, B. N. (1949), *La Philosophie byzantine* (Paris).
Oehler, K. (1969), *Antike Philosophie und byzantinisches Mittelalter* (Munich).
Lemerle, P. (1971), *Le Premier Humanisme byzantin* (Paris).
Podskalsky, G. (1977), *Theologie und Philosophie in Byzanz* (Munich).

Hunger, H. (1978), 'Philosophie', in his *Die hochsprachliche profane Literatur der Byzantiner*, i (Munich), 3–62.

Wilson, N. G. (1983), *Scholars of Byzantium* (London).

Benakis, L. (1987), 'Grundbibliographie zum Aristoteles-Studium in Byzanz', in J. Wiesner (ed.), *Aristoteles: Werk und Wirkung. Paul Moraux gewidmet* (Berlin and New York), 352–79.

——(1988), 'Commentaries and Commentators on the Logical Works of Aristotle in Byzantium', in R. Claussen and R. Daube-Schackat (eds.), *Gedankenzeichen. Festschrift für Klaus Oehler* (Tübingen), 3–12.

——(1991*a*), 'Commentaries and Commentators on the Works of Aristotle (Except the Logical Ones) in Byzantium', in B. Mojsisch and O. Pluta (eds.), *Historia Philosophiae Medii Aevi: Festschrift für Kurt Flasch* (Amsterdam), 45–54.

——(1991*b*), 'Bibliographie internationale sur la philosophie byzantine (1949–1990)', in *Bibliographie byzantine publié à l'occasion du XVIIIe Congrès Internationale d'Études Byzantines* (Athens), 319–77.

Of course, some of these works are already outdated again, since current research has come to question the views expressed in them, and more books and articles have been published in the last decade. Still, this short bibliography can at least serve as a first guide to a preliminary study of Byzantine philosophy; the general surveys and the bibliographical material which it includes provide valuable information for anyone who is interested in finding out where to look for the texts themselves and which books and articles to consult on specialized topics.

But most of the work still remains to be done, if we are to be able to understand and evaluate the distinctive character of Byzantine philosophy. Following the rising interest of the last decades, it now seems important to encourage further the systematic study and critical assessment of the original contributions of Byzantine philosophers. What we still need to do is to take their works seriously as philosophical writings; putting aside our prejudices and misconceptions, we need to make a renewed effort to reconstruct and to do justice to Byzantine philosophy. This volume was conceived as at least a concerted attempt in this direction.

II

This volume, in fact, grew out of some of the papers read and discussed at a conference in Thessaloniki in 1997, which also had been devoted to Byzantine philosophy and its relation to ancient philosophical thought. It was guided by the thought that, if it is our aim to recover and rethink Byzantine philosophy, it also is crucial to examine in detail the influence of earlier philosophical traditions on Byzantine philosophers. What is more, Byzantium's dependence in philosophy on its ancient heritage manifestly is an area of study which, in particular comparison with other aspects of Byzantine civilization, like the indebtedness of Byzantine to ancient art, has hardly received any attention. However, there is no doubt that it is the Byzantines who copied, studied, commented on, and taught the texts of ancient philosophers, and that it is mainly because of their efforts that the philosophical traditions of antiquity were transmitted and kept alive.

Investigating the ancient sources of Byzantine philosophy, we perhaps first should find out what the Byzantines themselves have to say about ancient philosophy, or, as they characteristically call it in contrast to Christian theology, 'the wisdom from without'. It soon becomes clear that Byzantine thinkers are by no means unanimous as to the importance of ancient philosophy; their views greatly differ on this matter. Some, under the influence of St Paul and authors like Tatian, consider ancient philosophy as useless or even dangerous, because it corrupts the Christian view of things and leads to heresies. Others, in particular Basil the Great and Gregory of Nyssa, claim that ancient philosophy, if used in a cautious and careful way, could be a preparation for the true faith, help in its elucidation, and serve as a dialectical weapon against heresies. After all, Pantaenus and Justin the Martyr had been philosophers. Clement of Alexandria clearly had been heavily influenced by Stoicism and Platonism. Origen had even taught philosophy to his students, and had gained a reputation as a philosopher, though precisely Origen's example, once his orthodoxy had become suspect, fuelled questions about the usefulness of ancient philosophy. Finally, Byzantine philosophers, like John Italos and Barlaam of Calabria, undertake the task, in some cases at high personal cost, to defend ancient philosophy in its own right, but also as a means for a better understanding of Christian dogma.

Such conflicting attitudes towards ancient philosophy usually depended on whether the aim of the Byzantine author was to clarify certain philosophical issues, or to rebut the pagans, or write against the heretics, or explain Christian dogmas, but also on the knowledge of ancient philosophy which at the time was available to the particular Byzantine thinker. In general, Byzantine philosophers had some direct knowledge of the works of ancient philosophers. They certainly had access to most of the major ancient texts we still have, and the continuity of the Greek language, of course, made it possible for them to study the ancients in the original. To take the obvious case of Plato's and Aristotle's works, at least a thousand Byzantine manuscripts have survived which either preserve Aristotle's text, or in addition also comment on it; in Plato's case there are more than 260 Byzantine manuscripts of his dialogues. Nevertheless, although all of Plato and Aristotle was in principle available, certainly in centres like Constantinople, Trebizond, Thessaloniki, and Mystras, in practice only some works were commonly read; for instance, the works of Aristotle which were widely read during Byzantine times were the *Categories*, the *De interpretatione*, the *Analytics*, the *Physics*, and the *Nicomachean Ethics*.

It is not by accident, of course, that the Byzantines had a preference for certain ancient philosophers, or even for certain works of these philosophers.

Indeed, they were quite selective and generally chose only those ancient philosophical texts which they regarded as compatible with their Christian faith. Thus, they taught Aristotle's logic as generally useful or as a preparation for more theoretical studies; but they disagreed with him on his theory of the eternity of the world or his understanding of God as the first unmoved mover who moves the heaven, but exerts no providence for individual human beings. Byzantine philosophers consider Plato's metaphysics to be closer to the Christian world-view, especially on issues like, for instance, the immortality of the soul and the creation of the world; still, though, for doctrinal reasons they cannot accept the Platonic theory of metempsychosis or the existence of eternal ideas or forms. Hence, Byzantine philosophers follow the eclectic tradition of later antiquity and combine aspects of Plato's and Aristotle's theories, at least up until the fifteenth century, when they start contrasting them and believe that they need to take sides, presenting themselves either as Platonists or as Aristotelians. Important though it may be, the influence of Plato and of Aristotle is not the only one which shapes Byzantine philosophical thought. For it is crucial here to keep in mind that the Byzantines also engage in a limited dialogue with the other schools of ancient philosophy. For instance, they are interested in criticizing or appropriating elements from the doctrines of the Epicureans and the Stoics, but in particular of the Neoplatonists, and they examine the implications of the Sceptics' views on the possibility of human knowledge.

But whatever attitude the Byzantines took towards ancient philosophy, and whatever the specific ancient sources which they relied on to form their theories, one thing is certain; it was impossible for Byzantine philosophers to escape altogether from the influence of ancient philosophy. For it was ancient philosophy which provided them with a well-articulated theoretical framework and with the philosophical language which had to serve as the basis for their own philosophical discourse. But does this mean that the Byzantines merely copied ancient philosophers, and hence that their philosophical writings altogether lacked originality? Do Byzantine philosophers interpret ancient philophical theories always in the same way, the way they had already been interpreted in late antiquity? Does Byzantine philosophy as a whole lack a distinctive character which differentiates it from the previous periods in the history of philosophy? Such general questions concerning the relation between ancient and Byzantine philosophy are constantly in the background of the articles of this volume. There is no doubt that these questions still remain open, but I think that the contributors to this volume manage to address some of them in the only way they at this point can be addressed, namely by thoroughly investigating particular topics which give us some insight as to the directions in which we should look for possible answers.

This volume contains eleven articles, mainly written by established scholars, but also by scholars belonging to the younger generation. They represent different disciplines, such as philosophy, history, classics, and medieval or Byzantine studies. The particular topics which they discuss range, in modern terms, from philosophy of language, theory of knowledge, and logic to political philosophy, ethics, natural philosophy, and metaphysics. As to the philosophers whose works our contributors study, they belong to all periods from the beginnings of Byzantine culture in the fourth century to the demise of the Byzantine Empire in the fifteenth century. In fact, the wide range of authors and texts which this volume covers becomes obvious when one just looks at the extensive indexes of names and of passages at the end of the volume. Perhaps the reader is introduced here, for the first time, to some Byzantine authors or to some of their writings. Most Byzantine philosophers definitely are not household names, not even among philosophers. So little attention has been given to their philosophical works that we do not even know whether they deserve to become a standard part of philosophical literature. This general unfamiliarity is reflected by the fact that there is not even a standard way in contemporary scholarship of rendering their Greek names. Thus, to further guide the reader in his or her attempt to learn more about these more or less unknown Byzantine philosophers as well as about the more familiar ones, we have added an epilogue in which Linos Benakis presents the most recent publications on Byzantine philosophy; these include the new critical editions of Byzantine philosophical texts, the introductory surveys of Byzantine philosophy, the up-to-date bibliographies, the entries in recently published dictionaries or encyclopedias, and the new journals which specialize on Byzantium.

The main contents of the volume are these. The first article by Sten Ebbesen raises the more general issue of the relation, or rather, it turns out, the lack of relation, between Byzantine philosophy and the West. It discusses the different paths which the Byzantines and the Western medieval philosophers took, especially in connection with their reliance on ancient philosophy. The second article closely examines a particular philosophical topic which occupied Basil the Great, namely whether proper names only designate substances or have a descriptive content. Paul Kalligas's treatment of the subject refers to the views both of ancient and of modern philosophers, in order to discover and elucidate the new elements which Basil brings into the ancient discussion. From the fourth-century philosophy of language we next move to the sixth century and to political philosophy in Dominic O'Meara's systematic analysis of an anonymous dialogue of the Justinian period, namely 'On Political Science'. The author of this dialogue, being concerned with the political problems of his time, suggests a new constitutional order; he seems to be very much influenced by Neoplatonism and by his own interpretation of the problems arising out of Plato's political philosophy. The last article on the early period focuses on John of Damascus in the eighth century, and in particular on his attempt to integrate a notion of a will into Aristotle's moral psychology and theory of action. The problem here is to explain why God would create human beings if they sooner or later would sin, but also to get a better grasp of the process of how we come to make a choice. According to Michael Frede, John's account of human freedom is quite novel in some ways, and this novelty had an important impact on Thomas Aquinas, and thus on the further development of thought about the will in traditional western philosophy.

Next, we turn to the eleventh century, and to an anonymous logical text which here for the first time is analysed in detail by Jonathan Barnes. Although this is an elementary handbook of logic written mainly in the Peripatetic tradition, it includes interesting divergences, like for instance the discussion of syllogisms with singular propositions, which show that logic in Byzantium had an interesting further development, though firmly based on Aristotle and the Stoics. John Duffy's article turns our attention to perhaps the central figure of Byzantine philosophy, namely Michael Psellos. The specific subject which concerns him is the status of philosophical discourse in Byzantium from the middle of the ninth century to the appearance of Psellos around 1040. He argues that there is a significant development from the rather humanistic character of Photios' and Arethas' interests to the way Psellos views the philosopher as someone with a hard-earned and unsurpassed knowledge in all branches of learning, and especially in the philosophy of the ancients. My article gives an example of Psellos' own knowledge and appropriation of the ancient philosophical traditions. I closely study his paraphrasis on Aristotle's *De interpretatione*, and try to show that, although Psellos' main aim is to promote a knowledge of Aristotle's logic, he also does express his own logical views, some of which originate in his attempt to reconcile the Christian tradition with the ancient philosophers.

The Palaeologan period is first represented by Theodore Metochites, and in particular by Börje Bydén's edition of and philosophical commentary on one of his shorter philosophical treatises, namely *Semeiosis* 61. In this text we find Metochites' account of ancient Scepticism, in which he attempts to present it not as the perverse cultivation of argument for argument's sake, and to vindicate it as the reasonable view that there exist things of which knowledge is impossible. My article also tries to shed light on some of the works of three Byzantine philosophers of the fourteenth century, namely Nikephoros Gregoras, Barlaam of Calabria, and Gregory Palamas. The issue here is the debate about the significance and use of Aristotelian syllogistic. Although Gregoras adopts an entirely negative attitude, Barlaam and Palamas disagree as to the limits of the use of logical reasoning in our attempt to understand God and his attributes. Their arguments and counter-arguments raise interesting questions as to the nature of demonstration and the connection between faith and reason. Polymnia Athanassiadi compares Michael Psellos and George Gemistos Plethon, another particularly important Byzantine philosopher, and like Psellos of an unusually independent mind. She considers their collections of the Chaldaean Oracles, which in her view from Iamblichus onwards served the Neoplatonists as the holy book *par excel-*

lence. Psellos and Plethon give us a substantially different interpretation of these texts; whereas Psellos directly follows the Neoplatonists in interpreting the Chaldaean Oracles in their own context, Plethon's account uses them as a companion to a new philosophical theology. George Karamanolis contrasts the work of Plethon with that of yet another major Byzantine author, namely George Scholarios Gennadios. In his article the general issue is the fifteenth-century controversy over the primacy of Plato or Aristotle, a controversy which is not so much about how Aristotle's philosophy compares with Plato's, but rather about which philosophical authority comes closer to Christian doctrine. To better illustrate the philosophical reasons presented by Plethon and Scholarios, the discussion here focuses on two particular topics, namely Aristotle's view about the world's constitution and the nature of the human soul.

If these articles persuade the reader that Byzantine philosophy is worth investigating, this volume has achieved its aim. Needless to say, most of the questions concerning either the general character of Byzantine philosophy or the specific doctrines of particular Byzantine philosophers cannot be settled here. We rather hope that this attempt will be found to be inviting and promising enough for others to join us in the study of Byzantine philosophy. Only in this way will we manage to completely bridge the gap between ancient philosophy and early modern philosophy. In this connection we have to keep in mind the profound impact Byzantine scholars and philosophers of the fifteenth century had on the revival of Platonic studies and Platonism in the Renaissance in the West.

I would like to close this introduction by acknowledging the help I have received in completing this project. I would like to thank all those who organized and participated in the conference in Thessaloniki, especially V. Kotzia-Panteli and S. Kotzabassi; I also thank Myles Burnyeat and Richard Sorabji who read the first draft of this volume, and made invaluable comments not only on particular articles, but also on its composition as a whole; Oxford University Press, and in particular Peter Momtchiloff who took the risk of publishing a collection of articles on as unusual a subject as Byzantine philosophy; finally, Michael Frede for his constant encouragement, but mainly for his unwavering conviction that Byzantine philosophers can be a pleasure to read and study, any time and any place.

Greek–Latin Philosophical Interaction

STEN EBBESEN

Introduction

In antiquity Europe was divided into a Greek and a Latin zone of influence. The limits of the Greek zone had been established about 300 BC. In the eastern Mediterranean Greek was the language of all central and much local administration, and it functioned as a lingua franca for all sorts of purposes. The Roman conquest changed nothing in that regard: it just put a wafer-thin layer of Latin administration on top of the Greek, and after less than a millennium that thin layer had worn off. But in the West, which prior to the advent of the Roman legions had no international language of administration, commerce, and higher culture, Latin filled the vacuum and obtained the role that Greek had in the East.

It makes sense to see a lot of European history, political and cultural alike, as a meeting between two cultures defined by the use of the Greek and the Latin language, respectively. This is the perspective that I now want to apply to the history of philosophy.[1] But it is only in a very long perspective that we can talk about the Greek and the Latin cultures as entities of the same rank. For most of history one of them has been dominant.

There was the time when the Latin world was in most matters at the receiving end. While avidly absorbing as much Greek culture as they possibly could, Romans like Cato the Elder would stiffen their sagging self-esteem by calling Greeks *Græculi* and extolling the superior virtues of *mos maiorum*. There came a time when the Greek world was in most matters at the receiving

---

[1] Proper documentation of the claims made in this article would require a book-length bibliography. References in the footnotes below will generally regard lesser known/accessible scholarly works and/or details rather than broad issues. Some general help, especially on the medieval Latin material, may be found in Kretzmann *et al.* (1982); Dronke (1988); De Libera (1993); Ebbesen (1995). I have compared certain aspects of the Byzantine and Latin traditions in Ebbesen (1992, 1996*a*).

end, and many Greeks would try to preserve their self-respect by pretending that this was not so; after all, the Latins were barbarians.

Such attitudes are not really helpful for anyone. People who realize that another culture has in some fields something better than their own are worthy of praise, especially if they actively do something to give other members of their linguistic community access to the foreign ways of thought through translations. Cicero is well spoken of for his role in transmitting Greek thought to the West. It might be time to honour those persons with a background in Greek culture who understood that they had something to learn from the Latins when that time arrived. Though less influential, George Scholarios deserves a place beside Cicero.

Stages of Latin Reception of Greek Philosophy

The main stages of the Latin reception of Greek philosophy are well known from current histories of philosophy. Nevertheless, let me repeat the story. The Greek influence came in five waves.

The first wave

In the first century BC Cicero, Varro, and Lucretius made a major effort to make Greek philosophical thought available in Latin. Their work was followed up by Seneca in the first century of the Christian era.

This first wave is characterized by the educative purpose—the purpose is to educate the a-philosophical Latin world. Especially in the Ciceronian age the Roman authors themselves think of the Latin world as purely receptive: it is a passive intellect, a *tabula rasa*, that must receive the imprint of the Greek agent intellect. Another characteristic of the first wave is the virtual absence of translations. Except for Cicero's translation of a major part of Plato's *Timæus* no text by any of the famous philosophers was translated—nor, for that matter, was any text by a second-rate thinker. What we find are popularizing accounts of Greek philosophy with liberal loans from Greek primary and secondary literature.

Greek culture was indisputably dominant at the time. The Greek lands had had a tradition for having professional philosophers since the fourth century BC. By 161 BC the philosophers had reached Rome—we know that because in that year a decree of the senate was needed to expel them from the city.[2]

The interest with which the upper echelons of Roman society greeted the famous philosophers' embassy some five years later might seem to indicate that Rome was ready to receive philosophical culture, create a class of Latin philosophers, and perhaps one day be able to rival the Greeks. Gellius tells us

---

[2] Gellius, *Noctes Atticae* 15. 11. 1; Suetonius, *De grammaticis et rhetoribus* 25. 1 = *De rhetoribus* 1. 1.

that the three 'philosophers—Carneades from the Academy, the Stoic Diogenes and the Peripatetic Critolaus—used the senator C. Acilius as an interpreter when they appeared in the senate, but before that happened they each gave separate presentation talks, drawing a numerous public'.[3] It is characteristic of the episode that in the senate the Greeks must have their speeches translated into the language of the political masters, but outside the senate the representatives of the dominant culture could perform in their own language and be understood by representatives of the subservient culture—including, no doubt, several senators who a short time afterwards would insist on the use of an interpreter in the senate.

The first wave did not create an innovative Latin-language philosophical tradition, nor even a noticeable tradition for non-innovative philosophical works in Latin. For centuries Greek continued to hold a monopoly as the language of learning. Romans with philosophical interest, such as Musonius Rufus and Marcus Aurelius, would tend to express themselves in Greek. The only known victim of the Emperor Domitian's expulsion of philosophers from Rome and all of Italy was a Greek, Epictetus.[4]

The long-term importance of the first wave lay primarily in its demonstration that it is possible to talk about philosophical matters in Latin. Cicero and his contemporaries did for Latin what Nicole Oresme and other fourteenth-century figures were to do for the Western vernaculars: they prepared the ground for the day when the monopoly of the one learned language would be broken.

Secondly, the first wave made elements of Greek ethics, Stoic ethics in particular, a part of any educated man's intellectual baggage. Cicero and Seneca made access to that part of education independent of a mastery of Greek. Ambrose and other Church Fathers had a good deal of Stoic ethics in their baggage. This was to be important in the Latin Middle Ages.

The second wave

This lasted from about 350 till 525.[5] It was actually a very composite wave, but let me separate just three main components. First, there were translations and adaptations of the Aristotelian *Organon* and related works. The best known, and for posterity by far the most important translator and adapter, was Boethius (consul in 510), who clearly saw himself as a second Cicero, bringing Greek philosophy to Latium.

---

[3] Gellius, *Noctes Atticae* 6. 14. 9.

[4] Gellius, *Noctes Atticae* 15. 11. 5: 'Qua tempestate Epictetus quoque philosophus propter id senatusconsultum Nicopolim Roma decessit.' Epictetus, *Dissertationes* 3. 8. 7, mentions one Italicus, whom he describes as the closest thing to a philosopher among the Romans (Ἰταλικὸς ὁ μάλιστα δοκῶν αὐτῶν—sc. τῶν Ῥωμαίων—φιλόσοφος εἶναι). This man may have been a native victim of Domitian's persecution.

[5] I put the beginning *c.*350 in order to be able to include such persons as Vettius Praetextatus and Marius Victorinus; 525 is the approximate year of Boethius' death.

The second component was the composition of a comprehensive scientific grammar of Latin by Priscian in Constantinople shortly after the year 500. The grammatical theory explicitly and implicitly taught by Priscian is almost totally derived from the works of Apollonius Dyscolus, an Alexandrian Greek from the second century AD. In Priscian's case it seems pretty obvious that it was his appointment to a job as teacher of Latin on a high level in Constantinople that occasioned the adoption of Greek theory. In late antiquity Constantinopolitan culture was Greek–Latin bilingual to an extent never seen anywhere before or since. Interestingly, the same Flavius Theodorus Dionisii who in 527 produced a copy of Priscian's *Institutiones grammaticae* was also responsible for a copy of Boethius' logical opuscula. Flavius Theodorus worked in Constantinople.[6]

The third component was the introduction of Neoplatonizing thought. The main medium was theological writings, and Augustine (354–430) overshadows all others.

Boethius and the other translators were not themselves philosophically innovative, and their work was little noticed by their contemporaries; it was centuries before the Latin world reaped the fruits of their toil in the shape of philosophical innovation. The same may be said about Priscian's grammar. Augustine was both a mediator and an innovator, and though it was to be a long time before he got worthy successors, he did start a living tradition of philosophizing theology in Latin.

The third wave

After a couple of genuinely dark centuries higher education began its comeback in the West in the days of Charlemagne. About the end of the tenth century the movement was beginning to pick up speed; a boom in higher education was starting, a boom that has lasted ever since. About this time the third Greek wave arrived. Not through new translations but because Boethius' Greek-inspired works and his translations of the *Ars Vetus* began to acquire a status as standard texts in higher education. The *Ars Vetus* is the truncated *Organon* that consists of Porphyry's *Isagoge*, and Aristotle's *Categories* and *De interpretatione*. The resuscitation of Boethius was soon followed by that of his contemporary Priscian.[7]

In the course of the tenth, eleventh, and early twelfth centuries a distinctive native Latin tradition grew up on soil fertilized with ancient Greek philosophy. It was scholastic in the same way that Greek philosophy had been at least since the second century AD, that is, in the sense that the foundation of teaching and discussion was a small set of authoritative books. The *Ars Vetus*, Boethius' logical monographs and Priscian's grammar were the central

---

[6] See Obertello (1974: i. 347–8).

[7] For the introduction of Boethius' works in the medieval schools, see Van de Vyver (1929); for Priscian, see Kneepkens (1995).

texts in the young Western scholasticism, but there were numerous other sources of inspiration. The key texts all contained Greek theory, but it was not a doctrinally uniform set of texts and the blend was different from that available in the Eastern empire.

The resulting native tradition of Latin philosophy had the following characteristics:

1. It was analytic. Painstaking analysis of propositions and concepts, of sentences and terms, dogged attempts to clarify the relationships between words, concepts, and extramental realities—that is what we find.

2. It was linguistic, both in the sense that there was an intense interest in the philosophy of language and in the sense that without copying grammar it relied heavily on grammatical research for its analytical tools and procedures.

3. It was logical in the sense that one of the favourite occupations of philosophers consisted in formulating logical rules and in exploring how well both new and traditional rules performed in extreme conditions. It was also logical in the sense that philosophers made an extraordinary effort to lay bare the structure both of their own argumentation and of that of their opponents.

4. It was imaginative. People would think up strange sentences and set up strange thought experiments to test hypotheses. While respectful towards the classics, men felt no fear of going beyond the ancients. They would talk about the ancients as giants on whose shoulders they were sitting, but an important point of the simile is that from that position they could see further than the ancients themselves.

5. From an early date there was a consciousness of philosophy being a different enterprise from theology, even if the difference was not institutionalized till the late twelfth or early thirteenth century. At the same time, however, there was a broad acceptance of the use of philosophical method in theology and a feedback resulting in the adoption in philosophical contexts of certain questions first raised and of certain conceptual tools first developed in theology. Theological irrationalists of the brand of Bernard of Clairvaux (*c*.1090–1153) had very limited success.

The philosophy that resulted from the third wave of Greek influence reached maturity in the twelfth century with people like Peter Abelard (1079–1142), Alberic of Paris, Adam Balsham Parvipontanus, and Gilbert of Poitiers (= Gilbertus Porretanus, d. 1154). I shall give a couple of examples of how they worked.

Perhaps the best known part of Abelard's work is his thoughts about signification and universals.[8] Wrestling with a problem whose roots in Porphyry and further back in ancient Greek philosophy are clear for everyone to see, and armed with both Aristotle's hierarchy of genera and species and his

---

[8] For an introduction to Abelard and references to further literature, see Marenbon (1997). For the problem of universals, see De Libera (1996).

flow-chart of signification in the *De interpretatione*, further with the Porphyr-ian notion of words of the second imposition—metalinguistic words, names of names—plus a few other things, Abelard and some near-contemporaries created a nominalism the like of which the world had not seen before: a genuine, and pretty coherent, nominalism. A new quasi-entity, the circum-stance (*status*) of being a man, was introduced to serve as that which is shared by the individuals picked out by a common term like 'man', while the word qua significative was distinguished from the word qua merely phonetically shaped. Another quasi-entity, the *dictum propositionis*, or *enuntiabile*, was introduced to be what propositions signify.[9]

Never since the days of Chrysippus in the third century BC had signification been so thoroughly analysed. And rarely since his days had philosophers advertised their views in such provocative ways. Each of the philosophical schools of the twelfth century had a list of paradoxical tenets, as outrageous as the Stoic paradoxes ('Only a sage is a rich man', etc.). To take just one example: the nominalists defended the thesis that nothing grows. A blatant falsehood! But if anyone was sufficiently intrigued to ask a nominalist what on earth he might mean by proclaiming such nonsense, the nominalist would introduce him to a problem about identity. The nominalists reasoned as follows: a thing equals the sum of its parts, growth is an addition of parts, consequently the result of growth is a different thing from the old one. This line of argument destroys the identity between a teenager and a full-grown man. To repair the damage done by their own argument, the nominalists used the notion of a person: a person (*persona*) can grow while preserving his identity, but he becomes a new thing (*essentia*).

Abelard's *Ethics* is a masterpiece of conceptual analysis resulting in the thesis that we need all the concepts of vicious disposition, of will to do wrong, and of wrong done, but none of the three can be the decisive criterion for the morally evil. The primary bearer of moral predicates is the agent's intention, his conscious acceptance of acting in some way. Abelard eliminates various plausible candidates for being the primary bearer of moral predicates by means of counter-examples. He could be quite imaginative in devising such examples. Thus in a subargument for the thesis that the agent's intention is decisive for the moral character of an act he asks if it can really be true that sexual pleasure is unconditionally evil, and he conjures up the picture of a religious who is bound in chains and placed in a bed with women. Suppose, he says, that the combination of the soft bed and his contact with the women brings him to pleasure, though not to consent, who will presume to call this pleasure, which comes by natural necessity, a fault?[10]

Abelard's conceptual apparatus for ethics has ancient roots, Greek roots, Stoic roots in particular. In spite of the special Christian colouring of his

---

[9] For 12th-cent. nominalism, see Courtenay (1992).
[10] Abelard, *Ethica*, ed. Luscombe, 20.

peccatum, the connection to the Stoic ἁμάρτημα is easily seen. There is some tortuous historical path connecting his *consensus* with the Stoic συγκατάθεσις. The Abelardian thought experiment in his *Ethics* is a counter-example against a very specific thesis. One branch of twelfth-century logic aimed at developing techniques for finding a counter-argument (*instantia*) against just any possible argument![11]

Pure logic was intensely cultivated, but I will not exemplify, because of limited space. Let me just mention a new branch of logic that began to appear in the twelfth century: the logic of 'syncategorematic' words, that is, words that neither have nor purport to have referents. The syncategoremata studied included the traditional 'logical words'—quantifiers (*omnis, quidam, nullus*), the negation *non*, and modal operators (*necessario* etc.)—but also such words as 'whether', 'both', 'except', 'only' (*an, uterque, praeter, tantum*) and many more as well.[12] The inspiration was partly drawn from Priscian's analyses of conjunctions and prepositions (and via him we may see a connection back to the Stoics), partly from the challenge posed by certain theological propositions.

By the twelfth century Latin philosophy, while owing an immense debt to Greek thought, had become emancipated and had moved from home to settle in Paris. She was the intelligent daughter of an intelligent mother; she revered her mother but she did much more than just copy her.

The question is: how was her mother doing? The shortest answer is: she was growing old. About the year 600 she had abandoned her Alexandrian residence to move permanently to Constantinople, which was an old people's home of the sort that intermittently lavishes care on its occupants, while all but forgetting them in the periods in between. She had until now learnt nothing from her daughter, but she could be excused for not doing so. There really was nothing of importance to learn. And if the Byzantine world had failed to build strong philosophical milieux that could survive the death of a master or temporary imperial indifference to the economic well-being of philosophers, the situation had not been much different in the West. But on Christmas night 1100 the alarm bells ought to have rung in Constantinople. It was time Ma started to listen to her daughter.

She didn't. Apparently, Greek intellectuals continued to believe theirs was the dominant culture, though Greek had been steadily losing terrain as a language of higher culture since the seventh century. Constantinople and Thessaloniki were the only important centres left, and the geographical area from which they could recruit new learned men had become severely restricted. Meanwhile Latin had spread over the whole of Central and Northern Europe. Schools in France or Italy could begin to recruit their students from as far away as Scandinavia, and they could benefit from the structure of

---

[11] See Iwakuma (1987).

[12] For an introduction to the lore of *syncategoremata*, see Kretzmann (1982).

Western society with its stable clerical authorities besides the more fickle secular ones.

By 1100 the Latin world was becoming a major producer of intellectual goods. Yet, to the best of my knowledge, there is no sign that anyone in Byzantium started to learn Latin to see what new discoveries their Western colleagues might have made. Paradoxically, at the same time, the Latin world was heading for the fourth wave of Greek influence.

The fourth wave

The formative phase of Latin scholasticism had drawn inspiration from a great many Greek sources, but Aristotle and the tradition of Aristotelian exegesis shaped the Western school tradition more than anything else. So when things really started to move fast in the twelfth century the natural thing for the Latins was to go looking for more Aristotle and more Aristotelian exegesis. And for the first time for 600 years they got into contact with living Greek intellectuals.[13]

Just as the Latin lands had started a return to learning and philosophy about 800, so had Byzantium, and just as the Latins were looking for more Aristotle in the early twelfth century, so were some Greeks. In principle, all of Aristotle was available in Constantinople, but in practice this was not the case except for a few commonly read works. Even if one could lay hands on a copy of the Stagirite's own text of the *Topics* or the *Metaphysics*, this was of little use if there was no commentary to dispel the mists of his famous obscurity.

With financial support, it seems, from Anna Comnena, Eustratios of Nicaea and Michael of Ephesus did a tremendous work in completing fragmentary commentaries handed down from antiquity and writing entirely new ones on works for which there was not even a fragmentary one from ancient days. Michael was still working on the project when one day, perhaps in the 1120s or 1130s, a stranger knocked at his door. The visitor was called James, an unusual man with one foot in the Latin and another in the Greek world. He was a Venetian, but also a Greek. He styled himself *Jacobus Veneticus Grecus*. In a public dispute about the procession of the Holy Ghost that took place in Constantinople in 1136 he was a member of the Latin delegation. At another time we find him in Italy.[14]

---

[13] There may have been some contacts in the 9th cent. John Scot Eurigena, the translator of Pseudo-Dionysius the Areopagite, is likely to have acquired his mastery of Greek with the help of Grecophone visitors to France, but there is no particular reason to believe that he knew anyone really steeped in philosophy or theology.

[14] For James of Venice, see Minio-Paluello (1952). There is no direct evidence that Michael and James ever met, but the idea—first proposed by Browning (1962)—is very tempting. It gives a simple explanation of how Michael got access to the manuscripts he used, some of which contained quite rare items. Cf. Ebbesen (1996c: 263) for indications that James used Michael's own working copy of his *Elenchi* commentary.

James had started or was considering to start translating some Aristotle from Greek into Latin, and Michael had what he needed: both manuscripts of Aristotle and commentaries. James' translations gave the Latins access to such *chefs d'œuvre* as the *Posterior Analytics*, *Physics*, and *Metaphysics*. But the one that immediately attracted their attention most was the *Sophistici elenchi*.[15] This is understandable, because among all the previously unknown Aristotelian writings this book with its analysis of fallacies was the one that was closest to the interests of the analytic Latin philosophers. The funny thing is that no one used James' translation. Everybody used Boethius', which had been forgotten for six centuries and now miraculously turned up. Nevertheless, it was James who secured the instant success of the rediscovered text. For he provided a first-aid kit to readers of the *Elenchi* by translating Michael of Ephesus' commentary.[16] In that way a Byzantine scholar, Michael, put his fingerprints on late medieval scholastic logic in the West.

For all the good things one can say about Michael, he was a compiler with no distinctive philosophical personality. The item from his commentary that was to become most deeply entrenched in the Western tradition was a classification of polysemy or ambiguity into actual, potential, and imaginary polysemy (διττὸν ἐνεργείᾳ, δυνάμει, φαντασίᾳ: *multiplicitas actualis, potentialis, fantastica*). Latin texts combine this piece of theory with others, but in Michael's own work the introduction of the classification has no further consequences for the theory of polysemy; it is just an isolated idea contained in a passage that is an excerpt from a work by old Galen.[17]

After some confusion in the twelfth century about how to integrate the new Aristotelian material, and after seeking help from Arabic Aristotelian philosophers, Latin scholars of the thirteenth century reached an Aristotle interpretation that was both more Aristotelian and more Neoplatonic than that of the preceding century. Until about 1280 they also continued to receive new translations; by that time the Latin *Corpus Aristotelicum* was complete and important late ancient commentaries had also been translated.[18] But apart from Michael's commentary on the *Elenchi*, only one near-contemporary Greek work made it to the West: the collection of commentaries on the *Ethics* known as 'Eustratius', in fact a composite work, a major part of which was due to Michael of Ephesus.[19]

[15] Cf. De Rijk (1962–7). De Rijk argued that the *Elenchi* brought about a major change in the development of Latin logic. This view is challenged in Ebbesen (forthcoming), but there is no denial that the book was intensely studied in both the 12th and the 13th cents.

[16] See Ebbesen (1981). The translation no longer exists, but it is often quoted by Latin authors, usually with ascription to Alexander (of Aphrodisias). For a quotation with the correct attribution to Michael, see Ebbesen (1996c: 255–7).

[17] For the Galenic classification of ambiguity and the excerpts from Galen's *De captionibus* in Byzantine scholia on the *Elenchi*, see Ebbesen (1981).

[18] For a convenient survey of the translations, see Dod (1982).

[19] The translation was done by Robert Grosseteste. See Mercken (1973–91). Notice that the preface of the volume from 1991 contains important corrections of the information about Michael given in the 1973 volume.

It was too late to change radically the course of Latin philosophy. New subjects came under scrutiny and the way people read Aristotle changed, but the analytical approach remained, and the new branches of philosophy that had developed in the twelfth century, especially within logic, survived in new contexts, though they were largely removed from the interpretation of Aristotle.

The fourth Greek wave left the Latins with a certain measure of schizo-phrenia—in some philosophical genres the native tradition lived on, in others it had been replaced by an approach that paid less attention to particulars and more to universals, ontological hierarchies, and the possibility of letting one's personal intellect disappear in the sea of some universal intellect.[20]

This schizophrenia was what fourteenth-century nominalists tried to over-come; to a large extent by relying on the native Latin tradition that had resulted from the third Greek wave rather than on the results of the fourth wave. They felt no need of more translated texts, and none were made for a century.[21] At the same time, a thirteenth-century translation of Proclus' *Elementatio theologica* acted as a virus in the body of Latin scholasticism, which slowly began to crave for more Platonism.

The final wave

The West did get more Platonism. It came, of course, with the movement we usually call the Renaissance. The last great wave of Greek influence reached the shores of Italy about 1400 and 150 years later the whole West was drenched. The effects on Latin philosophy were profound, I think, but not easy to describe.[22] The philosophical scene became more confusing than ever. Not only did all sorts of Greek texts become available, from Plato and Plutarch to Leo Magentinos from the thirteenth century, but a new class of learned men who were not academics started to dabble in philosophy alongside their other literary pursuits. These unprofessional philosophers or would-be philosophers shared important traits with the typical Byzantine learned man, who was never an academic philosopher for the simple reason that there was no academy for him to graduate from and to teach in later on.

The Renaissance is an untidy period. Its beauty is not in its collective achievements, but on the individual level its actors are often fascinating. Think of the *cardinalis Nicenus*, alias Bessarion (*c*.1403–72): not a great philosopher, but a man with a good training, a serious interest in philosophy, and the ability to move with ease both in Latin and in Greek circles.

---

[20] Cf. Ebbesen (1998) and—with stronger emphasis on the Arabic contribution—De Libera (1993).

[21] A Latin translation of Sextus Empiricus may be from *c*.1300 (though it could also be earlier), but it seems to have had few readers and exerted no detectable influence on 14th-cent. philosophy. See Cavini (1977).

[22] For a good introduction to the period, see Copenhaver and Schmitt (1992).

Latin Influence on Greek Intellectuals

Bessarion represents the class of Greeks who, without losing their attachment to their native culture had come to realize that the Latin culture had changed from being subservient to being dominant, or at least that Latin did not equal barbarian.

Until the eleventh century the Greek culture had been the dominant one. The scales tipped in the twelfth, but nobody seems to have really noticed before the thirteenth century. To all appearances, educated Greeks of the twelfth century continued to think of the Latins as representatives of a subservient culture, and so did the Latins; at least they did not yet feel that theirs was the dominant culture. They only started to feel that way in the thirteenth century, and still the reverence for the Greek past put a sordine on any trumpeting self-advertisement.

The fourth crusade not only brought home to the Greek world the truth that the West was economically and militarily stronger, it also made it more difficult for Greek intellectuals to ignore Western academe and its achievements. No university took root in the Greek world, but Latin schools of a certain, not quite elementary, level appeared, and Franks with a university degree or equivalent training from a religious school became a fairly common sight in the East.[23] Some of them learned Greek, and some Greeks learned Latin. A Latin wave started to wash the feet of the Greek intelligentsia, though few submerged their whole body in the wave.

I have looked in vain for clear signs of Latin influence in Nikephoros Blemmydes,[24] and, I may add, the thorough investigations of Greek writings on fallacies that I did in the 1970s did not turn up a single loan from the Latin tradition before the fifteenth century. On the other hand, there were people already in the thirteenth who translated Latin philosophical texts into Greek. Not contemporary ones, but Latin authoritative texts: Boethius' *On Topical Differences*, *Hypothetical Syllogisms*, and the *Consolation of Philosophy*, Macrobius on *Scipio's Dream*.[25]

The selection is interesting. For one thing, the translated texts are rather short. This suggests that the translators selected texts that might be incorporated in a teaching programme. For another, the translated texts are Latin classics rather than modern texts. This is not very surprising. The Westerners had acted in the same way—with the exception of a couple of recent Aristotle commentaries they had only translated ancient *auctores*. Moreover, with the translation of a few Latin *auctores* the Greek world would have access

---

[23] Cf. Schabel (1998).

[24] In Ebbesen (1996*b*: 182), I suggested that maybe Blemmydes had some (indirect) knowledge of Marius Victorinus' *De definitionibus* and Boethius' *De divisione*. I have to retract the suggestion. The passages in Blemmydes that reminded me of the Latin authors turn out to be loans from John of Damascus.

[25] See Nikitas (1982, 1990); Papathomopoulos (1999); Megas (1995).

to the majority of the authoritative philosophical texts used in the West since most of those were originally Greek. The only serious defect would be the absence of translations of Averroes and Avicenna. True, there would also be a conspicious lack of a modern handbook of logic, but even if a Byzantine scholar had realized that his culture might need a handbook including such subjects as 'properties of terms' (*proprietates terminorum*), it would not have been obvious to him what to translate. By the end of the thirteenth century Peter of Spain's *Summule* was only just beginning to establish itself as a classic.[26]

On the other hand, there is something else weird about the selection. The texts selected were not university texts. Neither Boethius' *Consolation* nor Macrobius figured in any normal university programme, and the two logical works were entirely marginal in late thirteenth-century university teaching. It is noteworthy that the most productive of the translators, Maximos Planoudes (*c*.1255–*c*.1305), also translated Donatus' *Ars grammatica*, Ovid's *Metamorphoses* and *Heroides*, and *Disticha Catonis*. Those were the sort of texts that were taught at cathedral school level.

Two other translations by Planoudes are theological. Augustine's *De Trinitate* and Thomas Aquinas' *Summa theologica* do not point to an ordinary cathedral school milieu but rather to a Dominican *studium*.[27] Planoudes and Manuel Holobolos (fl. 1267), the translator of two of Boethius' logical opuscula, probably depended on Latins established in Constantinople for their ideas about what to translate. The prime suspect is the Dominican house which had been in the City since 1232.

In the fourteenth century the Latin influence on Greek philosophical discourse still seems to be weak. In theology, the influence seems stronger. In the Hesychastic debate of the 1330s Barlaam of Calabria (*c*.1290–1348) brings with him a Latin approach, and even his opponent, Gregory Palamas (1296–1359), uses loans from Augustine. This is amply shown by Demetracopoulos (1997), who further argues that Palamas borrowed a Stoic division of signs into indicative (ἐνδεικτικόν) and commemorative (ὑπομνηστικόν) from Sextus Empiricus.[28] Now, one of Palamas' examples does point back to Sextus, and indisputably so, but the actual wording of the distinction does not. Palamas distinguishes between a natural and a non-natural symbol: φυσικὸν σύμβολον, μὴ φυσικὸν σύμβολον. The terminology takes us back

---

[26] See De Rijk (1972), which contains references to De Rijk's own ground-breaking studies. It should be noticed, however, that De Rijk gave a mistaken impression of an early tradition for commenting on the *Summule* by dating the commentary of Guillelmus Arnaldi to the 1230s, which is too early by half a century.

[27] If the Greek translation of the Pseudo-Aristotelian *De plantis* is also by Planoudes, as commonly assumed, this shows him 'bringing home' a Greek authoritative text not available in Greek. *De plantis* was read in Western universities, and it would not be a strange thing for a Dominican *studium* to possess.

[28] Demetracopoulos (1997: 73–9; 201–2). The passage about natural and non-natural signs occurs in Christou *et al.* (1962: 627). For Byzantine use of Sextus, cf. Ch. 8 by B. Bydén in this volume.

not to Sextus but rather to Augustine, whose distinction between natural and given signs was widely known in Latin scholasticism, but usually phrased as a division into *signa naturalia* and conventional signs, with varying terminology for the latter (*ex institutione, ad placitum*, and other expressions).

Of course, even if my suspicion of a Latin source of Palamas' natural symbol is correct, this does now show a major Latin influence. At most it shows that the Latin philosophical apparatus was sneaking into the thought patterns of Greek intellectuals.

Palamas is not my hero, but another pair of intellectuals from Thessaloniki have heroic status with me. They are Demetrios (*c*.1324–97/8) and Prochoros (*c*.1333–69/70) Kydones.[29] While Planoudes had no successor in Constantinople, the Kydones brothers from Thessaloniki continued his work, translating important Latin texts into Greek: this was the way to go if Greeks were to catch up with developments, just as the Latins had translated Greek works since antiquity.

The Kydones brothers translated theological works (by Augustine, Aquinas, Herveus Natalis, and others), most of which had a considerable amount of philosophical content, but apparently the fourteenth century did not bring any significant augmentation of the number of purely philosophical Latin texts in Greek translation, and it is a matter of speculation how influential the few existing ones were, or what the effects of Latin-language schools were. In the early 1430s George Scholarios (*c*.1400–72/4), also known as Gennadios, assures us that he was innovative when he started to teach a Latin-style philosophy course in his school, and lets us understand that his pupils had difficulties with his 'strange and foreign terminology' (ξέναι καὶ ὑπερόριοι φωναί).[30] There is no reason to disbelieve him.

Scholarios did not just follow the already beaten track by translating more Thomas Aquinas. He translated almost everything necessary for an arts school of university level that followed *via Thomae*: *Liber sex principiorum*, Peter of Spain's *Summule*, but with Thomas's treatise on fallacies inserted instead of Peter's; a commentary on the *Ars Vetus*, mainly taken from Radulphus Brito, a famous Parisian master from the 1290s; Thomas on *De anima* and *Physics*, *De ente et essentia*.[31]

Now, Scholarios did not have much success, and it might look as though the fall of Constantinople put a definite end to Latin influence among Greeks. But this is scarcely the right way to look upon things. For one thing, we have the highly interesting milieux in Italy in the mid–late fifteenth century in which learned Greek émigrés both taught Latins and themselves were taught Latin philosophy. For another, a Latin presence continued in the Greek area during the Ottoman period. Theophilos Korydaleus (1572–1646), who had

---

[29] For the Kydones brothers, see Beck (1959: 733–8).
[30] Petit *et al.* 1928–36: vii/4. Cf. Ebbesen and Pinborg (1982).
[31] Edns.: Petit *et al.* (1928–36: vi–viii). For the translations of Brito, and the relation to Italian school tradition, see Ebbesen and Pinborg (1982).

been trained in Rome and Padua, blessed his people with a number of works in Greek, and they were actually used, as a considerable number of seventeenth- and eighteenth-century manuscripts prove. With Korydallean Aristotelianism the Greek world had been brought closer to the West in two ways: not only did Korydaleus' works contain ideas that had first matured in Latin, but Greeks also came to participate in the 'back-to-Aristotle' movement that swept the Latin schools after men had seen the disastrous results of sixteenth-century attempts to get rid of The Philosopher.

Conclusions

Though Greek philosophy has influenced Latin philosophy and vice versa, the general tendency has been for the flow of influence to be one-directional at any given time. Milieux in which a Greek and a Latin scholar would naturally meet have been few. Some such milieux may have existed in ancient Rome, but since there was no indigenous Roman philosophy this hardly modified Greek philosophy. Late ancient Constantinople certainly offered an opportunity for exchange, but again the Latins had little to give. When the Latins finally had something to offer, it took some time before Greeks noticed the fact, but in the second half of the thirteenth century a tiny stream of Latin thought began to flow into the Greek environment. More research is needed to determine the importance of this tiny stream in the thirteenth–fifteenth centuries, as well as later. Only in fifteenth-century Italy do we find a noteworthy number of intellectuals of the two linguistic groups actually talking to each other, reading each other's books (whether classics or freshly composed), and each being influenced by the other side's traditions and views.

BIBLIOGRAPHY

Beck, H.-G. (1959), *Kirche und theologische Literatur im byzantinischen Reich* (Byzantinisches Handbuch, 2/1; Handbuch der Altertumswissenchaft, 12/2/1; Munich).

Browning, R. (1962), 'An Unpublished Funeral Oration on Anna Comnena', *Proceedings of the Cambridge Philological Society*, 188 (NS 8): 1–12. Repr. in Browning, *Studies on Byzantine History, Literature and Education* (London, 1977). Also repr. in Sorabji 1990.

Cavini, W. (1977), 'Appunti sulla prima diffusione in occidente delle opere di Sesto Empirico', *Medioevo*, 3: 1–20.

Christou, P. K., Bobrinsky, B., Papaevangelou, P., and Meyendorff, J. (eds.) (1962), Γρηγορίου τοῦ Παλαμᾶ Συγγράμματα, i (Thessaloniki).

CIMAGL = Cahiers de l'Institut du Moyen Age Grec et Latin, Université de Copenhague.

CLCAG = Corpus Latinum Commentariorum in Aristotelem Graecorum.

Copenhaver, B. P., and Schmitt, C. B. (1992), *Renaissance Philosophy* = *A History of Western Philosophy*, iii (Oxford and New York).

Courtenay, W. J. (ed.) (1992), Acts of the 1991 Madison Conference on Medieval Nominalism, *Vivarium*, 31/1: 1–215.

De Libera, A. (1993), *La Philosophie médiévale* (Paris).

—— (1996), *La Querelle des universaux: De Platon à la fin du Moyen Age* (Paris).

De Rijk, L. M. (1962–7), *Logica Modernorum*, i–ii (vol. ii in 2 parts) (Assen).

—— (ed.) (1972), *Peter of Spain, Tractatus, called afterwards Summule Logicales* (Wijsgerige teksten en studies, 23; Assen).

Demetracopoulos, J. (1997), *Αυγουστίνος και Γρηγόριος Παλαμάς* (Athens).

Dod, B. G. (1982), 'Aristoteles Latinus', in Kretzmann *et al.* (1982: 43–79).

Dronke, P. (ed.) (1988), *A History of Twelfth-Century Western Philosophy* (Cambridge).

Ebbesen, S. (1981), *Commentators and Commentaries on Aristotle's Sophistici Elenchi: A Study of Post-Aristotelian Ancient and Medieval Writings on Fallacies*, i–iii (CLCAG 7/1–3; Leiden).

—— (1992), 'Western and Byzantine Approaches to Logic', *CIMAGL* 62: 167–78.

—— (ed.) (1995), *Sprachtheorien in Spätantike und Mittelalter* (= P. Schmitter, ed., Geschichte der Sprachtheorie, 3; Tübingen).

—— (1996*a*), 'Greek and Latin Medieval Logic', *CIMAGL* 66: 67–95.

—— (1996*b*), 'George Pachymeres and the Topics', *CIMAGL* 66: 169–85.

—— (1996*c*), 'Anonymi Parisiensis Compendium Sophisticorum Elenchorum. The Uppsala Version', *CIMAGL* 66: 253–312.

—— (1998), 'The Paris Arts Faculty', in J. Marenbon (ed.), *Medieval Philosophy* = *Routledge History of Philosophy*, iii (London and New York), 269–90.

—— (forthcoming), 'The Role of Aristotle's *Sophistici Elenchi* in the Creation of Terminist Logic'.

Ebbesen, S., and Pinborg, J. (1981–2), 'Gennadios and Western Scholasticism: Radulphus Brito's *Ars Vetus* in Greek Translation', *Classica et Mediaevalia*, 33: 263–319.

Iwakuma, Y. (1987), '*Instantiae*: An Introduction to a Twelfth Century Technique of Argumentation', *Argumentation*, 1: 437–53.

Kneepkens, C. H. (1995), 'The Priscianic Tradition', in Ebbesen (1995: 239–64).

Kretzmann, N. (1982), 'Syncategoremata, exponibilia, sophismata', in Kretzmann *et al.* (1982: 211–45).

—— Kenny, A., and Pinborg, J. (eds.) (1982), *The Cambridge History of Later Medieval Philosophy* (Cambridge).

Luscombe, D. E. (ed. and tr.) (1971), *Peter Abelard's Ethics* (Oxford).

Marenbon, J. (1997), *The Philosophy of Peter Abelard* (Cambridge).

Megas, A. (ed.) (1995), *Μαξίμου Πλανούδη* (±1255 – ±1305) *Του υπομνήματος εις το "Ονειρον του Σκιπίωνος" μετάφρασῃ. Λατινο–ελληνική Βιβλιοθήκη* 8 (Thessaloniki).

Mercken, H. P. F. (1973–91), *The Greek Commentaries on the Nicomachean Ethics of Aristotle*, i, iii (CLCAG 6/1 and 6/3; Leiden).

Minio-Paluello, L. (1952), 'Iacobus Veneticus Grecus: Canonist and Translator of Aristotle', *Traditio*, 8: 265–304. Repr. in Minio-Paluello, *Opuscula, The Latin Aristotle* (Amsterdam, 1972).

Nikitas, D. Z. (ed.) (1982), *Eine byzantinische Übersetzung von Boethius' 'De hypotheticis syllogismis'* (Hypomnemata, 69; Göttingen).

—— (ed.) (1990), *Boethius De topicis differentiis* καὶ οἱ βυζαντινὲς μεταφράσεις τῶν Μανουὴλ Ὁλοβώλου καὶ Προχόρου Κυδώνη (Philosophi Byzantini, 5; Athens).

Obertello, L. (1974), *Severino Boezio*, 2 vols. (Collana di monographie, 1, Accademia ligure di scienze e lettere; Genoa).

Papathomopoulos, M. (ed.) (1999), *Anicii Manlii Severini Boethii De consolatione philosophiae. Traduction grecque de Maxime Planude* (Philosophi Byzantini, 9; Athens).

Petit, L., Sideridès, X. A., and Jugie, M. (eds.) (1928–36), *Œuvres complètes de Gennade Scholarios*, 8 vols. (Paris).

Schabel, C. (1998), 'Elias of Nabinaux, Archbishop of Nicosia, and the Intellectual History of Later Medieval Cyprus', *CIMAGL* 68: 35–52.

Sorabji, R. (ed.) (1990), *Aristotle Transformed: The Ancient Commentators and their Influence* (London).

Van de Vyver, A. (1929), 'Les Étapes du développement philosophique du haut Moyen-Age', *Revue belge de philologie et d'histoire*, 8/2: 425–52.

2

Basil of Caesarea on the Semantics of Proper Names

PAUL KALLIGAS

Philosophical literature in both late antiquity and early Byzantine times usually relies heavily on the tradition of which it forms part. This has sometimes been taken as a mark of lack in originality or even in proper philosophical insight, but it also has created the impression that the contribution made by some of the eminent figures of the period is either dauntingly obscure or hopelessly scholastic. However, not infrequently, the disparaging assessment of these philosophers is due to a misunderstanding of both their particular theoretical aims, and their perception concerning their own role as adherents of a given philosophical tradition. The fact that our knowledge of the developments in the history of philosophy during the vast period between Aristotle and Plotinus is based on evidence which is at best second-rate and at worst distressingly fragmentary deprives us of any real hope of realizing fully the complexities of the theoretical environment within which such thinkers found themselves embedded. Sometimes we get a glimpse of a seemingly arid landscape, ransacked by the intense crossfire of disputation between the various schools during the Hellenistic period, but we are rarely capable of discerning accurately the positions entrenched in it and figuring out the communication and supply lines which used to hold them together into often intricate and meticulously articulated theoretical systems. It is only after we have carefully examined the lacunose evidence concerning this long tradition that we can begin to understand and to evaluate properly the attempt of a thinker to contribute something new on an issue which had already been treated extensively by his predecessors—though, obviously, not to his own full satisfaction—while avoiding scores of well-trodden pitfalls. And it is only then that one can appreciate the originality or even the ingenuity of such a contribution, which often amounts to a development or fine adjustment within the confines of an already established broader theoretical network. Furthermore, in some instances, we can thus form a more concrete idea as to the subtlety and the complexity of the issues involved, and even to reconstruct a philosophically stimulating frame of discussion.

I believe that such a case is presented in Basil of Caesarea's treatment of the semantic function of proper names, which emerges as a side issue during a theological controversy, but appears to possess considerable philosophical interest when viewed within the context of related theories expounded until his time.

In modern theories of meaning proper names tend to take on a leading role. This is so because they are generally viewed as the semantically simplest and most transparent of terms, being the singular designators *par excellence*, which is to say, the expressions best-adapted for referring to unique objects, to individuals. By means of proper names we can indicate an object while uttering a name which applies to it and to it alone: what simpler semantic relation could we ever imagine? Given, further, that in recent times particular sense objects have come to be accorded both ontological and epistemological priority, proper names would appear to be, of all linguistic elements, the ones most directly and rigidly correlated to the extra-linguistic reality to which they refer.

Considerations such as these led in the nineteenth century to the formulation of the view that proper names, unlike general terms, possess denotation only, but no connotation.[1] Thus, for example, while the general term 'man' denotes Socrates, Alcibiades, and an indefinite number of other men, it also connotes those properties which are common to all these men and which differentiate them from other entities. On the other hand, the term 'Socrates' denotes only the particular man who is the bearer of this name, without connoting or ascribing to him any further property whatsoever. In other words, proper names refer to determinate individual entities as such, and not as bearers of any properties.

Though seductive in its simplicity, this 'classical' theory came up almost immediately against some severe difficulties, mainly with regard to the content of proper names which denote imaginary (i.e. non-existent) entities, such as 'Pegasus' or 'Chimaera',[2] or in explaining the information content of

---

[1] While this theory was articulated with greater precision by Mill (1872: I. ii. 5), it originates in medieval scholastic philosophy. See e.g. the first of the semantic levels of words distinguished by Henry of Ghent in his *Summa quaestionum ordinarium* (Paris, 1520), *apud* Knudsen (1982: 482–3). Mill does not of course deny that sometimes there may exist a specific reason why a proper name was given to some person or thing. He notes, however, that 'the name, once given, is independent of the reason'. Dartmouth will continue to be so named, even if the River Dart changes course and the city is no longer situated at its mouth. Cf. Kripke (1980: 26).

[2] During the discussion after the presentation of my paper at Thessaloniki, Prof. S. Ebbesen maintained that 'Chimaera' should not be considered as a proper name at all since, in his view, it stands for a whole kind of mythological beings, and he kindly referred me to his publication 'The Chimera's Diary', in S. Knuuttila and J. Hintikka (eds.), *The Logic of Being* (Dordrecht, 1986), 115–43. But I think that one might discern a significant lacuna between entries 1 and 2 of this 'Diary': verses 319–27 of Hesiod's *Theogony* make it quite clear that he, at least, considered the Chimaera as an identifiable particular monster, the offspring of Typhon and Hydra (or, perhaps, Echidna), begetter of the Boeotian Sphinx and the Nemean lion, and finally slain by Bellerophon and Pegasus.

statements of individual identity, such as 'Aldebaran is α-Tauri' or 'Clark Kent is Superman'. Accordingly, Frege advanced the alternative theory that while proper names are indeed singular designators, they possess not only reference (*Bedeutung*) but also meaning (*Sinn*), and are thus stand-ins for, or abbreviations of, descriptive expressions.[3] Nor was this view, however, spared its share of critical objections. How could we maintain the role of proper names as rigid designators—in other words, how could we justify our conviction that we continue to refer through them always to the selfsame objects, in spite of any transformations these objects may have undergone in respect of their descriptive elements? And how can we explain our incapacity to provide any usable definitions for them?

It is not my intention to review here the various solutions which have been proposed in recent times to these problems. I do however believe that these two theoretical poles, the 'designative' and the 'descriptive', provide us with a useful frame of reference for understanding the corresponding positions adopted by those who dealt with this issue in antiquity.

The fact is that ancient philosophers do not appear to have accorded similar importance to the issue of the semantics or even the logical behaviour of proper names.[4] Aristotle in chapter 7 of the *De interpretatione* (17ᵃ38–ᵇ3) attempts a distinction between 'universal' (καθόλου) and 'singular' (καθ' ἕκαστον) terms on the basis of the criterion of whether these are 'naturally predicable' (πέφυκε κατηγορεῖσθαι) 'of a number of things' (ἐπὶ πλειόνων) or not. Although the terminology he employs is too general to allow us directly to determine whether within the second category he would wish to include other singular designators such as definite descriptions, the example he cites ('Callias') reveals that what he principally has in mind are proper names. The crucial element he introduces here is the discrimination of such terms from those general terms whose reference is delimited by the use of quantifiers so that they may function as 'partial' (μερικαί)[5] terms in specific sentences. As Aristotle's commentator Ammonius has put it, 'partial (*sc.* sentences) differ from singular ones in that whereas singular sentences effect their assertion about one definite individual such as Socrates, partial ones, even if they assert something with regard to some one thing, do not signify anything definite, but may be true of any chance individual, as when we say "some man is just"'.[6] The distinguishing feature of proper names is

---

[3] See Frege, 'On Sense and Meaning', in Geach and Black (1980: 60–3); cf. Russell (1956: 200–1); McDowell (1977: 172–4).

[4] See Barnes (1996: 181–2).

[5] *De interpretatione* 17ᵇ7: καθόλου μέν, μὴ καθόλου δέ. On this see Ammonius, *In De int.* (CAG 4/5) 89. 8–17, 90. 7–20 Busse. Theophrastus appears to have introduced the term μερικὴ ἀπροσδιόριστος to characterize sentences of the form τὶς ἄνθρωπος ζῷόν ἐστιν (cf. fr. 82B–E FHS&G).

[6] *In De int.* 90. 12–16 B.: διαφέρουσι δὲ τῶν καθ' ἕκαστα αἱ μερικαὶ (*sc.* προτάσεις) τῷ τὰς μὲν καθ' ἕκαστα ἐπί τινος ἑνὸς ὡρισμένου ποιεῖσθαι τὴν ἀπόφανσιν, οἷον Σωκράτους, τὰς δὲ μερικάς, εἰ καὶ πρὸς ἕν τι βλέπουσαι ἀποφαίνοιντο, μηδὲν ὡρισμένον σημαίνειν, ἀλλ' ἐπί τινος τοῦ τυχόντος δύνασθαι ἀληθεύειν, ὡς ὅταν εἴπομεν 'τὶς ἄνθρωπος δίκαιός ἐστιν.

therefore, according to this view, that their denotation is from the start determinate and individuated; in other words, that they designate a definite, unique object.

This observation allows us here to juxtapose a passage from the *Prior Analytics* (1. 27, 43[a]25–35) in which Aristotle, embarking on a subdivision of 'all the things that are' (ἀπάντων τῶν ὄντων), distinguishes a class of entities 'such as Cleon and Callias and the singular and perceptible' (οἷον Κλέων καὶ Καλλίας καὶ τὸ καθ᾽ ἕκαστον καὶ αἰσθητόν) which 'are such that they cannot in truth be predicated universally of anything else … as others can of them' (ἔστι τοιαῦτα ὥστε κατὰ μηδενὸς ἄλλου κατηγορεῖσθαι ἀληθῶς καθόλου … κατὰ δὲ τούτων ἄλλα); in other words, they can function as subjects of sentences but not as predicates. This appears to imply that expressions which designate such entities lack descriptive content, because otherwise there would be no reason to deny them the role of predicate, that is, of the term which 'describes' something by ascribing a property to it. It seems therefore that if we had to place Aristotle somewhere along the spectrum of competing theories on the semantics of proper names which we posited at the start, it would have to be near the first, the 'classical' theory, according to which proper names lack connotative, that is, descriptive, content and are pure designators, indeed ones with an entirely determinate and unique denotation.

However, the first to recognize proper names as a particular category of expressions with a discrete semantic behaviour were the Stoics. Already Chrysippus (*SVF* ii. 147) had, it appears, distinguished the 'name' (ὄνομα) from the 'appellative' (προσηγορία) as separate parts of language, but the fullest pertinent testimony concerns Diogenes of Babylon, a thinker known for his involvement with questions of grammatical theory:[7] 'an appellative is … a part of language which signifies a common quality, e.g. "man", "horse"; a name is a part of language which indicates a peculiar quality, e.g. "Diogenes", "Socrates" '.

In order for us to grasp the import of these definitions, we must begin by recalling that, for the Stoics, to subsume an object under the first of their categories, 'substance' (οὐσία), implied no more about it than that it constitutes a real, material entity;[8] accordingly it is to this category that all material bodies belong (see *SVF* i. 396). It was to the second category, 'quality' (ποιότης), that corresponded those properties which determine the nature and the general or the particular attributes of each object. However, these qualities were not all regarded as occupying the same ontological level. The 'common qualities' (κοιναὶ ποιότητες) are merely abstract entities, 'conceptions' (ἐννοήματα) or even 'presentations' (φαντάσματα, *SVF* ii. 378 and

---

[7] Ἔστι δὲ προσηγορία μὲν … μέρος λόγου σημαῖνον κοινὴν ποιότητα, οἷον ἄνθρωπος ἵππος. ὄνομα δέ ἐστι μέρος λόγου δηλοῦν ἰδίαν ποιότητα, οἷον Διογένης, Σωκράτης, *apud* Diocl. Magn. *apud* Diog. Laert. 7.58. Cf. Brunschwig (1994: 44–5).

[8] See Sedley (1982: 260).

165),[9] which may possess 'subsistence' ($\dot{v}\pi\acute{o}\sigma\tau\alpha\sigma\iota\nu$) but no real 'existence' ($\ddot{v}\pi\alpha\rho\xi\iota\nu$), a state reserved for determinate material objects. The fundamental elements of Stoic ontology, the ones which secure the particular character and the individuation of these objects, are the 'peculiar qualities' ($\ddot{\iota}\delta\iota\alpha\iota$ $\pi o\iota\acute{o}\tau\eta\tau\epsilon s$). These have material subsistence and coexist with substance, or 'prime matter' ($\pi\rho\acute{\omega}\tau\eta\nu$ $\ddot{v}\lambda\eta\nu$, *SVF* i. 87), being totally mixed together with it (*SVF* i. 92).[10] They consist of 'breaths' ($\pi\nu\epsilon\acute{v}\mu\alpha\tau\alpha$) and 'air-like tensions' ($\dot{\alpha}\epsilon\rho\acute{\omega}\delta\epsilon\iota s$ $\tau\acute{o}\nu o\nu s$) which pervade matter and invest it with various characteristic properties (*SVF* ii. 449). The products of this mixture are the bodies, objects which have now become 'qualified entities' ($\pi o\iota\acute{\alpha}$) and have in this manner been individuated.

The constitutive character of these peculiar qualities is better revealed through one of the famous paradoxes of Chrysippus. According to this,[11] if we assume that we have a person, Theon, whose *unique* property is that he has only one foot, then he must 'perish' ($\ddot{\epsilon}\varphi\theta\alpha\rho\tau\alpha\iota$) from the moment that some other person, Dion, loses one of his feet and finds himself, also, with just one. The explanation of the paradox is that from the moment that Theon's peculiar quality ceases to characterize only a *single* person, it ceases to exist as such and becomes a common quality, which may well subsist, but, as we saw, lacks existence.[12] Thus Theon perishes, in the sense that he ceases to exist as a distinct entity with particular individual attributes.[13]

This example helps us to grasp some of the basic features of peculiar qualities:

1. They constitute particularities, by which the specific individual which alone possesses them is distinguished from all others.[14] As a result, they are of necessity entirely singular and unique entities, each one of which may only 'conceptually' ($\kappa\alpha\tau$' $\dot{\epsilon}\pi\acute{\iota}\nu o\iota\alpha\nu$) be analysed as a synthesis of various common qualities.

2. Furthermore, they designate their object *descriptively*, that is, by ascribing to it properties,[15] that is, attributes which are identical neither

---

[9] See Reesor (1954: 52–3).

[10] On these distinctions see Rist (1971: 43–4). Cf. Plut., *De comm. not.* 1083 c–D.

[11] *SVF* ii. 397, tr. Long and Sedley: 'For the sake of argument, let one individual be thought of as whole-limbed, the other as minus one foot. Let the whole-limbed one be called Dion, the defective one Theon. Then let one of Dion's feet be amputated.' The question arises which one of them has perished, and the claim is that Theon is the stronger candidate: 'for Dion, the one whose foot has been cut off, has collapsed into the defective substance of Theon. And two peculiarly qualified individuals cannot occupy the same substrate. Therefore it is necessary that Dion remains, while Theon has perished.'

[12] Cf. *SVF* i. 65.

[13] Cf. Mnesarchus *apud* Arium Didymum, *Epitome* fr. 27 (*Dox. Graec.* 463. 5, 13). Long and Sedley 1987: i. 175–6 offer a different interpretation of the paradox.

[14] See Sedley 1982: 264–7. We find an echo of this view in a testimony by Plutarch concerning Posidonius (fr. 264 E–K), according to which this Stoic philosopher refused to recognize as proper names Roman *cognomina* such as Cato or Cicero, because these were 'adjectival appellatives' ($\pi\rho o\sigma\eta\gamma o\rho\iota\kappa\grave{\alpha}$ $\dot{\epsilon}\xi$ $\dot{\epsilon}\pi\iota\theta\acute{\epsilon}\tau o\nu$).

[15] Brunschwig 1994: 41–3 and 56 has advanced the view that the Stoics maintained a distinction between the expressions (*a*) '$\Sigma\omega\kappa\rho\acute{\alpha}\tau\eta s$' (without the article) and (*b*) 'ὁ $\Sigma\omega\kappa\rho\acute{\alpha}\tau\eta s$' (with

with its matter nor with its existence—which for the Stoics were one and the same thing, namely, what they called 'substance' ($o\dot{v}\sigma\acute{\iota}a$).

3. Also, as a passage of Simplicius (*SVF* ii. 390) emphatically notes, peculiar qualities had to be distinguished by the 'stability' ($\dot{\epsilon}\mu\mu\omega\nu\acute{\eta}\nu$) they had, that is, to correspond to more or less permanent traits, differing thereby from those which fell under the third of the Stoic categories, the 'dispositions' ($\tau\grave{a} \pi\grave{\omega}s \,\dot{\epsilon}\chi o\nu\tau a$).

4. By the same token, we could say, roughly, that to these qualities must have corresponded one-place predicates, so that they could be differentiated thereby from those of the fourth category, the 'relative dispositions' ($\tau\grave{a} \pi\rho\acute{o}s \,\tau\acute{\iota} \pi\omega s \,\dot{\epsilon}\chi o\nu\tau a$).[16]

The Stoic position according to which proper names denominate qualities of this nature[17] could be considered to be more akin to the Fregean viewpoint presented earlier. Indeed, from the Stoic perspective, not only do proper names have a descriptive content, but they correspond to definite descriptions in the most radical sense of the term: peculiar qualities represent the totality of those attributes which, being stable and complete in themselves, determine the identity of the pertinent object or person, and at the same time differentiate it from all others, constituting and defining, we might say, its individuality or its personality.[18]

So great were the exigencies placed by the Stoics on the semantic content of proper names that it was natural they should have come up against powerful critical arguments, mainly from the side of their perennial opponents, the Academics. We saw to what acrobatic expedients Chrysippus was obliged to resort against such attacks, when it came to explaining what happens in the

---

the article), the first referring, according to them, to that quality which defines an *infima species* with one unique member, and the second designating this same member. In my opinion, this distinction corresponds, roughly, to the one between denotation (understood as a semantic property of a term) and reference (understood as the function this term performs as a component of a sentence structure). Hence the element of anaphoricity which, as Brunschwig 1994: 51 notes, informs the semantic function of type (*b*) expressions, arises only within determinate contexts, while type (*a*) expressions possess semantic content ('meaning') in and of themselves, which corresponds to a definite peculiar quality.

[16] See Sedley 1982: 262–3.

[17] Cf. Alex. Aphrod., *In An. pr.* (CAG ii. 1) 179. 11 Wallies, and Simpl., *In Cat.* (CAG viii) 35. 34 Kalbfleisch. A noteworthy application of this theory in the field of theology is to be found in Origen, *De oratione* 24. 2: after providing the definition 'a name is a principal appellation, representative of the peculiar quality of the named' ($\acute{o}\nu o\mu a \,\dot{\epsilon}\sigma\tau\grave{\iota} \,\kappa\epsilon\varphi a\lambda a\iota\acute{\omega}\delta\eta s \,\pi\rho o\sigma\eta\gamma o\rho\acute{\iota}a \,\tau\hat{\eta}s \,\dot{\iota}\delta\acute{\iota}as \,\pi o\iota\acute{o}\tau\eta\tau o s \,\tau o\hat{v} \,\dot{o}\nu o\mu a\zeta o\mu\acute{\epsilon}\nu o v \,\pi a\rho a\sigma\tau a\tau\iota\kappa\acute{\eta}$), he explains that the peculiar quality indicated must be entirely individuated in respect of the spiritual, intellectual and corporal attributes of the named, while any change in it should normally ($\dot{v}\gamma\iota\hat{\omega}s$) bring about a corresponding change in name, as happened in the cases of Simon/Peter and Saul/Paul. Accordingly, the only consistent bearer of a proper name is God, 'who is always the same, being unwavering and unchanging' ($\acute{o}\sigma\tau\iota s \,a\dot{v}\tau\acute{o}s \,\dot{\epsilon}\sigma\tau\iota\nu \,\acute{a}\tau\rho\epsilon\pi\tau o s \,\kappa a\grave{\iota} \,\dot{a}\nu a\lambda\lambda o\acute{\iota}\omega\tau o s \,\dot{a}\epsilon\grave{\iota} \,\tau v\gamma\chi\acute{a}\nu\omega\nu$)! A further theological precedent can be found in the Derveni Papyrus, xxii. 7–15; see Funghi 1997: 33.

[18] See Lloyd 1971: 66. However the notion of peculiar quality did not extend as well to variable or wholly chance properties, such as the space–time co-ordinates of a body. On this point, a different view is ascribed to Posidonius by Kessisoglou 1997: 103–6.

case of Dion's amputation. We can imagine that he must have confronted similar difficulties in the case of statements of the form 'Dion is dead' or 'Socrates is snub-nosed', since, based on their theory, the first would appear contradictory[19] and the second tautological.

It would be interesting to know what the Academics themselves had to counter-propose on the same subject. Regrettably, our evidence about them is even more lacunary than in the case of the Stoics. The only relevant clue I have in mind comes from Sextus Empiricus (*M*. 7. 176–9, tr. Bury adjusted) and concerns the views of Carneades on the second criterion of knowledge of sense objects:

But since no presentation is ever simple in form but, like links in a chain, one hangs from another, we have to add, as a second criterion, the presentation which is at once both probable and 'irreversible'. For example, he who receives the presentation of a man necessarily receives the presentation both of his own qualities and of the external conditions—of his own qualities, such as colour, size, shape, motion, speech, dress, foot-gear; and of the external conditions, such as air, light, day, heaven, earth, friends and all the rest. So whenever none of these presentations disturbs our faith by appearing false, but all with one accord appear true, our belief is the greater. For we believe that this man is Socrates from the fact that he possesses all his customary characteristics ($\tau\grave{\alpha}$ $\epsilon\grave{\iota}\omega\theta\acute{o}\tau\alpha$)—colour, size, shape, converse, coat, and his position in a place where there is no one exactly like him. And just as some doctors do not deduce that it is a true case of fever from one symptom only—such as too quick a pulse or a very high temperature—but from a concurrence ($\sigma\upsilon\nu\delta\rho\omega\mu\tilde{\eta}$), such as that of a high temperature with a rapid pulse and soreness to the touch and flushing and thirst and analogous symptoms; so also the Academic forms his judgement of truth by the concurrence of presentations, and when none of the presentations in the concurrence provokes in him a suspicion of its falsity he asserts that the impression is true.[20]

---

[19] As noted apparently by e.g. Alex. Aphrod., *In Anal. pr.* 179. 11 Wallies, when he states that 'if "Dion" is the name of the peculiar quality, then the carrier of the peculiar quality is living, and therefore one who spoke of Dion would speak of a living thing, if we must be precise in talking about names'. Brunschwig 1994: 52–3 has pointed out an extremely elegant solution the Stoics could appeal to in the face of this difficulty, on the basis of the distinction referred to in n. 15 above. However he, too, admits that, in case Dion has died, the statement $\dot\tau\acute{\epsilon}\theta\nu\eta\kappa\epsilon\nu$ $\dot{o}$ $\varDelta\acute{\iota}\omega\nu$' would be for them 'in principle as impossible as the statement "$\tau\acute{\epsilon}\theta\nu\eta\kappa\epsilon\nu$ $o\tilde{\upsilon}\tau o\varsigma$"'.

[20] $E\pi\epsilon\grave{\iota}$ $\delta\grave{\epsilon}$ $o\grave{\upsilon}\delta\acute{\epsilon}\pi o\tau\epsilon$ $\varphi\alpha\nu\tau\alpha\sigma\acute{\iota}\alpha$ $\mu o\nu o\epsilon\iota\delta\grave{\eta}\varsigma$ $\dot{\upsilon}\varphi\acute{\iota}\sigma\tau\alpha\tau\alpha\iota$ $\dot{\alpha}\lambda\lambda$' $\dot{\alpha}\lambda\acute{\upsilon}\sigma\epsilon\omega\varsigma$ $\tau\rho\acute{o}\pi o\nu$ $\ddot{\alpha}\lambda\lambda\eta$ $\dot{\epsilon}\xi$ $\ddot{\alpha}\lambda\lambda\eta\varsigma$ $\ddot{\eta}\rho\tau\eta\tau\alpha\iota$, $\delta\epsilon\acute{\upsilon}\tau\epsilon\rho o\nu$ $\pi\rho o\sigma\gamma\epsilon\nu\acute{\eta}\sigma\epsilon\tau\alpha\iota$ $\kappa\rho\iota\tau\acute{\eta}\rho\iota o\nu$ $\dot{\eta}$ $\pi\iota\theta\alpha\nu\grave{\eta}$ $\ddot{\alpha}\mu\alpha$ $\kappa\alpha\grave{\iota}$ $\dot{\alpha}\pi\epsilon\rho\acute{\iota}\sigma\pi\alpha\sigma\tau o\varsigma$ $\varphi\alpha\nu\tau\alpha\sigma\acute{\iota}\alpha$. $o\tilde{\iota}o\nu$ $\dot{\alpha}\nu\theta\rho\acute{\omega}\pi o\upsilon$ $\sigma\pi\tilde{\omega}\nu$ $\varphi\alpha\nu\tau\alpha\sigma\acute{\iota}\alpha\nu$ $\dot{\epsilon}\xi$ $\dot{\alpha}\nu\acute{\alpha}\gamma\kappa\eta\varsigma$ $\kappa\alpha\grave{\iota}$ $\tau\tilde{\omega}\nu$ $\pi\epsilon\rho\grave{\iota}$ $\alpha\dot{\upsilon}\tau\grave{o}\nu$ $\lambda\alpha\mu\beta\acute{\alpha}\nu\epsilon\iota$ $\varphi\alpha\nu\tau\alpha\sigma\acute{\iota}\alpha\nu$ $\kappa\alpha\grave{\iota}$ $\tau\tilde{\omega}\nu$ $\dot{\epsilon}\kappa\tau\acute{o}\varsigma$, $\tau\tilde{\omega}\nu$ $\mu\grave{\epsilon}\nu$ $\pi\epsilon\rho\grave{\iota}$ $\alpha\dot{\upsilon}\tau\grave{o}\nu$ $\dot{\omega}\varsigma$ $\chi\rho\acute{o}\alpha\varsigma$ $\mu\epsilon\gamma\acute{\epsilon}\theta o\upsilon\varsigma$ $\sigma\chi\acute{\eta}\mu\alpha\tau o\varsigma$ $\kappa\iota\nu\acute{\eta}\sigma\epsilon\omega\varsigma$ $\lambda\alpha\lambda\iota\tilde{\alpha}\varsigma$ $\dot{\epsilon}\sigma\theta\tilde{\eta}\tau o\varsigma$ $\dot{\upsilon}\pi o\delta\acute{\epsilon}\sigma\epsilon\omega\varsigma$, $\tau\tilde{\omega}\nu$ $\delta\grave{\epsilon}$ $\dot{\epsilon}\kappa\tau\grave{o}\varsigma$ $\dot{\omega}\varsigma$ $\dot{\alpha}\acute{\epsilon}\rho o\varsigma$ $\varphi\omega\tau\grave{o}\varsigma$ $\dot{\eta}\mu\acute{\epsilon}\rho\alpha\varsigma$ $o\dot{\upsilon}\rho\alpha\nu o\tilde{\upsilon}$ $\gamma\tilde{\eta}\varsigma$ $\varphi\acute{\iota}\lambda\omega\nu$, $\tau\tilde{\omega}\nu$ $\ddot{\alpha}\lambda\lambda\omega\nu$ $\dot{\alpha}\pi\acute{\alpha}\nu\tau\omega\nu$. $\ddot{o}\tau\alpha\nu$ $o\tilde{\upsilon}\nu$ $\mu\eta\delta\epsilon\mu\acute{\iota}\alpha$ $\tau o\acute{\upsilon}\tau\omega\nu$ $\tau\tilde{\omega}\nu$ $\varphi\alpha\nu\tau\alpha\sigma\iota\tilde{\omega}\nu$ $\pi\epsilon\rho\iota\acute{\epsilon}\lambda\kappa\eta$ $\dot{\eta}\mu\tilde{\alpha}\varsigma$ $\tau\tilde{\omega}$ $\varphi\alpha\acute{\iota}\nu\epsilon\sigma\theta\alpha\iota$ $\psi\epsilon\upsilon\delta\acute{\eta}\varsigma$, $\dot{\alpha}\lambda\lambda\grave{\alpha}$ $\pi\tilde{\alpha}\sigma\alpha\iota$ $\sigma\upsilon\mu\varphi\acute{\omega}\nu\omega\varsigma$ $\varphi\alpha\acute{\iota}\nu\omega\nu\tau\alpha\iota$ $\dot{\alpha}\lambda\eta\theta\epsilon\tilde{\iota}\varsigma$, $\mu\tilde{\alpha}\lambda\lambda o\nu$ $\pi\iota\sigma\tau\epsilon\acute{\upsilon}o\mu\epsilon\nu$. $\ddot{o}\tau\iota$ $\gamma\grave{\alpha}\rho$ $\alpha\dot{\upsilon}\tau\acute{o}\varsigma$ $\dot{\epsilon}\sigma\tau\iota$ $\Sigma\omega\kappa\rho\acute{\alpha}\tau\eta\varsigma$, $\pi\iota\sigma\tau\epsilon\acute{\upsilon}o\mu\epsilon\nu$ $\dot{\epsilon}\kappa$ $\tau o\tilde{\upsilon}$ $\pi\acute{\alpha}\nu\tau\alpha$ $\alpha\dot{\upsilon}\tau\tilde{\omega}$ $\pi\rho o\sigma\epsilon\tilde{\iota}\nu\alpha\iota$ $\tau\grave{\alpha}$ $\epsilon\dot{\iota}\omega\theta\acute{o}\tau\alpha$, $\chi\rho\tilde{\omega}\mu\alpha$ $\mu\acute{\epsilon}\gamma\epsilon\theta o\varsigma$ $\sigma\chi\tilde{\eta}\mu\alpha$ $\delta\iota\acute{\alpha}\lambda\eta\psi\iota\nu$ $\tau\rho\acute{\iota}\beta\omega\nu\alpha$, $\tau\grave{o}$ $\dot{\epsilon}\nu\theta\acute{\alpha}\delta\epsilon$ $\epsilon\tilde{\iota}\nu\alpha\iota$ $\ddot{o}\pi o\upsilon$ $o\dot{\upsilon}\theta\epsilon\acute{\iota}\varsigma$ $\dot{\epsilon}\sigma\tau\iota\nu$ $\alpha\dot{\upsilon}\tau\tilde{\omega}$ $\dot{\alpha}\pi\alpha\rho\acute{\alpha}\lambda\lambda\alpha\kappa\tau o\varsigma$. $\kappa\alpha\grave{\iota}$ $\ddot{o}\nu$ $\tau\rho\acute{o}\pi o\nu$ $\tau\iota\n\acute{\epsilon}\varsigma$ $\tau\tilde{\omega}\nu$ $\dot{\iota}\alpha\tau\rho\tilde{\omega}\nu$ $\tau\grave{o}\nu$ $\kappa\alpha\tau$' $\dot{\alpha}\lambda\acute{\eta}\theta\epsilon\iota\alpha\nu$ $\pi\upsilon\rho\acute{\epsilon}\sigma\sigma o\nu\tau\alpha$ $o\dot{\upsilon}\kappa$ $\dot{\epsilon}\xi$ $\dot{\epsilon}\nu\grave{o}\varsigma$ $\lambda\alpha\mu\beta\acute{\alpha}\nu o\upsilon\sigma\iota$ $\sigma\upsilon\mu\pi\tau\acute{\omega}\mu\alpha\tau o\varsigma$, $\kappa\alpha\theta\acute{\alpha}\pi\epsilon\rho$ $\sigma\varphi\upsilon\gamma\mu o\tilde{\upsilon}$ $\sigma\varphi o\delta\rho\acute{o}\tau\eta\tau o\varsigma$ $\ddot{\eta}$ $\delta\alpha\psi\iota\lambda o\tilde{\upsilon}\varsigma$ $\theta\epsilon\rho\mu\alpha\sigma\acute{\iota}\alpha\varsigma$, $\dot{\alpha}\lambda\lambda$' $\dot{\epsilon}\kappa$ $\sigma\upsilon\nu\delta\rho o\mu\tilde{\eta}\varsigma$, $o\tilde{\iota}o\nu$ $\theta\epsilon\rho\mu\alpha\sigma\acute{\iota}\alpha\varsigma$ $\ddot{\alpha}\mu\alpha$ $\kappa\alpha\grave{\iota}$ $\sigma\varphi\upsilon\gmma o\tilde{\upsilon}$ $\kappa\alpha\grave{\iota}$ $\dot{\epsilon}\lambda\kappa\acute{\omega}\delta o\upsilon\varsigma$ $\dot{\alpha}\varphi\tilde{\eta}\varsigma$ $\kappa\alpha\grave{\iota}$ $\dot{\epsilon}\rho\upsilon\theta\acute{\eta}\mu\alpha\tau o\varsigma$ $\kappa\alpha\grave{\iota}$ $\delta\acute{\iota}\psi o\upsilon\varsigma$ $\kappa\alpha\grave{\iota}$ $\tau\tilde{\omega}\nu$ $\dot{\alpha}\nu\acute{\alpha}\lambda o\gamma o\nu$, $o\ddot{\upsilon}\tau\omega$ $\kappa\alpha\grave{\iota}$ $\dot{o}$ $Á\kappa\alpha\delta\eta\mu\alpha\ddot{\iota}\kappa\grave{o}\varsigma$ $\tau\tilde{\eta}$ $\sigma\upsilon\nu\delta\rho o\mu\tilde{\eta}$ $\tau\tilde{\omega}\nu$ $\varphi\alpha\nu\tau\alpha\sigma\iota\tilde{\omega}\nu$ $\pi o\iota\epsilon\tilde{\iota}\tau\alpha\iota$ $\tau\grave{\eta}\nu$ $\kappa\rho\acute{\iota}\sigma\iota\nu$ $\tau\tilde{\eta}\varsigma$ $\dot{\alpha}\lambda\eta\theta\epsilon\acute{\iota}\alpha\varsigma$, $\mu\eta\delta\epsilon\mu\iota\tilde{\alpha}\varsigma$ $\tau\epsilon$ $\tau\tilde{\omega}\nu$ $\dot{\epsilon}\nu$ $\tau\tilde{\eta}$ $\sigma\upsilon\nu\delta\rho o\mu\tilde{\eta}$ $\varphi\alpha\nu\tau\alpha\sigma\iota\tilde{\omega}\nu$ $\pi\epsilon\rho\iota\sigma\pi\acute{\omega}\sigma\eta\varsigma$ $\alpha\dot{\upsilon}\tau\grave{o}\nu$ $\dot{\omega}\varsigma$ $\psi\epsilon\upsilon\delta o\tilde{\upsilon}\varsigma$, $\lambda\acute{\epsilon}\gamma\epsilon\iota$ $\dot{\alpha}\lambda\eta\theta\grave{\epsilon}\varsigma$ $\epsilon\tilde{\iota}\nu\alpha\iota$ $\tau\grave{o}$ $\pi\rho o\sigma\pi\tilde{\iota}\pi\tau o\nu$.

According to the argument here set out, the correct usage of a proper name such as 'Socrates' in order to refer to an object presupposes the association and common assessment of a multitude of sense perceptions—in Sextus' terms, a 'concurrence of presentations' ($\sigma\upsilon\nu\delta\rho\omega\mu\dot{\eta}$ $\varphi\alpha\nu\tau\alpha\sigma\iota\tilde{\omega}\nu$)[21]—with a view to establishing their reliability and agreement. The identification of a person by means of a name will thus be accomplished not through the determination of the presence of some specific, uniquely qualifying property, but instead through the conjoined ascertainment of a variety of particular distinguishing features, including some which may be entirely circumstantial and without any direct relation to the individual's personality, such as, for example, clothing or momentary surroundings.[22]

A specific interest in proper names as discrete grammatical entities with a distinctive semantic behaviour was shown, as is natural, by the Alexandrian Grammarians, and especially by those who held that the explanation of grammatical phenomena required an understanding of the internal semantic rules which underlie them. Thus, for example, in the *Ars grammatica* of Dionysius Thrax we observe an attempt to reform the distinction which, as we saw, was posed by the Stoics between 'proper names' ($\dot{\delta}\nu\dot{\delta}\mu\alpha\tau\alpha$) and 'appellatives' ($\pi\rho\sigma\eta\gamma\sigma\rho\dot{\iota}\alpha\iota$), and to adapt it to the Aristotelian system of categories. First of all, names are held to constitute a single part of speech,[23] with two subdivisions. We find, accordingly, the following definition (*Ars Gr.* 12. 24. 3–6 Uhlig): 'A name is an inflected part of speech, signifying a body or thing... being said both in common ($\kappa\sigma\iota\nu\tilde{\omega}\varsigma$) and individually ($\dot{\iota}\delta\dot{\iota}\omega\varsigma$)—in common, e.g. "man", "horse"; individually, e.g. "Socrates".'[24] Later on (*Ars Gr.* 12. 33. 6–34. 2 U.) the following clarification is provided with regard to names: 'A proper (*sc.* name) is therefore one which signifies the peculiar substance, e.g. "Homer", "Socrates". An appellative, on the other hand, is one which signifies the common substance, e.g. "man", "horse".'[25]

---

[21] This conception may well derive from Plato's *Theaetetus* (157 в8–c1), where the perception of sense-objects is depicted as an 'aggregate' ($\ddot{\alpha}\theta\rho\sigma\iota\sigma\mu\alpha$) of partial perceptual apprehensions. Cf. Albinus, *Didask.* 4. 156. 3–14 Whittaker, where the epistemological twist given to the theory does not, I believe, run counter to the intentions of the *Theaetetus, pace* Schrenk 1991: 498.

[22] This view bears some resemblance with the theory of names as representing clusters of descriptions (cf. Kripke 1980: 30–2 and 60–1), but its distinctive epistemological purport safeguards it against some of the shortcomings of the semantic version, such as the problem of analyticity extensively discussed by Kripke.

[23] i.e. one of the eight recognized by Dionysius (name, verb, participle, article, pronoun, preposition, adverb, connective: *Ars Gr.* 11. 23. 1–2 Uhlig), by contrast with the five of Diogenes of Babylon (name, appellative, verb, connective, article: *SVF* iii Diog. fr. 21). Dionysius indicates that he is being consciously innovative on this point by noting: 'the appellative as a form has been subordinated to that of the name' (*Ars Gr.* 11. 23. 2–3 U.). See also the Byzantine *scholion ad loc.* (*Schol. in Dion. Thr.* (*Gramm. Gr.* i. 3) 214. 17–19 Hilgard).

[24] Ὄνομά ἐστι μέρος λόγου πτωτικόν, σῶμα ἢ πρᾶγμα σημαῖνον... κοινῶς τε καὶ ἰδίως λεγόμενον, κοινῶς μὲν οἷον ἄνθρωπος ἵππος, ἰδίως δὲ οἷον Σωκράτης.

[25] Κύριον μὲν οὖν ἐστι τὸ τὴν ἰδίαν οὐσίαν σημαῖνον, οἷον Ὅμηρος Σωκράτης. προσηγορικὸν δέ ἐστι τὸ τὴν κοινὴν οὐσίαν σημαῖνον, οἷον ἄνθρωπος ἵππος.

We observe, therefore, a further significant divergence from the corresponding Stoic theory: names are by now considered to designate *substances* (οὐσίας); in other words, they are already on their way to becoming 'substantives' (οὐσιαστικά). Instead of a reference to 'peculiar' and 'common qualities', we are now dealing with 'peculiar' and 'common substances'. The hybrid formulation seeks to adapt the Stoic division to the Aristotelian distinction between primary or 'peculiar' and secondary or 'common' substance. However, this unshackling of proper names from descriptive elements and coupling of them solely to determinate existent objects[26] unavoidably ranges the above theory once again among the 'designative' ones, and exposes it thereby to the familiar difficulties: how can one justify, for example, the use of proper names to denote mythical or, more generally, nonexistent objects, such as Pegasus, the Chimaera, the *Nothung*, or Utopia, which (presumably) do not correspond to Aristotelian primary substances? And perhaps we should recall here Wittgenstein's argument concerning the identification of a word's meaning with the object to which it refers:

It is important to note that the word 'meaning' is being used illicitly if it is used to signify the thing that 'corresponds' to the word. That is to confound the meaning of the name with the *bearer* of the name. When Mr. N. N. dies one says that the bearer of the name dies, not that the meaning dies. And it would be nonsensical to say that, for if the name ceased to have meaning it would make no sense to say 'Mr. N. N. is dead.'[27]

So we find ourselves once more, having travelled along an entirely different road, face to face with the problem of interpreting the statement 'Dion is dead', which appears to resist equally both the descriptive and the designative theories of proper names; for the referring expression 'Dion' seems to designate something which differs as much from any definite description corresponding to the substantive attributes of the particular person (among which must unavoidably be included the property 'man', which implies 'living being'), as from the object itself to which it refers, since it would not then 'say' anything about it which would permit the name to be used even if its object were to prove non-existent.[28]

---

[26] A point especially stressed by the scholiast *ad loc.*: 'and it (*sc.* the proper name) is called the dominant (κύριον) form, because it dominates one existence and substance and denotes this alone, or because it rendered predominantly and assuredly distinct that substance and existence which it alone denotes, e.g. "Homer", "Socrates"' (385. 25–8 H. Cf. 552. 7–10 H.). These remarks bring us very close to the 'classical' theory I referred to at the start. It should also be mentioned that, according to the prevailing view, for Aristotle also the truth of an assertion with a proper name as subject implies the existence of the person or thing designated by the subject. See *Cat.* 13^b27–33 and Wedin 1978: 191–3.

[27] Wittgenstein 1967: i. 40. See also Strawson 1952: 190.

[28] Related to this, but not identical, was the problem formulated by Chrysippus concerning the use of the indicative expression 'he' (οὗτος) in the case of some dead person (*SVF* ii. 202*a*): 'because Dion being dead, there perishes the assertion "he died", the correspondent of the ostension no longer being in existence; for ostension is directed to the living and concerns the living'.

We are in ignorance of what Dionysius might have replied to such objections. We can, however, be certain he would not have agreed with a radical
solution of the type proposed in the recent past by G. E. M. Anscombe,[29]
whereby the only proper names recognized as 'genuine' are ones which refer
to existent objects. Adopting such a view would involve making the grammatical status of a part of speech dependent on extra-linguistic or even
metaphysical parameters, something which we know Dionysius tried by every
means to avoid.[30]

All these problems I have signalled make manifest that the issue of the
semantics of proper names remained disputed during the Hellenistic period,
without there having emerged any satisfactory or, at least, unanimous and
consistent approach. Nor, in so far as I am aware, can we discover some
evidence that the years following saw any coherent theories or even new ideas
being formulated. The first significant rekindling of the issue appears to have
been the one we find in a passage from the *Contra Eunomium* composed by
Basil of Caesarea around AD 365, where we also meet with some, in my
opinion, noteworthy divergences from the various positions outlined so far.
Before moving on to present the relevant passage, I feel that I should add a
few words by way of background concerning the object of the controversy
between Basil and Eunomius, in the context of which the specific viewpoint is
advanced.

Eunomius, who served for a short period as bishop of Cyzicus, was a
spokesman for the most extreme branch of Arianism, the so-called Anom-
oeans, who denied the existence even of any similarity between the substances
of the Father and the Son. As a disciple of Aetius, a personage whose
extraordinary erudition had impressed even Julian the Apostate,[31] Eunomius
acquired a considerable philosophical training, which he applied to the
construction of an impressive theological system resting on Neoplatonic
foundations.[32] In the course of buttressing an argument to the effect that
the term 'unborn' (ἀγέννητος) constitutes a name of God expressive and
revelatory of his substance, Eunomius has recourse to a theory concerning
the correspondence 'in accordance with truth' (κατ' ἀλήθειαν) of specific
names to the nature of the objects they designate, as opposed to the association 'in accordance with human conception' (κατ' ἐπίνοιαν ἀνθρωπίνην)
of all other names to things, towards which these have no semantic or other
objective relation, so that no sooner are they pronounced than they vanish.[33]
This theory has its roots, of course, in the 'teaching of Euthyphro' as pre-

---

[29] In her Introduction to Wittgenstein's *Tractatus* (London, 1959), ch. 2. See also Searle 1967: 489*a*.

[30] See Robins 1951: 42–3.

[31] See Julian, *Epist.* 46 Bidez–Cumont.

[32] See Daniélou 1956: 428–9. This view put forward by Daniélou has been challenged by Rist 1981: 185–8, without, however, especially convincing arguments.

[33] See Eunomius, *Apologeticus* 8, and Martzelos 1984: 149.

sented by Socrates in Plato's *Cratylus*,[34] and which was widely influential among the Neopythagoreans and certain Neoplatonists.[35] However much it served to support his views on the selective manifestation of divine providence in the universe through specific 'seminal words' (σπερματικοὶ λόγοι) which were implanted in the souls of Adam and Eve, it also led Eunomius to the blanket denial of the semantic function of all other common names, since for him the 'conception' (ἐπίνοια) they evoke adds up to no more than subjective invention or simple phantasy.[36] For to the nature of things correspond only those names which were established 'connately' (προσφυῶς) and 'appropriately' (οἰκείως) by God himself during their creation, and this nature may become known to man only through some kind of apocalyptic revelation.[37]

It is against this extreme position that Basil introduces his own semantic theory, which rests on an entirely different valuation of the notion of 'conception'. This is no longer considered as mere illusion or 'delusion' (παράνοια), but rather as a mental function which may, under certain preconditions, yield an accurate grasp of reality, that is, of the properties from which perceptible objects appear to be constituted.[38] On the other hand, Basil also disapproves of Eunomius' theory concerning the names 'in accordance with truth', asserting that knowledge of the 'substance' (οὐσία) of things is innately impossible for human intelligence and thus ineffectible through names, which, being 'posterior' (ὕστερα) to the nature of things, are incapable of revealing it, but may only approximate it through its properties.[39] With regard more particularly to proper names, Basil attempts to explain their semantic function as follows:[40]

[34] On which see Boyancé 1941: 141–75, where particular stress is laid on the relation of this teaching to Pythagorean beliefs. Cf. Proclus, *In Crat.* 16. 5. 25–6. 19 Pasquali.

[35] See Daniélou 1956: 424–8. Although this author considers the most likely indirect source to have been the (presumed) commentary of Iamblichus on the *Cratylus*, it seems to me more probable that this role was played by some work of Theodorus of Asine, about whom we have specific testimony that he had composed a treatise entitled *On Names* (in which, of course, the *Cratylus* was referred to), and that he advocated a theory according to which *omne nomen quod proprie dicitur natura, convenit nominato et est imago rationalis rei* (test. 8 and 9 Deuse). A similar theory concerning names as 'voiced statues' (ἀγάλματα φωνήεντα), with clear magico-religious overtones, appears also to have been formulated earlier on by an obscure Platonist named Democritus. See Damascius, *In Phlb.* 24 (Westerink). We find another interesting precedent in the Valentinian *Gospel of Truth* (Nag Hammadi Codex i. 3), 21. 25–23. 22, 27. 15–33, 38. 7–41. 14, while the alchemist Zosimus of Panopolis, *On the Letter Ω* 10. 1. 99–101 Mertens, seems to believe that a proper name (κύριον ὄνομα) divulges the innermost nature of man (ὁ ἔσω ἄνθρωπος). As for later Neoplatonism, see also Gersh 1978: 303–4; Dillon 1985: 209–12.

[36] Cf. Gregory of Nyssa, *Contra Eunomium*, 2. 264. 25–265. 2 Jaeger.

[37] See Martzelos 1984: 153–6.

[38] See Basil, *Contra Eun.* 1. 6.

[39] See Martzelos 1984: 160–3.

[40] Basil, *Contra Eun.* 2. 4. 1–26 Durand-Doutreleau: Καίτοι τίς ἂν τῷ λόγῳ τούτῳ σωφρονῶν πρόσθοιτο, ὅτι ὧν τὰ ὀνόματά ἐστι διάφορα, τούτων παρηλλάχθαι καὶ τὰς οὐσίας ἀνάγκη; Πέτρου γὰρ καὶ Παύλου καὶ ἁπαξαπλῶς ἀνθρώπων πάντων προσηγορίαι μὲν διάφοροι, οὐσία δὲ πάντων μία. διόπερ ἐν τοῖς πλείστοις οἱ αὐτοὶ ἀλλήλοις ἐσμέν· τοῖς δὲ ἰδιώμασι μόνοις τοῖς περὶ ἕκαστον θεωρουμένοις ἕτερος ἑτέρου διενηνόχαμεν. ὅθεν καὶ αἱ προσηγορίαι οὐχὶ τῶν οὐσιῶν εἰσι σημαντικαί, ἀλλὰ τῶν ἰδιοτήτων, αἳ τὸν καθ᾽

Yet, to this argument, who in his right mind would add, that they whose names are distinct, must necessarily differ also in their substances (κατὰ τὰς οὐσίας)? For the appellations (προσηγορίαι) of Peter and Paul and all persons in general are distinct, yet the substance of all is one. Hence we are identical to each other in most things; only in terms of what are considered each one's peculiarities (ἰδιώμασι) have we been made different one from the other. It follows that the appellations signify not the substances, but the properties which characterize (χαρακτηρίζουσιν) each one. So that when we hear 'Peter', we do not grasp (νοοῦμεν) his substance by means of his name (I here call 'substance' the material subject (τὸ ὑλικὸν ὑποκείμενον), which the name does not in the least signify), but we register the concept (τὴν ἔννοιαν ἐντυπούμεθα) of what are considered his peculiarities. For directly from this sound we grasp 'the son of Jonah', 'the one from Bethsaida', 'the brother of Andrew', 'the one who was invited from among the fishermen to apostolic service', 'the one who is due to the superiority of his faith received on himself the edifice of the Church'; of which none is substance, understood as subsistence. So that the name, on the one hand, demarcates (ἀφορίζει) for us the character (χαρακτήρ) of Peter, but, on the other hand, it in no way represents (παρίστησι) the substance itself. Again, hearing 'Paul', we grasped a concurrence (συνδρομήν) of other peculiarities: 'the one from Tarsus', 'the Jew', 'the Pharisee according to law', 'the student of Gamaliel', 'the zealous persecutor of the Church of God', 'the one who was brought to consciousness by the terrible vision', 'the apostle of the nations'. For all these are encompassed (περιορίζεται) by the single sound 'Paul'.

With this paragraph, Basil intervenes in the controversy we have previously described, aligning himself precisely with none of the viewpoints considered, and bringing into the discussion certain new elements which, in my opinion, present a particular interest.

First of all, with his explicitly formulated denial that proper names[41] can signify substances, he distinguishes his position not only from that of Eunomius with respect to the privileged names 'in accordance with truth', but also from that of the Peripatetics, according to which—at least in so far as we found it articulated by Dionysius Thrax—names designate primary sub-

---

ἕνα χαρακτηρίζουσιν. ὅταν οὖν ἀκούσωμεν Πέτρον, οὐ τὴν οὐσίαν αὐτοῦ νοοῦμεν ἐκ τοῦ ὀνόματος (οὐσίαν δὲ λέγω νῦν τὸ ὑλικὸν ὑποκείμενον, ὅπερ οὐδαμῶς σημαίνει τοὔνομα), ἀλλὰ τῶν ἰδιωμάτων ἃ περὶ αὐτὸν θεωρεῖται τὴν ἔννοιαν ἐντυπούμεθα. εὐθὺς γὰρ ἐκ τῆς φωνῆς ταύτης νοοῦμεν τὸν τοῦ Ἰωνᾶ, τὸν ἐκ τῆς Βηθσαϊδᾶ, τὸν ἀδελφὸν Ἀνδρέου, τὸν ἀπὸ ἁλιέων εἰς τὴν διακονίαν τῆς ἀποστολῆς προσκληθέντα, τὸν διὰ τῆς πίστεως ὑπεροχὴν ἐφ᾽ ἑαυτὸν τὴν οἰκοδομὴν τῆς Ἐκκλησίας δεξάμενον· ὧν οὐδέν ἐστιν οὐσία, ἢ ὡς ὑπόστασις νοουμένη. ὥστε τὸ ὄνομα τὸν χαρακτῆρα μὲν ἡμῖν ἀφορίζει τὸν Πέτρον, αὐτὴν δὲ οὐδαμοῦ παρίστησι τὴν οὐσίαν. πάλιν ἀκούσαντες Παῦλον, ἑτέρων ἰδιωμάτων συνδρομὴν ἐννοήσαμεν· τὸν Ταρσέα, τὸν Ἑβραῖον, τὸν κατὰ νόμον Φαρισαῖον, τὸν μαθητὴν Γαμαλιήλ, τὸν κατὰ ζῆλον διώκτην τῶν Ἐκκλησιῶν τοῦ Θεοῦ, τὸν ἐκ τῆς φοβερᾶς ὀπτασίας εἰς τὴν ἐπίγνωσιν ἐναχθέντα, τὸν ἀπόστολον τῶν ἐθνῶν. ταῦτα γὰρ πάντα ἐκ μιᾶς φωνῆς τῆς Παῦλος περιορίζεται.

[41] It is obvious that Basil does not here employ the term προσηγορία with the meaning which, as we saw, it held for the Stoics, but rather in order to refer to proper names (cf. above, n. 17 and Lampe 1961: s.v. προσηγορία, E), or, in other passages, to appellatives as well (see e.g. *Contra Eun.* 2. 8). The choice of examples cited shows that Basil must have had the passage from Origen in mind and that he consciously diverged from the theory therein contained.

stances, that is, their meaning is identical to their denotation. The parenthetical clarification of the meaning of the term 'substance' is intended to prevent confusion with the preceding usage of the term, where this designated a 'secondary' substance, the one corresponding to the general term 'man' and on the basis of which 'we are identical to each other'. By 'material subject' is not of course meant matter, which has never been considered by anyone to be what a name might possibly designate, but rather the material object, the 'peculiar substance', which is denotated by it. Basil's position is that the use of a proper name does not evoke this object *directly*, but only through the 'concept' (ἔννοια) of some of its particular attributes.[42]

Nevertheless, the examples Basil enumerates make it clear that these 'peculiarities' (ἰδιώματα) are not intended as either fundamental or constitutive properties of the object in question, as we saw was the case with the 'peculiar qualities' of the Stoics. Phrases such as 'the son of Jonah', 'the one from Bethsaida' (with regard to Peter) or 'the zealous persecutor of the Church of God' (with regard to Paul) correspond neither to one-place predicates[43] nor to exclusive, self-sufficient or stable properties. While they undoubtedly possess some descriptive content, they do not even attempt to define, by listing them exhaustively, the basic constituting properties of the object so as to determine its nature absolutely in its individuality, but only to individuate it, distinguishing it, by means of a sequence of *characterizations*, from its peers.[44] A proper name *evokes* these characterizations through a process which we will investigate below, succeeding thereby in focusing the reference of the proposition in which it appears to just a single object.

The first element I would like to take notice of here is one that Basil does not state explicitly, but which can be inferred from the indicativeness of the characterizations he enumerates. These lists are not, nor could they be, complete and exhaustive. Descriptive characterizations of this type can always be multiplied *ad libitum*; consequently, the corresponding lists can be extended *ad infinitum*. The field from which these characterizations are drawn must be, of course, a more or less uniform frame of reference, without

---

[42] An analogous position is maintained by Basil in a passage of his *Epistle* 236 to Amphilochius (5.6), where the topic under discussion is the distinction between οὐσία (in the sense of 'second substance') and (individual) ὑπόστασις. The latter is described as 'peculiar' (ἰδιάζουσα), and is said to be mentally grasped as a 'concept' (ἔννοια), on the basis of 'the characters marked off for each one' (τοὺς ἀφωρισμένους περὶ ἕκαστον χαρακτῆρας). Cf. also [Athanasius], *De termin.* 1. 8 and *De Sancta Trin. dial.* 1. 16 (PG 28. 539–40 and 1141).

[43] That Basil is fully aware of this fact is demonstrated by the distinction he draws later on between names 'pronounced absolutely and in themselves' (ἀπολελυμένως καὶ καθ᾿ ἑαυτὰ προφερόμενα) and names 'said in relation to others' (πρὸς ἕτερα λεγόμενα) (*Contra Eun.* 2. 9).

[44] They thereby bear some resemblance to the characteristics or marks that point out the 'differentness' (διαφορότης) of a particular object from its peers, according to the suggestion advanced in Plato's *Theaetetus* 209 ɒ1 ff. As Burnyeat 1990: 221–5, has noted, these form merely a 'set of recognitional cues', having no claim to representing all or any of the essential features of their bearer.

any blatant internal contradictions, but which for all that may embrace several blanks or obscurities. The latter feature permits its constant enrichment with new characterizations, by which some aspects of the object may be determined with greater completeness and precision. This process is not, however, necessary for a term to function as a proper name; it is sufficient that there should exist a minimum of contextual descriptions, such that together they may constitute what Basil terms a 'character' ($\chi\alpha\rho\alpha\kappa\tau\acute{\eta}\rho$). And this last need not, of course, comprise the sum of all characterizations which could be ascribed to an object, but may include any of its subsets. In other words, the set of all potential characters is equivalent, roughly,[45] to the *power set* of such characterizations.

A second element is that the characterizations are not presumed to correspond obligatorily to real properties determining the object in question. It suffices that they should have been ascribed to the object within the pertinent frame of reference as components of some relevant narrative. Their relation to it is determined by the broader context within which they appear and, therefore, it may be established by purely linguistic (or perhaps we should say literary) means. Hence they may be withdrawn at any time without damage, generating neither contradiction nor nonsense, but only the need to readapt the corresponding 'character'.

One of the important advantages this theory offers is that it ensures great flexibility in the use of proper names. Various speakers, with different frames of reference, have the possibility of connecting a given proper name to a variety of characters. If these characters fall within a uniform and consistent set of characterizations, then each speaker is in a position to formulate propositions with significant informational content for the others, without causing any misunderstandings.[46] On the other hand, of course, if these characters are inconsistent with one another, we may infer that we are dealing either with a disagreement or with homonymy.[47]

There remains outstanding the question I raised earlier, that is, how proper names are able to evoke the characterizations they represent, as well as the further question of how the accumulation of these characterizations is assured, that is, how they all come to be ascribed to a single object. If we are to

---

[45] Because it does not, of course, include the null set. Putting it differently, we might say that each character consists of the logical sum (understood as the inclusive disjunction) of these characteristics. On this point compare the view advocated by Searle, *apud* Kripke 1980: 61 and 74.

[46] If e.g. speaker S_1 makes use of the name 'N' in virtue of characterizations {A,B,C,D} and speaker S_2 in virtue of {A,C,E,F}, it is obvious that S_1 can formulate the proposition 'N is B' without this being either tautological or contradictory for S_2.

[47] Inconsistency of characters may be due either to subjective factors, in which case we have a disagreement, or to objective factors (alterity) in which case we have a homonymy. For homonymy with respect to proper names, see *Schol. in Dion. Thr.* 233. 3–6 and 389. 19 H. The demand for consistency among characterizations corresponds, more or less, to the requirement that the denotation of proper names be rigid, i.e. that the identity of denoted objects should not shift in response to every change in context.

answer these questions, we need to consider that the expressions *par excellence* which lend themselves to the association and accumulation of characterizations are the pronouns. Pronouns are the best-adapted instrument language offers us for enlarging a particular frame of reference by adding new characterizations, analyses, and descriptions. Whether demonstrative or personal, they serve to maintain the thread of a narrative unbroken, to assure its coherence and possibilities for extension, by acting as reminders of the unity of the subjects and objects it sets in motion. All this is achieved thanks to the property of *anaphoricity* they possess, by means of which their reference is determined each time, on the basis of specific rules,[48] from the context within which they appear, in correlation to the characterizations previously formulated.

We thus observe that, on the strength of the theory just presented, proper names function as pronouns of a special type, as representatives of a group of characterizations which constitute a frame of reference and the meaning of which is determined on the basis of rules of anaphoricity.[49] In other words we have here a theory which interprets the use of proper names on purely semantic criteria, without appealing to syntactic or ontological parameters, as Aristotle[50] and the Stoics[51] did respectively. This fact enables it to deal unproblematically even with cases where a proper name denotes something non-existent. For in such cases the name will evoke, through anaphoricity, a particular frame of reference, where the use of the name will have been established on the strength of various characterizations, the content of which is by no means binding to its subsequent use, functioning merely as a semantic connective thread. Hence the fact, for example, that Paul, at some particular moment, ceased being a persecutor of Christianity does not nullify the coherence of his life narrative, nor does it dispel the unity of his personality, of which, on the contrary, it constitutes an element. This leads us to remark that proper names, as characterizations not of a descriptive, but of a pronomial type, stand out both for the rigidity of their denotation and for their correlation to a particular frame of reference, within which they have been endowed with meaning[52] through what we could label a 'baptism'. And the fact that this semantic framework constitutes a narrative element

---

[48] These rules are primarily semantic, not syntactic, in character. This allows them to connect terms belonging to sentences which are syntactically entirely autonomous. On the other hand, it relates them to other factors, semantic, linguistic, or even social, which also determine the appropriateness of the usage of proper names; see Strawson 1974: 42–6.

[49] In recent times, the consideration of proper names as pronouns of a special type has been proposed by Sommers 1982: 227–50. See on this point my review in *Deucalion*, 10 (1984), 77–8 (in Modern Greek).

[50] See above the passage cited from *Anal. pr.* 1. 27.

[51] For whom, as we saw, the items signified by proper names, the 'peculiar qualities', constituted a special ontological category.

[52] As correctly noted by McDowell 1977: 170 and 177, this undoubtedly necessary correlation is limited to the domain of beliefs (possibly sketchy or false ones) without presuming any knowledge of any related truths.

confirms Basil's position with regard to the 'conventional' (θέσει) and not 'natural' (φύσει) character of naming.

It remains for us to ask ourselves what sources Basil may have drawn on for his theory. As we have already noted, there do not appear to have survived any indications of a similar theory on the semantics of proper names having been formulated before Basil. The closest testimony, the passage we cited from Sextus concerning Carneades, in spite of its equivalent terminology, deals with our *knowledge* of sense objects and not with the linguistic means we employ to refer to them. The fact, however, that Basil presents this theory without any special argumentation and with a fairly allusive introduction of crucial and, more or less, uninterpreted terms (such as, for example, 'peculiarities' (ἰδιώματα), 'character' (χαρακτήρ)), shows that, up to a point, he must be drawing on some earlier source.

One indication which might, perhaps, be able to direct us towards his sources is the expression 'concurrence of peculiarities' (ἰδιωμάτων συνδρομή), which designates the notion evoked by the name 'Paul'. In a passage from Porphyry's *Shorter Commentary* on Aristotle's *Categories* we find the following explanation of the discrimination 'in accordance with number' (κατ᾿ ἀριθμόν) of Socrates from Plato:[53] 'for Socrates did not differ from Plato in virtue of specific differentiae; but it was in virtue of a particular concurrence of qualities that Plato differed from Socrates'. We see here again that it is a 'concurrence of qualities' (συνδρομὴ ποιοτήτων) which constitutes the particularity that individuates each person, distinguishing it from its peers.[54] However, it is clear that the differentiation Porphyry talks about no longer has an epistemological character, but an ontological one.[55] The 'qualities' (ποιότητες) constituting the particular personality of each human being must be descriptive ones and, to this extent, deprived of the extraordinary flexibility possessed by the characterizations in Basil's purely semantic theory.

---

[53] Porph., *In Cat.* (CAG iv. 1) 129. 9–10 Busse: εἰδοποιοῖς μὲν γὰρ διαφοραῖς οὐ διενήνοχεν Σωκράτης Πλάτωνος, ἰδιότητι δὲ συνδρομῆς ποιοτήτων, καθ᾿ ἣν [εἰδοποιῷ] (seclusi: <οὐκ> εἰδοποιῷ Bogardus, Strange) διενήνοχεν Πλάτων Σωκράτους.

[54] Proclus, *apud* Olympiodorum, *In Alcib.* 204. 8–11 Creuzer, ascribed this position to the Peripatetics although, as Strange remarks *ad loc. cit.* (1992: 140 n. 431) this may be found in another work of Porphyry's, the famous *Isagoge* (CAG iv. 1), 7. 21–4 Busse: 'such things are called individuals because each of them consists of properties the aggregate of which can never be the same for anything else; for the properties of Socrates could never be the same for any other particular man ...' (ἄτομα οὖν λέγεται τὰ τοιαῦτα, ὅτι ἐξ ἰδιοτήτων συνέστηκεν ἕκαστον, ὧν ἄθροισμα οὐκ ἂν ἐπ᾿ ἄλλου τινὸς τῶν κατὰ μέρος γένοιντο ἂν αἱ αὐταί ...). Here we have a clearer reference to the passage from Plato's *Theaetetus* which we mentioned in note 21 above. But also in the *Cratylus*, 432 B4–C6, Plato appears to imply that the difference between the names of two persons depends on the peculiarities which render them distinct: Cratylus and his perfect simulacrum should accordingly share the same name. Cf. also Dexippus, *In Cat.* (CAG iv. 2), 30. 20–7 Busse.

[55] In Kalligas 1997: 404–6, I have argued that we already meet with a kindred ontological theory, as regards the nature of sensible objects, in Plotinus.

For lack of other evidence, we are led to the conclusion that Basil, in his attempt to rebut Eunomius' naturalist theory of names, extended the onto-logical theory we find in Porphyry, but which has its roots in the sceptical Academy, towards an extreme nominalist position as concerns the semantics of proper names—a position which stood as the most complete and the most seductive such contribution to philosophical thought, at least until the time of William of Ockham.[56]

BIBLIOGRAPHY

Barnes, J. (1996), 'Grammar on Aristotle's Terms', in M. Frede and G. Striker (eds.), *Rationality in Greek Thought* (Oxford), 175–202.

Boyancé, P. (1941), 'La "Doctrine d'Euthyphron" dans le *Cratyle*', *Revue des Études Grecques*, 54: 141–75.

Brunschwig, J. (1994), 'Remarks on the Stoic Theory of the Proper Noun', in Brunschwig, *Papers in Hellenistic Philosophy* (Cambridge), 39–56.

Burnyeat, M. (1990), *The Theaetetus of Plato* (Indianapolis and Cambridge).

Daniélou, J. (1956), 'Eunome l'Arien et l'exégèse néo-platonicienne du *Cratyle*', *Revue des Études Grecques*, 69: 412–32.

Dillon, J. M. (1985), 'The Magical Power of Names in Origen and Late Platonism', in R. Hanson and H. Crouzel (eds.), *Origeniana Tertia* (Rome), 203–16.

Funghi, M. S. (1997), 'The Derveni Papyrus', in A. Laks and G. W. Most (eds.), *Studies on the Derveni Papyrus* (Oxford), 25–37.

Geach, P., and Black, M. (eds.) (1980), *Translations from the Philosophical Writings of Gottlob Frege*, 3rd edn. (Oxford).

Gersh, S. (1978), *From Iamblichus to Eriugena* (Leiden).

Kalligas, P. (1997), '*Logos* and the Sensible Object in Plotinus', *Ancient Philosophy*, 17: 397–410.

Kessisoglou, A. (1997), Η Ποιητική του Ποσειδώνιου από την Απάμεια (Athens).

Knudsen, C. (1982), 'Intentions and Impositions', in N. Kretzmann, A. Kenny, and J. Pinborg (eds.), *The Cambridge History of Later Medieval Philosophy* (Cambridge), 479–95.

Kripke, S. (1980), *Naming and Necessity* (revised and enlarged edn. Oxford).

Lampe, G. W. H. (1961), *A Patristic Greek Lexicon* (Oxford).

Lloyd, A. C. (1971), 'Grammar and Metaphysics in the Stoa', in Long (1971: 58–74).

Long, A. A. (ed.) (1971), *Problems in Stoicism* (London).

——and Sedley, D. (1987), *The Hellenistic Philosophers*, 2 vols. (Cambridge).

McDowell, J. (1977), 'On the Sense and Reference of a Proper Name', *Mind*, 86: 159–85.

[56] The instigation for my involvement in the subject of this chapter came from some discussions I had with John Demetracopoulos. I owe thanks also to Soteria Triantari, who referred me to the important pertinent study by G. D. Martzelos. My greatest debt, however, is to Nicolas Pilavachi who not only undertook the task of translating my paper (originally written in Modern Greek), but also provided some valuable comments on its content. Needless to say, of course, I alone should be held responsible for its shortcomings.

Martzelos, G. D. (1984), *Οὐσία καί ἐνέργεια τοῦ Θεοῦ κατά τόν Μέγαν Βασίλειον* (Thessaloniki).

Mill, J. S. (1872), *A System of Logic*, 8th edn. (London).

Reesor, M. (1954), 'The Stoic Concept of Quality', *American Journal of Philology*, 75: 40–58.

Rist, J. M. (1971), 'Categories and their Uses', in Long (1971: 38–57).

——(1981), 'Basil's "Neoplatonism": Its Background and Nature', in P. J. Fedwick (ed.), *Basil of Caesarea: Christian, Humanist, Ascetic* (Toronto, 1981).

Robins, R. H. (1951), *Ancient and Medieval Grammatical Theory in Europe with Particular Reference to Modern Linguistic Doctrine* (London, 1951).

Russell, B. (1956), 'The Philosophy of Logical Atomism', in Russell, *Logic and Knowledge*, ed. R. C. Marsh (London), 177–281.

Schrenk, L. P. (1991), 'A Note on *ἄθροισμα* in *Didaskalikos* 4.7', *Hermes*, 119: 497–500.

Searle, J. R. (1967), 'Proper Names and Descriptions', in P. Edwards (ed.), *The Encyclopedia of Philosophy*, vi (New York and London), 487–91.

Sedley, D. (1982), 'The Stoic Criterion of Identity', *Phronesis*, 27: 255–75.

Sommers, F. (1982), *The Logic of Natural Language* (Oxford).

Strange, S. K. (1992), *Porphyry, On Aristotle Categories* (London).

Strawson, P. F. (1952), *Introduction to Logical Theory* (London).

——(1974), *Subject and Predicate in Logic and Grammar* (London).

Wedin, M. V. (1978), 'Aristotle on the Existential Import of Singular Sentences', *Phronesis*, 23: 179–96.

Wittgenstein, L. (1967), *Philosophical Investigations*, tr. G. E. M. Anscombe, 3rd edn. (Oxford).

3

The Justinianic Dialogue *On Political Science* and its Neoplatonic Sources

DOMINIC O'MEARA

This chapter concerns the fragments of an anonymous dialogue in Greek 'On political science' discovered by Angelo Mai in a Vatican palimpsest (Vat. gr. 1298) and first published by him in 1827. A more complete edition of the fragments was published in 1982 by Carlo Mazzucchi, together with an Italian translation.[1] Mai identified the author of the dialogue as Peter the Patrician, a high official in the court of Justinian. Although this particular identification is fairly speculative, there is at least agreement that the anonymous dialogue dates to the Justinianic period, given its references, as if to a recent past, to the Persian King Peroz (459–484) and to the Frankish King Clovis (481–511). Mazzucchi thinks that the dialogue was written in the earlier part of the Justinianic reign, before 535, deriving from the higher circles of Justinian's administration,[2] whereas Averil Cameron prefers to place it towards the end of the reign (565) and considers it as voicing the interests of a senatorial elite.[3] The later dating seems more plausible, since, as will be seen below, the two speakers in the dialogue appear to represent high officials active in Justinian's administration in 528–9 and it seems unlikely that the dialogue, in portraying them, would have been written close to the time of their activity.

Already in 1900, Karl Praechter showed that the fragments of the anonymous dialogue present many affinities with Neoplatonic philosophy as well as with the work of an author who is almost contemporary, or perhaps somewhat earlier, the Pseudo-Dionysius. Praechter concluded, despite these affinities, that the author of the dialogue 'On political science' was not a

---

[1] *Menae patricii cum Thoma referendario De scientia politica dialogus*, ed. C. Mazzucchi (Milan, 1982).
[2] Ibid., p. xiii.
[3] Cameron (1985: 250–1).

Neoplatonist philosopher and seems to have been a Christian.[4] In this chapter I would like to pursue Praechter's investigation further and offer some remarks concerning the conclusions he reached. Praechter demonstrated the Neoplatonic affinities of the anonymous dialogue by means of a long series of comparisons of specific concepts and terms. He did not, however, examine as a whole the political philosophy that is presented in the dialogue, as this might relate to something comparable in Neoplatonism. This has to do no doubt with the received opinion that, given its otherworldly interests, Neoplatonism has little to say in the area of political philosophy.[5] However, it can be shown that an otherworldly orientation does not exclude an interest in political questions, a good example being provided by the anonymous dialogue itself. And it is possible to bring together elements of a Neoplatonic political philosophy.[6] Using such elements, I therefore propose to review in this chapter the political theory of the anonymous dialogue so as to determine the extent to which this theory can be related to a Neoplatonic background. I will try to show in particular that the anonymous dialogue offers interesting solutions to problems that arise in connection with Plato's political philosophy and that these solutions are Neoplatonic in character. But at first it might be best to describe the general structure and contents of the dialogue.

I

The palimpsest fragments discovered by Mai have been identified by him (and there seems to be no good reason to reject this identification) with a work of the same title on which Photios reports in his *Bibliotheca* (cod. 37). The dialogue 'On political science' read by Photios involved, according to his report, two speakers, the patrician Menas and the referendarius Thomas. We know of no referendarius of this name for this period, but Cameron refers[7] to the quaestor Thomas who, as a pagan, was purged in 529—the year, we remember, of Justinian's anti-pagan legislation that precipitated the closing of the Neoplatonic school of Athens. Menas is likely to have been the praetorian prefect of the Orient of that name for 528-9. Photios also tells us that the dialogue was made up of six books (λόγοι) and that it introduced a type of constitution different from earlier constitutions. This constitution was called 'dicaearchic' and consisted of a mix of the best of royal, aristocratic, and democratic constitutions and thus was itself the best of constitutional

---

[4] Praechter (1900: 621–32).

[5] Cf. Valdenberg (1925: 56).

[6] See O'Meara 1998*a–c* for three articles attempting this and O'Meara (1999*a–b*). In what follows I will refer to the principal texts cited in these articles, where further references may be found.

[7] 1985: 249.

types. Finally Photios says that the dialogue rightly attacked Plato's (ideal) republic or constitution (πολιτεία).[8]

Turning now to the actual fragments of the dialogue surviving in the Vatican palimpsest, we find that only a small part of book 4 and somewhat more of book 5 are extant. The speakers of the dialogue are named Menodorus and Thaumasius, no doubt Platonized versions of Menas and Thomas, names which Photios is likely to have found noted at the beginning of the text. The fiction of the Platonic dialogue is pushed very far in the fragments. The atmosphere and language of the conversation between Menodorus and Thaumasius remind us very much of a Platonic dialogue of the middle period, in particular the *Republic*: Thaumasius closely follows Menodorus' speculations, asking for clarifications; Menodorus sometimes formulates general principles, which then require explanation and exemplification. The fragments from book 4 have to do with military science and virtue. Menodorus and Thaumasius discuss the conduct of military exercises, the importance of infantry, a military moral code, and the relations between the military and civilians. A list of the contents of book 5 survives in the fragments. According to this list,[9] book 5 dealt with kingship (βασιλεία) and kingly science (βασιλικὴ ἐπιστήμη): how this science relates to other sciences; its laws, doctrines and practices; how the king imitates God, knows the divine, and rules accordingly. These points are covered to some degree by the remaining fragments. The following items in the list of contents are not, however, represented in the fragments: how what is said about a constitution differs from what was said by others, with an objection to something in Plato; then a comparison between Plato's and Cicero's republic and between Plato's and Aristotle's philosophy in general. The reference to Cicero is matched by quotations from Cicero in the fragments, some of which have been thought to come from lost parts of Cicero's *De re publica*. Indeed, the author of the dialogue seems well read in Latin literature and quotes Juvenal, Seneca, and Livy as well.

II

Among the various topics covered in the fragments, three are of more direct interest here: the conception of political science which inspires the dialogue; the relation the author sees between political and kingly science; and the theory of kingly science as an imitation of the divine.

The conception of political science

Political science arises, according to a fragment from book 5 (46. 11–47. 12), as a consequence of the human condition, the predicament in which we find

---

[8] Photios, *Bibliotheca* cod. 37, ed. R. Henry, 22. On Menas, cf. Rashed (2000: 89–98).
[9] Mazzucchi edn. (cited also in what follows), 15. 2–15.

ourselves, midway between the rational and the irrational, between the divine life of pure intellect (νοῦς) and nature. If transcendent intellect and nature, being unmixed with each other, know peace, humanity however, torn between them, lives in turmoil and conflict, striving both up towards the divine life of intellect and down towards nature. In his goodness, however, God provided human reason with two aids, 'dialectical science', which relates to the incorporeal, and 'political science', which relates to the corporeal and concerns political action.

At this point the published text of the fragments is puzzling: it describes 'dialectic', which leads up to the divine, as prior in time and as 'for the sake of something else', whereas political science is said to be prior in act and in value and is that 'for the sake of which'.[10] We would have expected the reverse, that political science is prior in time and for the sake of something else, and that dialectic is prior in act and value and that for the sake of which. Our passage seems to invert the proper order of things and indeed the Greek text of the fragment does not seem to be secure. At any rate, it becomes clear a little later that the author of the dialogue has his priorities right, when he tells us (49. 15–22) that God devised political knowledge as a divine method for the use of men, in their exile here below, so that they may attain good order, through which to return to the transcendent metropolis, the dignity of the immortal city. Here, clearly, political knowledge prepares the way and is subordinate to a higher union with the divine; political knowledge, relating to the body, produces good order in our terrestial lives, which in turn provides the condition for a return to the divine homeland, that of divine intellect from which we are exiled here below.

If we turn now to the Neoplatonists of the fourth and fifth centuries, we find the same interpretation and gradation of sciences as that used in the anonymous dialogue. Beginning with Iamblichus, Neoplatonists standardly divided philosophy, following the Aristotelian model, into theoretical and practical sciences, the highest theoretical science being what Aristotle called 'theology', which the Neoplatonists identified with the 'dialectic' of Plato's *Republic*, whereas political philosophy encompassed the practical sciences.[11] The practical and theoretical sciences were understood as constituting a scale aiming at the progressive divinization of man, or assimilation of man to the divine. Political philosophy, as a practical science, has to do with man as soul related to the body, soul using body as an instrument. Its objective is to bring political virtue, that is, good order, to the incorporated life of soul. This good order prepares the access to higher knowledge and virtue, the theoretical sciences and virtues of which dialectic is the summit, where man, as intellect, attains the life of divine transcendent Intellect. As Hierocles explains, summing up this theory towards the middle of the fifth century: 'we must first put

---

[10] 47. 12–16; for the distinction οὗ ἕνεκα, ἕνεκά του, cf. Plato, *Philebus* 54c.

[11] On this and on the following cf. O'Meara (1998a). On the place of political philosophy in the practical sciences cf. Elias, *Prolegomena philosophiae*, ed. Busse, 32. 1–30.

in order the irrationality and slackness in us, and then in this way look to the knowledge of more divine things [. . .] The political virtues make a good man, the sciences that lead up to divine virtue make man a god.'[12]

The anonymous dialogue presents this theory of the hierarchy and anagogic function of political philosophy and dialectic as part of a quasi-mythical, cosmogonic account of the human condition. We are reminded of the forced combination of opposed constituents that go to make up human nature in Plato's *Timaeus* and of the turmoil, moral and epistemic, that ensues. What can serve to check this turmoil, according to the *Timaeus*, is the greatest gift of the gods to mortals, philosophy (47 B). But what philosophy? The *Timaeus* passage speaks of the observation of the orderly movements of the heavens which will bring order to the movements of our soul (47 B–C). The theme of a divine gift to humanity in perdition also occurs in the myth of Plato's *Protagoras* (322 C–D), where Zeus, through Hermes, supplies us with the means whereby we might live together without destroying each other, that is, justice and shame. Zeus' divine gift reappears in Julian the Emperor's vision, in which, following a Platonic ascent to the highest levels of the divine, Julian receives instruction, on Zeus' orders, on how to rule, that is, he is taught the political knowledge that will guide him as emperor.[13]

Here we are very near, I suggest, to the ideas of the anonymous dialogue. Since, for the Neoplatonists, philosophical knowledge in general is a divine gift to humanity, mediated by superior souls such as those of Pythagoras and Plato,[14] we can include political philosophy as part of this gift. Indeed Iamblichus claims that Pythagoras, as well as revealing other sciences, bestowed 'political science' on his followers, a science also revealed, for the later Neoplatonist, by Plato in the *Gorgias*, the *Republic*, and the *Laws*.[15]

Finally the metaphors of exile and return to a mother city above whereby the anonymous dialogue describes human existence also have a good Platonic pedigree. I am thinking not only of the transcendent or heavenly model on which is based Plato's ideal state and which Proclus describes as an intelligible city,[16] but also of Plotinus' magnificent reading of Odysseus' return to his homeland as the return of the soul to the One (*Enn.* 1. 6. 8). Julian, too, describes our present condition as that of an exile from which we seek to return.[17]

The broad context and specific function of political philosophy, as described by the anonymous dialogue, are thus profoundly Neoplatonic in inspiration. But what of the *content* of this philosophy? According to the fragments of the dialogue, political science seeks to achieve well-being, in

---

[12] Hierocles, *In Aureum Pythagoreorum carmen commentarius*, ed. Koehler, 6. 5–7 and 19–21.
[13] Cf. O'Meara (1999*b*: 284–7).
[14] Cf. O'Meara (1989: 36–9).
[15] Iamblichus, *Vita Pythagorica*, ed. Deubner, 18. 5–10, 96. 14–97. 19; O'Meara (1999*a*: 194).
[16] Plato, *Republic* 500 E3, 592 B2–3; Proclus, *In Timaeum*, ed. Diehl, 1. 32. 10–12.
[17] O'Meara (1999*b*: 290).

accord with justice, for the purpose of the salvation of humans.[18] It includes, in view of this purpose, laws, doctrines, and practices. Among the laws are those concerning the election of kings, the constitution of an elite (senatorial) body, the choice of church authorities and of the high officers of state, and the protection of the laws (19. 27–20. 10). 'Political philosophy' is claimed to be identical to kingship or 'kingly science', which in turn is described as an imitation of God (18. 5–7), two points I would like now to consider.

The relation between political and kingly science

The identity that is affirmed between political philosophy and kingly science might seem, at first glance, puzzling, if we assume that kingly science is merely a part of political science, which will also include, for example, military science such as is explored in book 4 of the dialogue. Military science can be expected to have its own specific concerns, as distinct from the concerns of kingship discussed in book 5 of the dialogue.[19] Plato, it is true, identifies in some places political with kingly science.[20] But how does the anonymous dialogue understand this identity?[21]

A fragment of the dialogue (27. 7–15) allows us to see how kingship can be both a part of, and identical to, political philosophy. Kingship is the fountain of political light (τὸ πολιτικὸν φῶς) which is communicated, by a scientific method, to the ranks subordinated to it in the state, rank after rank, so that each rank shares in the knowledge of the rank above it that rules it. Thus, we may infer, if kingship communicates political knowledge to the lower orders of the state, then the other parts of political philosophy derive from kingship as if from a source. The language of this fragment is very close to that of the Pseudo-Dionysius, particularly at the beginning of the *Celestial Hierarchy*. Both authors express a fundamental theory of Neoplatonic metaphysics, the theory of a series of terms in which the first member of the series precontains and produces the other members of the series. This type of series, dubbed a 'P-series' by A. C. Lloyd, is to be found, for example, in Proclus' *Elements of Theology*.[22] In the case of the anonymous dialogue, this means that kingship or kingly science is both a part of, and identical to, political philosophy: it is part of political philosophy, because there are other parts, such as military science; it *is* political philosophy, because it precontains, as the highest part and source of all political knowledge, the other parts. To see how this would work out in practice, we could try to see if the military science described in book 4 of the anonymous dialogue can indeed be derived from the kingly

---

[18]   19. 20–4; 47. 22–4.

[19]   Plato describes military science as a part of political knowledge in *Protagoras* 322 B5.

[20]   *Euthydemus* 291 C4–5; *Politicus* 259 C–D.

[21]   The question of the relation between kingly science and other sciences is listed in the table of contents of book 5 of the dialogue (15. 3–4).

[22]   Propositions 18–19; cf. Lloyd (1990: 76–8).

science of book 5, account being taken of the lower ranks that are concerned. I believe this can, in fact, be done, but would like at present to look more into the notion that kingly science is an imitation of God.

Kingly science as imitation of the divine

It is asserted, both in the list of contents and in the fragments of book 5, that kingly science is an imitation of God, or assimilation to God.[23] This is, of course, a banality in the literature of monarchy of the Hellenistic and Roman imperial periods. An influential expression of the idea is found in the Pseudo-Pythagorean treatises on kingship.[24] It is found again, for example, in Eusebius' *Praise of Constantine* and in the *Ekthesis*, or 'Mirror of princes', composed by Agapetus for Justinian's accession in 527. The Neoplatonic philosophers seem to have been aware of the Pseudo-Pythagorean treatises on kingship.[25] Indeed I would argue that it is due to Iamblichus' promotion of Pythagorean texts that these treatises, along with other Pseudo-Pythagorean texts, found their way into Stobaeus' anthology and thus survived.[26] At any rate, the Neoplatonists contributed an interesting interpretation of the theme of kingship as imitation of the divine. Relating it to their view of philosophy in general as an assimilation of man to the divine, they specified what this divinization might mean. Two aspects of the divine, of God, were distinguished, knowledge, or perfect thought, and providence, or care of what is lower. If the life of the divine has these two aspects, then the philosopher who is assimilated to the divine, or imitates it, will exhibit these two sorts of activity, theoretical activity, or knowledge, and providential activity, that is political rule. These ideas are found, for example, in Ammonius and Olympiodorus towards the beginning of the sixth century in Alexandria,[27] and the conception of divine imitation as providential activity also occurs in our anonymous dialogue (below, p.57).

However, to describe kingship as imitation of divine providential rule is not to explain *how*, in particular, kingship imitates the divine. A form of this problem must already arise for any reader of Plato's *Republic* who asks how precisely the philosopher-kings model their city according to a divine paradigm (500 E): do they copy the Platonic Forms in the exercise of their rule, and what does this mean? For the Neoplatonists, who knew well the relevant passages of the *Republic*, these questions cannot but have become more acute. Plotinus, for example, speaks in *Enn.* 6. 9. 7 of the legendary legislator Minos

---

[23] 15. 12; 16. 6–7; 18. 6–7; 37. 14–15.

[24] Delatte (1942).

[25] Cf. Olympiodorus, *In Platonis Gorgiam*, ed. Westerink, 221. 3–11; Diotogenes, *De regno*, ed. Thesleff, 72. 16–23.

[26] On Iamblichus' promotion of Pythagorean texts, cf. O'Meara (1989: 96–7; 102–3). Stobaeus' sources contained extracts from Iamblichus' correspondence and work.

[27] Ammonius, *In Porphyrii Isagogen*, ed. Busse, 3. 8–19; cf. Olympiodorus, *In Platonis Gorgiam*, 166. 14–16.

making laws in the image of his communion with Zeus, that is, the One. But if the One is beyond knowledge and determinate being, how can it be the paradigm of laws made in its image? The anonymous dialogue shows awareness of this problem and addresses directly the question of how, if unknown, God may nevertheless function as an archetype for kingly science (16. 13–17. 8).

Responding to the question as to how kingly science is to be discovered, if it is an imitation of God and God is unknown, Menodorus distinguishes what may be discovered *scientifically* by reason and what is found by mere correct *opinion* guided by divine creation.[28] This scale of knowledge reappears later in the fragments where an ascent of the intellect is described, going from opinion and reasoning (διάνοια) using hypotheses (ὑποθέσεσι) up to science, a vision of the light, of truth stamped in the resemblance of the Form of the Good (35. 16–36. 4). We are here clearly in the world of Plato's *Republic*, of the ascent of the future philosopher-king from the cave to the light of the sun, the Form of the Good, an ascent which, according to the image of the line, goes through reasoning from hypotheses up to intellection (*Rep.* 511 B–E). In an interior dialogue, the ascended intellect of our anonymous text (36. 6–37. 2) affirms the first cause of all beings, a cause beyond (ἐπέκεινα) all things, which does not go out of itself, but which contains within the λόγοι of all things, like the centre of a circle from which progress the radii, which is to say an intelligible sun and intelligible world, a rank of intellectual beings, the visible sun and world, all ordered, down to the elements, in a hierarchy of rule which includes humans, themselves ordered in a monarchic structure. This is without doubt a Neoplatonic metaphysical landscape, dominated by a supra-intelligible hidden first cause from which derives an elaborate gradation of intelligible, intellectual and visible being.

But what does the metaphysical knowledge thus attained by reason signify for political philosophy? Three political principles may be inferred, I suggest, from this metaphysical knowledge: (i) political order is monarchic in structure (cf. 37. 3–8); (ii) the monarch, the political 'first cause', is transcendent; and (iii) power is exercised through a system of mediating ranks. The first principle is subject to some restrictions, to which I will return later. The second principle will be considered shortly. As for the third principle, we can find its application in the dialogue's insistence that the king choose and deal *only* with the highest officers of the state administration and of the Church.[29] If the king rules correctly as regards the highest rank subordinate to him, then this rank will function correspondingly as regards the rank subordinate to it, and so on. We might note that the same Neoplatonic principle of mediate terms inspires the ecclesiology of the Pseudo-Dionysius.[30]

---

[28] 17. 21–4; cf. Plato, *Politicus* 301 A10–B3.   [29] 26. 23–27. 6; 28. 6–13.

[30] Cf. O'Meara (1998c: 79).

Returning to the anonymous dialogue, the question of how rulership is an imitation of God is raised again a little later in the fragments (38. 13–40. 8). Here, various divine attributes are picked out—goodness, wisdom, power, justice—attributes which are one in God, but which can only be conceived by us as distinct, and still less adequately expressed.[31] Regarding *goodness*, this means that the ruler, as imitator of God, must be good in terms of his moral integrity and in terms of providential care for his subjects, ruling for *their* good and not his own, a requirement of Plato's *Republic*[32] taken up by Iamblichus and Proclus.[33] As for divine *wisdom*, this means, for the ruler, respecting the third principle, that of mediated rule, for it is a wisdom manifest in God's creation. Thus the ruler will deal only with his immediate subordinates and they, in turn, will transmit his providential rule, creating thereby a harmonious political structure (39. 8–22). As regards divine *power*, this means, for the ruler, moral and intellectual excellence, qualities whereby he transcends his subjects such as courage, practical sense, daring, benevolence (39. 22–40. 2). Finally, divine *justice* involves for the ruler both internal justice of the soul, such as that described by Plato, and an external justice that assigns to each rank its due (40. 2–8). This we might describe as a fourth political principle, that of (distributive) justice, 'to each what is appropriate', that is, the principle of geometrical proportion that underlies Plato's ideal city.[34] This fourth principle is also exemplified in the metaphysical structure of reality.

Summarizing, we can say that the anonymous dialogue provides an answer to a question that must arise in a political philosophy inspired by Plato's *Republic*: how can political knowledge be modelled on a transcendent paradigm? Our dialogue refers to a scientific knowledge of intelligible principles and to the lower level of correct opinion. In both cases, the object grasped is the structure of reality deriving from a supra-intelligible first cause, the complete metaphysical structure in the case of scientific knowledge, the cosmic structure in the case of correct opinion. This structure manifests the first cause and, in its organizational principles (monarchic order, transcendence of the first cause, mediated transmission, ranked distribution), provides the principles of kingly science. It is in this way that kingly science imitates the divine. The idea that the king imitates the cosmic order in his rule can be found already in Stoicism and in the Pseudo-Pythagorean treatises on kingship.[35] However, this idea is extended in the anonymous dialogue to include the complete metaphysical structure of a Neoplatonic reality and is

---

[31] For an example of a conventional account of the king's imitation of divine attributes cf. Dio of Prusa, *Or.* 1. 37–47.

[32] 39. 5–8; cf. 25. 10–11, which refers to Plato, *Rep.* 342 E (rather than to *Politicus* 297 A–B [printed as 197 A–B] as given in Mazzucchi's apparatus).

[33] Iamblichus, *Letter to Dyscolius*, in Stobaeus, *Anthol.*, ed. Wachsmuth and Hense, 4. 222. 10–15; Proclus, *In Tim.* 2. 118. 10–17.

[34] Cf. Neschke-Hentschke (1995: 129–35).

[35] Cf. also Dio of Prusa, *Or.* 1. 42–5.

presented as a solution to the problem of how a supra-intelligible unknown first cause may be an object of imitation.

Before concluding I would like to return to what has been described above as a first political principle, that of order as monarchic in structure. The political application of this principle is subject to some restrictions in the anonymous dialogue: the access of the monarch to rule and the exercise of rule are subject to *law*, which itself expresses political philosophy. The author of the dialogue is of the opinion that the source of political evils, of the disease of the state, is the absence of the requisite political knowledge among rulers who seek to rule in their own interest, by the use of force, money, flattery.[36] A method has to be found, therefore, whereby Plato's dream of the union of philosophy and kingship (*Republic* 473 D) may be realized (52. 23–53. 4), that is, a method allowing for the selection of rulers among those best equipped, morally and intellectually, for a rule that they do not, of themselves, desire. The method proposed by the dialogue involves a complicated legislation regulating the identification of the best possible candidates, nomination of them by the heads of all groups of the state, and a divine sanction through a religiously conducted drawing of lots.[37] The legitimacy of the ruler depends therefore on his intrinsic moral and intellectual qualities; on his designation by the subjects, through their representatives, in whose interest he is to rule; and on the divine sanction to which he is subordinate in the cosmic order. The ruler is also expected to preserve the law (38. 23), as stipulated in the fifth fundamental law (20. 8–10). Another legal restriction on monarchic absolutism mentioned in the fragments concerns the age of retirement of the monarch (44. 1 ff.).

This primacy of law as regards rulers reminds us more of Plato's *Laws* than of Plato's *Republic*. In a passage of the *Laws* (739 A–E), Plato speaks of a range of cities going from the best, the city of gods or of children of gods, who share women and property, to second- and third-best cities, in which concessions are made, notably regarding family life and private property. The *Laws* discuss a second-best city, in abstraction from the particular circumstances that might concern the founding of a specific state (745 E–746 C). Our anonymous dialogue also claims to be abstract in this sense: it does not discuss the particulars of a specific state (27. 18–21). The Neoplatonists found in the passage of the *Laws* (739 A–E) a way of explaining the relation between the utopia of the *Republic* and the city of the *Laws*: the former is an unrestricted ideal, the latter involves compromises with what is given.[38] Damascius warns us against utopian mirages,[39] and it can be shown that the Neoplatonists took an interest in the second-best state developed in the *Laws*. It is on this or on

[36] 54. 17–55. 8; 24. 24–25. 4.
[37] 19. 27–21. 10; cf. 25. 20–26. 7.
[38] Cf. Anonymus, *Prolegomena to Platonic Philosophy*, ed. Westerink *et al.*, 26. 45–58 (40, with n. 226, and 77–8); Proclus, *In Remp.*, ed. Kroll, 1. 9. 17–11. 4.
[39] Damascius, *In Philebum*, ed. Westerink, 171. 5–7.

an even less ambitious level that Julian the Emperor's political project is, I believe, to be placed: Julian does not claim to be a philosopher-king; his is a more humble role, administering the state under the guidance of philosophers.[40] Before him, Iamblichus had emphasized, quite strikingly, the primacy and sovereignty of law, to which the ruler as guardian of the law is subordinate.[41] A further sign that the level of political reform described by the anonymous dialogue corresponds more to the city of Plato's *Laws* than to that of the *Republic* may be seen in the mixed constitution that it proposes, made up (as Photios also notes in his report) of royal, aristocratic, and democratic elements, a mixed constitution being also proposed in the *Laws*, as compared to the absolutism of the philosopher-kings of the *Republic*.

If the anonymous dialogue is seen in this way as describing a project comparable to the second- or third-best cities of Plato's *Laws*, then the rejection in the dialogue of the abolition of family life among the elite[42] can be read, not as an attack on Plato himself, but as a rejection of this hallmark of the highest, divine, and indeed impossible city for humans, a hallmark absent from the second-best city of the *Laws*. I do not therefore think that we should conclude, with Praechter,[43] that the author of the dialogue was not a Neoplatonist. Nor should we be too influenced by the negative tone of Photios' report on the dialogue's criticism of Plato: Photios was no friend of Plato's *Republic*,[44] and the list of contents of book 5 in the palimpsest (15. 17) suggests a more restricted critique. The second argument offered by Praechter against the author being a Neoplatonist is based on the dialogue's rejection of divination (41. 24–6). But here again the point at issue is too limited to yield such a conclusion. The dialogue rejects divination as a basis for political decisions, which should derive rather from political science. This does not in principle preclude the use of divination in other contexts, such as that of private religious practices answering specific needs.

Was the author of the dialogue a Christian? Praechter notes[45] what might be a reference to the doctrine of man as the image of God (37. 5–6). This may suggest Christianity, but it is an isolated and rather weak indication. The situation reminds one of that of Boethius' *Consolation of Philosophy*, where the religion of the author is not exactly evident. Boethius, a contemporary of, or slightly older than the author of our dialogue, was his peer and equivalent in the court of Theoderic, a philosopher trained in the schools of late antique Neoplatonism, at home both in Greek and Latin culture, also fascinated by

---

[40] Cf. O'Meara (1999*b*: 286).

[41] Iamblichus *Letter to Agrippa*, in Stobaeus *Anthol.*, 4. 223. 14–224. 7.

[42] 22. 22–5; the criticism of Plato noted in the table of contents of book 5 (15. 17) may refer to material similar to this, as may also Photios' mention of criticism of Plato in the anonymous dialogue.

[43] Praechter (1900: 629).

[44] Cf. Photios, *Letter* 187, 168–71, ed. Laourdas and Westerink, vol. ii.

[45] 1900: 631.

Plato's call for the union of philosophy and politics (*Consolation* 1. 4. 4–8), who found himself at the higher levels of an imperial administration.

III

I would like to conclude with a few additional remarks. I hope to have shown that the anonymous dialogue 'On political science' can be located firmly in the framework of Neoplatonic philosophy, as regards its conception of the structure and functions of the parts of philosophy, the place of political philosophy in this structure, its nature as an imitation of the divine, the divine as expressed in a metaphysical chain of being. If the anonymous dialogue, like Plato's *Laws*, makes abstraction of the particulars of a specific state, its author is nevertheless very much aware of the political problems of the time, of which his philosophical predecessors—Plato, Aristotle, Cicero—were ignorant, problems posed by factions in Constantinople, by large numbers of unemployed, unoccupied people, by unworthy monks.[46] It is in part with an eye to these problems, but mostly in relation to the fundamental question of the appropriate selection, lawful election, and proclamation of the monarch, that the dialogue proposes a new constitutional order. If the general principle of this order, that of a mixed constitution, is not new—we remember Plato's *Laws*, Aristotle, and Cicero, for example—the particular dispositions proposed do seem to constitute a new framework for reconciling a number of claims: that of the importance of political science and of law expressing this science; that of the moral and intellectual superiority of the ruler who will conform to this science and law; that of the citizens in whose interest rule is to be exercised; and that of the divine to which the human order is subordinate. I also believe that the dialogue introduces interesting ideas of a Neoplatonic character as regards political philosophy itself: what its place and function are in the philosophical sciences, how its parts are related to each other, how kingship can be an imitation of a divine principle transcending knowledge.

Finally a word as regards the Pseudo-Dionysius. I have suggested elsewhere[47] that the Pseudo-Dionysius transformed Neoplatonic political philosophy into a Christian ecclesiology: man is saved (that is, divinized) through an emanative order of illumination, purification, and perfection going from the ineffable Godhead, through the celestial hierarchy, down to a church structure in which the bishop takes the place of the philosopher-king in the political order. In this structure for the divinization of humanity, no room is provided, apparently, for the political order, for the state, in the salvation of man. In the anonymous dialogue, however, the Church is integrated in legislation expressing political science (as religion had been made part of

---

[46] 29. 4 and 9–12, 33. 7–26, 28. 15–20.   [47] O'Meara (1998c).

legislation in Plato's *Laws*) whose ultimate function is the divinization of man. The Church is the object of the king's attention and care (27. 31–28. 13). The two authors, the Pseudo-Dionysius and the author of the anonymous dialogue, are thus objectively opposed. Assuming that the Pseudo-Dionysius is the earlier of the two, we may conclude that the author of the anonymous dialogue advocated a subordination of the Church to the constitutional law of the state, in opposition to the primacy claimed by Dionysian ecclesiology. However our author also sought to subordinate monarchical absolutism to law. Both monarch and Church should find their place, the author suggests, in a constitutional legislation expressing a political philosophy whose Neo-platonic inspiration I have attempted to show.[48]

BIBLIOGRAPHY

TEXTS

Ammonius, *In Porphyrii Isagogen*, ed. A. Busse (Berlin, 1891).
Anonymus, *Prolegomena to Platonic Philosophy*, ed. L. Westerink, J. Trouillard, and A. Segonds (Paris, 1990).
—— *Menae patricii cum Thoma referendario De scientia politica dialogus*, ed. C. Mazzucchi (Milan, 1982).
Damascius, *In Philebum*, ed. L. Westerink (Amsterdam, 1982).
Diotogenes, *De regno*, ed. H. Thesleff, *The Pythagorean Texts of the Hellenistic Period* (Abo, 1965).
Elias, *Prolegomena philosophiae*, ed. A. Busse (Berlin, 1900).
Hierocles, *In Aureum Pythagoreorum carmen commentarius*, ed. F. Koehler (Stuttgart, 1974).
Iamblichus, *Vita Pythagorica*, ed. L. Deubner (Stuttgart, 1975).
Olympiodorus, *In Platonis Gorgiam*, ed. L. Westerink (Leipzig, 1970).
Photios, *Epistulae et Amphilochia*, ed. B. Laourdas and L. Westerink, ii (Leipzig, 1984).
—— *Bibliothèque*, ed. R. Henry, i (Paris, 1959).
Proclus, *In Platonis Timaeum*, ed. E. Diehl (Leipzig, 1903).
—— *In Rempublicam*, ed. W. Kroll (Leipzig, 1899).
Stobaeus, *Anthologium*, ed. C. Wachsmuth and O. Hense (Berlin, 1884–1912).

SECONDARY LITERATURE

Cameron, A. (1985), *Procopius and the Sixth Century* (London).
Delatte, L. (1942), *Les Traités de la Royauté d'Ecphante, Diotogène et Sthénidas* (Liège).

---

[48] I am grateful for suggestions made by my colleagues at the meeting at Thessaloniki, in particular those made by John Duffy.

Dvornik, F. (1966), *Early Christian and Byzantine Political Philosophy: Origins and Background* (Washington, DC).

Lloyd, A. C. (1990), *The Anatomy of Neoplatonism* (Oxford).

Neschke-Hentschke, A. (1995), *Platonisme politique et théorie du droit naturel*, i (Louvain).

O'Meara, D. (1989), *Pythagoras Revived* (Oxford).

——(1998*a*), 'Vie politique et divinisation dans la philosophie néoplatonicienne', in *The Structure of Being and the Search for the Good: Essays on Ancient and Early Medieval Platonism* (Aldershot), ch. 17.

——(1998*b*), 'Aspects of Political Philosophy in Iamblichus', in *The Structure of Being and the Search for the Good: Essays on Ancient and Early Medieval Platonism* (Aldershot), ch. 18.

——(1998*c*), 'Evêques et philosophes-rois: Philosophie politique néoplatonicienne chez le Pseudo-Denys', in *The Structure of Being and the Search for the Good: Essays on Ancient and Early Medieval Platonism* (Aldershot), ch. 19.

——(1999*a*), 'Plato's *Republic* in the School of Iamblichus', in M. Vegetti and M. Abbate (eds.), *La Repubblica di Platone nella tradizione antica* (Naples), 193–205.

——(1999*b*), 'Neoplatonist Conceptions of the Philosopher-King', in J. Van Ophuijsen, *Plato and Platonism* (Washington, DC), 278–91.

Pertusi, A. (1990), *Il pensiero politico bizantino* (Bologna).

Praechter, K. (1900), 'Zum Maischen Anonymus περὶ πολιτικῆς ἐπιστήμης', *Byzantinische Zeitschrift*, 9: 621–32.

Rashed, M. (2000), 'Menas, préfet du Prétoire (528–9) et philosophe: Une épigramme inconnue', *Elenchos*, 21: 89–98.

Valdenberg, V. (1925), 'Les Idées politiques dans les fragments attribués à Pierre le Patrice', *Byzantion*, 2: 55–76.

4

John of Damascus on Human Action, the Will, and Human Freedom

MICHAEL FREDE

John of Damascus (perhaps born as early as AD 650, but no later than AD 680, died in AD 749, or shortly thereafter) has a complex account of human behaviour and human action. This account is mainly to be found in his *Expositio fidei orthodoxae* (Ἔκδοσις ἀκριβὴς τῆς ὀρθοδόξου πίστεως), the third part of his tripartite *Fons sapientiae* (Πηγὴ γνώσεως). In this account a doctrine of the will (θέλησις) plays a crucial role, because John of Damascus believes that to understand human actions we have to see that they involve an exercise of the will, or at least a failure to exercise the will. It is because we have a will that we are responsible for what we are doing. For, if, for instance, we behave in a way which is open to criticism, it is either because we chose to act in this way or because we failed to exercise our will in such a way as to choose not to act in this way. Thus, how we behave depends on our will and the way we exercise it. In principle our will is such as to enable us to make the right choices. But we can fail to avail ourselves of this ability, or use this ability without the indicated care, with the result that we fail to make the right choice or that we make the wrong choice. Such failure to use the will, or to use it appropriately, in complex ways affects the will. It affects it in such a way that it diminishes our ability to make the right choices. A will is free (ἐλεύθερος), and correspondingly a person is free, if the will is not thus diminished or constrained, if one's ability to make the right choices is not thus reduced, for instance by having fallen into the habit of making in certain situations the wrong choices. But quite irrespective of whether or not one's will in this way is constrained, it remains the fact that how one behaves depends on oneself in the sense that it depends on oneself how one exercises one's will. This feature of a person John of Damascus calls τὸ αὐτεξούσιον. This term often is rendered by 'freedom' or even 'freedom of will' or 'freedom of choice'. But it should be clear already from what has been said that this is

Myles Burnyeat generously read and made helpful comments on this chapter.

rather misleading, since the exercise of one's will remains a matter of one's discretion, even if the will no longer is free.

It is not surprising that John of Damascus should assume that there is such a thing as the will, and that it is in virtue of having such a will that we are responsible for what we are doing. By John's time this was a standard assumption which could be taken for granted. Though not originally a Christian doctrine, but of Stoic origin, it had become a standard view in Christian authors from the end of the second century onwards. But we also do have to keep in mind that Aristotle, for instance, on whom John of Damascus, directly or indirectly, relies a good deal for his account of human behaviour, does not in his account appeal to a will. Aristotle, too, assumes that human beings will ($\beta o\acute{u}\lambda\epsilon\sigma\theta a\iota$) things and that they do things, because they will to do them. And Aristotle, too, of course, must assume that, if human beings do will things, it is possible for them to will things, they can will things, they are able to will things. But to assume that human beings have a will is to assume more than that human beings can, or are able to, will things in this weak, trivial sense, in the sense in which quite generally possibility follows from actuality. It is rather to assume that they have the ability to will things in the sense of a basic, distinct, positive ability, comparable to the ability to discriminate perceptual features or the ability to understand things. Aristotle did not assume that it takes a special, distinct ability to will things. He did assume that if one comes to think of something as good or as a good, one will naturally will it. But willing it for him does not seem to involve the exercise of some further special capacity, namely the will. We have the ability to recognize something as good or a good, but if, as a consequence, the mind wills it, it is not because of an exercise of a further ability, but because the mind is constructed in such a way that, if one believes one has recognized something as good or a good, one wills it. From the first century AD onwards, though, the ability to will things did become thought of as a distinct, special ability. Yet there were different ways in which different authors conceived of this ability. This is not surprising, given that different philosophers had very different views about the human mind and its role in determining our behaviour. Accordingly, the will was also conceived of in rather different ways. Among these different views there was one, to be found in Alexander of Aphrodisias' *De fato* and in the *De anima mantissa* ascribed to him, according to which it is in virtue of the will that we are able, in the very same circumstances in which we will and choose to behave in a certain way, not to will and to choose to act in this way, or to will and to choose not to act in this way. But this, at least in antiquity, was a very rare view. It is not John of Damascus' view. Nor, as far as I can see, does John of Damascus espouse any of the views we find in antiquity. It is rather the case that John of Damascus' account will strike one as significantly different and in some ways novel, if one compares it to the better-known ancient accounts. Admittedly this first impression quickly gives way to the impression that John of Damascus' originality in this matter is rather more limited, if one also takes into account the views of John of Damascus' more immediate predecessors, in particular those of Maximus the Confessor. Like the latter, John of Damascus is very much indebted to Nemesius of Emesa. And, like Nemesius of Emesa, he is very much indebted to Aristotle. But my concern here is not to show that John of Damascus was particularly original. I am rather interested in his account because, whether original or not, it significantly differs from ancient accounts of the same matter. It seems to me to be a good example of a piece of Byzantine philosophy which has its sources in antiquity, because, though it differs from ancient accounts, it extensively relies on identifiable ancient sources like Nemesius of Emesa, and in fact gains its distinctive character in part by relying on Aristotle. Nemesius had relied on Aristotle, but like Aristotle Nemesius does not appeal to a will. What gives John of Damascus' account some of its distinctive character is the fact that John of Damascus tries to integrate a notion of a will into Aristotle's moral psychology and theory of action. It thus, though Byzantine, crucially depends for its novelty in part on its recourse to an ancient, indeed pre-Christian source, namely Aristotle. John of Damascus tries to combine the results of a discussion which over the centuries had moved far beyond Aristotle, for instance in coming to presuppose the existence of a will, with substantial pieces of Aristotelian doctrine.

There is reason to think that John of Damascus' account of human action and the will deserves our particular interest quite independently of how original we take his account to be. It deserves this interest because of the remarkable status John attained as an authority in Christianity, both Eastern and Western, an authority which also seems to give special weight to his account of human action and the will. He sometimes, in the West, is said to be the last of the Fathers of the Church. He writes at a point when, at least as far as the great Trinitarian and Christological issues are concerned, what is to count as orthodox Christian doctrine has been settled by the authority of the Fathers and the Councils. The last of these controversies, concerning Monophysitism, Monoergism, Monotheletism, still were an issue in his lifetime. Though also the issue of the number of wills in Christ finally had been settled by the Council of Constantinople in 680, John of Damascus still felt called upon to devote to the clarification of this issue a special treatise, the *De duabus voluntatibus in Christo*. And there still was the iconoclast controversy. But it was a time in which one could think that the great controversies had been authoritatively settled, and that it now was possible to give an overall account of Christian doctrine, as it had emerged from the teaching of the great Fathers of the past and the decisions of the Oecumenical Councils. And this, it seems, is what John of Damascus set out to do in the third part of his *Fons sapientiae*, the so-called *Expositio*.

There was something novel about this attempt to give a reasonably complete and reliable account of the whole of Christian doctrine. There, of course, had been some earlier attempts to give an overall outline of the Christian position, like Origen's *De principiis* or Theodoretus' fifth book *On Heresies*. But, for chronological reasons, they could not be as comprehensive as John of Damascus'. Another feature crucially distinguishes John's *Exposition* from, for instance, Origen's treatise. Origen clearly separates out the unquestionable doctrine of the Church from the questions this doctrine raises which are not authoritatively settled—these are of great importance for our understanding of the Christian view, but about them there is a great deal of confusion among Christians. It is these questions which Origen tries to clarify and to answer. But he proceeds in such a way as to make it clear that these are his answers based on Scripture, the teaching of the Church, and his own thought, which patently is deeply influenced by philosophy. As Origen knew, and as it in any case turned out, his views were deeply controversial. By contrast John of Damascus goes out of his way to make it clear that in the *Fons sapientiae* he is refraining from stating his own views (*Dial. β′* 2, Prooem. 60) which might be questioned and lead to controversy. What he presents in the *Exposition* is supposed to be the unambiguous position of the Church as it has emerged, no more and no less. And this he means to set forth as clearly as possible.

This does not mean that we get a mere catalogue of isolated dogmata. The particular doctrines are presented as integrated into, and often forming the crucial links in, a reasonable, intelligible view of the world, to a good extent based on philosophy, which itself, though substantial, is regarded as uncontroversial. At least one enemy to true Christian doctrine is philosophical confusion. It is telling that the *Fons sapientiae* consists of three parts: (i) the *Capitula philosophica* (κεφάλαια φιλοσοφικά) or *Dialectic*, (ii) a treatise on the heresies, and (iii) the *Exposition*. The *Dialectic* for the most part does not offer more than an exposition of elementary notions of Aristotelian philosophy, as we find them in Aristotle's *Categories* and Porphyry's *Isagoge*, enriched by some further notions of late ancient philosophy like that of a *hypostasis*. But it is clear already from the way these notions are introduced that they are meant to be used in, among other places, an exposition of Trinitarian and Christological doctrine, and that familiarity with these notions is supposed to be crucial for a clear exposition of Christian doctrine which does not give rise to the kind of confusion on which Trinitarian and Christological heresies are based. It is in this sense and this spirit that the *Exposition* relies on philosophical notions, distinctions, and assumptions which John of Damascus regards as uncontroversial, but which nevertheless allow him to present Christian doctrine in a systematical, coherent, seemingly clear and precise fashion. He can at least think of the *Exposition* as a detailed, clear, precise, uncontroversial exposition and explication of the Creed orthodox Christians subscribe to.

Though John of Damascus' standing no doubt in part is due to his orthodox opposition against Monotheletism and his contributions to the iconoclast controversy, in the long run his authority seems to have been primarily based on the fact that Christians came to accept the *Exposition* as what it presents itself as: a systematical, reliable, clear exposition of Christian doctrine, rather than of John's own views on the matter.

At least Orthodox Christianity has come to regard his *Exposition*, and thus also the account of human action and the free will contained in it, as authoritative. It is telling that, when B. N. Tatakis[1] turns to John of Damascus, he prefaces his account of John's views by a sketch of what he, Tatakis, takes to be the essence of Orthodox Christianity (pp. 107–9), to then proceed to recount, *inter alia*, in some detail, John's doctrine of the will (pp. 119–25). There is a question as to when John of Damascus acquired this authoritative status in Orthodox thought. H.-G. Beck warns us against overestimating the influence of John of Damascus on the further evolution of Byzantine theology.[2] But already the sheer number of manuscripts of the *Exposition* (about 250), of which more than 200 predate the sixteenth century, leaves no doubt as to the importance attributed to the text as a compendium of Christian doctrine already in Byzantine times. The fact that John of Damascus' account of the will in the *Exposition* also is transmitted separately[3] seems to indicate a particular interest in John's account. I also note in passing that John of Damascus, in relying on Aristotle, must have contributed to the rather remarkable and somewhat surprising standing Aristotle has in Orthodox thought to the present day.

But more important perhaps is the reception of John of Damascus' work in Western Christianity. For there seems to be at least a prima-facie case for the assumption that John of Damascus' remarks in the *Exposition* specifically on the will had an impact on Western medieval thought, for instance on Thomas Aquinas, and in this way on the further development of thought about the will in traditional Western philosophy. If this were true, we would have here the rather rare case of a piece of Byzantine philosophy which, on an important topic, has had an influence on Western thought and also for this reason deserves our interest.

John of Damascus seems to be the last Greek author Western Latin Christianity accepted as an authority. Both the *Dialectica* and the *Expositio* were translated into Latin. A version of the *Dialectica* is still extant in a translation by Robert Grosseteste, produced about 1240. It is unclear, though, whether this is not just a revision of an already earlier translation. Of more importance for our purposes is the *Exposition*. Of this, in whole or in part, several Latin translations were produced. Already by the middle of the twelfth century, a partial translation by Cerbanus was available. But the most influential one was the one produced by Burgundio of Pisa around 1150 at the

---

[1] Tatakis (1949): in spite of its obvious shortcomings still the standard modern account of Byzantine philosophy.

[2] Beck (1959: 476; 480); and more recent authors.

[3] Cf. Beck (1959: 481).

instigation of a fellow Pisan, Pope Eugenius III. One can see why there would be such interest in the *Exposition*. As scholastic theology began to develop, John's account must have met a strongly felt need for a reliable, compact, but sufficiently detailed and systematic account of the whole of Christian doctrine, and though serious tensions between Eastern and Western Christianity had been developing for some time, John of Damascus seemed to be far enough removed in time from the emerging controversies not to appear suspect. What came to guarantee John of Damascus, but in particular the *Exposition*, a place in Western thought for the rest of the Middle Ages was the fact that Peter Lombard in the middle of the twelfth century made extensive use of the *Exposition* as an authority in his *Sentences*, first in Cerbanus' partial translation and then in Burgundio's complete version. For since theology came to be taught by lecturing on Peter Lombard's *Sentences*, every theologian at some level was exposed to John of Damascus' views or even had to form an opinion about them himself. There are some twenty-six references in Peter Lombard to John of Damascus. It is telling for the view which one took of the *Exposition* as a compendium of Christian doctrine that Grosseteste in his commentary on Pseudo-Dionysius' *Celestial Hierarchy* at one point refers to the *Exposition* as John's *Sententiae*.[4] Indeed, it seems that the use of the title *Sententiae* or *Liber Sententiarum* for the *Exposition* was not uncommon in scholasticism, suggesting its association with Peter Lombard's *Sentences*.[5]

But quite independently of Lombard's *Sentences* there was a considerable interest in John of Damascus, in particular the *Exposition*. Grosseteste, for instance, extensively used the *Exposition*. The tabula produced by Grosseteste and Adam of Marsh which constitutes an index of theological subjects with relevant references on each subject to passages in the authorities has 280 references to John of Damascus' *Exposition* on seventy-four subjects. By comparison the numbers for Ambrose are thirty-three references on seventeen subjects, for Anselm 124 references on forty-eight subjects. The list, not surprisingly, is headed by Augustine, Gregory the Great, and Jerome, but John of Damascus in the number of references among ecclesiastical authors follows in fourth place. There are some seventeen references to the *Exposition* in Grosseteste's *Hexaemeron*. Indeed, Grosseteste was interested enough, it seems, to produce another Latin version of the text, based on Burgundio's translation.[6] That John of Damascus was regarded as an authority we can, for instance, see not just from the fact that he is constantly referred to in Thomas Aquinas' *Summa theologica*, but also from the fact that at least in one place we find Thomas making, or at least reporting, an effort to defend John against the charge of unorthodoxy on a point which, by Thomas' time,

---

[4] MS Merton College 86, fo. 86ʳ, quoted by Callus (1955: 46).

[5] Cf. *Die Schriften des Johannes von Damaskos*, ed. B. Kotter (Berlin, 1973), ii, p. xxii, who refers to De Ghellinck (1948: 414).

[6] Cf. Callus (1955: 46–54).

had become perhaps the most serious cause of division between Greek East and Latin West. In *Summa theologica* I, q. 36, a. 2, concerning the procession of the Spirit also from the Son, the *filioque* of the Western version of the Creed, John is quoted as an authority for the view that the Spirit does not proceed from the Son, because he is saying 'ex Filio autem Spiritum Sanctum non dicimus'. In his response (ad 3) Thomas refers to the Nestorians and to Theodoretus as having denied the procession from the Son. He also says that John followed Theodoretus, but adds that some might argue that, though John does not confess that the Spirit proceeds from the Son, at least the words quoted cannot be taken to mean that John denies the procession from the Son. There is perhaps at least this much truth in the suggestion, namely that Easterners refused to say, as part of the Creed—the Constantinopolitan or the so-called Nicene or Niceno-Constantinopolitan Creed, as read at and accepted by the Council of Chalcedon (451)—that the Spirit also proceeds from the Son. The reason for this, in the first place, was that this Creed, as accepted in Chalcedon by East and West, in fact did not contain the *filioque*, and that there was no authority recognized on all sides to justify the addition of the *filioque* as representing the commonly held doctrine of the Church. From an Eastern point of view its addition, whatever its merits or errors, in the first place constituted an uncanonical tampering with the Creed and a disregard for the authority of the Fathers. The monks of St Sabbas, John's monastery, protested as early as 807 against its use by Western monks in Jerusalem.

It is remarkable, and an indication of the regard in which John of Damascus is held in the West, how cautiously Thomas treats John of Damascus' position on the *filioque* which by this point had become a matter of deeply divisive controversy, settled for the West by the Lateran Council of 1215. In this context it is interesting that when Grosseteste translated John's *Trishagion*, he appended a note to it, referring to the dispute between the Latins and the Greeks whose 'view it is that the Holy Spirit is the Spirit of the Son (*Spiritus Filii*), but does not procede from the Son, but only from the Father, though through the Son (*per Filium*)'. But Grosseteste goes on to explain that the truth probably is that, though the Latins and the Greeks differ in their wording and thus seem to say things contrary to each other, there is no disagreement in the view expressed in contrary fashion. And he points out the multiple ambiguity of expressions like 'huius', 'ex hoc', 'illo', 'ab illo'. He asks 'who dares to accuse this author, *scilicet* Johannes Damascenus, and the blessed Basil, Gregory the Theologian, Cyril and similar Greek Fathers of heresy?' In his lectures on Peter Lombard (I, dist. 11, q. 1) Duns Scotus takes up the question of the procession of the Spirit. In setting out the view against the procession from the Son he starts out questioning John's *Exposition* ('He rests in the Son', 'we do not say "out of the Son"') and the *On the Trishagion* ('the Holy Spirit is of the Son, not out of the Son'). In answering the question he points out that there is disagreement between some of the Greeks and the

Latins, briefly quotes Grosseteste's note on John's explanation of the *Trisha-gion*, then paraphrases it as saying 'it is unbelievable that these Greek saints and doctors (who, after all, have canonical status, as one can see from distinctions 15 and 16 of the *Decreta*) should have been heretics, last of all such a great doctor as the Damascene was, and others'. Duns Scotus himself comments that perhaps earlier Greek authors, like John of Damascus, expressed themselves cautiously using phrases like 'of the Son' and others, because the matter was not settled. And he considers that whatever they meant to say, it is an article of faith that the Spirit proceeds from the Son.[7] When Duns Scotus produces the *Ordinatio*, he is more ample in quoting what John actually said, and also in giving authoritative evidence for the view he defends, but now he quotes Grosseteste for eighteen printed lines, adding himself that however this may be, it is clear what the doctrine of the Church is.[8]

Of particular relevance, though, for our purposes is the way John of Damascus' *Exposition* was drawn on especially in discussions concerning voluntary action and free will, and this at a time when Western doctrine on the matter was remarkable fluid. A good example is Thomas Aquinas. Needless to say, his Commentary on the *Sentences* contains references to John of Damascus, and Thomas's discussion of human action in the Commentary also reflects his awareness of John's discussion. If we look at the *Summa theologica*, we find that Thomas in the section on voluntary human action (II.1, qq. 6–17) refers at least nineteen times to John of Damascus; in the section on the powers of the intellect, the will, and the freedom of the will (I, qq. 79–83) at least twelve times. Not surprisingly, the discussion whether Christ is one in will (III, q. 3, a. 18) contains some six references to John. Similarly q. 24 of Thomas's *De veritate*, on free choice, has some fourteen references to John of Damascus. So there is at least some prima-facie reason to believe that John of Damascus was one of the few Byzantine authors who also on this topic had some influence on Western thought. Indeed, it seems fair to say that the long sequence of different kinds of mental acts which Thomas presents as being involved in choice, which gives Thomas's account of choice its distinctive character and which continues to puzzle his commentators, has its origin largely in John of Damascus, though John himself derives it from Maximus the Confessor.

It is easy to see why Latin authors in the thirteenth century would take a particular interest in John of Damascus' account of human action and the will. They had some doctrine of the will or other, ultimately relying for this on Augustine. They also came to rely on Aristotle's *Nicomachean Ethics* which does not, certainly not explicitly, involve a doctrine of a will. So there was a problem about interpreting Aristotle's moral psychology in such a way as to

---

[7] Duns Scotus, *Opera omnia* (Vatican City, 1966), xvii, *Lectura*, 127–8.
[8] Cf. on all this Southern (1992: 231–2).

involve a doctrine of the will. Before they had Aristotle's *Nicomachean Ethics* available to them, they already had had for some time a Latin version of Nemesius of Emesa's *De natura hominis*. The treatment of human action in this treatise, heavily indebted as it is to Aristotle, must have greatly facilitated the reception of Aristotle's account. That Nemesius of Emesa obviously was an orthodox Christian author and at least sometimes seems to have been confused with Gregory of Nyssa must have helped in establishing Nemesius as an authority, and hence the readiness to look at the relevant parts of Aristotle's *Ethics*. But Nemesius does not have, at least explicitly, a doctrine of the will. The four authorities Thomas is mainly relying on for human action, the will, and choice, are Augustine, Aristotle, Nemesius, and John of Damascus. It seems to me to be easy to see which role John of Damascus must have played in this context. Not only, like Nemesius, did he facilitate the reception of Aristotle's moral psychology. He also offered an account, heavily based on Nemesius and Aristotle, which already involved a richly structured doctrine of a will meant to fit into Aristotle's moral psychology. So now the task was to integrate a somewhat simple model of the will inherited from the Augustinian tradition with the rather complicated, but also only very roughly sketched, model offered by John of Damascus.[9]

Unfortunately, though, the literature on Latin medieval philosophy and in particular on Thomas Aquinas, does not, as far as I can see, have much of substance to say on John of Damascus' influence in this regard. In fact, standard accounts of, for instance, Thomas Aquinas' position just pass him over in silence. This is not a matter which we have to pursue here. I will just quote from Gauthier:

This conception of the will, worked out by Saint Maximus, and taken up by Saint John of Damascus, has imposed itself on Christian theology, not only with the Greeks, but also with the Latins, and the form of long habit nowadays makes it appear so natural to those minds which have been formed in the school of scholasticism (only to those, though; for it has become alien again to modern philosophy) that it seems to them to be just a matter of good sense.[10]

But, if we do not have a better understanding of the precise impact John of Damascus had in this regard on Latin medieval thought, this in good part seems to be due to the fact that we really do not know much about John of Damascus' doctrine on human action and the will, let alone understand it. The literature offers very little guidance and help.[11] For these reasons, then, it seems to me to be a worthwhile task to try again to provide a more detailed account of John of Damascus' view on human action, the will, and human freedom.

[9] On how one proceeded to do this see useful remarks in Lottin (1931: 631–61).

[10] Introduction to R. A. Gauthier and J. Jolif, *Commentary on Aristotle's Nicomachean Ethics*, 2nd edn. (Louvain, 1970), 266.

[11] There are the remarks in Tatakis (1949: 119–24) and Lottin (1931), whose title promises more than the article delivers.

The importance John of Damascus attributes to the topic of the will is reflected by the fact that it is the subject of the final chapter 10 of the *Institutio elementaris*, a very brief (in Kotter's edition seven pages long) exposition of some basic notions like 'substance' or 'consubstantial' or 'hypostasis', an exposition which parallels the *Dialectic*, but is more narrowly focused on what is of use for a clear account of Christian doctrine. It is easy to see why John of Damascus would take such an interest in the topic. There was a simple reason why Christian authors since the second part of the second century had taken an interest in the doctrine of a free will: orthodox Christians had to explain why God would create human beings if they sooner or later would sin and if he then was going to punish them for their sins. John of Damascus himself in his *Dialogue against the Manichaeans* (34. 1540C ff.) has the Manichaean raise the question why God created the devil and human beings if he knew that they were going to sin. Christians from the second century onwards had to explain this in the face of a variety of so-called 'Gnostic' doctrines, according to which the world, including human beings, was not created by God, but by an imperfect Demiurge who, with the powers subordinate to him, had created and ruled the world in such a way that human beings could not but sin, perhaps even systematically were made to sin. Sometimes this view went hand in hand with a belief in astral determinism, the view that this world is governed by the planets who, pursuing their own interests, determine our lives, perhaps even our choices. But astral determinism, to be distinguished from the view that astrologers can infer our future from the constellation of the stars, was quite widespread independently of Gnosticism. There also emerged, at the end of the third century, under the influence of a particular form of Gnosticism, Manichaeism, according to which most human beings in this life, given their constitution, could not but sin.

Against such views it was crucial for orthodox Christians to maintain that God had created the world, including human beings, and that he had created human beings in such a way that they were not bound by their very nature and constitution or their circumstances to do wrong. They did so by appealing to the view that all human beings have been created with a will in virtue of which they are able to choose the right thing to do, and which no power in the world can overcome so as to make them choose the wrong thing, unless they themselves surrender their will and let it be enslaved. So John of Damascus has this traditional interest in a doctrine of the will to explain how God's goodness is perfectly compatible with his creating human beings which will sin and which he will punish for their sins, because they are responsible for their sins, since they have been created with a free will. But it seems that John of Damascus' interest in the will to justify human responsibility may not just be this by his day very traditional interest. For John of Damascus, perhaps in part because of his location, Manichaeism still seems to be a live concern, as shown for instance by his *Dialogue against the Manichaeans* just referred to.

More important, though, is his concern with Monotheletism, the doctrine that there is just one will in Christ. Against this John of Damascus argues at great length that, given Christ's two natures, his divine and his human nature, we also correspondingly have to assume two wills, a divine will and a human will. Hence we need enough of a doctrine of a will to distinguish between the divine and the human will. What is more, we need a doctrine of a will with enough structure to explain why the ordinary human will would be liable to sin, whereas Christ's human will would not go wrong, though its nature would not prevent it from doing wrong. John of Damascus devoted a special treatise to this problem, the *De duabus voluntatibus in Christo*, but also dealt with it at some length in the third book of the *Exposition*. So for these reasons John has a particular interest in the will and its freedom.

Perhaps the best way to approach John of Damascus' view, or rather, the view he sets forth, is to begin with his terminology. John's term for the will is θέλησις. The terms the ancients had used for the will were προαίρεσις and βούλησις. Θέλησις is formed analogously to these terms. Βούλεσθαι means 'to will, to want', but in philosophical language at least from Plato onwards 'to rationally desire'. Hence βούλησις is used to refer to a particular rational desire, a desire of reason, as opposed to a non-rational desire, a desire which arises in one perhaps independently of one's reason. But βούλησις also comes to be used for the ability or faculty in virtue of which one has, or forms, such rational desires, perhaps even for the disposition to have or form such desires. The same with προαίρεσις. προαιρεῖσθαι means 'to choose'; προαίρεσις is used to refer to a particular choice, but also comes to be used to refer to a disposition to make certain choices and, finally, to one's ability and disposition quite generally to make choices. ἐθέλειν or θέλειν means 'to want', a θέλησις is one's wanting something or other, a particular want or wish one has, but the term, analogously to βούλησις and προαίρεσις, can be used to refer to one's ability and disposition to will things quite generally. The question is why John of Damascus uses this term, rather than either of the old terms. The reason for this by no means is that for John of Damascus, as for many in antiquity, θέλησις is just a more colloquial variant of βούλησις. Nor is it that θέλησις and its cognates have the authority of New Testament use. It is rather that it is crucial for John's theory that certain beings, namely God and Christ have a will, but make no choices. So the term προαίρεσις as a general term for the will, covering God's will, would be highly misleading. But it is also crucial to John's theory that all created rational beings have to make choices, and that making choices presupposes rationally willing things. Hence the term βούλησις would be misleading. Though it would cover the case of God who wills things, it would not do justice to the fact that the will of creatures involves two distinct functions, the ability to rationally desire things, and the further ability to make choices to satisfy one's rational desires. It should be noted that for John of Damascus the will is not to be identified with the ability to make choices, neither in general, nor in the case of created rational beings, nor even just the case of human beings. The term θέλησις in part is chosen precisely to mark this.

John of Damascus assumes, following a long Platonist tradition, that reality divides into an intelligible world and a sensible world. The intelligible world is inhabited by intellects, the sensible world by bodies, some of them living bodies, for instance animals with a non-rational soul. Human beings straddle the two worlds in having an intellect and a body. In this way they have a privileged position. Now according to John of Damascus all intellects have a will. This may seem curious to us, but if it does, it is because we have a rather 'intellectualistic' view of the intellect or of reason. We think of reason in purely cognitive terms, and perhaps even in purely instrumental terms. This is not how the ancients thought of the intellect or of reason. I have already alluded to the fact that at least from Plato onwards most ancient philosophers thought that the intellect or reason has its own desires, its own specific form of desire, namely βούλησις. The intellect is thought to do things, namely for instance, to contemplate the truth; it is thought to enjoy doing this, and hence to will or rationally desire to do this. We have to remember that for many ancient philosophers intellects do not just exist as the capacities of some corporeal organism but by themselves, with a life of and on their own. In this light we more easily understand the assumption that all intellects have a will.

For John of Damascus, as opposed to most Platonists, the most radical divide is not that between the intelligible world and the sensible world, but the divide between God and his creation, and this creation contains both the intellects other than God and the visible world. Correspondingly there is supposed to be a radical difference between God's intellect and his will and created intellects and their will. John of Damascus marks this distinction by calling created intellects, or beings with a created intellect, 'rational' (λογικόν), as opposed to 'intellectual' (νοερόν), though he does not always consistently maintain this distinction in terminology. A being may be intellectual without being rational in this sense. A being, in virtue of being intellectual, has a will; a being, in virtue of being rational, has a certain kind of will, namely the will in virtue of which it can make choices, the choices a rational being has to make. John explains in *Expos.* 2. 27 what it is to be rational, rather than merely intellectual:

of the rational one aspect (or part) is the theoretical (θεωρητικόν), the other the practical (πρακτικόν); theoretical is that which understands how things are, practical is that which is deliberative (βουλευτικόν), that which determines for things to be done the way they should be. And one calls the theoretical aspect (or part) intellect (νοῦς), but the practical reason (λόγος).

Part of the background of this is the Platonist view that the intellect contemplates eternal truth, but that the rational soul not only contemplates the truth, but also concerns itself with ordering the visible world in such a way as to reflect eternal truth; which, at least in the case of a soul like the human soul, involves it in λογισμοί and deliberation.

To better understand how John of Damascus sees this, we have to take into account that for John of Damascus, as opposed to most Platonists, all intellects, apart from the divine intellect, are created and for this reason rational in such a way as to engage in deliberation and choice. It is not just human beings which are rational in this way, but also angels and demons (cf. *Exp.* 2. 27, last paragraph), that is, all created intellects. Not being God, but created beings, they lack the perfection of God, in this case specifically God's omnipotence and omniscience. God's willing something (βούλεσθαι) is tantamount to its being the case, for there is nothing to stand in the way of his will. But created beings have limited abilities, both in the sense that they do not have abilities for everything, and in the sense that, even if they have the ability for something, this ability might be limited. Thus a created intellect may will something, but not have the ability to attain, or to realize, what he wills. But even if he has this ability, he has to figure out whether and how he might attain or realize what he wills. This might be a complex and tedious task. Given its complexity, it is possible for one to go wrong at many points along the way. To avoid mistakes, one has to go about it with great care.

Now, it also is of relevance that John of Damascus in this context emphasizes that all created beings, having been created, are subject to change and thus to corruption and ultimately destruction. They are τρεπτά, as John of Damascus puts it (*Exp.* 2. 27). There is nothing about their nature which guarantees their continued existence. Thus human souls are not by nature immortal; they are, being created, as far as their nature is concerned, subject to corruption and destruction. Now physical objects are subject to corruption by being subject to physical change. But rational beings are turnable, subject to corruption by turning one way rather than another in their choices, or the way they make choices (κατὰ προαίρεσιν, *Exp.* 2. 27; 960C). They may make the right choice, but they also may make the wrong choice. And if they make the wrong choice, corruption sets in. One wrong choice gives rise to another, and quickly one's ability to make choices is completely corrupt. It may be worth noting, though this is not the place to pursue this in detail, that it is an old theorem of ancient philosophy that all things which come into being also pass away. It is also relevant that Plato in the myth of creation in the *Timaeus* qualifies this theorem to the effect that all the things the Demiurge creates, though they, as far as their nature is concerned, are subject to corruption and destruction, will not pass away, since the Demiurge orders and arranges things in such a way that they will not get destroyed. In Christian authors from an early point onwards, for instance in Origen, we find the idea that all created beings as such are liable to corruption and destruction, an idea expressed by using the very term John of Damascus uses, τρεπτόν; we also find this very term used, for instance, in Origen, to refer to the 'moral' corruptibility of rationality, and we also find the connection between the two ideas that the corruptibility of rationality has its source in the creation of rational beings out of nothing.

It is important to get at least somewhat clearer about this complicated matter. God created beings whose being consists either wholly or partially in their rationality. This rationality, not being divine, does not have the perfection of the divine intellect; it is limited. Being created, it is subject to change and thus also to corruption. There cannot be a created being which by its nature is incorruptible. Thus even God cannot create such a being. But what he can do, and what he does do, is create rational beings in such a way that they are able not to get corrupted, though they are corruptible. Now the change of physical objects is such that, though ultimately it involves their destruction, it, to a large extent, at least from the perspective of the object, is neutral, neither for the better nor for the worse for the object. But change in one's rationality does seem to be for the better or the worse. It is a matter of progressing or regressing in one's understanding and knowledge, a matter of progressing or regressing in developing an attitude towards things which is adequate to them, does justice to them. Thus the rationality we have been endowed with at creation is good enough to avoid mistakes and to make the right choices. But it changes for better or worse. And, of course, it does not change by itself. It changes by the way we make use of it. It improves as we manage to avoid mistakes and to make the right choices. In doing so our understanding and knowledge increases, we form the right habits in going about deciding matters. It correspondingly deteriorates if, due to lack of care, we make mistakes. In this way, we not only have control over our rational activity, but also, indirectly, over the state of our rationality, whether it improves or deteriorates. We, for instance, can get better and better at making the right choices. Thus we can perfect our rationality in such a way that it becomes our second nature to make the right choices. But this 'second nature' is not a real nature. It can never be our real nature to make the right choices unfailingly. For our rationality is created and thus turnable. And it remains so, however much we manage to perfect it. It always as such remains liable to corruption. So it is by an act of divine grace that rational beings, having reached a certain state of perfection of their rationality, as a reward as it were for their involving themselves in the appropriate way in the perfection of their rationality, are made to be no longer liable to corruption, and thus become immortal and divine, able to enjoy a life of eternal bliss. Short of such an act of divine grace we would get a view as we seem to find it in Origen, according to which created intellects forever can rise and fall, however far they have risen. This raises the question why God did not create the rational beings in such a way and arrange things in such a way right from the start that, though corruptible, they would not in fact get corrupted. The answer would seem to be that they would not have deserved their immortality and divinity.

It is a crucial part of John's view, then, that the rationality with which we have been endowed in creation does enable us to get things right and to make the right choices. It is not imperfect in the sense that it is so insufficient that we are bound in some cases to make a mistake, because we are just not sufficiently equipped to deal with such complicated cases. We are created with all the knowledge and all the right attitudes we need to deal with any case we might encounter, if we apply ourselves appropriately. But it also is crucial that the rationality we are created with is imperfect in the sense that it admits of perfection, and that we have been given control over our rational activity. For instance, we know what it is to think properly, and can make the required efforts to do so.

There is a detail here which is of sufficient general importance and of relevance to our topic not to be passed over in silence altogether, though it is of such complexity that it cannot be dealt with here. When I talk about the rationality with which we have been endowed at creation, I am not talking about the rationality with which each of us after the Fall is born. When the Fathers talk about the creation of Adam, or the first human beings, and with them of mankind, they do not talk about the creation of an infant, but about the creation of a mature human being which *ab initio* is endowed with everything it needs to do right, to make the right choices. In this sense mankind at creation was endowed with a sufficient degree of rationality, wisdom, and virtue. But this does not mean that we, after the Fall, are born with this rationality, wisdom, and virtue. There is agreement that all of us who are affected by the Fall are born in a condition or in a situation in which our rationality will be severely limited and more or less seriously damaged. Precisely how this is thought to come about depends on the view one takes of the origin of the soul. But on the view which became dominant, namely the view that each soul is created by God *ad hoc* at conception, or at least at birth, the soul does not benefit from the wisdom and virtue with which Adam's soul was endowed from its very beginning when mankind was created. This invites the view that the soul which is created after the Fall is created endowed with reason and hence a will, but not with the knowledge and the virtue with which Adam's soul was endowed. And this in turn invites the view that the soul is created without knowledge, let alone wisdom and virtue, but rather given the mere capacity to know and to will or to choose. It is noteworthy that John of Damascus, like the Greek Fathers in general, in comparison for instance to Augustine, is rather reticent about the effect of the Fall on the capacities of the soul.

John of Damascus assumes, then, that created rational beings, because created out of nothing, rather than having proceeded from God, are 'turnable', corruptible, but also perfectible, in their rationality. Since their rationality crucially involves deliberation and choice, they are corruptible in the way they make choices. Now John of Damascus closely connects the two features of being rational (λογικόν) and being turnable (τρεπτόν) with a further feature, the feature of being αὐτεξούσιον, of having control over what one does, of determining oneself what one does. *Exp.* 2. 27 starts out with the claim 'Now we say that the feature of being αὐτεξούσιος is an immediate concomitant of being rational. For everything which is generated also is subject to corruption.' And the last paragraph of *Exp.* 2. 27 begins: 'One has to recognize that the angels, too, being rational, are αὐτεξούσιοι, and because they are created, turnable.' We have to be clear about the precise nature of this third feature and its relation to rationality and to turnability. The term αὐτεξούσιος seems to be of Stoic origin. It occurs repeatedly in Musonius and frequently in Epictetus. It is taken up by Christian authors; we find it already in Justin Martyr, Tatian, and then frequently, for instance in Origen. It is standardly rendered by 'freedom of will' or 'freedom of choice'. Already Rufinus had translated Origen in this way. But this seems highly misleading in general, and it is misleading in John of Damascus.

John of Damascus (*Exp.* 2. 27) explains 'a being, being rational, will be in charge or control (κύριον) of what it does and αὐτεξούσιον. And this is why non-rational beings are not αὐτεξούσια.' This suggests that the character of being αὐτεξούσιος is closely connected with, or even to be identified with, one's having some control over what one is doing. And this control is linked to one's rationality. It is because of one's rationality that one has some control over what one is doing. And this is due to the fact that rationality, as opposed to intellectuality, essentially has a practical aspect. Its very function is to determine what one is to do. Non-rational beings do not have this kind of control over what they are doing. They, in an important sense, do not act at all, but are made to do what they do. An animal sees an appetizing object. The object triggers an appetite in the animal and, given this appetite, the animal cannot but move after the object. The right thing to say here is not that the animal has no choice but to move after the object, but that the animal has no choice. It does not move by rational choice, but is made to move by something outside it. For if it moved by choice it would have some control over what it is doing. Perhaps this is intuitively clearer, if we adopt an originally Stoic way of looking at the matter. According to the Stoics, both animals and rational creatures are meant to display a certain kind of behaviour as part of the divine general order of things. But animals are created in such a way that they in general will display the desired kind of behaviour, because their response to a situation is fixed by the situation and the way they have been constructed. The animal is constructed in such a way that, if it finds itself in a situation in which there is appropriate food for it, then, if it needs food, it will find it and go after it. Its appetite is just part of the mechanism to ensure that animals, when needed, go after food. By contrast, rational beings are meant to do what they do, not because things have been set up in such a way as to make them display the desired behaviour, but because they of their own accord want to act in this way; because of their understanding of and attitude towards things, they choose to act in this way. This is why they have been given rationality. And because of their rationality, their response to a situation is not fixed by the situation and the way they have been constructed and created. It is, rather, crucially determined by their rationality. Now it is true that they have been created rational, but it also is the case that, as we have seen, and as John of Damascus is emphasizing, this rationality is turnable, subject to change. But we have control over the way it does change. What we think about something is not just a matter of the thing we think about and our intellectual ability, but also of the care and the attention with which we think about it. So how we behaviourally respond to a situation also depends on the way we think about it, and the way we think about it depends on the care with which we think about it. It is in this way that we, in being rational, are αὐτεξούσιοι. We are in control of what we are doing, rather than being made to do what we are doing by something outside us to which, given the way we have been constructed or created, we can only respond to in one particular way. That we have this control shows itself paradigmatically in the fact that we can do what we do, because we want to do it, because we choose to do it, when, if we had not chosen to do it, it would not have been done by us.

Actually this way of presenting John's view is not quite correct. It is true that John repeatedly contrasts human beings and animals in that human beings at least are supposed to guide nature, whereas animals are guided or led by nature in their behaviour. In presenting the matter this way I am emphasizing the fact that animal behaviour is fixed, as it were, by factors outside the particular animal, its circumstances and its genetic origin, here collectively referred to as 'nature'. But even in the animal case John of Damascus distinguishes between behaviour which has its origin in the animal itself, because the animal, given its nature, is inclined towards it, and behaviour which is forced upon the animal by something outside it. For even in the animal case John, like Aristotle, distinguishes between 'voluntary' and 'involuntary' behaviour. So the crucial difference here is not the difference between having one's behaviour forced upon oneself and its having its origin in one's own inclinations, but between one's behaviour in one's non-rational inclinations over which the animal has no control, or in one's inclinations over which one has some control, because one is rational.

It seems to me to be a mistake, though, to identify the feature of being αὐτεξούσιον with the freedom of the will, or the freedom of choice, let alone the freedom of choice understood in the sense that whatever the circumstances or the situation, and whatever the state of our soul, that is to say the state of our rationality and the state of our disposition to have non-rational desires, we can always choose to act in a given way, but also choose not to act in this way. That this is not what John of Damascus has in mind seems to me to be clear from the following. John of Damascus also applies the term αὐτεξούσιος to God. Given that God does not make any choices, the basic meaning of αὐτεξούσιον cannot be 'able to freely choose', let alone 'be able to freely choose' in the sense 'being equally able to choose not to do something when one, in fact, chooses to do something'. For even if God made choices, they would be free, not because God could equally make a different choice, but because whatever choice God would make, it would not be a choice he is made to make. For God, given his goodness, will not and cannot make any other choices than he does. This is not a matter of an inability or some limitation. Let alone does it mean that his choices are forced upon him by some necessity. Now, John of Damascus, closely following Maximus the Confessor (cf. *Pyrrh.* 324D ff.) in one place (*Exp.* 3. 14 = 58. 122 K) tells us that the term αὐτεξούσιος is homonymous. It is one thing for God to be αὐτεξούσιος, another for angels, and another for human beings. In the case of God the term applies superessentially (ὑπερουσίως). That is to say that it is of the very essence of God that he is αὐτεξούσιος, but in such a way that he is not just another thing which is αὐτεξούσιος, but rather the source and the paradigm of all αὐτεξουσιότης, as is the case with God's goodness. In the preceding paragraph, John had talked about the way αὐτεξούσιος applies to Christ as God. God does what is good. But there is nothing to force doing this upon him. And there is nothing which forced this upon him by giving him this nature such that, given this nature and/or this situation, he is forced to do what is good. For being God, he by nature is good, is the Creator, is divine, rather than having this imposed on him by something antecedent. The central idea then is that whatever God does is not forced upon him. This is the paradigm of αὐτεξουσιότης. There is homonymy, because God cannot but do what he does, namely what is good. But this is not because this is forced upon him from the outside, either by something in the situation or something which gave him this nature. Nor does he have a need for any rational control over what he does. For by his very nature he will not do but what is good. There is no choice. *A fortiori*, there is no freedom of choice, let alone a 'libertarian' kind of freedom. There rather is the feature of the person doing what he does without its being forced upon him, and the feature of what he does that it is not something which he is forced to do. So we rather are dealing with a certain kind of freedom in and of what one does. This is the paradigmatic case.

If we turn to the homonymous, derived case of created rational beings, the situation is different. Their αὐτεξουσιότης takes a different form which is an image, something derivate, of its paradigm. They, not being by their very nature good, as they are not God, are not guaranteed to do what is good. But they also, being God's creatures, are not by their very nature guaranteed to do what is evil. This would be incompatible with God's goodness in creating them. Whether they do good or evil is not forced on them by their nature which has been imposed on them by something else. Nor is it forced on them by the situation, or a combination of their situation and their nature. For in the same situation different rational beings behave quite differently. Rather they have control over what they do. They most importantly have control over their actions. But this is a certain kind of freedom of action, of what one does, not the freedom of choice. It is true that a certain kind of freedom of choice crucially is involved in this freedom of action. For, if the choice to act in this way were forced on them, then the action itself indirectly would be forced on them. But what one can say about choice in relation to action, one can equally say about other things a rational being does in relation to its choice. It comes to think about a situation in a certain way. If it did not think about this situation in this way, it would not make this choice. That it thinks about the situation in this way is not forced upon it by something in the situation or in its nature, or both. For, if the thought were forced upon it, to that extent also the choice and the action would be forced upon it. But the thought is not forced upon it. The way it thinks about the situation depends on the care with which it thinks about it and the way it has developed its ability to think about situations. In *Exp*. 2. 22 (= 36. 90 ff. K) John explicitly says that one freely ($a\vec{v}\tau\epsilon\xi o\upsilon\sigma\iota\omega\varsigma$) rationally desires, freely inquires, freely considers, freely deliberates, freely judges, freely takes an affective attitude towards something, for instance consents, freely chooses, freely is impelled towards something, freely acts. It is true that for John the freedom of choice in the sense indicated has a privileged position in this list. This is why he can say *Exp*. 3. 14 (= 58. 56 ff. K) that there are three forms of life, the vegetative, the sensitive, and the intellectual or rational, and that there are certain motions, activities, doings characteristic of each form of life, for instance growth of vegetative life, motion on impulse of sensitive life, but free ($a\vec{v}\tau\epsilon\xi o\upsilon\sigma\iota o\varsigma$) motion of intellectual or rational life. But, he says, if any motion of an intellectual or rational being is of this kind, it is its willing something ($\theta\acute{\epsilon}\lambda\eta\sigma\iota\varsigma$), that is, in the case of rational beings, for instance humans, choosing something. There are various reasons for this privileged position of choice. It is choice which distinguishes created intellectual beings, that is, rational beings, from God on the one hand, and animals on the other. If we also take into account John's doctrine of providence, it turns out that John is following a long tradition in Christian thought, already manifest in Origen, based in part on Stoicism, and in part on St Paul, according to which our action, as opposed to what we ordinarily think, is not as free as our choice, since it, even in ideal circumstances, would not come to fruition without at least divine cooperation. So we may choose to act in a certain way, but it is a matter of God's will and providence whether we manage to. If we do, it is perhaps because he acts through us, because in this regard we are his agents, because at least in some regard we do his will. We do not do his will in murdering somebody, but it perhaps is the case that we cannot but do his will in killing somebody. By contrast, it is at least questionable whether one could, in making the wrong choice, be doing God's will. Moreover, all the different things a rational being may be doing, apart from engaging in contemplation and theoretical inquiry, have as their natural end point a choice which results in action. So choice has a privileged place in the life of a rational being. But this does not mean that the αὐτεξούσιον involved in it is the freedom specifically of choice. It is the sort of freedom which quite generally characterizes all the doings which are characteristic of a rational being, or rational activity, and thus also of choice. For the same reason it is also not specifically the freedom of the will in general, though one freely wills and freely wants or chooses. For one equally freely theoretically inquires. *A fortiori*, αὐτεξουσιότης is not the freedom of the will or the freedom of choice in the 'libertarian' sense. John of Damascus clearly takes the view (cf. *Exp*. 2. 22) that one's choice may be or even is settled by one's judgement (κρίσις) and one's consent (γνώμη). If, upon deliberating the matter of how to attain an end one wills, one has come to the judgement that a certain course of action is the indicated way to attain the end, and if one finds that the idea of pursuing one's end in this way is to one's liking, one will choose to act in the indicated way. This does not make the choice one which is forced upon one by something else, by something in the situation, or by God who has given one this nature; it rather is the natural consequence of one's judgement and one's consent, over both of which one has some control. But, given this judgement and given this consent, one could not choose otherwise in this situation. One's rationality could have taken a different disposition, in which case one might have judged otherwise and not consented. But this is an entirely different matter.

That the freedom in question is not the freedom of the will or the freedom of choice is not affected by John of Damascus' claim that the term αὐτεξούσιον in the case of human beings does not refer to quite the same feature, is not used in quite the same way, as in the case of angels. The case of human beings is complicated by the fact that human beings have a body. Their having a body gives rise to non-rational desires. Hence human beings not only need to be in control of their rational activity, but also of their body and their non-rational desires. To have this control they need to be able to choose not to act on their bodily desires, not to have it forced upon them by a desirable object to go after it. This is a problem angels do not face. And there is another problem angels do not face. They do not have to be able to resist the temptation of the devil and the demons. All this means, though, is that we have to exercise our abilities for the various rational functions with even more care to maintain a firm control over them, and that reason not only has control over itself and its activities, but also over the body and its motions. The latter point matters particularly to John of Damascus, because he thinks that human souls are more in the image of God than angels precisely because they rule over something other than themselves.

So God created rational beings and thus also human beings in such a way that they are αὐτεξούσιοι, that they have some kind of freedom in their activity, because their activity is not forced upon them and because they have some control over what they are doing. They are not in what they are doing the victims of their circumstances or their nature or the combination of both.

They, in what they are doing, are determined by their own rationality, and the state of their rationality, though not its nature, is crucially their own, because of their own doing. The freedom in question shows itself in particular in their choice. They are free in their choice. I have already said something negatively about what this does not mean. But I now need to say more about this, both negatively and positively.

It is often said that freedom in choice is freedom of choice, and this is taken to mean that we are free to choose between good and evil, that we are free to choose the good, but also to choose the evil. In good part this is due to the way we think about choice. We think of choice as a matter of considering two or more, at least prima facie, viable options with their pros and cons, and then choosing between them. And if we actually have several options and thus a choice, there seems to be a sense in which we are free to choose between the options. And since in general we make the choice at least in part on the basis of which option we deem better or worse, we also think that in crucial cases of choice we either opt for the good or for the bad. I doubt whether this is a good way of looking at things. If I want, or choose, to tell you the truth about John of Damascus, as well as I can in my circumstances and with my abilities, it is not that it ever came to my mind to consider the possibility not to tell you the truth. But this does not mean that I do not want to, or choose, to tell you the truth, as well as I can. For it to be a choice there has to be an alternative possibility. The alternative possibility is not to tell you the truth. But for me to act by choice, I do not have to have considered, or even thought of, this alternative. If I choose an apple, there has to be a variety of items, for instance apples, to choose from. But I do not have to consider the various items to choose from, let alone to reject them all but one. I have to choose one rather than another. If I say that I want this one, I do not mean to say that I do not like the others. But, however this may be, I do not think that the ancients or John of Damascus thought of choice in the way we standardly seem to think of it.

Let us go back to creation. God created rational beings with a set of abilities which would allow them to do the things he meant them to do, and this not because things were set up in such a way that they were made to do them, but because they wanted to, because they chose to do them of their own accord. Now this presupposes that the world is not arranged in such a way that, quite independently of what we will and want, it already is a settled matter what is going to happen in the world, including what we are going to do in the world. John of Damascus in *Exp.* 2. 25 argues against this possibility, especially since there are many, as he claims, who believe that all that happens in the world is antecedently settled. Obviously he is thinking of various forms of determinism or fatalism. By contrast he argues that there are things such that it depends on us (is ἐφ' ἡμῖν) whether they get done by us or not. More specifically, if we choose to do them, they get done; if we do not choose to do them, or choose not to do them, they do not get done by us, and thus do not happen. So the world must be such that we can do the things we are meant to do, namely the right things to do, if we choose to. But this obviously is not enough. We also have to be able to choose to do them. We have to be able to choose to do what we are meant to do by our own choice. Now, to assume that we have the ability to choose correctly, at least in the world of late antiquity, but also in the world of John of Damascus, and perhaps even in our world, is by no means a trivial assumption. It is to rule out the possibility that at least in the state of creation one's ability to make the right choice was not pre-empted by the fact that the wrong action was forced on us anyway, independently of what we would have wanted. But it also, and this is more relevant now, could be pre-empted in another way. One might assume, as many did assume, that the wrong choice can be forced on us. One might think, for instance, that the planets or other questionable powers, or the devil, are so powerful as to be able to make us choose the wrong thing. Against this background it is a substantial claim to say that, at least in the state we are created in, we are able to make the right choice, that we have been given all the abilities we need to be able to make the right choice, that there is no power in the world which can force the wrong choice on us. To say this is not at all to say that we have been given the ability to choose between the right and the wrong thing to do, such that we might, by virtue of this ability, choose the right thing, but also by virtue of this ability choose the wrong thing. It is true that we have not been given a nature such as always to choose the right thing, but we at least have been given the ability, or rather the abilities which enable us, always to choose the right thing, though this often might be quite difficult. That it is also possible for us not to choose the right, but the wrong thing, is not due to the ability we have been given, but due to the fact that the proper exercise of the ability is often difficult, requires a great deal of care and devotion to the task, that our rationality is subject to change and corruption, that we can be distracted, and due to many other factors. Looking at John of Damascus' account shows us that he does not construe choice as inherently a choice between two options, the good and the evil. According to John of Damascus, by the time we come to make a choice, having deliberated a matter, we are only considering one option, and the only question is whether this option, a suggested course of action to attain the end we will or want, is to our liking or not. If it is sufficiently to our liking, we choose to act in the suggested way. If it is not to our liking, we do not choose to act in this way. This is not the same as to choose not to act in this way. And John of Damascus does not say that, if the suggested action is not to our liking, we choose not to act in this way. Nor is there any reason why he should say this. He has reason to say that, if we sufficiently dislike the proposed course of action, we choose not to follow it. For he wants to account for choice, and if there is a choice, it is either a choice to pursue the suggested course of action or a choice not to pursue the suggested course of action. And so he needs an explanation as to how one might come to choose not to act in the suggested way. This is particularly important, because it plays a crucial role in his account of how we are not bound to act on inordinate non-rational desires. On his view we block them by choosing not to act this way. But the only resource his account offers for explaining this is that we sufficiently dislike the course of action suggested by the non-rational desire. But we may neither sufficiently like nor sufficiently dislike a proposed course of action. Hence, if we do not choose to act in this way, this does not mean that we have to choose not to act in this way. There may be no choice at all. Moreover, if there is a choice, though it will be a choice to act in this way or a choice not to act in this way, it will not be a choice between the two alternatives. For one's choice, on John's view, is a matter of whether one sufficiently likes or sufficiently dislikes a proposed course of action. But taking a liking or taking a disliking to a course of action is not as such a choice. John's account does leave space for the possibility of considering various options in the course of deliberation. But, on his account, by the time we come to choose, they all could have been eliminated, not by choice, but by some other rational activity. So I take it that for John choice is not a choice between two or more options, let alone between the good and the evil, though choice presupposes that there is an alternative option, at least in the form of not pursuing the first option.

So, given what I have said so far, the freedom with which we are created is not the freedom to make the right choice or the wrong choice. It is rather the freedom to do what one is meant to do in the sense that one has the ability to do it, and that one's ability to do it is not pre-empted by the fact that it is forced upon one not to do it. It moreover is the freedom to choose to do what one is meant to do (one is meant to do what one is meant to do of one's own choice), in the sense that one has the ability to choose to do what one is meant to do and that this ability is not pre-empted by the fact that it is forced upon one to choose not to do it. This, then, is the freedom of choice with which we originally have been created. It should be clear that this does not amount to the freedom either to do what we are meant to do or to do what we are not meant to do. God, for instance, did not guarantee that we would always be able to do what we are not meant to do, or to choose to do what we are not meant to do. Nor does it mean that the freedom with which human beings have been created will always be retained. But before we turn to this, we should first consider how, according to John of Damascus, rational beings do make choices, and what in the state in which they have been created would enable them to make the right choices, to do what they are meant to do from choice.

Perhaps the most important piece of evidence for John's account of how we come to make a choice is found in *Exp*. 2. 22 (36. 71ff. K). But there are parallels offered by *Exp*. 3. 14 and *De duabus voluntatibus* 18 *bis* (148 B ff. M). It may also be of some help to compare *Barlaam and Ioasaph* II. 132–3, though this text clearly draws on the first passage from the *Exposition* just referred to. Now it is well known and obvious that, for the distinctions which John draws in his account, he relies on Maximus the Confessor (cf. *Ad Marinum* 13 B ff.). But it is to be noted that many of these distinctions, and most of the terms to mark the distinctions, are already there in Nemesius (*De nat. hom.* 2. 33) and hence, not surprisingly, also to be found in texts like Meletius' *De natura hominis*. So we have to wonder how original Maximus Confessor is in this regard. Absolutely crucial for this account, it seems to me, is that any choice presupposes that there are things which we will, rationally desire (βουλήσεις). There is no choosing or wanting without a willing. All intellectual beings will things, but rational beings in the narrow sense of the term then, at least as a rule, have to make a choice to attain what they will, if it is attainable. Now rational beings can perfectly reasonably and appropriately will something which, though, is not within their reach, which however they might try, they cannot attain. They also, quite unreasonably and inappropriately, can will something which is, or is not, within their reach. So there in principle is the possibility of a discrepancy between what they will and what they actually can do: (i) they will something, but they lack the ability to do any of the things which would lead to the attainment of what one wills; (ii) they will something, but all or some of the things they could do to attain what they will are things they are not meant to do, are, though real options, not legitimate options. Hence, if we will something, it requires some thought as to whether we can do anything to attain what we will, and if so, what the different options are, if there should be more than one, and whether they are acceptable. It is on the basis of these considerations that we make a choice and act from choice. The way John of Damascus, following Maximus, tries to analyse the whole process which begins with one's having a rational desire (βούλησις) and leads to a choice and, beyond the choice, to an action and its conclusion is this. We first of all (i) have to consider whether what we will in principle is the sort of thing which it is in our power, or up to us, to attain. This sort of consideration according to John is called ζήτησις or σκέψις. Given a positive answer, we can then proceed to (ii) counsel or deliberation (βουλή, βούλευσις). We know that we can attain what we want, but we now have to deliberate whether we should pursue that matter to attain what we want or not (cf. 36. 76–7 K). From this deliberation John explicitly distinguishes (cf. εἶτα 36. 77 K) a third step: (iii) we have to form a judgement (κρίσις), as to which of the possible options is the best to pursue. There is a question here as to what the options in question are supposed to be and as to the sense of 'the best' (τὸ κρεῖττον). If we distinguish between deliberation and judgement as two distinct parts of the process, it would seem that deliberation is supposed to settle the question whether or not we want to do something or other to attain what we will. The view seems to be that the process only continues if this question is settled positively. So the options in question in coming to a judgement cannot include the option of not doing anything. They rather must be the different courses of action which might be open to one to attain what one wills. And the judgement as to the best must be a judgement as to the relative merits of the different courses of action to attain the end which one can think of. That it is judged the best is, hence, perfectly compatible with its being bad and even with one's thought that it is bad. It is just the best by comparison. Fortunately it is not the judgement which decides one's choice and one's action. For that we need (iv) the γνώμη, that is we have to be favourably disposed (διατίθεται) towards the envisaged action, we have to love it (ἀγαπᾶν). We are told that we may judge a course of action to be the best, but fail to like it. It is only if we like it that we will choose the course of action. In Burgundio of Pisa's translation γνώμη is rendered by 'sententia'. This seems to correspond to the use of the word 'sense' in which we to the present day might say of a group which has not yet formally decided a course of action that it is the sense of the group that one ought to proceed in such-and-such a way. In Thomas Aquinas (e.g. *Summa theologica* II.1, q. 15 a. 1) γνώμη is understood as constituting 'consent'. With this a crucial connection to Augustine's doctrine, but also implicitly to Stoic doctrine, is established. In Stoic doctrine choice is a matter of a simple act of assent to a thought (φαντασία). But this single assent involves both the acceptance of a proposition (that the thing to do is to act in this way) as true and the acceptance of one's attitude towards this proposition reflected in the way one thinks of the proposition. This single assent in John of Damascus seems to be split up into the assent constituted by the judgement and the consent constituted by the attitude one takes to the content of the judgement. Depending on one's disposition we, then, get (v) a choice (προαίρεσις) or selection or election (ἐπιλογή). John of Damascus explains that it is a matter of choosing or electing one thing rather than another. Here the two options are to take the course of action or not to take it. To choose is to choose to do it or to choose not to do it, when it is an option not to do it or to do it respectively. Having made a choice, one is (vi) impelled towards action, and this is called an 'impulse' (ὁρμή). That is, we are actually trying to do, set out to do, what we have chosen to do. That this is what we have chosen to do does not necessarily mean that we actually manage to do it. But it does mean, according to John of Damascus, that we actually move to do it, try to do it. In doing what one does, one (vii) makes use (χρῆσις) of one's ability to desire things, for instance one's ability to have a non-rational appetite for something, or an aversion against something (cf. *De duab. volunt.* 18*bis*, 149 C). Thus one's action may constitute a good use or a misuse of one's desiderative abilities. Having availed oneself of them, the desire which motivated the action subsides. This is the very sketchy, but detailed account of choice Latin medieval philosophers were particularly interested in. Unfortunately I here do not have the space to work out its details. I should just note that John of Damascus at least presents the matter in such a way as to suggest that we are dealing with a sequence of episodes in a process, as if there were all these things we had to do before we could do something by choice. But we should also note that matters even in John of Damascus' mind must be a lot more complicated. For clearly he does not think that one's action is something different from one's use of one's abilities to desire things. And there is at least a question whether he does not think that the choice itself constitutes an impulse. So we should at least consider the possibility that John of Damascus presents things as if they formed a temporal sequence for reasons of exposition to point out at how many places things could go wrong and hence at how many places we had a chance to avoid wrong-doing.

The next question to ask is what it is about human beings in the state they have been created in which is supposed to enable them always to make the right choices. John of Damascus tells us (*Exp.* 2. 12 = 26. 37 ff. K) that God created man to be of such a nature as to be able not to sin (ἀναμάρτητον), explaining immediately that this does not mean that man does not admit of sinning, but that it is not part of the nature of human beings to sin, but a matter of their choice. They have the ability (ἐξουσία) to stay in the good state they have been created in and to advance in perfection. Now the reason why rational beings have to make the choices in the first place is that they are not omniscient, that they are lacking in knowledge and understanding (*Exp.* 2. 22 = 36. 100–1 K). So God must have endowed them at their creation at least with the knowledge and understanding which would allow them to make the right choices. It helps at this point to keep in mind that it is the view of Plato, Aristotle, the Stoics, and their later followers that it is consti-tutive of the intellect and reason to dispose of a basic knowledge and under-standing of the world. Hence God does not create the angels or Adam with a mind which is a *tabula rasa*, but with a mind which has the requisite general knowledge and understanding to be able to act reasonably. Obviously, to have this general knowledge is not yet actually to know what to do in the particular situation in which one finds oneself. The individual has to supply the further thought which is needed for this. It is here that things can go wrong, but the task is not beyond natural human intellectual ability. Man in creation has been given this cognitive ability. But choice is not just a matter of cognition. Even the fact that one judges that a certain course of action is the best one available in a given situation does not in itself suffice in choosing this course of action. There must be some inclination, some desire, to act in this way. To make the right choices one also must be able to be inclined towards, to have some desire for doing, the right things. And John of Damascus, *Exp.* 2. 22 (36. 51 ff. K) tells us that the soul has sown into it as part of its nature an ability to desire what is appropriate for something of the nature of the living being, an ability to hold together all those things which are constitutive of the being of something of this nature, namely the will. So to have a will is to be able to desire what is appropriate, to be concerned with one's integrity. Note that here the will is characterized as the ability to desire what it is good for one to desire, rather than as the ability to desire what it is good for one to desire or to desire what it is bad for one to desire. The will essentially is an ability to be inclined to the good, to be inclined, to begin with, towards what furthers one in one's being and integrity, and against what is detrimental to one's being and integrity, what leads to corruption and destruction. John of Damascus does not say that one, as part of one's nature, desires what it is good to desire. He just says that, as part of one's nature, one is able to desire what it is good for one to desire. But there is the clear suggestion that one naturally would desire what it is good for one to desire, and that if one does not, one somewhere must have made a mistake, must have lapsed, a mistake or lapse one could have avoided. But we can say more about how concretely John of Damascus must conceive of this ability to desire what it is good for one to desire. As far as rational beings quite generally are concerned, the source of this ability must lie in this ability to have the right rational desires, that is the right βουλήσεις. And this will be a function of their knowledge and understanding, in particular their knowledge and understanding of the good. The better they understand the good the more attractive they will find it. In any case, when they come to see something as good or a good, they will rationally desire it. And this will give rise to deliberation as to how they might attain it. How good the deliberation and its result is will depend on the quality of their thinking and the care they expend on it. But the motivation should come from the fact that one is attracted by the good to be attained by the proposed course of action, that is, from the rational desire for this good. So one can see how John of Damascus might think that we are created so as to be endowed with the ability to make the right choices.

To this we should perhaps add for clarification that John of Damascus does not think of a created rational being like Adam as created in a neutral state from which then, by its own choices, it turns to good or to evil. It is very clear that John of Damascus thinks of created rational beings as being already at creation endowed with a certain amount of wisdom and virtue, set on the path to perfection on which they can continue, though they also can regress. We also should add that John of Damascus tells us that the divine commandments are meant to serve as guidance so that in our ignorance we do not lose the right path.

So far I have been talking about rational beings quite generally. I now have to turn to the special case of human beings, a special case, since human being have a body and the non-rational desires which come with having a body. Human beings not only have to be concerned with their integrity as rational beings and to exercise the appropriate control over the activity of their reason, they also have to look after their body and its integrity and to control the activity, that is primarily the desires, of the non-rational part of the soul which having a body gives rise to. The responsibility of reason or the intellect for the body gives rise to two problems. If the body is depleted, this naturally gives rise to a non-rational desire for food or drink, as it may be. If one's physical existence is threatened this naturally gives rise to a non-rational desire to avoid physical mutilation or destruction. If one's body is exhausted this naturally gives rise to a non-rational desire to sleep. These may be all perfectly natural and in some sense even 'reasonable' desires to have. But they may be in conflict with the desires of reason. To protect one's rationality, to protect oneself as a rational being, and given one's attachment to the good or what one conceives of as such, an attachment which is inherent in one's rationality, one may think in certain circumstances that it is unreasonable to act on one's non-rational desire for food or drink, for sleep, even for physical survival, if it is detrimental to one's integrity as a rational being. Hence the will in the case of rational beings with a body has to involve the ability to make the right choice even in the face of a non-rational, but perfectly natural desire to the contrary. A fortiori, given that non-rational desires may be inordinate and unreasonable, the will has to be such that we are able to make the right choices, even when presented with unreasonable desires.

Now, in the state in which man is created, the rational soul rules or governs the body and the non-rational the desires it gives rise to. For this to work it must be the case that human beings differ from animals in that, whereas with animals non-rational desires in themselves constitute an impulse ($\delta\rho\mu\acute{\eta}$) which makes the animal move after something or away from it, in human beings the presence of the non-rational desire does not as such and by itself mean that the human being acts as suggested by the desire (*Inst. elem.* 10). For how the human being acts in the state we are created in is determined by reason, more specifically the will. Now at this point we also need to take account of the fact that John of Damascus distinguishes, both in the case of animals and of human beings, two forms of non-rational desire, appetite ($\dot{\epsilon}\pi\iota\theta\upsilon\mu\acute{\iota}\alpha$) and aversion ($\theta\upsilon\mu\acute{o}s$). The first is a desire for something, the second a desire against something, the desire to avoid or get rid of something. In animals, naturally, these two basic forms of desire are directed towards objects conducive to or detrimental to their physical integrity and well-being. But in human beings, John of Damascus assumes, following a long tradition we already encounter in Gregory of Nyssa, these non-rational desires are not restricted to bodily things, but can extend to everything whatsoever which is good or bad, or at least is perceived as such. Indeed, John of Damascus tells us that God gave us these desires to love God and hate the devil. In the state we are created in, these non-rational desires are meant to feed into the way the will operates in the following way. As we saw, we have to make a judgement as to the best course to proceed to attain our objective. But this judgement does not suffice to produce a choice in favour of the course of action, unless we take a liking to this course of action. Now this affective attitude towards the proposed course of action in the case of human beings is not just a matter of our rational desires, but also of our non-rational affect. In this way the course of action we choose also, in principle, can be a function of our non-rational love of God and our non-rational aversion to the devil. But, equally, in principle, it can be a function of some powerful entirely misguided non-rational appetite or aversion. Even in the state we are created in, there is nothing to prevent us from having a non-rational desire which is unreasonable, though we are entirely reasonable. There is one further matter which we have to clear up about the way we function as long as we have managed to be entirely reasonable. Suppose we had a perfectly natural non-rational desire to eat. How would this get blocked? It would get blocked by a choice not to eat in these circumstances. But we have a complex account of choice, and it is part of the interest of this account that it, at least implicitly, claims that one cannot just make a choice out of the blue. A choice, any choice, presupposes the prior exercise of any number of abilities, for instance, one's judgement, but ultimately one's ability to form rational desires, βουλήσεις. Now, when reason does, as it should, govern the body, what we do is determined by reason. John of Damascus defines an action, properly speaking, as having its origin in the intellect. This can be understood in a weaker and a stronger sense. One way of understanding it is this. Reason, if it is not corrupted, will understand that it is good to provide the body with food, if it is depleted. It is sensitive to the state of the body and hence aware of whether the body is depleted. If it is, it will form the rational desire to provide the body with food, if there is no overriding concern. This rational desire will set in process deliberation which will end in the choice to eat. On this account one's eating has its origin entirely in the intellect. But on this account whatever appetite for food one may have is entirely irrelevant. How, then, could we provide for a role for appetite which still is compatible with the claim that action has its source in the intellect or the rational part of the soul? Here it may be relevant to refer to a remark in John according to which the activity of one part of the soul is an affection of the other parts (*Exp.* 2. 22, second paragraph). I take this to mean that if we have an appetite for food, which is an activity of the ἐπιθυμητικόν, the part of the soul in virtue of which, or in which, we form appetites, this affects the rational part of the soul and the θυμητικόν. One way in which it might be thought to affect them is this. Depending on their disposition, it might produce a desire in them, a non-rational aversion in the spirited part, but also one or more desires in the rational part. It will be these different and possibly conflicting desires which will help to determine the affective attitude we take to a proposed course of action which in turn will determine our choice. But what matters at this point is that the appetite in a sufficiently developed reason, other things being equal, would provoke in the intellect the rational desire to provide the body with food. So one's eating would have its origin in reason, in a rational desire, but the non-rational appetite would serve a double function: it would provoke a rational desire to eat, if this was appropriate, and it would help to strengthen the affective attitude in favour of eating in the face of a possible aversion. In this way, I take it, non-rational desire is made to play a substantive role in rational activity and rational behaviour.

The next question, then, is how we are to imagine that corruption comes about; with this comes the further question as to what the effect of corruption is. John of Damascus clearly focuses on choice as the source of corruption. It is in choosing that we go wrong. But this does not necessarily mean that we go wrong in making the wrong choice. This might just be a consequence of having gone wrong at any place on the way to making a choice. One might easily make a mistake in one's judgement as the best course of action available to one in the circumstances to attain the objective. But things also may go wrong in forming an affective attitude towards the course of action envisaged. It is at this point that the non-rational desires come in. And it would seem to be at this point that insinuations from outside will be most effective. There is a question not just about the different places something may go wrong, but also as to whether the place at which we make a wrong choice is particularly privileged, since making a wrong choice is particularly damaging and corruptive. After all, making the wrong judgement also would seem to be damaging and corruptive, and open to blame. For if one had gone about making the judgement with more care, if one had cared more about making the right judgement, one would have avoided making the wrong judgement. Still, presumably choice is deemed to have a privileged place, since it is the choice which in giving rise to an action has a direct impact on the world and on other human beings, and since, because of its impact, it also in turn has a special impact on the soul. Be this as it may, a mistake in making a choice is prejudicial for further mistakes. It affects in a variety of ways the exercise of the ability in exercising which we made a mistake, but also the other abilities involved in making a choice. It may, for instance, encourage and strengthen the non-rational desires whose presence led to our taking the wrong affective attitude towards the envisaged course of action, and thus loosen the grip reason has. It may lead to rationalization of the mistake, if it is not perceived and acknowledged as such. It thus may have an effect on what one regards as good or a good. It thereby has an influence on what one wills, on one's βουλήσεις. It is clear from the examples John gives in *Exp.* 2. 22 (36. 65 ff. K) that he believes that even one's ability to form rational desires does get corrupted in such a way as to make us desire to do things which we are not meant to do. But careless reasoning may also lead us to misevaluate things and correspondingly to form inappropriate rational desires. And once our rational desires are inappropriate, we are bound to make the wrong choices, because we are going to consider the wrong courses of action and are liable to take the wrong affective attitude towards them. And this will have a distorting effect on our non-rational desires.

Choices are habit-forming. They not only lead to a disposition or habit of the ability to make choices as a whole, but they also lead to a disposition of the various abilities involved in making a choice. This seriously does affect our ability to make the right choices with which we originally were created. It is not the case that now our choice is forced upon us by the circumstances or our nature or the combination of both. But given the shape and disposition our rationality, in particular our will, has acquired by our wrongdoing, by the choices we have made, it may now be factually no longer possible for us to make the right choices. We become easily manipulated for those who understand the habits of our mind. So in this sense we have lost our freedom. But, since it remains the case that neither our doing, nor our choosing is forced upon us, but determined by the disposition of our rationality, over which, moreover, we retain some control, we remain αὐτεξούσιος in the sense we have defined. And the weaker sense of 'freedom' which comes with this suffices to make us responsible for our actions, even if we now could not choose otherwise. For it remains the case that the explanation for our action lies in the particular disposition of our own rationality, in particular our will, for which we ourselves are responsible.

If we now look back on this account, it is obvious that, in spite of its reliance on Aristotle in many regards, it is in crucial regards quite un-Aristotelian, not just in its introduction of a notion of a will, but also in its understanding of non-rational desire and its forms, and of the way it may prevail over rational desire. It relies on Nemesius of Emesa, but the account is not that of Nemesius. It is heavily indebted to Maximus the Confessor, in particular for the details of the faculties involved in choice. But, though John of Damascus does nothing to point this out, his account of the will also subtly, but significantly seems to me to differ from Maximus' account. The highly compilatory character of the account John offers should not make us overlook that, in spite of all the internal tensions and unclarities which arise from John's use of disparate sources, the account which emerges in some ways is novel. It certainly does make us look differently at some of the doctrines of earlier authors it relies on precisely by integrating them into a new context. Thus one crucial difference between Aristotle and John of Damascus is that John does not allow for any action against one's choice. He allows for action, or rather behaviour, entirely guided by one's non-rational desire. And he allows for action guided by one's non-rational desire in the face of a countervailing rational desire, but not for action against one's choice. But this is how Aristotle characterizes acratic behaviour, cases in which one acts on a non-rational desire against one's better knowledge. The way Aristotle discusses these cases, in particular cases in which spirited desire prevails, we get little sense of what we emphasize in considering such cases, namely the internal psychological conflict, the sense of feeling pulled in different directions, involved in the cases we tend to focus on. By contrast John of Damascus creates a place for such conflict with his doctrine that choice presupposes an affective attitude towards the proposed course of action, where this affective attitude reflects the way a balance between the conflicting desires has been reached, if there is a conflict.

What perhaps also is important is that, if one looks at John of Damascus' account, one can see how this sort of account, if one espoused it, would naturally lead one to a certain interpretation of Aristotle which still is quite widespread, but which I take to be quite mistaken. Aristotle notoriously also characterizes a choice as a deliberative desire (*EN* 1113^{a}10–11) and as a 'desiderative understanding or a considered desire' (1139^{b}4–5). I take it that the desire in question in Aristotle, that which gives motive force to the choice, is the rational desire, the βούλησις, which underlies one's choice in the first place. This is why one's choice may or may not prevail in the face of non-rational desire to the contrary. If one's non-rational desire is in line with one's rational desire it adds a further motive to one's choice. If not, it may make one act against one's choice. But John of Damascus and many modern commentators seem to interpret Aristotle as assuming that choice is a prod-uct of reason and desire where reason supplies the deliberation and non-rational desire at least part of the motive force.

If one takes this view, one is a crucial step nearer to a whole variety of positions which will later be taken up. In a further step one might come to think that the desire of John's reason in choice is a non-rational desire, especially if one conceives of human non-rational desire as of the kind which finds one's fullest and highest expression in the love of God. In this case one has taken a major step towards separating the intellect or reason from the will. For we now have reason with its rational desire, but all this desire seems to do is to move us to ponder as to how we might attain what we rationally desire. The choice is made by the will which is the ability and disposition to make choices. It is the will which determines how we act, and its causal or motive force is derived from non-rational desire. If one took this view, one might easily, instead of one will, postulate two wills, the ability to form rational desires, but much more crucially, and distinct from this ability, the ability to make choices, the *liberum arbitrium*. Once we have gone this far, we might as well strip reason of its own desire and content ourselves with the view that reason can form beliefs about what is good or a good and that such a belief will suffice to make us deliberate. Now reason has become an exclu-sively cognitive ability which supplies us with the beliefs requisite for action. The will, on the basis of these, provides us with choices. The motive force which makes a choice an impulse will be derived from non-rational desire. But once we have arrived at this view, it will be tempting either to dispense with the will altogether and explain everything in terms of beliefs and desires, or to keep the will, but conceive of it as independent from both the beliefs and the desires by turning it into an ability to make choices which are not determined by one's beliefs or desires.

Thus John of Damascus' account seems to constitute an important link in the history of the notion of the will between ancient and later thought on the matter. The fact that medieval Latin authors did refer to his views on the will and choice extensively, and at least in some cases demonstrably availed themselves of them, at least suggests that he historically did play such a role.

BIBLIOGRAPHY

T<small>EXTS</small>

John of Damascus, *Expositio fidei orthodoxae*, ed. M. Lequien (*Patrologia Graeca*, 94. 790–1228; Paris, 1860); ed. B. Kotter, *Die Schriften des Johannes von Damaskos* (Berlin, 1973), ii.
—— *De duabus voluntatibus*, ed. M. Lequien (*Patrologia Graeca*, 95. 127–86; Paris, 1860).
—— *Institutio elementaris*, ed. M. Lequien (*Patrologia Graeca*, 94. 99–112; Paris, 1860); *Die Schriften des Johannes von Damaskos*, ed. B. Kotter (Berlin, 1969), i. 20–6.
—— *Capita philosophica (Dialectica)*, ed. M. Lequien (*Patrologia Graeca*, 94. 525–676; Paris, 1860); *Die Schriften des Johannes von Damaskos*, ed. B. Kotter (Berlin, 1969), i. 51–146.
—— *Dialogus contra Manicheos*, ed. M. Lequien (*Patrologia Graeca*, 94. 1503–84; Paris, 1860).
—— *De hymno trisagio*, ed. M. Lequien (*Patrologia Graeca*, 95. 22–62; Paris, 1860).
Duns Scotus, *Opera omnia*, xvii. *Lectura* (Vatican City, 1966).
—— *Opera omnia*, v. *Ordinatio* (Vatican City, 1959).

S<small>ECONDARY</small> L<small>ITERATURE</small>

Beck, H.-G. (1959), *Kirche und theologische Literatur im byzantinischen Reich* (Byzantinisches Handbuch, 2/1; Munich).
Callus, D. A. (1955), *Robert Grosseteste* (Oxford).
De Ghellinck, J. (1948), *Le Mouvement theologique du XIIe siècle*, 2nd edn. (Brussels).
Lottin, O., 'L'Analyse de l'acte humain chez St. Jean Damascène', *Revue Thomiste*, 36 (1931), 631–61.
Southern, R. W. (1992), *Robert Grosseteste*, 2nd edn. (Oxford).
Tatakis, B. N. (1949), *La Philosophie byzantine* (Paris).

5

Syllogistic in the anon Heiberg

JONATHAN BARNES

The anon Heiberg is a short text in five parts or Chapters: Logic, Arithmetic, Music, Geometry, Astronomy. The parts are of unequal size, the first being by far the longest.[1] The edition prepared by Heiberg and published post-humously in 1929 is based on seven MSS, the earliest of which is dated to 1040. Heiberg describes a further fifteen MSS. I do not know if any more have since been discovered.

Although Heiberg's was the first critical edition of the text, the work was not previously unknown: Chapter 1 had been published in 1600 and ascribed to Gregory;[2] Chapters 2–5 had been published in 1533, and again in 1556, under the name of Michael Psellos.[3] The ascription to Psellos can hardly be correct, for chronological reasons. Heiberg rejects the ascription to Gregory, apparently because the work is left anonymous in the oldest MSS. But perhaps the author was the monk Gregory Aneponymus.[4] As for the date, the astronomical Chapter of the work gives 6516 as 'the present year' (5. 8 (p. 108. 14 H), 9 (p. 109. 9–10 H)), and the Byzantine year 6516 ran from 1 September 1007 to 31 August 1008 in the Julian calendar. The same Chapter also establishes some correlations between the Byzantine and the Egyptian calendars, and these indicate a period between 1 September and 14 December 1007.[5] Hence if the five Chapters of the work form a unitary composition, the date is fixed.

Each chapter of the work has its own title (each title is an iambic trimeter); but no MS offers a title for the work as a whole. Is the piece a conjunction of five independent essays? Several MSS contain only a selection of the Chapters, which clearly had some independent circulation. Again, some

---

[1] In Heiberg's edn., Logic occupies some 50 pp., Arithmetic 15, Music 7, Geometry 30, Astronomy 18. References to the anonymus will be given by chapter-, section-, page- and line-numbers in Heiberg's edn.

[2] The ascription is found in two late MSS: Heiberg (1929: XV). Full bibliographical references in the Bibliography.

[3] I take this information from Heiberg (1929: XIX).

[4] So Benakis (1988: 5).

[5] I lift all this from Taisbak (1981).

minor differences of style may be observed. For example, Chapter 4 contains ten references to early authorities—six of them to Euclid—whereas in the other chapters references are sparse.[6] On the other hand, the first section of Chapter 2 explicitly announces a discussion of all four parts of the *quadrivium*, so that the last four Chapters at any rate appear to have been conceived of as a unitary whole. Chapter 1 does not introduce itself as the first of five discussions, nor do I find any clear reference in 2–5 to a preceding account of logic;[7] but in 1. 12, and again in 1. 67 (the last section of the chapter), the four sciences of the *quadrivium* are mentioned and logic is said to be the instrument for their discovery. On the whole, then, it seems reasonable to think that the five essays were written as parts of a single treatise.[8]

The treatise is unoriginal.[9] I have not tried to elicit its sources—about which its author is elegantly silent.[10] But there are numerous parallels to be found in the earlier literature, and for the chapter on logic it is plain—and unremarkable—that the author is writing in the Peripatetic tradition: most of his ideas surely derive from the commentaries on the *Organon*, and I guess that he often copies closely.[11]

The chapter on logic, to which the following pages restrict themselves, carries the title: συνοπτικὸν σύνταγμα τῆς φιλοσοφίας. It seems as though logic were identical with philosophy, as though 'logic' and 'philosophy' were synonyms.[12] But the first section addresses itself to 'those who are seeking the instrument of philosophy (τὸ τῆς φιλοσοφίας ... ὄργανον)' (1. 1 (p. 1. 5 H)); and the last section informs the reader that he now possesses a summary account 'of the whole instrumental philosophy (τῆς ὅλης ὀργανικῆς φιλοσοφίας)' (1. 67 (p. 50. 12–13 H)). So the 'φιλοσοφία' of the title is presumably short for 'instrumental philosophy'; and instrumental philosophy

---

[6] In Ch. 1 Aristotle is named four times (and 'the Stoics' once); in 2, the Pythagoreans; in 3, Plato; in 5, Ptolemy (twice); in 4 we find Archimedes (§51), Euclid (§§10, 18, 29 [twice], 30, 39), Plato (§§21, 33), Theo (§22—the commentator on Ptolemy); and note the epigram in §26.

[7] The first sentence of 2. 1 begins thus:

μέλλοντί μοι καὶ περὶ τῶν τεσσάρων μαθηματικῶν ... διαλαβεῖν ... (p. 50. 26–7 H).

You might take 'καί' to mean 'also', and hence to imply that Ch. 2 had been preceded by something else—a chapter on logic, say. But this is at best a veiled hint, not a clear reference.

[8] See, with further argument, Ebbesen (1981: i. 262–5).

[9] Several of the symposiasts at Thessaloniki, where a version of this essay was presented, spoke as though Byzantine philosophy must be original if it is to be worthy of praise—or even of study. Originality is the rarest of philosophical commodities. It is also an over-rated virtue: a thinker who strives to understand, to conserve, and to transmit the philosophy of the past is engaged in no humdrum or unmeritorious occupation. At any rate, most of my fellow symposiasts have the same reason as I for hoping that this is true.

[10] The references listed in n. 6 do not imply that the author used those texts as his own sources of information.

[11] See in general Praechter (1931*b*); and for the source of 1. 59 see Praechter (1931*a*: 2–6); Ebbesen (1981: i. 269, 274–9).

[12] Note also 1. 39 (at p. 32. 8 H and p. 32. 17 H 'φιλοσοφία' refers specifically to logic), and 1. 48 (at p. 39. 8 H ἡ ὅλη φιλοσοφία is logic). So too in a 9th-cent. biography of St John Psichaites: Ebbesen (1981: i. 257).

is the philosophical study of the instrument of the sciences—in other words, it is logic.

For logic is conceived of as a tool or instrument. The text affirms roundly that 'all sciences were discovered by the ancients' by means of logic (1. 67 (p. 50. 16–17 H)). And it adds that while those who have set out unversed in logic may indeed have arrived at 'experience ($\pi\epsilon\hat{\iota}\rho\alpha$)', they have certainly not attained 'knowledge ($\dot{\epsilon}\pi\iota\sigma\tau\acute{\eta}\mu\eta$)' (p. 50. 18 H). Only the trained logician, 'with the unwavering and necessitating guides of the syllogisms, is able to track down every science and art' (p. 50. 21–3 H). It would be unfair to ask the author to explain or justify these large and agreeable claims—he is, and he surely takes himself to be, parroting a commonplace.[13]

The plan of the chapter is equally traditional. When you learn to read, you start with letters, move up to syllables, and finally reach whole expressions. So, when you learn logic, you start with the ten categories, move up to 'matters concerning interpretation', and finally reach the figures of the syllogism (1. 1; cf. 25 (p. 18. 4–7 H)). In other words, you study the matter of Aristotle's *Categories*, of his *De interpretatione*, and of his *Prior Analytics*.

The programme announced in the opening section is carried out in §§2–48: first, a discussion of the categories—prefaced by an account of the Porphyrean *quinque voces* (§§2–20); then, material deriving from *De interpretatione* (§§21–4); and finally, the syllogistic (§§25–48). The programme is done, but there is a supplement: just as there are tares among the wheat,[14] so there are fallacies among the syllogisms—and 'expert philosophers must know the types of paralogisms so that they will not stumble into falsity instead of truth' (1. 49 (p. 39. 21–3 H)).[15] There follows a long account of fallacies and sophisms, based ultimately on Aristotle's *Sophistici Elenchi* (§§49–63). And the chapter is rounded off by a summary description of the different types of syllogism—probative, dialectical, rhetorical, sophistical, poetical (§§64–7).[16]

Of the six books of Aristotle's *Organon*, three form the background to the items promised in the programme, and a fourth lies behind the supplementary matter. The work contains no hint of the *Topics*—perhaps because the *Topics* deals with dialectical syllogisms and our text sees itself as a preparation for scientific study.[17] But equally, the work contains no hint of the *Posterior Analytics*—the Aristotelian treatise which deals expressly with scientific syllogisms and in which, on the traditional interpretation, Aristotle shows how logic serves as the instrument of the sciences. To be sure, our text

[13] For the commonplace see e.g. Lee (1984: 44–54).

[14] Matthew 13: 24–30: already applied to philosophy by Clement, *strom* 6. 8, 67. 2.

[15] See Ebbesen (1981: i. 88–9; iii. 116–17).

[16] On these five types, which are found earlier in Elias, see Praechter (1931*b*: 87–9); Ebbesen (1981: i. 102–5).

[17] One of the scholia printed by Heiberg lists the contents of the *Topics* (p. 134. 19–135. 6 H); and most of the scholia attached to Ch. 1 refer to matters discussed in the *Topics* and have no visible connection to our treatise.

makes a passing reference to probative syllogisms; but its characterization of them is cursory and inadequate, and it betrays no acquaintance with Aristotle's subtle account.[18] Why is *APst* thus cold-shouldered? 'Ignorance, Madam, pure ignorance'?[19]

It would be false to suggest that the chapter offers rich treasures to the logician, or even to the historian of logic.[20] Its intellectual pretensions are modest. To be sure, it purports to give the pious reader all he needs to know about the subject; but it presupposes no anterior knowledge, and it rarely engages in any deep or difficult matter. Occasionally an ἀπορία is discussed—e.g. 1. 2; sometimes differences in opinion are noted—e.g. 1. 13; and there is one long and detailed exegesis of an Aristotelian definition—at 1. 59.[21] But for the most part, the chapter is purely expository in style and elementary in scope.

I here discuss six issues, of unequal magnitude. All are drawn from the syllogistic sections of the chapter. The first four concern what might be termed the range of the syllogistic; the fifth centres about proofs of non-concludency; and the sixth occupies itself with what later mediaeval logicians called the bridge of asses.

Undetermined Syllogisms

A contemporary presentation of Aristotle's categorical syllogistic is likely to explain that a categorical syllogism consists of three categorical propositions, and that a categorical proposition links two terms in a certain quality and a certain quantity. There are two qualities: a term may be either affirmed or denied of a term. There are two quantities: a term may be predicated either universally or particularly of a term. There are thus four types of categorical proposition: universal affirmative, universal negative, particular affirmative, particular negative.[22] I shall represent such propositional forms by way of schematic letters[23] and standard abbreviations, thus:

---

[18] 'Syllogisms put together from true premisses are themselves true and are called probative (ἀποδεικτικοί)': 1. 64 (p. 48. 2–4 H); contrast e.g. Psellos, *Philosophica minora* 1. 13 (p. 41. 35–42. 2 Duffy); John Italos, *dialectica* §2. The inadequate definition is not idiosyncratic: see e.g. Clement, *strom* 8.3, 6. 2–4.

[19] Ebbesen (1981: i. 264), seconded by Benakis (1988: 6), says that the neglect of *Top* and *APst* 'was hardly remarkable in the 11th century'; and he supplies parallels. Note that John Italos was well acquainted with *Top*: *dialectica* §§4–12.

[20] I do not know how well the work sold: Benakis (1988: 8), thinks that Blemmydes probably made use of it. (See below, n. 64.)

[21] Taken from a commentary on *SEl* 167ª21: parallels in Ebbesen (1981: i. 172 n. 2).

[22] This is the roughest of characterizations; but the refinements which a serious exposition of the syllogistic would require may here be left aside.

[23] In its exposition of the syllogistic, our text does not use schematic letters (but see below, p. 131): like most ancient accounts of logic, it prefers metalogical description. The use of letters has certain familiar advantages; and for the moment it will be harmless; but see below, n. 69.

AaB, AeB, AiB, AoB

—'A holds of every B', 'A holds of no B', 'A holds of some B', 'A does not hold of some B'.[24]

Our text is more generous. It asserts that Aristotle built his syllogistic about not a tetrad but a hexad of types of proposition;[25] for in addition to the four types which I have just enumerated, there are two more, 'the undetermined ($\dot{\alpha}\pi\rho o\sigma\delta\iota\acute{o}\rho\iota\sigma\tau os$) affirmative and the undetermined negative' (1. 28 (p. 20. 11–14 H)). A proposition is undetermined if it lacks a determinator or $\pi\rho o\sigma\delta\iota o\rho\iota\sigma\mu\acute{o}s$, if it lacks a sign of quantity.[26] As an example of an undetermined affirmative we are offered:

Men walk ($\mathring{\alpha}\nu\theta\rho\omega\pi os$ $\pi\epsilon\rho\iota\pi\alpha\tau\epsilon\hat{\iota}$)

and for an undetermined negative:

Men do not walk ($\mathring{\alpha}\nu\theta\rho\omega\pi os$ $o\mathring{\upsilon}$ $\pi\epsilon\rho\iota\pi\alpha\tau\epsilon\hat{\iota}$)[27]

(1. 24 (p. 17. 1–5 H)). I introduce the formulae

AuB

and

AyB

to present such propositional forms.

Categorical syllogistic, as our text develops it, will thus be more bulky than the standard contemporary version; and our text finds types of syllogism unrecognized in contemporary accounts.[28] In the first and second figures there are six valid moods, whereas the contemporary version allows only four valid moods in each. In the third figure there are ten valid moods,

---

[24] In the Peripatetic style, the predicate is presented before the subject (see Apuleius, *int* 13 (p. 212. 4–10 Moreschini)—here and hereafter I write 'Apuleius' rather than '[Apuleius]' for convenience rather than from conviction). Note that 'A does not hold of some B' is to be construed as 'Of some B, A does not hold'.

[25] I return to this assertion below, p. 112.

[26] The $\pi\rho o\sigma\delta\iota o\rho\iota\sigma\mu o\acute{\iota}$ are introduced in 1. 21, where there are said to be two of them, the universal and the particular (p. 13. 26–8 H); at 1. 22 (p. 15. 11–12 H), it is said that there are affirmations and negations 'both without determinators and with determinators'. Singular propositions ('Socrates walks'), although they do not carry determinators, do not count as undetermined: an undetermined proposition is one which might but does not sport a determinator. At 1. 24, at the end of the enumeration of the different types of proposition (on which see below, p. 112), our author remarks that he has not included singular propositions 'which Aristotle does not use in his exposition of the syllogisms, since he constructs the syllogisms from what is universal and eternal' (p. 17. 24–7 H)—a commonplace (e.g. Philoponus, *in APr* 12. 22–3), which goes back ultimately to Aristotle, *APr* 43^{a}40–3.

[27] The Greek sentences are not barbarisms—hence I use the English plural to translate them. 'Man walks' is strained English. 'Horse sleeps' is babu.

[28] i.e. contemporary versions of Aristotle's assertoric syllogistic: categorical syllogistic had a long history, and different logicians discovered different numbers of moods (the differences depending in part on their attitude to the 'fourth figure').

whereas the contemporary version allows only six. Thus to the fourteen valid moods of contemporary accounts, our text adds eight undetermined moods (as I shall call them), bringing the total to twenty-two.

The third and fourth moods of the first figure—Darii and Ferio—may be presented schematically as follows:

AaB, BiC:: AiC
AeB, BiC:: AoC

Our text subjoins a fifth and a sixth mood, to wit:

AaB, BuC:: AuC
AeB, BuC:: AyC

I dub these moods Daruu and Feruy. The extra moods in the second figure are Festuny and Barycy:

BeA, BuC:: AyC
BaA, ByC:: AyC

And in the third figure we meet Datusu, Dusamu, Ferusyn, and Bycardy:

AaB, CuB:: AuC
AuB, CaB:: AuC
AeB, CyB:: AyC
AyB, CaB:: AyC

Why consider these moods to be valid? Although the treatise offers no formal proof, its description of Daruu provides a broad hint:

Fifth is the combination which deduces an undetermined affirmative conclusion from a universal affirmative major and an undetermined affirmative minor. The terms are those of the third combination:

Animal to every man
Man in white (this is the undetermined item)
Therefore: man in animal[29]

---

[29] In our text, examples of a, e, i, and o propositions are regularly expressed by verbless sentences of the form

τὸ Α παντὶ [οὐδενὶ, τινι, οὐ παντὶ] B.

You would expect undetermined examples to be expressed thus:

τὸ Α [οὐ] B.

In fact we get

τὸ Α [οὐκ] ἐν B.

It is tempting to connect this use of 'ἐν' with Porphyry's thesis that affirmations and negations signify *aliquid alicui inesse* or *non inesse* (see Boethius, *in Int*² 122. 7–15—Boethius connects the thesis with the ἔν τινι εἶναι of *Cat* 1ª20–ᵇ9: *in Int*² 68. 4–69. 22; and in fact it is already found in Apuleius, *int* 3 (p. 191. 1–6 M)); but it is difficult to make anything out of this.

This is equivalent to ($\emph{ἰσοδυναμεῖ}$) 'to some'; for the undetermined propositions are equivalent to particulars. (1. 30 (p. 22. 3–9 H))[30]

Thus we are invited to accept the two equivalences:

AuB ⇔ AiB

and

AyB ⇔ AoB.

Whence it is easy to see that Daruu is a valid mood: its validity follows directly from the validity of Darii and the equivalence between 'AuB' and 'AiB'. The same holds for all the extra moods.

But then is not our text a niggard? It does not, for example, mention Daraptu—

AaB, CaB:: AuC

—which, given the equivalences, follows directly from Darapti. It does not mention Dariu or Darui, or Feriy or Feruo, or ... In short, its system appears to be radically incomplete. Hence when the text explicitly claims to have given an exhaustive account of the contents of each figure,[31] this seems to be an egregious error.

An explanation for these apparent omissions might be sought in 1. 33. There, after the exposition of the valid moods, the text propounds the so-called *peiorem* rules (*peiorem semper conclusio sequitur partem*.)

You must know that it is common to the concludent combinations[32] of the three figures that the conclusion follows the worse of the premisses ... A particular is worse than a universal, a negative than an affirmative, and an undetermined than a determined. (p. 26. 5–9 H)

Hence, in particular,

if one of the premisses is assumed in undetermined form, the conclusion will follow undetermined'. (p. 26. 23–4 H)

Now in Darui—

AaB, BuC:: AiC

—the conclusion is determined and the second premiss undetermined. The *peiorem* rule is violated—and Darui is therefore not valid. If our text

---

[30] Cf. 1. 36 (p. 28. 13–14 H): 'the undetermined propositions are equivalent to the particulars'; 1. 32 (p. 25. 13–14 H): 'we said that the undetermined items are taken as ($\emph{λαμβάνεσθαι ἀντί}$) particulars'. See also 1. 59 (p. 44. 13–17 H), with Ebbesen (1981: i. 197–9).

[31] See 1. 30 (p. 22. 13–14 H), 31 (p. 23. 19 H), 32 (p. 25. 14–15 H).

[32] $\emph{συλλογιστικοὶ τρόποι}$: (i) the text uses '$\emph{τρόπος}$' for the traditional '$\emph{συζυγία}$', and I translate it accordingly; (ii) a combination is $\emph{συλλογιστικός}$ if it yields a conclusion of the form 'AxC'—I use 'concludent' for '$\emph{συλλογιστικός}$' and 'non-concludent' for '$\emph{ἀσυλλόγιστος}$'.

implicitly rejects Darui and its fellows, that is not the result of oversight: rather, the text explicitly adopts a rule which outlaws such moods.

But if the *peiorem* rule outlaws Darui, it does not outlaw Dariu—

AaB, BiC:: AuC

—for here the conclusion is 'worse' than each premiss. Then why omit Dariu? Perhaps our author implicitly strengthens the *peiorem* rule so that it requires the conclusion to be neither better nor worse than the worse of the premisses? Such a strengthened rule will outlaw Dariu; and many formulations of the *peiorem* rule—including the formulation in our text—appear to propose it.[33] But it cannot be right; for it will also outlaw Darapti.[34]

Then recall the fact that our text ignores the subaltern moods—moods such as Barbari,

AaB, BaC:: AiC,

which may be derived from a canonical mood by applying one of the rules of subalternation[35] to its conclusion. These moods, we happen to know, were added to the syllogistic by Aristo of Alexandria; but standard ancient accounts do not mention them, and Apuleius, who does, rejects them as 'utterly stupid' (*int* 13 (p. 213. 9 M)). Now, given the *peiorem* rule of our text, Dariu and its fellows might be considered to be special types of subaltern mood; and the fact that the text does not mention Dariu is of a piece with the fact that it does not mention Barbari.

But this seems to increase rather than decrease the difficulty. Perhaps Barbari is 'utterly stupid'; but it is assuredly valid. Why reject it? Well, our text does not explicitly reject Barbari; and although it pretends to give a complete treatment of the syllogistic figures, it does not explicitly claim to have listed all the valid moods: it explicitly claims to have listed all the concludent combinations. The combination for Barbari is not overlooked: it is the same as the combination for Barbara. And although the text does not expressly indicate that this combination will yield 'AiC' as well as 'AaC', neither does it expressly deny the entailment; for it does not explicitly claim to have listed every conclusion which may be inferred from a given combination. What holds for Barbari holds equally for Dariu: its combination is listed (it is the combination for Darii); and nothing in the text expressly states that Dariu is not a valid mood. So perhaps Dariu is implicitly accepted?

No. In 1. 27, having computed the number of concludent combinations, the text observes that 'the syllogisms in abstraction from perceptible matter [i.e. the valid moods] are thus many and no more' (p. 20. 2–4 H); that is to say, here at least the text implicitly supposes that each concludent combination

---

[33] See e.g. Alexander, *in APr* 51. 31–2: 'It seems that the conclusion is always similar to the worse of the items assumed in the premisses, both in quantity and in quality'.

[34] As well as other, less celebrated, moods: Baralipton, Fapesmo, . . .

[35] i.e. AaB:: AiB, and AeB:: AoB (see Aristotle, *Top* 109^{a}3–6).

answers to precisely one valid mood. The combination 'AaB, BiC' certainly answers to Darii: it does not, therefore, answer to Dariu. Unless we dismiss the remark in 1. 27 as a passing negligence, we must conclude that our text implicitly outlaws Dariu (and also the subaltern moods).

However that may be, we must revisit Darui. Our text implicitly rejects Darui, on the basis of the *peiorem* rule. But the rule—the pertinent part of the rule—is false. A universal proposition is better than a particular in this sense: from 'AaB' or 'AeB' you may infer 'AiB' or 'AoB', but not *vice versa*. Our text insists that undetermined propositions are equivalent to particular propositions: from 'AiB' or 'AoB' you may infer 'AuB' or 'AyB' and also *vice versa*. Undetermined propositions are not worse than particulars: they are no better either—they are much the same.

Perhaps they are worse in some other fashion? After all, negatives are worse than affirmatives; but that cannot be because 'AaB' entails 'AeB' but not *vice versa*. There is another canon of goodness operating here—and so also, perhaps, in the case of the undetermined items. Well, no doubt we could discover or invent a criterion according to which the undetermined is worse than the particular. But no such discovery or invention will do any good: given the equivalences, then Dariu is valid—and that's an end on it.

I conclude that, in the matter of undetermined syllogisms, our text is logically inept.[36]

Undetermined moods had been considered by every Peripatetic logician since Aristotle. Aristotle introduces undetermined propositions at the beginning of *APr*.[37] And at 26ª28–30, after expounding Darii and Ferio, he remarks:

Similarly if BC is undetermined, being affirmative—for there will be the same syllogism whether it is taken as undetermined or as particular.

Undetermined propositions do not reappear in the exposition of the valid moods in A 4–6;[38] but in A 7 we find a general claim:

it is evident that if an undetermined item is posited instead of an affirmative particular, it will produce the same syllogism in all the figures. (29ª27–9)

Each of the two passages I have just quoted is puzzling.

[36] The same ineptitude recurs in Blemmydes: at *epit log* 29. 917AC, he remarks that Aristotle subscribed to both the pertinent equivalences; but he adds that although the u–i equivalence is evidently true, the y–o equivalence is not: y-propositions are sometimes equivalent to o-propositions but more often equivalent to e-propositions. When he develops categorical syllogistic in 31–4, he constructs it around the four standard propositions (and hence allows only the 14 canonical moods: 32. 944B). But at the end of the exposition, he announces that thus far he has dealt with syllogisms of which the premisses are determined: as for those with undetermined premisses, what has already been said will serve—providing the reader bears in mind the relevant *peiorem* rules, on which Blemmydes takes the same view as our text (34. 961A). No reader will be able to elaborate the undetermined moods on the basis of Blemmydes' several remarks.

[37] 24ª16–20: his term 'ἀδιόριστος' was later enlarged to 'ἀπροσδιόριστος'.

[38] But they are sometimes noticed in connexion with non-concludent combinations: 26ª30–2, ᵇ21–5; 27ᵇ36–9; 29ª8–10.

In A 7 Aristotle mentions only affirmative undetermined propositions,[39] and he speaks only of undetermined premisses. Thus you would take him to be giving the accolade to Darui, Feruo, Festuno, Dusamis, Datusi, and Feruson—and by implication to be rejecting Daruu, Dariu, ..., Feruy, Feriy, ... and all the rest. Yet it is desperately difficult to conjure up a justification for such a view. As for 26ᵃ28–30, it is not clear to me whether the word 'similarly' invites us to consider one mood or two—a mood similar to Ferio, or moods similar to Darii and to Ferio. The former I find an easier construal of the Greek; but most commentators opt for the latter.[40] Nor is it clear whether we should think of Feruo (and Darui) or of Feruy (and Daruu). If, in the expression 'the same syllogism', the word '$\sigma\upsilon\lambda\lambda o\gamma\iota\sigma\mu\acute{o}s$' means 'conclusion', then Feruo (and Darui) are presumably intended. On the other hand, if '$\sigma\upsilon\lambda\lambda o\gamma\iota\sigma\mu\acute{o}s$' means 'syllogism', then A 4 claims that Feruo (or Feruy) is the same mood as Ferio; and A 7 claims that Darui and its congeners are the same as Darii and its congeners.

It may reasonably be said that there is a lacuna—or at least a vagueness—in Aristotle's treatment of the categorical moods. Theophrastus, we should expect, will have tried to fill the gap—that was his general *modus operandi*. And in fact it is clear that he said something on the subject of undetermined moods; more particularly, that he explicitly admitted at least one undetermined mood to the first figure. Only one short text on the matter survives, and that text is wretchedly corrupt.[41] But whatever we do with it, Theophrastus was certainly prepared to acknowledge undetermined moods as superadditions to the canonical moods.

Many later logicians followed Theophrastus' lead. But there were some dissenters—thus according to Apuleius, the undetermined moods

are otiose (*supervacaneus*), since the undetermined (*indefinitus*) is taken for a particular,[42] and the same moods will come about as from particulars. (*int* 13 (p. 212. 15–213. 5 M))

And some logicians havered.[43]

---

[39] Alexander pertinently asks why he did not add 'and negative' at 29ᵃ28; but he returns no satisfactory answer (*in APr* 111. 13–27).

[40] e.g. Alexander, *in APr* 61. 1–3; Philoponus, *in APr* 79. 6–9.

[41] Apuleius, *int* 13 (p. 212. 12–213. 5 M). *Pace* Barnes *et al.* (1991: 136 n. 157), this text has nothing to do with the five moods which Theophrastus added to the first figure (on which see Alexander, *in APr* 69. 27–70. 20, and other texts in Fortenbaugh *et al.* (1994: 91A–91E)).

[42] *pro particulari accepi*: cf. $\lambda\alpha\mu\beta\acute{\alpha}\nu\epsilon\sigma\theta\alpha\iota$ $\grave{\alpha}\nu\tau\grave{\iota}$ $\mu\epsilon\rho\iota\kappa\hat{\omega}\nu$ (above, n. 30).

[43] Undetermined moods are implicitly rejected by e.g. Galen (*inst log* 2. 4: if you predicate A of B and B is a general term, then 'it must be determined ($\delta\iota\omega\rho\acute{\iota}\sigma\theta\alpha\iota$) whether it is said of all or of some'; 11. 2: there are only 16 combinations, although there are several equivalent expressions for them); Boethius, *syll cat* 813C. They are implicitly accepted by e.g. the Ammonian scholia (see Ammonius, *in APr* IX. 34: there are 36 combinations—so also Philoponus, *in APr* 68. 30–4); and explicitly accepted by e.g. Philoponus (the first figure contains six valid moods (*in APr* 79. 4–9), the second six (94. 32–95. 7), and the third ten (110. 8–11)); and they are later expressly noted by Blemmydes, *epit log* 34. 961A (see above, n. 36). Alexander is ambivalent: at *in APr* 51. 24–5, he remarks, neutrally, that 'if we count in the combinations of undetermined propositions', then we

The issue depends on the status of the two equivalences,

AiB ⇔ AuB

and

AoB ⇔ AyB.

Most, but not all, ancient logicians took both equivalences to be true; and they ascribed the two truths to Aristotle.[44] The ascription is not without textual support;[45] and if it goes beyond what the words of *APr* explicitly supply, it is, I suppose, the most plausible way of squeezing a precise thesis out of Aristotle's various remarks.[46]

If the equivalences are not true, then evidently there may in principle be further moods to add to the canonical fourteen. Whether or not there are in fact further moods to be added will depend on the sense which is assigned to the undetermined sentences. If the equivalences are true, then—as I have already observed—Daruu, Darui, and Dariu and the rest are all of them valid moods; but the truth of the equivalences does

shall get more concludent pairings; at 61. 1–3 (commenting on *APr* 26ᵃ28–30) he says that with undetermined premisses we get deductions 'similar to (ὅμοιος)'—and hence, by implication, not identical with—Darii and Ferio; and at 94. 18–20 and 112. 1–2 he implies that the undetermined moods are identical with their particular counterparts.

[44] e.g. Alexander, *in APr* 30. 29–31; 62. 22–4; Apuleius, *int* 3 (p. 190. 21–2 M); 5 (p. 196. 5–8 M); 13 (p. 213. 1 M); Martianus Capella, 4. 396; Boethius, *int syll cat* 776C; *syll cat* 802C; Ammonius, *in Int* 116. 7–8; [Ammonius], *in APr* 70. 20–2; 71. 3–4; Philoponus, *in APr* 79. 4–5; 110. 10–11, 27; 203. 6–8; 222. 14; 228. 10; 277. 12–13; 323. 3–4; 349. 9–10—but at 42. 31–3 he states that undetermined propositions, as Aristotle has remarked in *Int*, ἀναλογοῦσι . . . ἢ ταῖς καθόλου ἢ ταῖς μερικαῖς. But note the long discussion in Ammonius, *in Int* 111. 10–120. 12: some had contended that 'AoB' and 'AyB' are not equivalent, appealing both to theoretical considerations (cf. e.g. Boethius, *in Int²* 152. 12–161. 18; anon, *in Int* 45. 12–46. 5 Tarán; 87. 2–14 T). I note that Whitaker 1996, 86–92, argues that, at least in *Int*, Aristotle accepted neither equivalence. (It is plain that if AuB then AiB and that if AyB then AoB: it is the reverse implications which are contested.)

[45] The interpretation is based not only on *APr* 26ᵃ28–30 and 29ᵃ27–9, but also on *de Int* 17ᵇ29–37. There Aristotle states that it is possible that sentences of the form 'AuB' and 'AyB' should be true at the same time; he admits that this may seem odd, since 'AyB' appears to mean that AeB; but in point of fact—or so he claims—'AyB' does not mean the same as 'AeB' nor is it even the case that

AeB ⇔ AyB.

Plainly, these remarks do not entail the two equivalences. But they are most satisfactorily explained on the hypothesis that in fact Aristotle did accept the two equivalences.

[46] Why not propose that Aristotle accepted

AiB ⇔ AuB,

but rejected

AoB ⇔ AyB,

as some later logicians did (above, n. 44)? Well, he certainly did not accept

AeB ⇔ AyB

(above, n. 45); and when he refers to y-propositions in his proofs of non-concludence (above, n. 38), he implicitly treats them as equivalent to o-propositions.

not in itself establish whether these moods must be added to the canonical fourteen.

Suppose that the equivalences are grounded on synonymies, that undetermined sentences are synonymous with their particular counterparts. 'Men walk', for example, is shorthand for 'Some men walk'; and in general, between 'AiB' and 'AuB', while there may be some difference of nuance or of colour, there is no difference of sense. In that case Daruu, Darui, and Dariu are not three additional moods, to be annexed to Darii: they are all one mood, and the mood is Darii. The validity of Daruu and the rest does not mean that the syllogistic of Aristotle must be enlarged; for Aristotle has already mentioned Daruu—he has mentioned Darii, and Darii is identical with Daruu. Suppose—as Theophrastus perhaps supposed—that the undetermined propositions are equivalent to their particular counterparts, but that undetermined sentences are not synonymous with their particular counterparts: then Daruu and the rest are plausibly taken to be additional moods.[47] In this way the distinction between synonymy and the weaker relation of expressing equivalent propositions is fundamental to the dispute over the status of undetermined moods. Yet no ancient text ever makes the distinction plain, or offers a clear and unambiguous gloss on '$\iota\sigma\sigma\delta\nu\nu\alpha\mu\epsilon\hat{\iota}\nu$'. Ammonius, for example, ascribes the equivalences to Aristotle: first he uses the phrase '$\tau\dot{\eta}\nu$ $\alpha\dot{\nu}\tau\dot{\eta}\nu$ $\delta\dot{\nu}\nu\alpha\mu\iota\nu$ $\check{\epsilon}\chi\epsilon\iota\nu$' which he apparently glosses in terms of having the same truth-value (*in Int* 110. 24–5; cf. 114. 22–3); a page later he affirms that, according to Aristotle, 'AiB' and 'AuB' 'say ($\phi\theta\check{\epsilon}\gamma\gamma\epsilon\sigma\theta\alpha\iota$)' or 'signify ($\sigma\eta\mu\alpha\acute{\iota}\nu\epsilon\iota\nu$) the same thing' (111. 10–15).

The undetermined moods are an intriguing ripple on the surface of categorical syllogistic; but it must be confessed that an ancient logician who wished to replace the Aristotelian tetrad by a hexad might rather have considered other non-standard types of determined proposition.[48]

Singular Syllogisms

Tacked on to the end of the discussion of the third figure comes the following short and perplexing paragraph:

[47] Suppose that the expressions E and E* each formulate a syllogism, and that they differ from one another in that where E contains the sentence S, E* contains the sentence S*. (1) If S and S* are synonymous, then E expresses the same syllogism as E*—thus, almost explicitly, our text (1. 59 (p. 44. 21–45. 5 H), on 'begging the question'; cf. the scholium at p. 139. 12–13 H). (2) If S and S* are not synonymous but express propositions which are logically equivalent to one another, then E and E* express different syllogisms.

[48] Most obviously, in view of Aristotle's interest in 'what holds for the most part', propositions of the form 'A holds of most Bs'. Such items were discussed in the context of modal logic. So far as I am aware, no ancient logician ever thought of treating them as a type of non-modal determined proposition.

Syllogisms consisting wholly of singulars (οἱ ... ἐκ τῶν καθ᾽ ἕκαστα δι᾽ ὅλου συλλογισμοί), about which not even Aristotle said anything, resemble universal syllogisms: just as the latter embrace all the subject kind, so the former embrace the whole person. E.g.

Levi of Jacob
Jacob of Isaac
Isaac of Abraham
Therefore: Levi of Abraham

(Hence the noble Paul says: And as I may so say, Levi also, who receiveth tithes, payed tithes in Abraham (*Hebr.* 7: 9).) Similarly, the negative syllogisms consisting of singulars are compared to the negative universals. (1. 32 (p. 25. 26–26. 4 H))

The only thing which is clear in this paragraph is the remark about Aristotle: he did not mention purely singular syllogisms—no doubt because, as our text has already reported (1. 24 (p. 17. 24–7 H)), he did not use singular propositions at all in his syllogistic.

It seems improbable that our author is himself responsible for the invention of wholly singular syllogisms; but I can recall no close parallel to the paragraph in any ancient logic text. By way of comment I offer three guesses, none of which is very satisfactory.

The first two guesses start from the comparison which the text draws between singulars and universals. Although our author speaks explicitly of singular syllogisms and universal syllogisms, it is easy to swallow the suggestion that there is an underlying comparison between singular propositions and universal propositions. Just as 'All men are mortal' ascribes something, namely mortality, to the whole ensemble of men (and not just to one or two of its component parts), so 'Socrates is mortal' ascribes something, namely mortality, to the whole of Socrates (and not just to one or two of his component parts). Just as 'No men are mortal' denies mortality of the whole human ensemble, so 'Socrates is not mortal' denies mortality of the whole individual. In general, there is a parallel between 'AaB' and 'Fx', and between 'AeB' and 'not-Fx'. The parallel is rough; and there is no call to make it more precise by invoking notions taken from set theory or mereology.

The first guess now recalls that for centuries a stock example of a syllogism in Barbara was this:[49]

All men are mortal
Socrates is a man
Therefore: Socrates is mortal

This syllogism does not—or does not evidently—possess the canonical form of Barbara,

---

[49] It is the illustrative syllogism, e.g. in John Italos, *dialectica* §15 (but Italos does not say that it is in Barbara).

AaB, BaC:: AaC;

but it does possess the form

AaB, Bx:: Ax.

And you might call this form quasi-Barbara. Quasi-Celarent will look like this:

AeB, Bx:: not-Ax

And there are several other quasi-moods, among them quasi-Darapti:

Ax, Cx:: AiC

Hence—the first guess—it is such quasi-moods which underlie our text.

The guess has two advantages: it gives sense to the comparison between singulars and universals; and it presents us with moods, with (as our text calls them) 'syllogisms in abstraction from perceptible matter' (1. 27 (p. 20. 2–3 H)). Its disadvantages are equally evident: it does not fit the illustrative example; and the quasi-moods are not properly described as wholly singular—each contains a non-singular proposition.

The second guess is free from the second of these disadvantages. Contemporary logic offers us any number of wholly singular inferences—for example, the schema:

Fx, Gx:: Fx & Gx

In general, take any valid schema in propositional logic, replace the Ps and the Qs by an 'Fx' and a 'Gx', and you have a wholly singular inference schema. Perhaps such things lie behind our text? They are moods, and they are wholly singular moods. But they suffer from at least one disadvantage of their own: all such schemata will contain complex propositions ('hypothetical' propositions, in the ancient jargon); and it seems certain that in our text wholly singular syllogisms need not contain—and probable that they may not contain—complex propositions as components.

The third guess forgets the parallel between singular and universal propositions and instead fastens its attention on the illustrative example. It is expressed with less than perfect limpidity. I suppose that the telegraphic 'Levi of Jacob (ὁ Λευὶ τοῦ Ἰακώβ)' means 'Levi is of the house of Jacob'; and in any event it must express some relation between Levi and Jacob. Thus the text offers an example of what Galen called relational syllogisms.[50] For the example has the form:

xRy, yRz, zRw:: xRw.

You might reasonably analyse this as a polysyllogism, taking it to be the copulation of two arguments of the form:

---

[50] On which see Barnes (1993).

xRy, yRz:: xRz.

And a negative singular syllogism? Consider the example:

Caesar not of Ptolemy
Ptolemy of Cleopatra
Therefore: Caesar not of Cleopatra

And then the general formula:

not-xRy, yRz:: not-xRz.

Such relational syllogisms may now be compared to universal syllogisms, not in virtue of any parallel between singular and universal propositions, but rather for the following reason: just as the validity of Barbara and of Celarent depends on the logical properties of the term-connexion marked by 'a' and 'e', so the validity of the two argument forms I have given depends on the logical properties of the relation marked by 'R'. (The affirmative argument is valid inasmuch as 'R' marks a transitive relation; the negative argument is valid inasmuch as the relation is also symmetrical.[51])

So the third guess finds Galen's relational syllogisms behind our text. It may be objected that the two schemata which I have given are not formally valid, and that, according to the third guess, the text does not concern itself with moods but rather with 'concrete' arguments. Perhaps that is so[52]—but exactly the same can be said of Galen's examples. It may also be objected that our text does not explicitly talk of relations or of τὰ πρός τι, and that Galen does not talk of wholly singular syllogisms. This is a serious objection. Nonetheless, the third guess is the best that I can do. I am too timid to speculate that relational syllogisms found their way into Christian texts thanks to the Theodotian heretics who used Galen's logic in their biblical exegesis.[53]

Two Million More Moods

Near the beginning of its formal development of the syllogistic our text makes the following declaration:

---

[51] A simple proof:

1 (1)	xRy	premiss
2 (2)	not-yRz	premiss
3 (3)	xRz	hypothesis
3 (4)	zRx	3, symmetry
1, 3 (5)	zRy	1, 4, transitivity
1, 3 (6)	yRz	5, symmetry
1, 2 (7)	not-zRx	1, 2, 3, 6 reductio

[52] But the notion of 'formal' validity is notoriously hard to capture: see Barnes (1990).
[53] On them see Eusebius, *h.e.* 5. 28. 13–14; cf. Walzer (1949: 75–86).

Such being the number of the syllogisms,[54] Aristotle, for the sake of simplicity, takes up a single hexad of propositions—the one consisting of two unquantified propositions and four quantified ones, with definite names—and illustrates the syllogisms by way of these, supposing that by way of them the others too will be made clear. (1. 28 (p. 20. 11–15 H))

There is a comparable passage at the end of the discussion of syllogistic:

If to these combinations you join those from the other hexads—not only those depending on subject and predicate but also those compounded from a third item co-predicated—and if you attach and count in those with modes and their mixtures, and if you are ready to put together those thousands of syllogisms...(1. 48 (p. 39. 1–7 H))

then you will have brought your study of syllogisms to its completion.

In 1. 24 our text computed the total number of types of categorical proposition. There is the basic hexad in which all the terms are simple names and verbs ('Men walk'); then there are propositions with indefinite names ('Not-men walk'); then those in which there is a third item co-predicated—these being simple ('Men are just'), or metathetic ('Men are not-just'), or privative ('Men are unjust'). In addition, categorical propositions of any of these varieties may carry a modal operator ('Necessarily...', 'Possibly...', ...); and finally, every proposition must bear one of three tenses. The various permutations which these possibilities allow yield in all 576 types of categorical proposition.[55] 1. 26–7 then compute the total number of combinations: $576 \times 576 = 331,776$ (p. 18. 27–8 H)—a figure which must be multiplied by 12, to take care of the modalities,[56] and then by 3 for the figures. The result is 11,943,936 combinations (p. 19. 16–17 H), of which 2,433,552 are concludent.[57] According to our text, Aristotle's syllogistic, as he presents it in *APr*, concerns itself with a mere six of the 576 types of proposition, and with a mere 108 of the 12 million combinations. Aristotle therefore elaborates only a minute fragment of categorical syllogistic.

The suggestion that Aristotle restricts himself, 'for the sake of simplicity', to six types of proposition is surprising—on several counts. First, our text plainly implies that Aristotle did not discuss modal syllogisms in *APr*. And

---

[54] Here, as often, '*συλλογισμός*' means 'syllogism in abstraction from perceptible matter' or 'mood'.

[55] Syrianus did not get past 144 (see Boethius, *in Int*[2] 321. 20–323. 13), while Ammonius managed to arrive at the figure of 3,024 (*in Int* 219. 19–21). Our text confesses that it omits certain further complications: p. 17. 21–8 H.

[56] p. 19. 7 H: the modalities are already catered for in the 576 types of proposition: I suppose—the text is not clear on the point—that modality comes into the picture twice, first with reference to the modal status of the 'matter' of the proposition (thus e.g. '2 + 2 = 4' has a necessary matter), and secondly with reference to the form of the proposition (thus e.g. 'Necessarily 2 + 2 = 4' has a necessary form): see e.g. Alexander, *in APr* 27. 1–5; Ammonius, *in Int* 88. 18–28; Philoponus, *in APr* 43. 18–44. 1; John Italos, *dialectica* §§25, 31.

[57] p. 19. 20–1 H—but the total must be modified in some unspecified ways to account for the vagaries of certain modal combinations.

this is bizarre. It is not in the least odd that our text does not discuss modal syllogistic—such an *arcanum* has no place in an elementary text.[58] The oddity lies in the implication that Aristotle was mum on the subject. For no one who had read the *Analytics*—or who had seen any ancient commentary on the work—could conceivably have thought that Aristotle had said nothing about modal syllogistic. It appears to follow that the author of our text had not read either Aristotle's work or any commentary on it—a consequence which is awkward. I have no explanation worth recording.

Secondly, the text plainly implies that an extension of the syllogistic to cover all 576 types of proposition is a simple enough task—or so at least I understand the remark that 'the others too will be made clear' by way of the basic syllogisms. Again, no one familiar with the *Analytics*, or with the commentatorial tradition, could have thought such a thing. Aristotle's account of modal syllogisms is notoriously difficult, and evidently it does not depend on a simple transposition from the non-modal to the modal. The commentators show how the Peripatetic tradition was in a state of perplexity.

Thirdly, our text plainly implies that the syllogistic expounded by Aristotle in *APr*—and taken over by itself in 1. 30–2—concerns only those combinations each of whose propositions consists of a simple name and a simple verb (plus determinators). 'Every man runs' but not 'Every man is an animal', nor 'Some man is unjust', nor 'No non-man is just', nor 'No non-man laughs', ... This is plainly false. Not only does Aristotle explicitly remark, in the later parts of *APr*, that the component propositions of syllogisms may have any degree of complexity,[59] but the illustrative examples in the formal exposition of the syllogistic are rarely of the simple 'noun plus verb' structure. Rather, they usually contain, at least implicitly, a copula or 'third item co-predicated'.

The same is true of our text itself. Not one of its illustrative examples contains a verb. The example of a syllogism in Barbara—typical for all the subsequent examples—is this:

Substance to every animal
Animal to every man
Therefore: substance to every man[60]

True, the example is expressed in telegraphese rather than in Greek, and there is nothing in it which answers to the copula. Nonetheless, the jargon expressions correspond to Greek sentences in which a third item is co-predicated: they do not correspond to Greek sentences of the structure 'noun plus verb'. Here it appears that the author of our text has not merely not read

---

[58] But the text does say something about the modalities, and in particular about modal conversion: 1. 22 (p. 15. 12–14 H), 1. 36 (p. 28. 21–29. 4 H).

[59] See esp. *APr* A 36–8.

[60] 1. 30 (p. 21. 22–3 H)—already at 1. 25 (p. 18. 11–12 H); see above, n. 29.

his Aristotle—he has not looked at the text which he is in the course of writing.

How, in any event, might you think that Aristotle's syllogistic would need an extension in order to accommodate propositions outside the basic hexad? In order to accommodate, say, the proposition 'Every man is unjust'? Here an exciting answer suggests itself: propositions of this sort have logical properties which are not shared by all universal affirmative propositions. For example, from 'Every man is unjust' we may infer 'No man is just'; and in general, from '$\tilde{A}aB$' we may infer 'AeB'.[61] This formal inference is not recognized in basic syllogistic. An extension of syllogistic might come to display it—and might therefore open the way to some extra moods. Thus an extended syllogistic might acknowledge the validity of, say:

$$\tilde{A}aB, BaC :: AeC$$

which follows from Celarent together with the inference in question.

This idea was to have a future, and perhaps it—or something like it—lies darkly behind our text. But nothing in basic syllogistic could be said to 'make clear' the validity of

$$\tilde{A}aB, BaC :: AeC,$$

which depends on a rule beyond its ken. If our author did have such moods in mind, he failed to see—or contrived to hide—their relation to what he took to be the basic moods of the syllogistic.

Hypothetical Moods

They occupy 1. 38. There are precisely six of them. They are said to be 'different from the syllogisms we have just described' (p. 30. 16 H); but the first is 'similar' to a categorical mood. Our text does not trouble to explain what a hypothetical syllogism is.[62] A curious sentence which announces that such things contain five distinct features[63] clearly implies that every hypothetical syllogism contains a conditional proposition (p. 31. 26–32. 2 H).[64]

---

[61] The equivalence between 'AaB' and '$\tilde{A}eB$' is noted by Psellos: *Philosophica minora* 1. 15; earlier essays in the same field include Apuleius, *int* 6 (p. 198. 7–17 M); Boethius, *int syll cat* 785A; and the thing goes back ultimately to Aristotle, *int* 19^{b}32–20^{a}15.

[62] Normally—and roughly—a hypothetical syllogism is a syllogism at least one of whose premisses is a hypothetical proposition; and a proposition is hypothetical if it is of the form '$f(P_1, P_2, \ldots, P_n)$'—where each 'P_i' is a proposition and 'f' is an n-placed sentential connector.

[63] Cf. Boethius, *hyp syll* 2.1. 1: 'some think that hypothetical syllogisms consist of five parts, others of three'; in his discussion of the controversy (§§1–6), Boethius refers to Cicero *in rhetoricis* (i.e. *inv* 1. 37. 67–39. 72; cf. Marius Victorinus, *in Cic rhet* 1 (pp. 102–4 Orelli)), and I suppose that the issue derives from the rhetorical tradition.

[64] Each such syllogism is declared to contain an antecedent and a consequent—and hence, by implication, a conditional proposition. Unless our author thinks that disjunctions and conjunctions also divide into antecedents and consequents? Blemmydes, *epit log* 36. 973BC, says that in

But this is true of only half the types of hypothetical syllogism which the text has just enumerated. Again, no explanation is offered of why there are only six kinds of hypothetical syllogism—and precisely these six kinds. There was no unanimity on the point in the Peripatetic tradition.[65]

Modern scholarship tends to associate hypothetical syllogistic with the Stoics; but although the Stoics are mentioned in our text (p. 31. 28–9 H), it is only as the users of a variant terminology.[66] Hypothetical syllogistic is not presented as a Stoic annexe to a Peripatetic system—and in fact Peripatetic logic, since the time of Theophrastus, had always incorporated a treatment of hypothetical syllogisms.[67] The Peripatetics generally supposed that hypothetical syllogisms were in some fashion subordinate, or even reducible, to categorical syllogisms.[68] The claim in our text that hypothetical syllogisms of the first type are 'similar' to categoricals perhaps hints at some sort of reduction. An obscure remark at the end of l. 38 claims—traditionally and falsely—that the premisses of a hypothetical syllogism, when they are contested, are proved by way of categorical syllogisms;[69] and this, too, may be taken to hint at a thesis of reduction or subordination. But there is nothing explicit on the subject in our text.

The five hypothetical moods which are not similar to categoricals are closely related to the five kinds of 'indemonstrable' argument which formed the basis of classical Stoic logic. These kinds are sometimes presented by way of the following schemata:

(1) If P, Q; P:: Q
(2) If P, Q; Not-Q:: Not-P
(3) Not-(both P and Q); P:: Not-Q

---

the disjunctive proposition 'δέκα ἢ ἄρτιός ἐστιν ἢ περιττός', 'δέκα' is the antecedent and 'ἢ ἄρτιός ἐστιν ἢ περιττός' the consequent.

[65] Alexander, for example, lists eight forms of hypothetical syllogism; but his extra hypothetical items concern such things as arguments based on 'the more and the less': *in APr* 389. 31–390. 9 (= Theophrastus, 111E, in Fortenbaugh *et al.* (1994)). Some later texts recognize seven types of hypothetical syllogism: Martianus Capella, 4. 420; Marius Victorinus, *apud* Cassiodorus, *inst* 2. 3. 13 [= Isidore, *etym* 2. 28. 23–6])—ultimately from Cicero, *Top* 13. 53–14. 57 (cf. Boethius, *in Cic Top* 5 (pp. 353–9 Orelli)). See below, p. 118. Others acknowledge six: the Ammonian scholia (*apud* Ammonius, *in APr* XI 1–36)—one 'wholly hypothetical' syllogism and five 'mixed' (but very different from what is to be found in our text); cf. Philoponus, *in APr* 243. 11–246. 14. Some like five: [Ammonius], *in APr* 68.23–6 (corresponding, but not precisely, to items (1)–(5) below—wholly hypothetical syllogisms being noted separately at 67. 29–30); Boethius (?), *in APr* 304. 5–19 Minio-Paluello (for the authorship see Minio-Paluello (1957: 95); (1962: lxxix–lxxxviii); Shiel 1982). Blemmydes, *epit log* 36, recognizes the same six syllogisms as our author, to whom in this chapter he is very close. (But he has not simply copied our text, and I imagine that he and our author depend on a common source.)

[66] Cf. e.g. [Ammonius], *in APr* 68. 4–14.

[67] See Barnes (1985); Maróth (1989).

[68] The supposition is founded on Aristotle, *APr* A 23; see Barnes (1997); Barnes (1983: 286 n. 3); Maróth (1989: 74–81).

[69] p. 32. 2–7 H: so too e.g. Alexander, *in APr* 262. 32–263. 25; Ammonius, *in Int* 3. 22–8; Philoponus, *in APr* 301. 2–5.

(4) Either P or Q; P:: Not-Q
(5) Either P or Q; Not-P:: Q[70]

The first two of our author's pentad are indeed completely stoical.[71] The presentation of the other three is in one respect different inasmuch as it is explicitly allowed that the conjunction and the disjunctions which they contain may have more than two members (p. 31. 15, 18, 21 H).[72] Thus instead of (4) we have a mood which may be described as follows:

> Given a disjunction (with any number of disjuncts) and also any one of the disjuncts, infer the conjunction of the negations of each of the other disjuncts. (See p. 31. 17–21 H.)

Schematically, and for the particular case of a triple disjunction, we might write:

(4*) Either P or Q or R; P:: Not-Q and not-R.[73]

Disjunction in ancient logic is standardly taken to be 'exclusive'; that is to say, a disjunction is true if and only if precisely one of its disjuncts is true. Hence (4*) is valid.

There is thus no difficulty with the transformation of (4) into (4*)—or, more generally, with its extension to multiple disjunctions of any degree of complexity. For (5) the case is more complicated. The best generalization might be thought to be something like this:

---

[70] The schematic versions are unhistorical, and in the case of (3)–(5) they are inaccurate: e.g. if the fourth indemonstrable is to be presented schematically rather than metalogically (see above, n. 23), then it must be given by a pair of schemata:

(4a) Either P or Q; P:: Not-Q
(4b) Either P or Q; Q:: Not-P

For a careful account see Bobzien (1996: 134–41).

[71] But the name of (2) is unusual: 'this is also called conversion with contradiction (σὺν ἀντιθέσει ἀντιστροφή) inasmuch as we convert from animal to man but contradictorily' (p. 31. 6–8 H). The same name is found in [Ammonius], *in APr* 68. 28, and in the Ammonian scholia, *apud* Ammonius, *in APr* XI. 8–13 ('it is called the second hypothetical and, παρὰ τοῖς νεωτέροις, conversion with contradiction'). Earlier 'conversion with contradiction' describes either the operation of contraposition, which takes us from 'If P, Q' to 'If not-Q, not-P', or else the contrapositive itself (e.g. Alexander, *in APr* 29. 15–17; 46. 6–8). And this presumably explains the origin of the unusual nomenclature; for in fact [Ammonius] offers us not (2) but rather

(2*) If not-P, not-Q; Q:: P

So too in Cicero, *Top* 13. 53, we find (2*) rather than (2); and also Martianus Capella, 4. 420. Boethius, *in Cic Top* 5 (p. 356 O), gives (2); and in his comment on Cicero's text he explains that (2*) is a special case of (2) (p. 361 O). The Ammonian scholia give (2), and then offer (2*) as another example of the same mood. Marius Victorinus apparently offered (2): Cassiodorus, *inst* 2. 3. 13 (cf. Isidore, *etym* 2. 28. 23).

[72] So too e.g. Sextus, *PH* 2. 191; Galen, *inst log* 6. 6; Augustine, *c Acad* 3. 13. 29; Philoponus, *in APr* 245. 23–4, 31–5; Blemmydes, *epit log* 36. 976D-977B.

[73] This is not exact, for the reason given in n. 70 with reference to (4); and the same inexactitude will mark the following schemata. (And it is not at all easy to produce a perspicuous schematic representation of the generalization of (4).) If I nonetheless persist with schemata, that is because their disadvantages do not affect the points which I am concerned to bring out.

Given a disjunction (with any number of disjuncts) and also the negations of at least one but not all of the disjuncts, infer the disjunction of the remaining disjuncts (or, if only one disjunct remains, the remaining disjunct).

A schematic version of this, for the particular case of triple disjunctions, requires two schemata:

(5*) Either P or Q or R; Not-P and not-Q:: R
(5+) Either P or Q or R; Not-P:: Either Q or R.

Each of these schemata is valid. Our text (p. 31. 21–6 H) offers a generalization of (5*) and ignores (5+). It has, to be sure, precedents for so proceeding;[74] but from a logical point of view the procedure is arbitrary.

The case of (3) is more serious. The generalization of (3) might be thought to look like this:

Given the negation of a conjunction (with any number of conjuncts) and also at least one but not all of the conjuncts, infer the negation of the conjunction of the remaining conjuncts (or, if only one conjunct remains, the negation of the remaining conjunct).

For triple conjunctions consider the pair of schemata:

(3*) Not-(P and Q and R); P and Q:: Not-R
(3+) Not-(P and Q and R); P:: Not-(Q and R)

Our text offers something different:

The fourth mood is the one which, from a negated conjunction and the positing of one of the conjuncts, rejects the others (τὰ λοιπά); e.g.

It is not the case that the same thing is a man and a horse and an ox.
But it is a man.
Therefore: it is not the others. (p. 31. 13–17 H)

In other words, for triple conjunctions it suggests neither (3*) nor (3+) but rather:

(3%) Not-(P and Q and R); P:: Not-Q and not-R.[75]

And this is surely invalid. A conjunction is true if and only if each of its conjuncts is true. Hence the negation of a conjunction is true if and only if at least one of its conjuncts is false. Hence a proposition of the form

Not-(P and Q and R)

---

[74] e.g. Philoponus, *in APr* 245. 34–5; cf. Galen, *inst log* 6. 6.
[75] To be sure, the example rather suggests a schema from predicate logic, to wit:

(3P) $(\forall x) \neg (Fx \wedge Gx \wedge Hx)$; Fa:: $\neg Ga \wedge \neg Ha$

Similarly with one of the two examples which illustrate (4*) and (5*). Are the examples merely careless? I doubt it—but the matter is too intricate to be broached here.

may be true when both 'P' and 'Q' are true. Hence from

Not-(P and Q and R)

together with 'P' we cannot validly infer 'Not-Q'.

The error is not peculiar to our author. In his *Topics* Cicero lists seven hypothetical moods.[76] The first of the seven is (1) and the second is (2*); the fourth is (4), the fifth (5), the sixth (3). As for the third, it may be represented by

(3C) Not-(P and not-Q); P:: Q.[77]

This is not identical with (3); but it is either a special case or else an immediate consequence of (3); and its presence in the list has, for that reason, been found odd.[78] Finally, this is Cicero's seventh mood:

(7) Not-(P and Q); Not-P:: Q.[79]

The mood is invalid: if both 'P' and 'Q' are false, then

Not-(P and Q)

is true.

Cicero does not explain why he takes (7) to be valid; but Boethius correctly observes that the mood may be accepted if 'P' and 'Q' are restricted to propositions which are jointly exclusive and mutually exhaustive. Hence it is tempting to guess that Cicero presupposed that a negated conjunction is true if and only if exactly one of its conjuncts is true;[80] in other words, that he took

---

[76] See above, n. 65.

[77] So at least Cicero's example suggests; and so Martianus Capella, Marius Victorinus, and Boethius certainly understood the text. Cicero's description of the inference, as the MSS present it, is this:

When you negate certain conjuncts and assume one or several of them [*ex eis unum aut plura sumpseris*] so that what is left is rejected, that is called the third type of argument. (*Top* 13. 54)

That is, I suppose:

Given a negated conjunction (with any number of conjuncts) and also all but one of the conjuncts, infer the negation of the remaining conjunct.

This does not fit the example: excision of *aut plura* clears up the difficulty (but see Frede 1974: 160–1).

[78] Boethius, *in Cic Top* 5 (pp. 356–7 O), replaces (3C) by

(3B) Not-(if P, not-Q); P:: Q

—which (pp. 364–5 O) he seems to take to be the correct interpretation of Cicero's text. Marius Victorinus retains (3C) but replaces (6) by something which is not formally valid: Cassiodorus, *inst* 2. 3. 13 (cf. Isidore, *etym* 2. 28. 24).

[79] So the MSS; and the text is protected by the parallels in Martianus Capella, 4. 420, Marius Victorinus (Cassiodorus, *inst* 2. 3. 13; cf. Isidore, *etym* 2. 28. 25), and Boethius, *in Cic Top* 5 (p. 359 O); see Frede 1974: 161–7 (who also refers to Philoponus, *in APr* 246. 5–16).

[80] Note that he calls his third type of argument *illa ex repugnantibus sententiis conclusio* (*Top* 14. 56).

Not-(P and Q and R and . . .)

to be equivalent to:

Exactly one of: P, Q, R, . . .

Given such an equivalence, (7) is valid. Given such an equivalence—to return to our text—(3%) is valid.

In our text, then, I suppose that (3%) is not a carelessness or a casual error: rather, it derives from a tradition which took a non-Stoic view of negated conjunctions, and which is represented for us in certain Latin logic texts. Perhaps the tradition itself depends on nothing more diverting than a simple carelessness, a trivial logical howler? I suspect not: rather, someone considered various ordinary sentences of the sort 'You can't have an entrée and a dessert with this menu, you know'; and he decided that such negated conjunctions were true when exactly one of the conjuncts was true. Not an implausible decision—but discussion would lead to distant and deepish waters.

The five Stoic indemonstrables do not constitute the sum of their hypothetical syllogistic. On the contrary, in calling the five moods 'indemonstrable' the Stoics suggest—what they also roundly affirm—that there are many other demonstrable syllogisms. (Indeed, infinitely many.) Why does our text limit itself to its versions of the five indemonstrables, suggesting that they (together with one further item) constitute the whole of hypothetical syllogistic? Perhaps our author thought it enough to list the moods of the indemonstrables: inasmuch as all other hypothetical moods can be derived from them, he has, in listing them, potentially encompassed all possible hypothetical moods. But in that case why did he not do the same thing with categoricals? Why, that is to say, did he not content himself with giving the indemonstrables of the first figure? (Or, come to that, Barbara and Celarent?)

Categorical syllogistic recognizes compound inferences. For example,

AaB, BaC, CaD:: AaD

is a valid mood.[81] But compound categoricals—as their name suggests—were construed as abbreviated strings of simple syllogisms. My example is an abbreviation of a pair of Barbaras, which you might write thus:

AaB, BaC:: AaC, CaD:: AaD

If a Peripatetic logician affirms that there are precisely n valid categorical moods, he means that there are n simple categorical moods: the compound

---

[81] For compound categorical syllogisms see the Ammonian scholia, *apud* Ammonius, *in APr* IX. 41–X. 28; [Ammonius], *in APr* 65. 29–31; Blemmydes, *epit log* 31. 933B. For compound hypotheticals: the Ammonian scholia, *apud* Ammonius, *in APr* XI. 37–XII. 3.

moods, infinite in number, do not count, they are not conceived of as additions to the logical repertoire.

Perhaps the Peripatetics took a similar view with regard to the hypothetical syllogisms. There are n simple moods. Any other valid moods are compound. For example,

If P, Q; Either R or P; Not-R:: Q

is an abbreviated version of:

Either R or P; Not-R:: P; If P, Q:: Q

Hence the limitation to five hypotheticals.

Or rather, to six—for there is also the first of the hypotheticals mentioned in our text, the one which is not a version of a Stoic indemonstrable but is 'similar' to a categorical.

First, let us introduce the syllogism similar to the categoricals:

If God is just, there are courts of justice in the hereafter
If there are courts of justice in the hereafter, souls are immortal
If God is just, souls therefore are immortal[82]

This appears in the first combination of the first figure of the categorical syllogisms, differing only in being hypothetical, as I have said. If the problem in question is negative, it will be established hypothetically either through the first figure or through the others. (p. 30. 20–8 H)

The example is a case of what the Peripatetics called a 'wholly hypothetical syllogism'.[83]

Wherein lies the similarity between such syllogisms and categorical syllogisms?[84] Most presentations of wholly hypothetical syllogistic operate with telegraphic examples, of which the following is typical:

If man, then animal
If animal, then substance
Therefore: if man, then substance[85]

You might be prepared to accept the following schema as the pertinent logical form of the argument:

If Fx, Gx; If Gx, Hx:: If Fx, Hx;

and you might be tempted to say of the schema that it is nothing other than Barbara in hypothetical dress. For 'If Fx, Gx' is best construed universally, so that 'If man, then animal' amounts to 'Anything is, if a man, then an animal';

---

[82] Similar examples in Philoponus, *in APr* 243. 25–32.
[83] See Barnes (1983); Ierodiakonou (1990)—who discusses our text at 140–1.
[84] [Ammonius], *in APr* 68. 15–23, which also talks of such similarities, does not help.
[85] e.g. Alexander, *in APr* 326. 23–5—see Barnes (1983: 289–95); Ebert (1991: 17 n. 16).

and that—according to some ancient logicians—is tantamount to the categorical sentence 'Every man is an animal'.[86] In general, 'If Bx, Ax' is equivalent to—if not synonymous with—'AaB'. Wholly hypothetical syllogisms—of this particular sort—are 'similar to' categorical syllogisms inasmuch as they are lightly disguised instances of the categorical mood Barbara.

This conclusion is pleasingly close to the claim made in our text. But it cannot be correct. The example given in the text[87] has the form:

If P, Q; If Q, R:: If P, R.

It does not have the form

If Fx, Gx; If Gx, Hx:: If Fx, Hx.

Thus the alleged equivalence between 'If Bx, Ax' and 'AaB' cannot be the explanation of the similarity which our text claims to hold between wholly hypothetical syllogisms and categoricals.

A second attempt to unearth the similarity calls on Theophrastus. Alexander reports that Theophrastus had examined wholly hypothetical syllogisms, and that he had established certain analogies between conditional propositions and categorical propositions.[88]

Being a consequent or apodosis is analogous to being predicated, and being antecedent to being subject—for in a way it is subject for what is inferred from it. (Alexander, *in APr* 326. 31–2)

'AaB' sets down B and says A of it. 'If P, Q' sets down P and says Q on its basis. Aristotle had allowed himself the locution 'A follows B' as an expression of universal affirmative propositions:[89] just as 'AaB' says that A follows B, so (and more obviously) 'If P, Q' says that Q follows P. The schema

If P, Q; If Q, R:: If P, R

is similar to Barbara

AaB, BaC:: AaC

inasmuch as 'If P, Q' is analogous to 'BaC', 'If Q, R' to 'AaB', and 'If P, R' to 'AaC'. So Theophrastus; and it is reasonable to conclude that our author works in the Theophrastan tradition.

Thus one sort of wholly hypothetical syllogism is similar to Barbara. A second sort is then described: 'If the problem in question is negative, it will be established hypothetically either through the first figure or through the others'. What does it mean to say that 'the problem in question is negative'?

---

[86] See e.g. Galen, *simp med temp* 11. 499 K; Boethius, *hyp syll* 1. 1. 6.

[87] Compare the example in the Ammonian scholia, *apud* Ammonius, *in APr* XI. 2–3; cf. Boethius, *hyp syll* 1. 3. 5.

[88] *in APr* 325. 31–328. 7 (see Theophrastus, 113ʙ, in Fortenbaugh *et al.* (1994)); cf. Philoponus, *in APr* 302. 6–23 (= Theophrastus, 113ᴄ, in Fortenbaugh *et al.* (1994)); see Barnes (1983).

[89] See below, p. 131.

A 'problem (πρόβλημα)' is, on Aristotle's definition, a question of the form: Is it the case that P or not? And syllogisms were construed as answers to problems—that is to say, you solve the 'problem' by finding an appropriate syllogism the conclusion of which is either 'P' or 'Not-P'.[90] Hence the word 'problem' came to be used as a general designation for the conclusion of a syllogism. We might therefore imagine that the 'problem' in the illustrative example is:

If God is just, souls therefore are immortal;

and we might then guess that an example of a negative problem might be:

It is not the case that if God is just, souls therefore are immortal.

But it is evident that the 'problem' in the example is not the conditional proposition but rather its consequent, 'Souls are immortal'. Note the position of 'ἄρα' in the last line: εἰ ὁ θεὸς δίκαιος, ἀθάνατοι ἄρα αἱ ψυχαί (p. 30. 23 H). This clearly suggests that the 'real' conclusion of the argument—and hence the substance of the problem—is 'Souls are immortal'. The underlying idea is this: the conclusion of a wholly hypothetical argument is not a conditional proposition, it is not 'If P, R'. Rather, the conclusion is the consequent of the conditional proposition, 'R'. The last line of the wholly hypothetical argument presents the conclusion, but presents it hypothetically. The argument is not taken to establish that if P, then R: it is taken to establish that R—on the hypothesis that P.[91]

A negative problem will then be something of the form 'Not-R'; for example: 'Souls are not immortal' and the conclusion—the last line—of a negative wholly hypothetical argument will therefore have the form:

If P, not-R

Given that 'If P, Q' is analogous to 'AaB', presumably 'If P, not-Q' will be analogous to 'AeB'. And corresponding to Celarent we shall find the wholly hypothetical schema:

If P, Q; If Q, not-R:: If P, not-R.

Two other categorical moods conclude to propositions of the form 'AeC', namely Cesare

BeA, BaC:: AeC

and Camestres

BaA, BeC:: AeC.

---

[90] For 'πρόβλημα' see also 1. 39 (p. 32. 12 H), below, p. 130.

[91] The same idea is found in Alexander: *in APr* 265. 15–17; 326. 12–17; Philoponus, *in APr* 243. 32–6; 244. 16–21; cf. Boethius (?), *in APr* 320. 7–16 M–P (= Theophrastus, 113D, in Fortenbaugh *et al.* (1994)): *Alexander et plurimus chorus philosophorum nec syllogismos huiusmodi contendunt: nil enim nisi consequentiam eos aiunt ostendere* (320. 14–16). See Barnes (1983: 307–9).

Corresponding to them we may invent the schemata

If P, Q; If R, not-Q:: If P, not-R

and

If P, not-Q; If R, Q:: If P, not-R,

each of which is valid.

No doubt our text has these three negative schemata in mind. But it actually says that a negative problem 'will be established hypothetically either through the first figure or through the others';[92] and 'the others' must refer to the second and the third figures. Yet no third figure mood yields a universal negative conclusion. Our author has blundered—but it is perhaps no more than a careless slip.

Our text explicitly takes wholly hypothetical syllogisms to constitute a single type of syllogism; yet Barbara, Celarent, Cesare, and Camestres are four distinct categorical moods: why not embrace four distinct wholly hypothetical moods? To be sure, the hypothetical companion of Celarent might be regarded as a special case of the hypothetical companion of Barbara; but the same is not true of the other two negative moods.[93] More generally, our text offers no hint that wholly hypothetical syllogisms had once been elaborated in a systematic fashion.[94]

Non-Concludent Combinations

Our text works with a hexad of categorical propositions, and it affirms that the six varieties of categorical proposition allow the construction of thirty-six combinations, thus:

aa ae ai ao au ay
ee ea ei eo eu ey
ii ia ie io iu iy
oo oa oe oi ou oy
uu ua ue ui uo uy
yy ya ye yi yo yu

---

[92] Theophrastus invented three hypothetical figures corresponding to the three categorical figures. Yet we should not be tempted to think that our text refers to the hypothetical figures: to change reference without warning and in the space of three lines would be unpardonable; and the text clearly supposes that affirmative problems can be proved only in the first figure—which is false of the hypothetical figures.

[93] Blemmydes, *epit log* 36. 977D–979A (cf. Philoponus, *in APr* 243. 13–15), recognizes four types of wholly hypothetical mood, inasmuch as the conclusion of such a syllogism may have any of the four forms 'If P, Q', 'If P, not-Q', 'If not-P, Q', and 'If not-P, not-Q'.

[94] Contrast e.g. Boethius, *hyp syll* 2. 9. 1–3. 6. 4.

The calculation presupposes that an ea pairing, say, is distinct from an ae pairing. The pairing which yields Cesare is

{BeA, BaC}.

The pairing which yields Camestres is

{BaA, BeC}.

And these two sets are supposedly distinct. Most, but not all, ancient accounts of the syllogistic took this line. It is not immediately evident how the two pairings were thought to be distinguished. This does not concern me here. But I venture to add that the orthodox line does not imply that combinations are ordered pairings: the pairing for Cesare is

{BeA, BaC},

not

<BeA, BaC>.

There is no such thing as 'the first premiss' of a syllogism.[95]

However that may be, our text informs us which combinations in each figure are concludent, and then affirms that all the rest are non-concludent. It offers no systematic proofs for the concludence of concludent combinations or for the non-concludence of non-concludent combinations. But it offers a sketch of the ways in which concludence may be proved, and it passes some remarks on the manner of proving non-concludence. I shall say something about the latter remarks—and first it is worth saying what a proof of non-concludence ought to establish.

To say that a combination is non-concludent is not to say that nothing can be deduced from it: trivially, from any combination an infinite number of propositions can be deduced. Rather, a combination is non-concludent if and only if it is not concludent; and a combination is concludent if and only if it entails a categorical proposition the two terms of which are identical with the two extreme terms of the combination. For example, a combination of the type ae in the first figure is concludent if and only if at least one of the following twelve schemata is a valid mood:

(1) AaB, BeC:: AaC
(2) AaB, BeC:: AeC
(3) AaB, BeC:: AiC
(4) AaB, BeC:: AoC
(5) AaB, BeC:: AuC
(6) AaB, BeC:: AyC

---

[95] See Barnes (1997a: 121–5).

  (7) AaB, BeC:: CaA
  (8) AaB, BeC:: CeA
  (9) AaB, BeC:: CiA
 (10) AaB, BeC:: CoA
 (11) AaB, BeC:: CuA
 (12) AaB, BeC:: CyA

Consequently, the combination is non-concludent if and only if each of the twelve schemata is invalid.

To prove non-concludence, then, we shall apparently need to produce no fewer than twelve distinct demonstrations, one for each schema. Aristotle made the task lighter for himself: in *APr* A 4–6 he restricts his attention to six of the twelve schemata; and he supposes that the first figure combination ae is concludent if and only if at least one of schemata (1)–(6) is valid. Moreover, he saw that the task could be made lighter still. Given the equivalences between 'AiB' and 'AuB' and between 'AoB' and 'AyB', (5) is invalid if and only if (3) is invalid, and (6) is invalid if and only if (4) is invalid. And given the rules of subalternation, if (3) is invalid then (1) is invalid, and if (4) is invalid then (2) is invalid. Hence if we can show that (3) and (4) are invalid, the invalidity of all six schemata will have been demonstrated.

How might the invalidity of, say, (3), be proved? In several ways. One of them—the way which Aristotle himself trod—relies on the production of counterexamples. If (3) is valid, then any triad of terms whatever has the following property: if, when the terms are substituted for 'A', 'B', and 'C' in the premisses of the mood, two truths result, then when the appropriate two terms are substituted for 'A' and 'C' in the conclusion of the mood a truth results. Hence (3) is invalid if there is at least one triad of concrete terms—say 'X', 'Y', 'Z'—such that 'XaY' and 'YeZ' are both true and 'XiZ' is false; or, equivalently, if there is at least one triad such that all of

  XaY, YeZ, XeZ

are true.

How might we show that there is such a triad? By producing one—for example, the triad 'Animal', 'Man', 'Inanimate'. The following three propositions are all true:

  Animal holds of every man
  Man holds of nothing inanimate
  Animal holds of nothing inanimate

Hence not all concrete triads which make 'AaB' and 'BeC' true also make 'AiC' true. Hence (3) is not valid.

The invalidity of (4) can be shown in the same way—say by means of the triad 'Substance', 'Animal', 'Inanimate'.

Hence—or so Aristotle concludes[96]—the combination in question is non-concludent.[97]

So much for what must be done, and for one way of doing it. Here is the passage in which our text remarks on proofs of non-concludence in the first figure:

All the combinations apart from these are non-concludent. They are called non-concludent because they infer to contrary and incompatible conclusions. So—to take as a single example the second combination of the first hexad in this first figure—

Substance to every animal
Animal to no inanimate
Therefore: substance to every inanimate

And again, for the same combination:

Animal to every man
Man to no inanimate
Therefore: animal to no inanimate

Observe how, for the same combination and the same quality and quantity, contrary conclusions have been inferred. (1. 30 (p. 22, 14–22 H))[98]

[96] Had he considered all twelve schemata, he would have come to a different conclusion; for schema (10) is a valid mood—it is the mood called Fapesmo. Here is a proof:

1 (1)	AaB	premiss
2 (2)	BeC	premiss
3 (3)	not-CoA	hypothesis
3 (4)	CaA	3, square of opposition
1, 3 (5)	CaB	1, 4 Barbara
1, 3 (6)	not-CoB	5, square of opposition
2 (7)	CeB	2, conversion
2 (8)	CoB	7, subalternation
1, 2 (9)	CoA	1, 2, 3, 6, 8 reductio

[97] Here is Aristotle's version of the proof:

If the first follows each of the middle and the middle holds of none of the last, then there will not be a syllogism of the extremes; for nothing necessary results by virtue of the fact that this is so.

That is, the combination {AaB, BeC} is non-concludent insofar as there is no valid mood of the form 'AaB, BeC:: AxC'.

For it is possible for the first to hold of each of the last and of none of it, so that neither the particular nor the universal is necessary.

That is, possibly (AaB and BeC and AaC), so that 'AaB, BeC:: AoC' is not valid (and hence 'AaB, BeC:: AeC' is not valid either); and possibly(AaB and BeC and AeC), so that 'AaB, BeC:: AiC' is not valid (and hence 'AaB, BeC:: AaC' is not valid either).

And if nothing is necessary, there will not be a syllogism by way of these items. Terms for holding of each: Animal, Man, Horse. Of none: Animal, Man, Stone. (*APr* 26ª2–9)

This is Aristotle's most elaborate exposition of a proof of non-concludence. It is nothing if not concise, and it has often been misunderstood. On Aristotle's method see Patzig (1968: 168–92); Lear (1980: 54–75); Thom (1981: 56–64).

[98] Cf. 1. 31 (p. 23. 19–25 H), on the second figure, and 1. 32 (p. 25. 14–26 H), on the third. In the case of the second figure the text simply gives us two triads of true propositions and leaves us to decide what to make of them. In the case of the third figure there are two triads, and then the statement that, in the case of all the non-concludent combinations, an appropriate choice of terms will show that 'they do not always infer to the same conclusions'. Note also the scholium

These remarks have some affinity with the Aristotelian method which I have just sketched; but they do not reproduce that method, and the method which they describe is doubly bizarre. First, the reason for denying that a combination is concludent is precisely the fact that certain propositions of the form 'AxC' can be inferred from it. Secondly, the conclusions which our text invites us to draw quite evidently do not follow from the premisses which it offers us.

It is worth citing a second passage. After a description of Darapti,

AaB, CaB:: AiC

we find this:

Sometimes 'to every' is also concluded, the terms or the matter being responsible and not the combination nor the structure of the syllogism—for in that case 'to every' would always be inferred. E.g.

Substance to every man
Animal to every man
Therefore: substance to every animal. (1. 32 (p. 24. 1–5 H))

The pseudo-mood Darapta—

AaB, CaB:: AaC

—is not valid. It is not valid because you cannot always infer a universal affirmative conclusion from premisses of that form. But sometimes a universal affirmative conclusion can be inferred; and in such cases it is the 'matter' of the particular concrete argument, or the particular concrete propositions which are its premisses, which account for the validity.[99]

The connexion between this passage and the proofs of non-concludence is plain;[100] and the passage shares one of the oddities of the proofs—for it approves an argument which is evidently invalid. Given

Substance to every man

and

Animal to every man,

you may not infer

Substance to every animal,

even though this third proposition is also true.

(p. 130. 18–21 H—virtually identical with Philoponus, *in APr* 34. 7–10): 'The word "τι" [in Aristotle's definition of the syllogism] is taken for "the conclusion which is inferred ought to be a single determined item"—it is there to distinguish syllogisms from non-concludent combinations [here called "συζυγίαι"] which conclude both to "to every" and also to "to no"'.

[99] On matter and form in ancient logic see Barnes (1990: 39–65); Flannery (1995: 109–45).
[100] The connexion is explicitly noted at p. 25. 19–26 H.

In order to prove the non-concludence of the first figure combination in ae, the text purports to produce a triad of concrete terms such that the concrete argument

XaY, YeZ:: XaZ

is valid; and a second concrete triad such that

X*aY*, Y*eZ*:: X*eZ*

is valid. Although the text fails to produce such triads, we may still ask why such things—were they to be found—should be thought to prove non-concludence. The underlying idea is surely this: the first argument shows that arguments of the form (4) are not always valid, and the second argument shows that arguments of the form (3) are not always valid. Hence the schemata (4) and (3) are not valid moods. Hence the combination is non-concludent.

Both Aristotle's method and the method indicated by our text hunt for pairs of triads. But the methods differ in this respect: Aristotle requires triads of terms which make certain triads of propositions true; our text requires triads of terms which make certain arguments valid.

Our text is not innovative. On the contrary, the method which it patronizes is found in Alexander, and then in most later Peripatetic texts which deal with non-concludence.[101] It is, in short, the orthodox method of the late Peripatos[102]—where it began life as an interpretation of Aristotle. It is a false interpretation of Aristotle. Moreover, it is a method which is invariably bungled in its application inasmuch as we are urged to accept arguments which are invalid.[103] None the less, the method need not be considered as an interpretation of Aristotle (nor does our text offer it as such); and even if its applications are bungled, the method might itself be acceptable.

At the heart of the method there lies a certain thesis, never explicit but clearly implicit in our texts. It is this:

If propositions of the form P and Q sometimes entail a proposition of the form R, then the schema
    P, Q:: Not-R
is not a valid mood.

---

[101] See e.g. Alexander, *in APr* 52. 22–4 ('combinations which change and are reshaped along with their matter and have different and conflicting conclusions at different times are non-concludent and unreliable'); cf. 55. 21–32; 57. 3–4; 61. 18–20; Philoponus, *in APr* 34. 7–10; 75. 3–7 , 25–30; 76. 6–20; 80. 25–81. 21; [Ammonius], *in APr* 48. 40–49. 6; 62. 12–14—see Patzig (1968: 171–2); Barnes (1990: 58–62); Barnes *et al.* (1991: 12–14, which the present pages amplify and correct); Flannery (1995: 136–42).

[102] But perhaps not the only method. Thus Apuleius holds that a combination is non-concludent 'because it can infer a falsity from truths' (*int* 14 (p. 215. 6–7 M); cf. 8 (p. 203. 5–6 M)). Or is Apuleius merely proposing the orthodox method in a confused manner?

[103] The two points are connected: the applications are bungled because they use Aristotle's triads, or triads closely modelled on them.

The thesis has a certain plausibility. But it is false. It is worth showing that it is false—and first it is worth showing that one seductive objection to it is itself false.

The seductive objection suggests that the antecedent of the thesis can never be given a true instantiation; for it makes no sense to suppose that propositions of a given form might sometimes entail a certain form of proposition and sometimes not entail one. Entailment, after all, is an all or nothing affair: items do not 'sometimes' entail other items.

The objection is false. Consider again the schema

AaB, BeC:: AeC.

The schema is not a valid mood—that has already been demonstrated. But now take the concrete triad of terms 'Man', 'Man', and 'Stone'; and construct the argument:

MaM, MeS:: MeS.

That argument is an instance of the invalid schema. It is also—and trivially—a valid argument. (It is not a syllogism, you will say. True—it does not satisfy the conditions laid down by Aristotle in his definition of the syllogism. But no matter. The question is not: Is the argument an Aristotelian syllogism? But rather: Is the argument valid?) An invalid schema may have instances which are formally valid deductions; and the seductive objection is false.[104]

There is a true objection. As terms take 'Man', 'Man', and 'Greek'. Consider the argument:

MeM, MaG:: MaG

This argument is evidently and trivially valid. Now the argument is an instance of the schema

AeB, BaC:: AaC.

Hence arguments which instantiate this schema are sometimes valid. But then, if we accept the thesis which lies at the heart of the late Peripatetic method, we shall be obliged to reject the schema

AeB, BaC:: AoC

—and *a fortiori* the schema

AeB, BaC:: AeC.

But the first of these schemata is Celaront and the second Celarent. Thus the thesis at the heart of the orthodox method is false, and the method itself is to be rejected.

---

[104] The schema

P, Q:: R

is not a valid mood. Every valid syllogism is an instance of the schema . . .

The Colophon of Philosophy

1. 39–48 contains a continuous argument. It is the most technically sophisticated part of the treatise; it is presented as the summit or culmination—the κολοφών—of the study; and it purveys a 'remarkable method' which rests on 'a genuinely profound and most scientific consideration'. It is evidently the most important part of the Chapter in its author's eyes.

So that we may have a ready supply (εὐπορία) of premisses for any disputed problem which is put forward, a remarkable method has been discovered: by way of it we have a ready supply of premisses and thus can demonstrate by way of a conclusion the communality or the alienation of the terms in the problem. He hands this method down by way of a certain consideration ... (1. 39 (p. 32. 10–15 H))

'He hands down'—who does? Aristotle, although our text does not say so; and the ultimate source of the discussion in 1. 39–48 is *APr* A 27–8,[105] where Aristotle explains 'how we shall have a ready supply (εὐπορήσομεν) of syllogisms in relation to whatever may be posited' (43ᵃ20–1). That is to say, the colophon of philosophy is what the Middle Ages later pictured as the *pons asinorum*.[106]

The method or μέθοδος is apparently distinguished from the consideration or θεώρημα; and at p. 32. 18 H the text announces: 'This is the θεώρημα'. Since there is nothing answering to a theorem in the following lines, I take the word 'θεώρημα' in a relaxed sense—a certain heuristic method is to be based on certain logical considerations. It is difficult to say where the account of the θεώρημα ends and the account of the method begins. Indeed, I incline to think that there is no exposition of the method itself: we get the θεώρημα and are left to deduce the method for ourselves.

However that may be, the method must sound like a piece of hocus-pocus. How could any method help me to solve every problem, to prove every provable truth?[107] To be sure the method is less audacious than first appears. Every problem is said to be 'contained in two terms'; and every solution to a problem consists of a syllogism, the conclusion of which is an appropriate proposition of the form 'AxC':

Since each problem in dispute is contained in two terms, we need another term to mediate and either to connect the extremes to one another or else to separate and dissever them. (1. 39 (p. 32. 18–21 H))

---

[105] Which Alexander, *in APr* 290. 16–18, and Philoponus, *in APr* 270. 10, 273. 21, explicitly characterize as a μέθοδος.

[106] The diagram—or at any rate, a diagram—was used by Alexander (*in APr* 301. 10—but it is not preserved in our MSS of the commentary), and by Philoponus (*in APr* 274. 7—with a diagram in the MSS); and it is found in many MSS of *APr* itself (Minio-Paluello 1957: 97 n. 7). See e.g. Thom (1981: 73–5).

[107] The method is presented as a method of proof: cf. p. 32. 14 H ('ἀποδείκνυμεν'); *APr* 43ᵃ38, ᵇ11 (cf. 43ᵃ21–2: τὰς περὶ ἕκαστον ἀρχάς). But Aristotle's method, in virtue of the division which he makes in the lists of terms (see below, p. 131), will enable us to supply both demonstrative and non-demonstrative syllogisms: see 43ᵇ9–11; Philoponus, *in APr* 280. 11–27.

The question is, how do we find such a middle term? And the method answers the question. If the question is sensibly less daunting than its first expression suggested,[108] it is none the less daunting enough—how could any method be devised to answer it? Surely each science will have its own methods?

The θεώρημα on which the method is based is complex; and the exposition in our elementary text is (or so I have found) more difficult to follow than Aristotle's original version.

We start with a problem, the terms of which will be designated 'A' and 'E'. (This is the first time in our text that schematic letters have been used: they are not explained.) And we construct—or discover—six sets of terms, BΓΔ and ZHΘ, three of them associated with A and three with E (1. 39 (p. 32. 21–6 H)).[109]

> For the middle term has three qualities in relation to each of the two extremes: either the middle is one of the terms which follows them, i.e. one of the more universal terms, or it is one of those which they follow,[110] i.e. one of the more particular terms, or it is one of the alien terms. (p. 32. 26–33. 1 H)

B, Γ, and Δ terms associate with A; Z, H and Θ terms with E. X is a B-term if it 'follows' or is 'more universal than' A. In Peripatetic jargon, 'X follows Y' normally means 'XaY'.[111] But from 'XaY' it does not follow that X is more universal than Y; for 'XaY' is compatible with 'YaX', in which case the two terms are equally universal. X is more universal than Y if it holds of every Y and also of some non-Y. Hence X is a B-term if XaA and also AoX. Similarly, X is a Z-term if XaE and EoX. If X is a Γ-term, it is 'more particular' than A; that is to say, X is a Γ-term if AaX and also XoA. And X is an H-term if EaX and XoE. As for 'alien' terms, it emerges that X is a Δ-term if XeA and X is a Θ-term if XeE.

It is evident that the three 'qualities' do not exhaust the relations in which the middle term may stand to the extremes. (Although the run of the text may suggest exhaustivity, there is no explicit claim to this effect—and the word 'τινας' at p. 32. 26 H perhaps insinuates non-exhaustivity.) Why, for example, not construct sets of terms such that XiA or XiE? On this point our text is at one with Aristotle, who remarks that 'we should not select terms which follow some, but rather those which follow all the object' (*APr* 43^b 11–12).[112] None the less, our text is at once more generous and more sparing than Aristotle. The touches of generosity are harmless;[113] but the omission of

---

[108] Not, to be sure, in Aristotle's view; for he has already purportedly shown that every proof must take such a form (*APr* A 23). See Barnes (1997*b*).

[109] Cf. *APr* 44^{a}11–17—at p. 32. 22 H 'ὁ φιλόσοφος' designates Aristotle.

[110] Omitting 'ἐν' before 'οἷς' at p. 32. 28: cf. p. 33. 3, 5, 14, 18, 25.

[111] See e.g. Aristotle, *APr* 43^{b}3; 44^{a}13; Alexander, *in APr* 55. 10–11; 294. 1–2 (with reference to 43^{b}3); see above, p. 121.

[112] Nor need we select terms such that AeX and EeX, for 'the negative converts' (*APr* 43^{b}5–6)—i.e. such terms are identical with Δ-terms and Θ-terms.

[113] e.g. our text will require 'substance' to appear among the B-terms for 'animal' and also among the B-terms for 'man': according to Aristotle, if X is a B-term for Y and YaZ, then X should not appear among the B-terms for Z (*APr* 43^{b}22–6).

certain types of term which Aristotle includes is another matter—an elementary treatise may perhaps suppress the refinement which calls for sets of $\dot{\omega}_S$ $\dot{\epsilon}\pi\grave{\iota}$ $\tau\grave{o}$ $\pi o\lambda\acute{v}$ predicates (*APr* 43^{b}32–6); but it is strange—and potentially disastrous—to exclude co-extensive terms.[114]

Having constructed the six sets of terms, consider next those terms which are found both in one of the sets associated with A and in one of the sets associated with E.[115] Our text gives the impression that, for any A and any E, there will always be at least one such term. In any event, the $\theta\epsilon\dot{\omega}\rho\eta\mu\alpha$ implicitly limits itself to pairs of terms, A and E, for which that holds true.[116] Any such common term must fall into one of nine classes: either it is both a B-term and a Z-term—either, as the text puts it, it is a BZ term, or it is a ΓZ term, or a ΔZ, or a BH, or a ΓH, or a ΔH, or a BΘ, or a ΓΘ, or a ΔΘ. The text develops an illustrative example of a ΓH term; and it then goes through, in schematic fashion, each of the nine classes in the order in which I have listed them.[117]

The $\theta\epsilon\dot{\omega}\rho\eta\mu\alpha$ is most easily presented by way of an example. Suppose that the problem is this: What is the connexion between pipe-smoking and affability, between being a pipe-smoker and being affable? In other words, for what x do we have it that PxA? We consult the pertinent sets of terms for P and A; and we find that the term 'contented' appears both as a B-term and as an H-term. What next? Well, in this particular case, you might well imagine the following response: 'Since C is a B-term, CaP and PoC, and since C is also an H-term,

---

[114] Aristotle explicitly requires us to list $\ddot{\iota}\delta\iota\alpha$ (*APr* 43^{b}2–3, 26–9), which our text implicitly excludes. Here *APr* distinguishes between $\dot{o}\rho\iota\sigma\mu o\acute{\iota}$, $\ddot{\iota}\delta\iota\alpha$ and $\ddot{o}\sigma\alpha$ $\ddot{\epsilon}\pi\epsilon\tau\alpha\iota$ $\tau\hat{\omega}$ $\pi\rho\acute{\alpha}\gamma\mu\alpha\tau\iota$ (43^{b}2–4), so that you might reasonably infer that, in this context at least, $\ddot{o}\sigma\alpha$ $\ddot{\epsilon}\pi\epsilon\tau\alpha\iota$ are always taken to be $\kappa\alpha\theta o\lambda\iota\kappa\dot{\omega}\tau\epsilon\rho\alpha$. Now when in A 28 the $\theta\epsilon\dot{\omega}\rho\eta\mu\alpha$ is developed, Aristotle speaks exclusively of $\ddot{o}\sigma\alpha$ $\ddot{\epsilon}\pi\epsilon\tau\alpha\iota$: a reader might naturally suppose that $\ddot{o}\sigma\alpha$ $\ddot{\epsilon}\pi\epsilon\tau\alpha\iota$ here are the same items as $\ddot{o}\sigma\alpha$ $\ddot{\epsilon}\pi\epsilon\tau\alpha\iota$ at 43^{b}2–4; and so he might conclude that the $\theta\epsilon\dot{\omega}\rho\eta\mu\alpha$ applies only to $\kappa\alpha\theta o\lambda\iota\kappa\dot{\omega}\tau\epsilon\rho\alpha$ terms. Thus Alexander, *in APr* 306. 24–307. 7, takes *APr* 44^{a}38–^{b}5 to restrict the sets of terms to $\kappa\alpha\theta o\lambda\iota\kappa\dot{\omega}\tau\epsilon\rho\alpha$. Later, at 309. 11–35, he rightly concludes that the sets will contain co-extensional terms as well as $\kappa\alpha\theta o\lambda\iota\kappa\dot{\omega}\tau\epsilon\rho\alpha$ (something he had already stated plainly enough at 295. 1–3). None the less, he still gives a certain preference to $\kappa\alpha\theta o\lambda\iota\kappa\dot{\omega}\tau\epsilon\rho\alpha$ inasmuch as, according to him, the method requires us to look first for $\kappa\alpha\theta o\lambda\iota\kappa\dot{\omega}\tau\epsilon\rho\alpha$ and to take in co-extensional terms only if no $\kappa\alpha\theta o\lambda\iota\kappa\dot{\omega}\tau\epsilon\rho\alpha$ are to be found. In sum: our text is mistaken when it excludes co-extensional terms. But Aristotle's text invites the mistake. Alexander narrowly avoids it. And Philoponus in effect warns against it: 'It is clear that what follows something either extends further or is equal—animal, which extends further, follows man, and so does laughing, which is equal' (*in APr* 273. 30–3, on *APr* 43^{b}4).

[115] Cf. *APr* 43^{b}42; 44^{a}1, 6, 11.

[116] So, explicitly, Alexander, *in APr* 294. 21–2.

[117] Aristotle goes through the classes first at *APr* 43^{b}39–44^{a}11, using metalogical descriptions, and then at 44^{a}11–35, using schematic letters. In the metalogical treatment he mentions ΓZ, ΓH, ΔZ, BΘ and ΔH, which he uses to generate syllogisms in Barbara, Darapti, Celarent, Camestres, and Felapton. In the schematic treatment he lists the same five classes and moods, and adds to them BH and Baralipton. Later, at 44^{b}25–37, he remarks that BZ, ΓΘ, and ΔΘ terms are 'useless for making syllogisms'. Aristotle is interested in the production of (demonstrative) syllogisms: for each of the four types of categorical proposition, his procedure identifies (at least one) class of common term which will serve for its deduction. Our text—in the interest of a scientific hunt and discovery (1. 39 (p. 33. 26–7 H))—wants to ensure that every combination (and hence every concludent combination) has been considered.

AaC and CoA. Now, by Barbara, we may infer that AaP (from 'AaC' and 'CaP'); and then—if you insist—we may convert and assert that PiA.'

Now that is exactly what Aristotle does with BH terms.[118] But it is not how the $\theta\epsilon\acute{\omega}\rho\eta\mu\alpha$ proceeds in our text. Rather, we find this:

From BH terms there are generated sixteen non-concludent combinations in the first figure: with a particular affirmative major and a minor which is either particular affirmative or particular negative or undetermined affirmative or undetermined negative; or with a particular negative major and . . . (1. 43 (p. 35. 24–8 H))

It would be tedious to quote the whole passage. The sum of it is this:

A BH term generates
—in the first figure: ii, io, iu, iy, oo, oi, ou, oy, uu, ui, uo, uy, yy, yi, yo, yu—all of which are non-concludent;
—in the second figure: ao, ay—both concludent; and ai, au—both non-concludent;
—in the third figure: ia, oa, ua, ya—all concludent.

In all, then, a BH term generates twenty-four combinations, six of which are concludent. Similar accounts are given of the eight other classes. Taken together—what magic—they generate all 192 combinations.

What is going on? Let us return to our example. The BH term ensures that CaP, PoC, AaC, and CoA. It also, according to our text, generates twenty-four combinations—among which the combination for Barbara is not to be found. First, why not Barbara? I suppose, with little confidence, that the answer is this: the $\theta\epsilon\acute{\omega}\rho\eta\mu\alpha$ generates only those combinations which have a configuration appropriate to the problem. The problem—the conclusion to any pertinent syllogism—must have the form 'PxA'. In the first figure, every combination appropriate to this problem must have the form

$Px_1C, Cx_2A.$

The combination

AaC, CaP

does not have this configuration. Hence the $\theta\epsilon\acute{\omega}\rho\eta\mu\alpha$ does not generate it. ('So much the worse for the $\theta\epsilon\acute{\omega}\rho\eta\mu\alpha$: the restriction which it places on the generation of combinations is wholly arbitrary; and although there is nothing thereby logically amiss with it, the arbitrariness makes it an implausible candidate for the founding of a useful method.')

However that may be, a BH term does not generate the combination for Barbara. But it does generate twenty-four other combinations—how? The text says nothing on the matter; and it is not easy to devise a convincing answer.

[118] 'If B is the same as H, there will be a converted syllogism. For E will hold of every A—since B of A and E of B (it is the same as H)—whereas A will not necessarily hold of every E but will necessarily hold of some since a universal affirmative predication converts to a particular' (*APr* 44^{a}30–5).

It will seem plausible to think along the following lines. The definition of a BH term guarantees four propositions, which constitute what I shall call the 'basic group'. In our case:

CaP, PoC, AaC, CoA.

The members of this group entail various other propositions by way of the conversion laws and the equivalences for unquantified propositions. Adding all the entailed propositions to the basic group, we arrive at the 'extended group', in our case:

CaP, PiC, CiP, PuC, CuP, PoC, PyC, AaC, CiA, AiC, CuA, AuC, CoA, CyA

Pair off the members of this extended group to form combinations in the various figures, and all the twenty-four combinations listed in the text are generated.

That is satisfactory enough in itself. But it does not meet all the demands of the text. For the extended group generates more than the twenty-four desiderated combinations. For example, it generates

PiC, AiC

which is a non-concludent third figure combination. According to our text, this combination is generated not by a BH term but rather by a BZ term (1. 40 (p. 34. 11–13 H)). The procedure I have rehearsed may generate all the combinations listed—but it does not generate only those combinations. We need something more sophisticated.

No simple procedure will do the trick. Here is one complex procedure. The key to it is this: although we start, as before, with the basic group, we construct three extended groups, not one—and the construction is done under certain restrictions.

I start with the notion of a 'serviceable' proposition: a proposition is serviceable for a given figure if it may serve as a member of an appropriate combination in that figure. Next, consider, for each figure, the universal propositions in the basic group. (1) If both these propositions are serviceable, they alone form the extended group. (2) If one of the propositions is serviceable, then the extended group is formed from that proposition together with all the entailments of the other propositions in the basic group which are serviceable in tandem with the first proposition. (3) If neither of the propositions is serviceable, then the extended group consists of all the serviceable entailments of the universal members of the basic group together with the serviceable non-universal members of the basic group and their serviceable entailments.

The basic group for the BH term C was

CaP, PoC, AaC, CoA.

For the first figure, neither universal proposition is serviceable. Hence rule (3) applies and we generate the following extended group:

PiC, PuC, PoC, PyC, CiA, CuA, CoA, CyA

—which yields the sixteen listed combinations. For the second figure 'CaP' is serviceable; rule (2) applies; we get:

CaP, CiA, CuA, CoA, CyA

—and hence the four listed combinations. For the third figure 'AaC' is serviceable. Rule (2) gives

AaC, PiC, PuC, PoC, PyC

—hence, again, the listed combinations.

The rules I have laid down are tortuous and arbitrary. I do not suppose that our author had thought them out—and I have not found them in any other ancient text. But at least, the procedure I have sketched gives the desired results for BH terms; and I hope that it gives the desired results for the other eight classes of common term. But I am sure that it is possible to invent other complex procedures; and in all probability there are some which are superior to the one I have here set out.

So much for the θεώρημα. I am not sure why it should be called deep and scientific—unless those two words mean something like 'contorted'. In any event, the θεώρημα is presented as the basis for a method. The method will give us a ready supply of premisses for any problem (p. 32. 12–14 H); and the text also assures us that

if we consider [ἀναθεωροῦντες] matters in this way, we shall discover all the combinations, both concludent and non-concludent, by the little—and not so little—method, and not one of all of them will be able to escape or run away from us. (p. 34. 3–6 H)

The θεώρημα purports to show that, for any problem, the nine classes of associated middle terms will yield all possible combinations. The method, then, is presumably to be described in something like the following way: 'If you want to solve the problem "For what x is it the case that AxC?", then make the six sets, construct the nine classes, produce the groups, assemble the combinations, select the concludent combinations, and embrace the concludent combination which yields a syllogistic proof for the problem.'

I am not sure whether the method is offered as a sure-fire way of finding a proof, as the best possible way, or simply as one good way among others. It seems to me evident that it is not a good way—certainly not as good as Aristotle's original way; but I shall limit myself to showing that it is not a sure-fire way.

The value of the method depends on the nature of the sets of terms on which it draws. In order to guarantee a proof of a problem, the sets must be complete: every middle term of every type must be found among them. It is wildly unreasonable to imagine that such complete sets are ever available.[119] But even if the sets were complete, there would be no guarantee of a proof; for the three qualities which determine the construction of the classes are three among many, and the terms needed for a proof might exhibit one of the other sorts of quality. In particular, the sets contain no co-extensive terms; and yet, according to Aristotle, many proofs use counterpredicable terms. Finally, even if the sets of terms were extended to include all the possible qualities, the method would not guarantee that we hit on a proof: the most it could hope to guarantee is that we should hit upon at least one syllogism with true premisses.[120] But a syllogism with true premisses is not thereby a proof.[121]

In short, the colophon of philosophy is a curious item. The $\theta\epsilon\omega\rho\eta\mu\alpha$ which it rehearses is serpentine and inexplicably arbitrary. The method which it trumpets is of no scientific value. Logic, in the Peripatetic tradition, purports to be the instrument of the sciences; in particular, its value is measured by its capacity to formulate scientific proofs. Notoriously, in Aristotle's own writings there is a gap between the scientific pretensions and the logical content of the syllogistic. As the Peripatetic tradition developed, so the gap widened.

BIBLIOGRAPHY

Barnes, J. (1983), 'Terms and Sentences', *Proceedings of the British Academy*, 69: 279–326.

——(1985), 'Theophrastus and Hypothetical Syllogistic', in W. W. Fortenbaugh (ed.), *Theophrastus of Eresus* (Rutgers University Studies in Classical Humanities, 2; New Brunswick, NJ).

——(1990), 'Logical Form and Logical Matter', in A. Alberti (ed.), *Logica mente e persona* (Florence).

——(1993), '"A Third Sort of Syllogism": Galen and the Logic of Relations', in R. W. Sharples (ed.), *Modern Thinkers and Ancient Thinkers* (London).

——(1997a), *Logic and the Imperial Stoa* (Philosophia Antiqua, 75; Leiden).

——(1997b), 'Proofs and the Syllogistic Figures', in H.-C. Günther and A. Rengakos (eds.), *Beiträge zur antiken Philosophie: Festschrift für Wolfgang Kullmann* (Stuttgart).

---

[119] To be sure, each set, according to Aristotle (and doubtless according to our text) can have only a finite number of members (*APost* A 19–22). But there is no upper limit to the number of members of any set, and no way of ensuring that all have been discovered. Moreover, there is (according to our text) an infinite number of problems and hence of sets of terms (1. 27 (p. 20. 4–10H)). Alexander's illustrative examples of sets list a certain number of concrete terms and then add '$\kappa\alpha\grave{\iota}$ $\tau\grave{\alpha}$ $\tau o\iota\alpha\hat{v}\tau\alpha$' (*in APr* 301. 21, 23, 31).

[120] Aristotle's sets of terms are differentiated into $\kappa\alpha\theta$' $\alpha\grave{v}\tau\acute{o}$ and $\kappa\alpha\tau\grave{\alpha}$ $\sigma v\mu\beta\epsilon\beta\eta\kappa\acute{o}s$ predicates (*APr* 43^{b}6–11—cf. 44^{a}36–^{b}5; Alexander, *in APr* 295. 28–296. 19); and the provenance of a middle term will thus indicate whether or not it is suitable material for a demonstrative syllogism.

[121] But see above, p. 100.

—— Bobzien S., Flannery K., and Ierodiakonou K. (1991), *Alexander of Aphrodisias: On Aristotle Prior Analytics 1. 1–7* (London).

Benakis, L. (1988), 'Commentaries and Commentators on the Logical Works of Aristotle in Byzantium', in R. Claussen and R. Daube-Schackat (eds.), *Gedanken-zeichen: Festschrift für Klaus Oehler* (Tübingen).

Bobzien, S. (1996), 'Stoic Syllogistic', *Oxford Studies in Ancient Philosophy*, 14: 133–92.

Ebbesen, S. (1981), *Commentators and Commentaries on Aristotle's Sophistici Elenchi* (Corpus latinum commentariorum in Aristotelem graecorum, 7; Leiden).

Ebert, T. (1991), *Dialektiker und frühe Stoiker bei Sextus Empiricus: Untersuchungen zur Entstehung der Aussagenlogik* (Hypomnemata, 95; Göttingen).

Flannery, K. (1995), *Ways into the Logic of Alexander of Aphrodisias* (Philosophia Antiqua, 62; Leiden).

Fortenbaugh, W. W., Huby, P. M., Sharples, R. W. and Gutas, D. (eds.) (1994), *Theophrastus of Ephesus: Sources for his Life, Writings, Thought and Influence* (Philosophia Antiqua, 54; Leiden).

Frede, M. (1974), *Die stoische Logik* (Abhandlungen der Akademie der Wissenschaften in Göttingen, phil.-hist.Klasse, 88; Göttingen).

Heiberg, J. L. (1929), *Anonymi logica et quadrivium cum scholiis antiquis* (Det kgl. Danske Videnskabernes Selskab., Historisk-filologiske Meddeleser, 15/1; Copenhagen).

Ierodiakonou, K. (1990), 'Rediscovering some Stoic Arguments', in P. Nicolacopoulos (ed.), *Greek Studies in the Philosophy and History of Science* (Boston Studies in the Philosophy of Science, 121; Dordrecht).

Lear, J. (1980), *Aristotle and Logical Theory* (Cambridge).

Lee, T.-S. (1984), *Die griechische Tradition der aristotelischen Syllogistik in der Spätantike* (Hypomnemata, 79; Göttingen).

Maróth, M. (1989), *Ibn Sina und die peripatetische 'Aussagenlogik'* (Budapest).

Minio-Paluello, L. (1957), 'A Latin Commentary (? translated by Boethius) on the *Prior Analytics*, and its Greek Sources', *Journal of Hellenic Studies*, 77: 93–102.

—— (1962), *Aristoteles Latinus*, iii 1–4: *Analytica Priora* (Leiden).

Patzig, G. (1968), *Aristotle's Theory of the Syllogism* (Dordrecht).

Praechter, K. (1931*a*), 'Michael von Ephesos und Psellos', *Byzantinische Zeitschrift*, 31: 1–12.

—— (1931*b*), Review of Heiberg, *Byzantinische Zeitschrift*, 31: 82–90.

Shiel, J. (1982), 'A Recent Discovery: Boethius' Notes on the *Prior Analytics*', *Vivarium*, 20: 128–41.

Taisbak, C. M. (1981), 'The Date of Anonymus Heiberg, Anonymi logica et quadrivium', *Cahiers du Moyen-Age Grec et Latin*, 39: 97–102.

Thom, P. (1981), *The Syllogism* (Munich).

Walzer, R. (1949), *Galen on Jews and Christians* (Oxford Classical and Philosophical Monographs; Oxford).

Whitaker, C. W. A. (1996), *Aristotle's de Interpretatione: Contradiction and Dialectic* (Oxford Aristotle Studies; Oxford).

6

Hellenic Philosophy in Byzantium and the Lonely Mission of Michael Psellos

JOHN DUFFY

In one of his books Cyril Mango makes the interesting observation that for the two centuries between 843 and *c.*1050 no additions were made to the *Synodikon of Orthodoxy*.[1] The *Synodikon*, a major liturgical manifesto of the Byzantine Church, was first promulgated at the end of the iconoclasm controversy, one of the most serious cultural upheavals of the Middle Ages. 'The Triumph of Orthodoxy', as the outcome is known, celebrated originally in the church of Hagia Sophia, in Constantinople, in 843, some years later became established as an annual feast falling on the first Sunday of Lent. The celebration consisted of a solemn procession and liturgical service which included a reading of anathemas against heretics and enemies of true doctrine. By the second half of the eleventh century certain versions of the *Synodikon* began to feature condemnations of contemporary 'enemies of the truth'. The most interesting instance is Michael Psellos' former student, John Italos who became the unfortunate target of no less than twelve citations in the anathemas of the year 1082.[2] Whatever the precise merits of the case, which is still a matter of some dispute, the proclaimed root of the charges against Italos was his dealings with ancient, that is, in Byzantine terminology, 'Hellenic' philosophy.

With Mango's observation as a suggestive backdrop, let us enquire briefly into the status and life of philosophy in Byzantium, giving particular attention to the two hundred years between 843 and the appearance of Michael Psellos on the scene as a maturing philosopher, let's say in the 1040s.

---

[1] Mango (1980: 102). See also Magdalino (1993: 383–4).
[2] A notorious event in Byzantine cultural history and often described. The text of the anathemas is in Gouillard (1967: 57–61; commentary 188–202). For a succinct recent account, with relevant references, see Agapitos (1998: 184–7).

As a starting-point we may look at the way that philosophy is defined in a very popular medieval Greek reference dictionary, the Suda lexicon, created from a wide variey of ancient and medieval sources sometime in the second half of the tenth century.[3] According to the Suda's formulation, philosophy is 'correct moral practice combined with a doctrine of true knowledge about Being'.[4] There are several points worth noticing in that description. For one thing it does not immediately ring a bell—at least in the context of the six traditional, non-confrontational, definitions of philosophy that were inherited from the late antique scholastics and that still show up in fully fledged form in the work of the theologian John of Damascus in the eighth century.[5] Nor, on the other hand, does it look particularly close to the common Byzantine, reduced, formula according to which philosophy equals monastic asceticism.[6] However, it does have a relative in a sixth-century treatment. In the commentator David's *Prolegomena*, philosophy is divided, in normal scholastic fashion, into theoretical and practical branches; in its theoretical aspect it aims to know all beings (γινώσκει πάντα τὰ ὄντα), while through the practical side it leads to correct morals (κατόρθωσιν ποιεῖται τῶν ἠθῶν).[7] So in a way the Suda's version could be said to parallel that of the late Alexandrian teacher. But, there is at least one major difference, and that is the phrase 'true knowledge' (τῆς γνώσεως ἀληθοῦς) in the Suda version, which sends an unmistakable signal about the definition's overtly Christian orientation.

It will be useful to stay with this David for a short while in view of our general interest in how Hellenic philosophy fared in Byzantium. David is a fairly typical representative of the last phase of the old academic tradition, in major cities like Alexandria and Athens, that was destined to die out for ever by the early seventh century. Like many of his colleagues in Alexandria in the late sixth century, whether they were teachers of philosophy or of medicine, David (as the name would imply) was probably a Christian, but the student body he addressed would have been composed of pagans and Christians, and teachers strictly maintained a posture of impartiality. This studied neutrality was so successfully pursued that it is usually impossible to single out indisputable traces of religious affiliation in the lecture notes or commentaries that have survived from the period. Looking at the two components of David's definition of philosophy one could argue in this instance that there is indeed a

---

[3] *Suidae Lexicon*, ed. A. Adler, 5 vols. (Leipzig, 1928–38).

[4] The full entry (4: 733) reads: Φιλοσοφία. Φιλοσοφία ἐστὶν ἠθῶν κατόρθωσις μετὰ δόξης τῆς περὶ τοῦ ὄντος γνώσεως ἀληθοῦς. ταύτης δὲ ἀπεσφάλησαν Ἰουδαῖοι καὶ Ἕλληνες.

[5] Ed. Kotter, 56 and 136–7; complete details conveniently collected in Podskalsky (1977: 22 n. 63).

[6] See e.g. Sevčenko (1956: 449–57, esp. 449–50), still worth reading after nearly fifty years. Again, extensive further references in Podskalsky (1977: 21 n. 61).

[7] David, *Prol.* 55. 17–19: οὕτως οὖν καὶ ἡ φιλοσοφία διαιρεῖται εἰς θεωρητικὸν καὶ πρακτικόν. καὶ διὰ μὲν τοῦ θεωρητικοῦ γινώσκει πάντα τὰ ὄντα, διὰ δὲ τοῦ πρακτικοῦ κατόρθωσιν ποιεῖται τῶν ἠθῶν.

subtle hint of Christian influence, not in πάντα τὰ ὄντα, which is at least neutral, but in the phrase κατόρθωσιν τῶν ἠθῶν, which seems to first become common in the fourth century, in the writings of Eusebius of Caesarea, Basil the Great, and Gregory of Nyssa.[8]

I will use David too for a look at those six, more traditional, definitions that were commonly discussed in the introductions to philosophy in the schools. As presented by him they identify philosophy as:

  (i) knowledge of beings qua beings;
 (ii) knowledge of things divine and human;
(iii) practice of death;
(iv) assimilation to God as far as humanly possible;
 (v) art of arts and science of sciences;
(vi) love of wisdom.[9]

There is no need for present purposes to review all of them and I may limit myself to a few remarks on the first four. The first two are attributed by David and his predecessors to Pythagoras, and since they are knowlege-based that would explain why they show up, in one form or another, in certain Christian writings which have more of an intellectual bent. The third and fourth on the other hand, which come from, respectively, the *Phaedo* and *Theaetetus* of Plato, are geared to action and the practical part of philosophy;[10] it should not be a great surprise, then, that they are commonly adopted by writers dealing with the monastic life in particular.

To give an example, they can be found in the widely read classic on monastic spirituality, the *Heavenly Ladder* of John Climacus, written in the first half of the seventh century. In the opening chapter or step of the *Ladder*, which is distinguished by a string of definitions, we encounter the following description of a Christian: 'A Christian is an imitator of Christ in thought, word and deed, as far as this is humanly possible';[11] and in the final chapter, which is on Love or Agape, the supreme goal of the spiritual climb is defined in part as 'assimilation to God as far as that is attainable by mortals'.[12] It is more than likely that Climacus was aware of the ancient origin of the formulation because we find him, in the chapter on Remembrance of Death (Μνήμη θανάτου), making the statement, 'Someone has remarked that it is fully impossible for us to live each day devoutly unless we consider it the last one of our lives. And it is amazing that the Hellenes as well had

---

[8] An impression based on a search in the electronic version of the *Thesaurus Linguae Graecae*.

[9] David, *Prol*. 20. 27–31: 1. γνῶσις τῶν ὄντων ᾗ ὄντα ἐστί. 2. γνῶσις θείων τε καὶ ἀνθρωπίνων πραγμάτων. 3. μελέτη θανάτου. 4. ὁμοίωσις θεῷ κατὰ τὸ δυνατὸν ἀνθρώπῳ. 5. τέχνη τεχνῶν καὶ ἐπιστήμη ἐπιστημῶν. 6. φιλία σοφίας.

[10] *Phaedo* 81*a*; *Theaetetus* 176*b* (cf. *Republic* 613*b*). For the arguments used to support a Pythagorean origin of the first two see David, *Prol*. 25. 25–26. 12.

[11] Ed. Trevisan, i. 45: Χριστιανός ἐστιν μίμημα Χριστοῦ κατὰ τὸ δυνατὸν ἀνθρώπων (sic) λόγοις καὶ ἔργοις καὶ ἐννοίᾳ.

[12] Ibid. ii. 307: Ἀγάπη ... ὁμοίωσις θεοῦ (sic) καθ᾽ ὅσον βροτοῖς ἐφικτόν.

a similar idea, seeing that they define philosophy as practice of death.'[13] If David's posture can be called studied neutrality, the adoption of parts of the words and spirit of the secular pagan definitions by Byzantine Christian authors could be characterized as a selective appropriation in which there is a firm taking over of useful pagan elements without any sign of apology.

Let us return to the definition of the Suda lexicon, our original point of departure. Here we noticed a clear indication of its orientation in the key phrase 'true knowledge' and the message is confirmed by the following terse sentence where the implications are that Jewish and pagan philosophers have clearly fallen short of the truth which, by definition we could say, is in the sole possession of the Orthodox.

Now, the material of the Suda lexicon is a compilation from earlier sources and indeed, as Paul Lemerle has remarked, 'it is a compilation of compilations', meaning that it frequently draws its entries from other collections such as lexica, scholia, and excerpta.[14] Its definition of philosophy that we have just examined is a word for word borrowing from the so-called *Excerpta de virtutibus et vitiis*; in other words it comes from a part of the encyclopedia produced in Constantinople, close to the year 950, under the auspices of Emperor Constantine VII Porphyrogennetos.[15] The encyclopedia's text reads: 'For philosophy is correct moral practice combined with a doctrine of true knowledge about Being. But both Jews and Hellenes fell short of this, since they rejected the Wisdom that came from heaven and tried to philosophize without Christ who was the only one to offer a paradigm, in word and deed, of the true philosophy.'[16] We see now that the Suda actually stopped short in its second sentence; here, in the longer version, the Jews and Hellenes are faulted in a more explicit way—they rejected the heavenly *sophia* and attempted to practise a philosophy in which Christ had no part. And there is more in the encyclopedia's text in the same vein, but it will be sufficient and appropriate for us to end the extract with its resounding phrase 'the true philosophy'.

And the Constantinian *Excerpta* in turn, as the term implies, are derived from earlier material. In this instance the discussion of philosophy comes verbatim from the historian George the Monk, the author of a universal chronicle covering the period from Adam to the year 842.[17] George himself

---

[13] Ed. Trevisan, i. 253: καὶ θαῦμα ὄντως πῶς καὶ Ἕλληνές τι τοιοῦτον ἐφθέγξαντο, ἐπεὶ καὶ φιλοσοφίαν τοῦτο εἶναι ὁρίζονται μελέτην θανάτου.

[14] Lemerle (1971: 299).

[15] Constantine Porphyrogennetos, *De virtutibus et vitiis*, i, ed. Th. Büttner-Wobst (Berlin, 1906).

[16] Ibid. 129: φιλοσοφία γάρ ἐστιν ἠθῶν κατόρθωσις μετὰ δόξης τῆς περὶ τοῦ ὄντος γνώσεως ἀληθοῦς. ταύτης δὲ ἀπεσφάλησαν ἄμφω καὶ Ἰουδαῖοι καὶ Ἕλληνες, τὴν ἀπ' οὐρανοῦ παραγενομένην σοφίαν παραιτησάμενοι καὶ χωρὶς Χριστοῦ φιλοσοφεῖν ἐπιχειρήσαντες τοῦ μόνου παραδείξαντος ἔργῳ καὶ λόγῳ τὴν ἀληθῆ φιλοσοφίαν.

[17] *Georgii Monachi Chronicon*, ed. C. de Boor, i. (Leipzig, 1904).

was writing in the 860s or 870s and, like his fellow chroniclers, he offers a text that is often a patchwork of borrowed pieces, arranged with a certain *Tendenz*. In fact, the whole section on philosophy,[18] and much else besides, is lifted by George word for word from the fifth-century ascetical author, Neilos of Ankyra.[19]

So what is going on here? One might well ask. It is not a case of intellectual laziness on George's part, because he knows exactly what he is doing and what his message is. After all, he is the one who, in the feisty prologue of his chronicle, coins the memorable slogan 'better a mumbler in truth than a Plato in falsehood'.[20] Rather, George, and the others who latched on to the same description of philosophy, used this material because it was readymade, expressed sentiments that they were comfortable with, and contained a formulation that they were more than happy to transmit. Putting it another way, we may suggest that it represented part of the cultural Zeitgeist of the ninth and tenth centuries.

Another text exhibiting the spirit of the times sends out the message more explicitly and, among other things, delivers a direct hit on Plato. In the life of St John Psichaites from the ninth century, the anonymous hagiographer describes how the holy man aimed at the heavenly philosophy, studiously avoiding all contact with the paltry earthly version. It is an entertaining and instructive passage, with the writer displaying, in the name of saintly obscurantism, both considerable rhetorical flourish and some acquaintance with the technicalities of the secular sciences. Here are his own words:

And practising the very highest philosophy he assimilated himself to God as far as he could and was content with a single syllogism: 'God is the Creator of all, the Creator is a judge, therefore God is the judge of all.' But propositions, syllogisms, and sophisms—which he regarded as the weavings of spiders—he consigned to the rubbish on the manure heap. Astronomy, geometry, and arithmetic he despised as dealing with the non-existent. For how could the likes of 'momentanea', 'even lines', and 'odd-even numbers' really subsist, if they have no separate substantial existence? And how can Plato, the expert in such things, use them as a means to ascend to the intelligibles, the same fellow who, like a serpent, slithers in the slime of the passions, with his belly stuffed and his mouth gaping?'[21]

---

[18] Ibid. i. 345, 3–8.
[19] Neilos of Ankyra, *Logos Asketikos* (*PG* 79), 721A–C.
[20] Ed. de Boor, i, 2, 9–10: κρεῖσσον γὰρ μετὰ ἀληθείας ψελλίζειν ἢ μετὰ ψεύδους πλατωνίζειν.
[21] Ed. Van den Ven, 109. 13–23: φιλοσοφίαν δὲ τὴν ἀνωτάτω ἀσκῶν ὡμοιοῦτο θεῷ κατὰ τὸ δυνατόν, ἓν μόνον συλλογιζόμενος τὸ τὸν θεὸν ἁπάντων εἶναι ποιητήν, τὸν ποιητὴν κριτήν, τὸν θεὸν πάντως (leg. ἁπάντων?) κριτὴν εἶναι. τὰς δὲ προτάσεις καὶ τοὺς συλλογισμοὺς καὶ τὰ σοφίσματα ὡς ἀραχνῶν ὄντα ὑφάσματα τοῖς ἐπὶ κοπρίας κειμένοις παρῆκεν. ἀστρονομίας δὲ καὶ γεωμετρίας καὶ ἀριθμητικῆς κατεφρόνησεν ὡς ἀνυπάρκτων ὄντων· πῶς γὰρ ἂν ὑποσταίη ἀκαριαῖα καὶ γραμμαὶ ἄρτιοί τε καὶ περισσάρτιοι καθ᾽ ἑαυτὰ ἐν ὑποστάσει μὴ ὄντα; πῶς δαὶ καὶ Πλάτων ὁ τούτων ἐπιστήμων δι᾽ αὐτῶν ἐπὶ τὰ νοητὰ ἀνάγεται, ὁ τοῖς ὄφεσιν ὁμοίως ἐν τῇ τῶν παθῶν ἰλυσπώμενος ἰλύι καὶ ἀποπληθούσης γατρὸς καὶ γνάθων ἀποφαινόμενος;

In view of the tightly constricted form of philosophy that is being sanctioned in those works of the ninth and tenth centuries that we have been citing, it is natural to ask what, if anything, is happening to the non-Christian tradition in the age of post-iconoclasm. How are mainstream authors like Plato and Aristotle actually faring in Byzantium? Here the answer will depend to some extent on what one means by philosophy. But let us take the term in the broadest sense, allowing us to include meaningful contact or interaction with any facet of the Hellenic tradition in that field of learning.

The two principal figures for consideration, because of ample documentation, are the Patriarch Photios who died at the end of the ninth and Arethas of Caesarea who was still active in the first three decades of the tenth century. In the case of Photios we can say that, probably in the earlier part of his career, he was involved in teaching Aristotelian logic; the physical evidence for that activity is in the form of extant comments on the *Categories* of Aristotle[22] and related scholia, the latter not yet systematically collected from the manuscripts. Though the material does not amount to very much in the larger picture of Greek philosophy in Byzantium, it is important as evidence for both teaching and general humanistic activity in the first half of the ninth century. And while it is always possible that lost works will have done away with evidence for an interest in other figures, such as Plato, it is highly unlikely, for several reasons, that Photios had anything serious to do with Platonism. For one thing, his nemesis, Niketas David, the biographer of rival Patriarch Ignatios, would surely not have passed over such an opportunity, if it was available. As it is, the best he can do, apart from sneering at his learning, is to paint Photios as a kind of bibliomaniac.[23]

Arethas, for his part, not only had clear dealings with Aristotelian logic but was instrumental too in helping the Platonic corpus to pass unscathed through a period when active friends of ancient philosophy were not plentiful. The recent publication of his scholia on logic is a welcome development[24] and lovers of Plato will always be grateful to the distinguished Byzantine churchman who, when still only a deacon, spent a considerable sum of money to have a complete copy of Plato's works made in the waning years of the ninth century. This is the marvel of big book production that can still be seen in the Bodleian Library at Oxford under the title E. D. Clarke ms. 39. The marginal notes in the deacon's own hand may be taken as proof of his scholarly concern for the text and its contents.

The only other candidates whose names at least deserve to be raised in this discussion are a trio of near contemporaries who all happened to die in the decade between 860 and 870. They are, first, John Grammatikos, the icono-

[22] *Photii Epistulae et Amphilochia*, ed. L. G. Westerink, v (Leipzig, 1986), quaestiones 137–47.
[23] Niketas David, *Vita Ignatii* (*PG* 105); 509B and 532D.
[24] M. Share (ed.), *Arethas of Caesarea's Scholia on Porphyry's Isagoge and Aristotle's Categories* (Athens and Brussels, 1994).

clast patriarch deposed at the restoration of image worship, who is said to
have had an active interest in, among other things, occult subjects—meaning,
perhaps, that he included Neoplatonic material in his reading and studies.
Next there is the relative of John, known variously as Leo the Philosopher or
Leo the Mathematician who taught at the so-called Magnaura school in the
capital, where he is reputed to have fostered the study of ancient mathematics
and philosophy. And thirdly a man who may have been a student of Leo,
namely, Constantine the Philosopher, the future missionary to the Slavs,
who, while still in Constantinople was appointed teacher of philosophy at
the Magnaura school. Unfortunately, as the choice of words already indicates, there is a tremendous amount of uncertainty about the facts of the
careers and activities of these three individuals; in addition, each of them, for
different reasons (e.g. John because he was a prominent iconoclast, Constantine thanks to his status as a major missionary), attracted legendary treatment of a negative or positive kind, which makes it very difficult to unearth
hard-and-fast details about their lives. It may be that Leo, for instance,
deserves an honourable place in the history of Byzantine Platonism, but we
are far from being able to secure the merits of the case.[25]

This, then, is the picture that can be reconstructed for roughly the two
centuries following the settlement of the icon question. There is, to put it
bluntly, not a lot of verifiable interaction with ancient philosophical texts or
ideas and even the two prominent intellectuals, Photios and Arethas, might
be more accurately depicted as humanists, because it would be an undue
strain on the available evidence to make them out to be anything like major
representatives of Byzantine philosophy. It is not my purpose here to explain
this state of affairs nor to explore to what extent it might be linked to the fact,
as stated by Mango, that the period witnessed no additions to the *Synodikon
of Orthodoxy*. Suffice it to comment that, if one were to include Photios and
Arethas under the heading of philosophers, it would have to be with the
qualification that they confined themselves fairly much to the preliminary
parts of the subject.

All of this takes on a certain significance after we turn to the era following
1050, when, from our point of view, Michael Psellos has already burst on the
scene and is lighting up the sky. Psellos is without question one of the most
intellectually flamboyant and intriguing figures of the Middle Ages and he
has been written about and discussed on many occasions. However, the last
word has not, by a long shot, been said on him and even if the general outlines
of his personality and thought have been fairly well delineated, two factors
will make him a fit subject for further scrutiny for some time to come. One is
that he is a complex and almost protean character who is hard to pin down
and it will take a number of scholars, coming from widely different angles, to

---

[25] For further information on these three figures the reader may consult the useful entries in
the *Oxford Dictionary of Byzantium* (New York and Oxford, 1991).

finally get the measure of him.[26] Another, not unrelated factor is the circumstance that quite a few of his writings are only now, for the first time, receiving basic critical treatment; they are gradually being added to a corpus of his works that will provide the surest foundation for approaching the man through his own public record.[27]

In that body of writings the ones that have received the least attention are the treatises that can be labelled theological. This may be illustrated by the simple statement that, in the first Teubner volume of Psellos' *Theologica*, published by Paul Gautier in 1989, of the 114 short treatises edited there 102 were seeing the light of printed day for the first time. A second volume will also contain a number of new items alongside of treatises that are more or less known already.[28] In view of the fact that these texts have until now been relatively inaccessible, it seems a good idea to bring them into play in a discussion of Psellos as *philosophos*.[29] Hence, for the remarks that follow, the main body of evidence will be the theological writings, though other works will on occasion be included in the picture as well. Another feature of the theological material, apart from the interest of the contents, is the fact that many of the individual works are pieces of exegesis that have their origin in the classroom and are therefore primary evidence for Psellos' activities as a teacher or tutor of higher education in the Byzantine capital in the middle decades of the eleventh century.[30]

In what sense are these theological works in the first place? Well they qualify as such, in terms of classification, because they all take their starting-point from a recognized document of Christian literature. And the range of writings discussed is quite broad, running the gamut from Old and New Testament to the Cappadocian Fathers to individual hymns of John of Damascus and Cosmas the Melode, to even a passage of the *Ladder of Divine Ascent* by John Climacus. By far the most common texts treated are the *Homilies* of the theologian *par excellence*, Gregory of Nazianzus, several of which, such as homilies 28 and 29, are the focus of repeated attention. But the reader of Psellos' *Theologica* soon comes to a realization that a major place is accorded in these exegetical writings to all kinds of what the Byzantines

---

[26] Recently published is a stimulating and attractively written monograph by A. Kaldellis, *The Argument of Psellos' Chronographia* (Leiden, Boston, and Cologne, 1999). The writer, presenting Psellos as a Platonist and political philosopher, goes out on a limb to paint him also as a revolutionary and subversive who essentially renounced Christianity in favour of Hellenic religion. It remains to be seen how much of this view of Psellos as a cultural extremist will be accepted by the scholarly world. Kaldellis himself, in the closing section of his book, seems to retreat to a somewhat safer position, recognizing that his picture is based on 'a single text from a corpus of thousands of pages, which contain a multitude of different Psellos' (197).

[27] The late L. G. Westerink initiated and guided the ongoing series of critical edns. of works by Psellos published by Teubnerverlag of Leipzig and Stuttgart.

[28] *Michaelis Pselli Theologica II*, ed. L. G. Westerink and J. M. Duffy, *Bibliotheca Teubneriana* (in press).

[29] A very good start on the study and appreciation of Psellos' theological writings has been made by Maltese (1994: 289–309).

[30] The point is justly stressed by Maltese (1994: 297–9).

would call Hellenic material, specifically ancient philosophy. And it is not just mainstream figures that are represented—Plato, Aristotle, and the leading Neoplatonists—but even the more arcane subject-matter, the *aporreta* as Psellos would call it, Chaldaean Oracles, Orphica, and Hermetica. Obviously we are, at this stage, light years away from the situation in the ninth and tenth centuries. And the Hellenic material is not simply included in the discussion in order to be refuted, which it frequently is, but Psellos a good number of times goes out of his way to say positive things about, and to be accommodating to, these 'aliens' and to some of their ideas. His fascination with Proclus in particular is a familiar fact and has been well documented over the years.[31] It will suffice here to illustrate the general phenomenon of Psellos' openness to the Hellenes with a couple of representative passages chosen from the theological writings.

The first appears in a discussion of a text by Gregory of Nazianzus in which Psellos bases his exegesis on the symbolic meaning of numbers; in the course of it he passes over the treatment by Maximus the Confessor in favour of Plato who is handed the clear compliment that he had already come close to the truth of the Christian position. Psellos, addressing his student audience, comments 'Do you see how Plato is not very far removed from the truth? That's the kind of man he is; in an alien guise he mystically discourses on our theology and grasps no small fraction of the truth.'[32]

The second example is from an unpublished exegesis of the episode in the gospel according to Mark where Jesus rejects the designation of 'good'. 'Why do you call me good?', he objects to the man who used the word, 'None is good except God alone' (οὐδεὶς ἀγαθὸς εἰ μὴ εἷς ὁ θεός).[33] In his effort to explain why Jesus objected to being called 'good', Psellos digs deep into outside sources, citing ancient discussions of the 'good'. And in this connection he invokes directly the testimony of both Hermes Trismegistos and Proclus, quoting towards the end the *On Providence* of Proclus on the identity of the One (τὸ ἕν) and the Good (τὸ ἀγαθόν):

In addition to all the others there is the philosopher Proclus too, both in his Platonic exegesis and in his work *On Providence*; it is in the third chapter in particular, I think, that he makes the statement 'the Good is identical with the One, as we have said numerous times.' Those are the man's own words. And I have gone somewhat out of the way to give you this information in order to make clear why the Lord was not happy with the compliment 'good'.[34]

---

[31] For example by D. J. O'Meara, *Michaelis Pselli Philosophica minora II* (Leipzig, 1989); see the *index locorum*. Similarly in *Theologica I*, ed. Gautier (Leipzig, 1989).

[32] *Theologica I*, op. 78, 107–9: ὁρᾷς Πλάτωνα οὐ πολὺ τῆς ἀληθείας ἀπῳκισμένον; τοιοῦτος γὰρ ὁ ἀνήρ, ἐν ἀλλοτρίῳ σχήματι ἀπορρήτως θεολογῶν τὰ ἡμέτερα καὶ οὐ πολλοστόν τι τῆς ἀληθείας καταλαμβάνων.

[33] Mark 10: 17–18.

[34] *Theologica II*, op. 18, 33–40: ἐπὶ πᾶσι δὲ τοῖς εἰρημένοις καὶ ὁ φιλόσοφος Πρόκλος ἐν οἷς τε στοιχειοῖ τὸν φιλόσοφον καὶ ἐν τοῖς Περὶ προνοίας αὐτοῦ λόγοις, ἐν τῷ τρίτῳ καὶ μάλιστα κεφαλαίῳ, ὡς οἶμαι, "ταὐτόν" φησι "τἀγαθὸν τῷ ἑνί, τοῦτο δὴ τὸ μυριόλεκτον"· οὕτως γὰρ

And this brings me to another issue of some importance, namely, what is it that Psellos had in mind when introducing at every conceivable opportunity the ideas of pagan philosophy and mysticism? The question would seem to be particularly appropriate when raised in conjunction with his teaching activity; obviously in Byzantium at almost any period it was at least a delicate matter to consort with the likes of Plato and Proclus, not to speak of the Chaldaean Oracles and other occult writings—but in front of students and in the context of the sacred documents of Orthodox Christianity? The answer or answers to this question, which was never far from his consciousness, are supplied in the first instance by Psellos himself and I will turn now to a consideration of his form of self-defence. The justification will hinge in large part on his conception of what it means to be a philosopher.

I will consider a series of passages, from both the theological texts and other writings, that bear directly on the point. The first appears at the end of a short treatise that Psellos has addressed to someone whom he does not identify, but who may well be the future emperor and his one-time student, Michael VII Doukas. It is a collection of information from various sources, but mainly the *Kestoi* of Julius Africanus, on all kinds of magical and, as Psellos himself admits, forbidden lore. At the conclusion he goes to great pains to make a clear public statement about the innocence of his dealings with material of this kind:

I solemnly assure you, it was not out of idle curiosity that I collected most of this lore but from love of learning. You see, by nature I have an insatiable appetite for every kind of subject and I would not want to miss anything, but would like even to know what is under the earth. And in my studies I did not, like most people, accept this and reject that, but made an effort to understand the methods of even disreputable or otherwise objectionable arts, in order to be able to refute their practitioners.[35]

Two points in particular call for comment. One is the charming confession of his insatiable curiosity about things and how he would like nothing better than to peek under the earth to see what is going on there. The other, of even greater importance to note, is his justification for collecting this set of arcana. It is stated in the single term *philomatheia* and is directly set against an opposite which is called *periergasia*. Now *periergasia* is a charged word which certainly includes, within its narrow range of meanings, magical lore and even magical practices. It is clear, then, that when Psellos is setting these terms in opposition, he is investing a lot of meaning in *philomatheia*, to convey the

---

ἐκεῖνος εἴρηκεν ἐπὶ λέξεως. παρεκβατικώτερον δὲ ταῦτα εἴρηκα, ἵν᾿ ᾖ δῆλον, ὁπόθεν ὁ κύριος τὴν τοῦ ἀγαθοῦ μαρτυρίαν μὴ προσηκάμενος φαίνεται.

[35] *Philosophica minora I*, op. 32, 100–6: Ἐγὼ δὲ οὐ περιεργασίας ἕνεκα, νὴ τὴν ἱεράν σου ψυχήν, ἀλλὰ φιλομαθείας τὰ πλείω τῶν μαθημάτων συνελεξάμην· ἐγένετο γάρ μοι ἡ φύσις ἀκόρεστος πρὸς ὁτιοῦν σπούδασμα καὶ οὐδὲν ἄν με βουλοίμην διαλαθεῖν, ἀλλ᾿ ἀγαπῴην ἂν εἰ καὶ τὰ νέρθεν εἰδείην τῆς γῆς. καὶ οὐχ ὥσπερ οἱ πολλοὶ περὶ τοῦτο μὲν ἐσπούδακα, ἐκεῖνο δὲ ἀπωσάμην, ἀλλὰ καὶ τῶν φαύλων ἢ ἄλλως ἀποτροπαίων ἐπιγνῶναι τὰς μεθόδους ἐσπούδακα, ἵν᾿ ἔχω ἐντεῦθεν ἀντιλέγειν τοῖς χρωμένοις αὐτοῖς.

sense of a laudable, and maybe even, a necessary curiosity about the world and everything in it, good, bad, and mysterious. And for good measure he assures his addressee and the wider world that a goal of this learning beyond the pale was to provide himself with a weapon against the promoters of forbidden arts.

I turn next to some other passages, all connected with Psellos in his teaching capacity and addressed directly to his students. One of the manuscripts in the library of the Greek Patriarchate in Istanbul contains a unique piece of Psellan exegesis with the title 'To his students on the ventriloquist' (Πρὸς τοὺς μαθητὰς περὶ τῆς ἐγγαστριμύθου).[36] The text is concerned with an Old Testament passage, the account of the Witch of Endor in *1 Kings*, and is of particular interest in that it owes nothing to previous commentaries on the story, including the one by Gregory of Nyssa. In fact Psellos faults the earlier commentators with failing to explore the origin of the term ἐγγαστρίμυθος and then sets out himself on a search, plunging into an excursus on demonology and bringing in along the way a brief discussion of the Chaldaean books. The closing paragraph shows our author staunchly defending his use of this kind of occult material. He proclaims (to paraphrase him) that he is sharing it with his students but is not in any way propounding it as doctrine; it is a display of *polymatheia* and done on their behalf. He is not hiding his knowledge of these things; in fact having even a smattering of expertise in arcane and occult topics is praiseworthy, enabling one to discern what is beyond the clouds and inside the ether.[37]

However, in Psellos' scheme of things, as he presents it, it is not simply a matter of the teacher's ability to display a boundless curiosity and wide knowledge; in his view this is something desirable in the student as well. Nor, when he evokes the principle of *polymatheia*, is his purpose solely to defend the knowledge of arcane learning. Two further texts will help to convince us of both of those points. Treatise 114 of the *Theologica I* collection, addressed to his student audience, has as its subject the genealogy of Christ starting from the time of Adam. This brief work opens with the banner statement that 'the philosopher must be a man of all sorts' and then goes on to spell out just how broad the concept of 'learning' is for Psellos. Beyond the arts and sciences in general it embraces, according to this formulation, history (which justifies the excursion into genealogy), geography and other forms of literary culture.[38] In this spirit one could justly translate the opening

---

[36] Published for the first time by Littlewood (1990: 225–31).

[37] Ibid. 231. 105–11: ὅσα μὲν ἀναγνοὺς ἔσχηκα ταῦτα δὴ κοινοῦμαι καὶ πρὸς ὑμᾶς, οὔτε δογματίζων οὔτε ἀποφαινόμενος, μόνον δὲ πολυμάθειαν ἐνδεικνύμενος καὶ τοῦτο δι' ὑμᾶς· οὐ γὰρ ἔγωγε φιλοτιμοῦμαι πάλαι τὴν περὶ τοῦτο σπουδὴν καταλελυκώς, τὸ δ' ἔχειν ἐπιστήμην καὶ τούτων οὐ πάνυ ἀποπροσποιοῦμαι· περὶ γὰρ τῶν ἀρρήτων καὶ ἀπορρήτων καὶ ὁ βραχύ τι κατειληφὼς ἐπαίνων ἄξιος ὅτι, τῶν πολλῶν οὐδὲ τὰ ἐν ποσὶ μόνον ὁρώντων, αὐτὸς ὑπερνεφὴς ὥσπερ γενόμενος καὶ τὰ ἐντὸς τοῦ αἰθέρος ἑώρακεν.

[38] *Theologica I*, op. 114, 1–8: Δεῖ τὸν φιλόσοφον παντοδαπὸν εἶναι καὶ φιλοτιμεῖσθαι μὴ μόνον ἐπιστήμας καὶ τέχνας εἰδέναι, ἐξ ὧν σοφία καὶ φρόνησις τὸ συναγόμενον πέφυκεν,

proclamation as 'the philosopher must be a man for all learning'. Psellos uses an almost identical formula in another work, on a homily of Gregory of Nazianzus, when he comments δεῖ τὸν σοφὸν παντοδαπὸν εἶναι.[39] It is appropriate to recall as well that one of his best known works on philosophy, the *De omnifaria doctrina*, has the original title Διδασκαλία παντοδαπή.[40] In a real sense, then, he is using *pantodapos* as a synonym of *polymathes*.

Lastly, in this particular chain of texts, I cite a section from the *Philosophica minora*. It is part of a short treatise, again addressed to his students, on the question, often dealt with in Greek theological writings, as to whether 'being' (οὐσία) is self-subsistent. On this occasion Psellos goes out of his way to stress his belief that certain Hellenic ideas can be helpful in theology and can contribute positively to Christian doctrine. Using that thought as a basis he introduces an account of Being, One, and Soul in terms taken from Neoplatonism and Plato's *Timaeus* and brings the discussion to a close with the following paragraph:

> I have enumerated all these things both to bring you to a state of broad learning and to make you familiar with Hellenic doctrines. Now I realize that our Christian teaching will clash with some of those doctrines, but it was not my intention to have you exchange the one for the other—that would be madness on my part; rather, I wanted you to become devoted to the former and merely take cognizance of the latter. And if they somehow stand a chance of helping you towards the truth, then make use of them.[41]

The purpose of the exercise, then, is twofold: to make his students *polymatheis* and have them well versed in Hellenic doctrines. What is left unsaid but understood is that the first is not possible without the second.

Several conclusions may be drawn from the pieces of evidence we have examined. First, Psellos consistently sees himself as a philosopher whether he be explaining a doctrine of Aristotle or commenting on a passage of the *New Testament*. His stance may be partly explained by a looseness in distinction between the two fields at a certain level within Byzantine thinking, though it

---

ἀλλὰ καὶ ἱστορίαν συλλέγειν καὶ γεωγραφίας ἔχεσθαι καὶ τῆς ἄλλης μουσικῆς μὴ ἀπείρως ἔχειν· μουσικὴν δέ φημι οὐ τὴν ἐν καθαπτοῖς ὀργάνοις μελοποιίαν καὶ χρῆσιν ἁπλῶς, ἀλλὰ πᾶσαν τὴν ἐκ λόγων συναγομένην ἱστορίαν τε καὶ παιδείαν καὶ τὴν ἄλλην ἁπλῶς εὐμάθειάν τε καὶ πολυμάθειαν. 'The philosopher must be a man of all sorts and strive not only to know sciences and arts whose natural product is wisdom and understanding, but also to study history, to be keen on geography, and to have some expertise in the rest of "music", by which I mean not just music making with physical instruments but all word-based history and culture and, in a word, the whole complex of deep and broad learning.'

[39] *Theologica I*, op. 68, 86.

[40] Michael Psellos, *De omnifaria doctrina*, ed. L. G. Westerink (Nijmegen, 1948).

[41] *Philosophica minora I*, ed. Duffy, op. 7, 117–23: Ταῦτα δὲ πάντα διηριθμησάμην ὁμοῦ μὲν ὑμᾶς εἰς πολυμάθειαν ἄγων, ὁμοῦ δὲ καὶ ταῖς Ἑλληνικαῖς δόξαις ποιούμενος ἐντριβεῖς. καὶ οἶδα ὡς ἐνίαις γε τούτων ἀντιπεσεῖται τὰ ἡμέτερα δόγματα. ἐγὼ γὰρ οὐχ ὥστε τούτων ἐκεῖνα ἀνταλλάξασθαι διεσπούδασα πρὸς ὑμᾶς—μαινοίμην γὰρ ἄν—, ἀλλ' ἵνα τούτοις μὲν ἦτε προσκείμενοι, ἐκείνων δὲ μόνον τὴν εἴδησιν ἔχητε. εἰ δέ πῃ καὶ συνεργοῖεν ὑμῖν πρὸς τὸν ἀληθῆ λόγον διακινδυνεύοντα, καὶ χρήσασθε.

may also be a deliberate bow to the Hellenic notion which regards theology as but a branch of the broader enterprise of philosophy. In the Christian understanding of things the tables are turned, philosophy being merely the servant of theology.[42]

Secondly, his idea of what characterizes a philosopher seems to be summed up in the single word *polymatheia*. This equation—*philosophia/polymatheia*—is obviously close to Psellos' heart and one more illustration may be offered from a totally different context, to drive the point home. In his early thirties Psellos was given the title *hypatos ton philosophon*, 'consul of the philosophers', by the Emperor Constantine Monomachos, but not everyone was pleased by this turn of events. A friend, one Machetarios, begrudged him the new honour and presumably made his resentment known either by letter or in some public way. We still have the reply that Psellos penned in response to this development, and it begins on a note of amical indignation: is this the way (to paraphrase him) a highly intelligent, dear friend reacts? Does this come from a man who has himself won every honour and rank? And you say these things against a philosopher? (καὶ ταῦτα κατὰ φιλοσόφου) Then, in order to remove any doubt about what that term means in his own case, Psellos proceeds to spell out exactly its implications and the accomplishments that underlie it: namely, a hard earned and unsurpassed knowledge in all brances of learning extending from rhetoric, through the arts and sciences, all the way to *hieratike* and *theologike*.[43] These last two are particularly suggestive, because *hieratike* is not only the art of magic, but may be a specific nod to Proclus' treatise on the subject (Περὶ τῆς ἱερατικῆς τέχνης); and *theologike*, in this form and immediately next to *hieratike*, also stands a good chance of being, in part at least, a shorthand reference to Proclus' *Elements of Theology* (Θεολογικὴ στοιχείωσις).[44] If that is an accurate assessement, it is but one more indication of the extraordinary position that Proclus, and Proclus-related material, came to hold in the hierarchy of Psellos' intellectual values.[45]

---

[42] Cf. Maltese (1994: 297).

[43] Psellos, *Letters*, no. 108 (Sathas v. 353): Οὕτως ὁ συνετώτατος, οὕτως ὁ φίλτατος ἐμοὶ Μαχητάριος; οὕτως ὁ κανὼν παντὸς λόγου καὶ τάξεως; καὶ ταῦτα κατὰ φιλοσόφου; ἀλλὰ δεῖ με καὶ πλείονα ἀριθμήσασθαι, ἵνα γνῷς οἷος εἰμὶ καὶ μὴ δυσχεραίνῃς τὴν προεδρίαν· κατὰ τοῦ πᾶν ἀνεγνωκότος μάθημα καὶ ὑπὲρ πάντας ἀνθρώπους ταλαιπωρήσαντος, φημὶ δὴ ῥητορικήν, γεωμετρίαν, μουσικήν, ῥυθμικήν, ἀριθμητικήν, σφαιρικήν, νομικήν, κἂν Ἕλληνες ἀπαρέσκωνται, ἱερατικήν, θεολογικήν, ὅσα ἔγνωσται, ὅσα οὐκ ἔγνωσται, ὅσα μηδεὶς τῶν πάντων.

[44] For broader evocative references to 'theological' and 'hieratical' matters, and specifically in Hellenic terms, see *Philosophica minora I*, op. 3, 125–47; ibid. 46, 28–51.

[45] This is a good opportunity to point to another striking instance of Psellos' drawing on Proclus even in discussions that go to the very heart of Orthodox beliefs. In a largely dogmatic treatise on the Incarnation, first published by P. Gautier (1977), Psellos, who openly declares his intention to bring in evidence and arguments based on 'alien' sources (ll. 164–79), at one point in the document, describing the power of God, uses the three-word formula ὑπερούσιος, ὑπέρζωος, ὑπέρνους (118–19); this comes directly from Proclus' *Elements of Theology*, prop. 115, and not via the Christian intermediary Ps. Dionysius the Areopagite. Elsewhere Proclus is

Thirdly, Psellos claims to want to make philosophers out of his students and on the same model as himself.[46] And he does not back down at all in his insistence on the full formula. We have seen several instances of it. In another case, commenting on a passage of Gregory of Nazianzus, he includes a description of the main tenets of the Chaldaean system, and then, as often, he justifies his procedure. He wants, he tells the students, to have them fully trained and for them not to lack any of the vital components of their education.[47]

This is robust language, but Psellos was no weakling either as an intellectual or as a defender of philosophy. To what extent he really expected to be able to produce others like himself is a question that would be difficult to answer. What cannot be doubted is the zeal of his efforts to promote philosophy in all its ramifications; and it was probably a lonely mission to judge both by what we know from other sources and by the words of the man himself who on one occasion was moved to comment 'I am a lone philosopher in an age without philosophy.'[48]

The word 'lone' here that Psellos uses of himself will serve us to draw attention to one of his special identifying characteristics, namely his uniqueness; he was indeed a *rara avis* and Byzantium did not see the likes of him either before or after his time. That feature of the man is not always sufficiently taken into account when questions of authorship and authenticity of texts arise, as they quite often do in his case. As an example we may take a recent work on Byzantine philosophy of the period that touches directly on the issue. In 1992 I. N. Pontikos published an edition and study of a collection of short philosophical treatises from the well-known Oxford manuscript, *Barocci* 131, which was copied in the thirteenth century.[49] Though transmitted anonymously, the miscellany of treatises preserved in the Barocci codex has in the past been attributed by various scholars to Psellos. Pontikos was the first to edit critically the complete set of texts and his work is of a high quality. Particularly valuable is the third chapter of his lengthy introduction in which he expertly explores in detail the philosophical background of the material. What must be judged somewhat disappointing, however, is his reluctance to accept the possibility that Psellos was directly involved in the

accorded special recognition as theologian or philosopher: *Theologica I*, op. 22, 38–9 (for a student audience) οἱ τοίνυν θεολογικώτατοι τῶν Ἑλλήνων, ὧν δὴ Πρόκλος κατὰ τὴν ἐμὴν ψῆφον τὸ κεφάλαιον...; and *Historia Syntomos*, ed. W. J. Aerts (Berlin and New York, 1990), 52. 37 Πρόκλος ὁ μέγας... φιλόσοφος, ὃν ἐγὼ μετά γε Πλάτωνα τίθημι.

[46] Cf. *Theologica I*, op. 20, 2–3: οὐκ ἀποκρύψομαι πρὸς ὑμᾶς, ὦ φίλτατοι παῖδες, οὓς διὰ τῆς φιλοσοφίας ὠδίνησα... Ibid. op. 89, 85–6: χρή γε ὑμᾶς, φιλοσόφους ὄντας... Ibid., op. 91, 3: ὦ φιλοσοφώτατοι παῖδες... Ibid., op. 76, 11–12: ἐπεὶ δὲ Ἀριστοτελικοὶ πάντες ὑμεῖς τὴν παιδείαν...

[47] *Theologica I*, op. 51, 103–4: βούλομαι γὰρ τελέους ὑμᾶς ἐκ τελέων εἶναι καὶ μὴ τοῖς καιριωτάτοις ἐλλείποντας μέρεσιν.

[48] *Oratoria minora*, ed. A. R. Littlewood (Leipzig, 1985), op. 6, 52–3: φιλοσοφῶ μόνος ἐν ἀφιλοσόφοις καιροῖς.

[49] *Anonymi Miscellanea Philosophica* (Athens and Brussels, 1992).

compilation. The most Pontikos is willing to concede is that it belongs to the philosophical tradition of Psellos, but that its anonymous author cannot be identified and that author—in the estimation of Pontikos—may well have been one of the scholars who witnessed the revival of Aristotelianism in the twelfth century.[50]

The fact is, however, that the unmistakable fingerprints of Psellos are detectable all over the philosophical writings in the Barocci collection; in other words, they show most of the characteristics of Psellan authorship, large and small. In the first instance, one may point to the range of topics explored—such as the nature of the soul, meteorology, the heresy of Euno-mius—and to the tell-tale cast of philosophers and other authors who are cited or brought into the discussion. Then there is the concern evinced for reconciling Greek and Christian ideas; in addition we are faced with the fact that, like many of Psellos' uncontested opuscula, the great majority of pieces in the Barocci collection have the literary form of replies (often drafted as a letter) to a question or problem raised by an unidentified correspondent. Add to that little stylistic touches and choice of vocabulary, and one comes away with the overwhelming impression that these documents, whatever small difficulties may seem to stand in the way, cannot be anything other than the writings or, in some instances probably, the working notes of Psellos.

A further stumbling block to Pontikos is the amount of attention paid to Aristotle, which leads him to assume that some of the texts were added in the twelfth century. 'The evidence for this assumption', he comments, 'rests on the use made of Aristotle's work and the commentaries on it. We know that Psellos had evidenced a strong preference for Plato as against Aristotle. Therefore, the Aristotelian material must derive from elsewhere.'[51] This, one would have to say in a word, is not a convincing argument; a glance at the sources listed, for example, in Gautier's edition of the *Theologica* would show just how much of the Aristotelian corpus comes into play in Psellos' presentations, and other evidence of the same kind is abundantly available in the two volumes of *Philosophica minora*.

These comments are not meant to cast doubts on the overall quality of Pontikos' work, which is in other respects well executed and very valuable. They are voiced rather in the conviction that Psellos was *sui generis* and against an assumption that there was some unknown figure out there, so to say, in the eleventh or early twelfth century who could in all essentials be another Psellos.

Some final observations should be made. The ninth and tenth centuries in Byzantium were not bad ones by any means for Greek culture, even for the Hellenic heritage in philosophy. Major figures like Photios and Arethas are honourable representatives of a Christian humanism that promoted the welfare of Greek books and, within certain limits, helped to sustain the role of

---

[50] Ibid., p. xl.   [51] Ibid., p. xxxix.

Aristotle and, to a lesser extent, Plato in the sphere of higher education. But no one will deny that a huge sea change came with Psellos in the eleventh century. Here was, for the first time in ages, a philosopher who took the trouble to give the subject a more substantial role in intellectual life and who actively re-established contact with the exegetical tradition of the late antique and early Byzantine centuries.

In one of the autobiographical sections of his *Chronographia* he pays a clear tribute to the Greek commentators and acknowledges their help as guides to the works of Plato and Aristotle.[52] And it is not a gratuitous mention by Psellos nor an empty compliment to himself. His minor philosophical treatises show an intimate familiarity with several commentators, including Philoponus and Olympiodorus, from whose works he draws extensively. But he does more than restore the link with that tradition; he picks up from where the Alexandrians left off in the seventh century. We have from his pen two substantial pieces of exegesis on Aristotle: one is a full-blown commentary on the *Physics*, still awaiting publication in the original Greek;[53] the other is a so-called paraphrase of the logical treatise *De interpretatione*, which survives in about thirty manuscripts, was first printed by Aldus Manutius in Italy, and was even the subject of a special poem by the twelfth century author John Tzetzes.[54] The ultimate recognition, perhaps, is to be found in a Jerusalem manuscript of the thirteenth century where Psellos is cited on the list of Aristotle's works and their commentators used in higher education; this is canonization—to be named in the same company with the likes of Porphyry and Ammonius.[55]

But going even beyond the parameters represented by the Alexandrian and Athenian school traditions, Psellos became imaginatively engaged with the full range of Greek thinkers, from the Presocratics to the later Neoplatonists. Among his cultural heroes were two that occupied very special places. One was Gregory of Nazianzus who represented for him the ideal model of Christian *rhetor* and *philosophos*. That was an easy choice. The other was Proclus, a different kettle of fish altogether. Proclus was a suspect resident alien in a Greek Christian world whom Psellos, in the interest of keeping him as a friend, was obliged to beat over the head from time to time with the big stick of orthodoxy. In order to retain Proclus within the frame of his unique brand of humanism, Psellos had to tread a fine line and he managed to do this with agility. He had the courage on occasion to go to bat for Proclus, even to praise him to the sky, but at other times he was clever enough to brand some

---

[52] *Chron.* 6. 37 = *Michele Psello: Imperatori di Bisanzio*, ed. S. Impellizzeri *et al.*, i (Milan, 1984), 284: ὡς δέ τισι τῶν ἐξηγησαμένων τὴν ἐπιστήμην ἐνέτυχον, τὴν ὁδὸν παρ' αὐτῶν ἐδιδασκόμην τῆς γνώσεως, καί με ἄλλος εἰς ἄλλον παρέπεμπον, ὁ χείρων πρὸς τὸν κρείττονα, κἀκεῖνος αὖθις εἰς ἕτερον, καὶ οὗτος εἰς Ἀριστοτέλην καὶ Πλάτωνα.

[53] The first edn. is being prepared by Linos Benakis.

[54] See Duffy (1998: 441–5).

[55] See *Commentaria in Aristotelem Graeca*, iii/1, ed. P. Wendland (Berlin, 1901), pp. xv–xix (here p. xviii). The manuscript in question is Jerusalem Taph. 106.

of his ideas as nonsense. His larger intention was to revive a moribund part of the Hellenic heritage; it was a solo mission and one that he puts on record, this time as a fait accompli, in the *Chronographia* where he tells his contemporaries: 'You who read my history today will bear witness to the truth of my words. Philosophy, by the time I came upon it, had already expired . . . ; but I brought it back to life, all by myself.'[56] Psellos was no stranger to exaggeration, particularly on the subject of his own role in Byzantine life and letters. Be that as it may, on the issue of philosophy the evidence suggests that what he is telling us is nothing but the truth.[57]

BIBLIOGRAPHY

A. TEXTS

Anonymi Miscellanea Philosophica, ed. I. N. Pontikos (Athens and Brussels, 1992).
Arethas, *Scholia on Porphyry's Isagoge and Aristotle's Categories*, ed. M. Share (Athens and Brussels, 1994).
Constantine Porphyrogennetos, *De virtutibus et vitiis*, ed. Th. Büttner-Wobst, i (Berlin, 1906).
David, *Prolegomena*, ed. A. Busse (CAG 18/2; Berlin, 1904).
George the Monk, *Chronicon*, ed. C. de Boor, i (Leipzig, 1904).
John Climacus, *Scala paradisi*, ed. S. Trevisan, 2 vols. (Turin, 1941).
John of Damascus, *Die Schriften des Johannes von Damaskos*, ed. B. Kotter, i (Berlin, 1969).
Michael Psellos, *Chronographie*, ed. É. Renauld, i (Paris, 1926).
—— *Imperatori di Bizanzio*, ed. S. Impellizzeri *et al.*, i (Milan, 1984).
—— *De omnifaria doctrina*, ed. L. G. Westerink (Nijmegen, 1948).
—— *Historia Syntomos*, ed. W. J. Aerts (Berlin and New York, 1990).
—— *Miscellanea*, ed. K. N. Sathas, in Μεσαιωνικὴ Βιβλιοθήκη, v (Paris, 1876).
—— *Oratoria minora*, ed. A. R. Littlewood (Leipzig, 1985).
—— *Philosophica minora I*, ed. J. M. Duffy (Stuttgart and Leipzig, 1992).
—— *Philosophica minora II*, ed. D. J. O'Meara (Leipzig, 1989).
—— *Theologica I*, ed. P. Gautier (Leipzig, 1989).
Neilos of Ankyra, *Logos Asketikos*, ed. J.-P. Migne (*PG* 79; Paris, 1860).
Niketas David, *Vita Ignatii*, ed. J.-P. Migne (*PG* 105; Paris, n.d. (*c.*1860)).
Photios, *Epistulae et Amphilochia*, ed. L. G. Westerink, v (Leipzig, 1986).

---

[56] Chron. 6. 37 = ed. Impellizzeri *et al.*, i. 284: καί μοι συμμαρτυρήσατε οἱ τήμερον τὸν λόγον ἀναγινώσκοντες, ὅτι ἐκπνεύσασαν τὴν σοφίαν καταλαβών . . ., αὐτὸς ἀνεζωπύρησα οἴκοθεν.

[57] The question of whether Psellos was in any sense an independent thinker has been squarely faced in a recent study by D. O'Meara (1998: 431–9). The author, basing himself on the texts in *Philosophica minora II*, shows that in his solutions to certain problems Psellos, while no innovator, does display a scientific and philosophical spirit that is in keeping with the best Greek traditions. The article also makes a significant contribution to the continuing debate about Psellos' real stance on the relationship between pagan philosophy and the Christian religion.

Proclus, *Elements of Theology*, ed. E. R. Dodds, 2nd edn. (Oxford, 1963).

Suidae Lexicon, ed. A. Adler, 5 vols. (Leipzig, 1928–38).

B. SECONDARY LITERATURE

Agapitos, P. A. (1998), 'Teachers, Pupils and Imperial Power in Eleventh-Century Byzantium', in Y. L. Too and N. Livingstone (eds.), *Pedagogy and Power: Rhetorics of Classical Learning* (Cambridge), 170–91.

Duffy, J. M. (1998), 'Tzetzes on Psellos', in C. F. Collatz, J. Dummer, J. Kollesch, and M.-L. Werlitz (eds.), *Dissertatiunculae criticae: Festschrift für Günther Christian Hansen* (Würzburg), 441–5.

Gautier, P. (1977), 'Lettre au sultan Malik-shah rédigée par Michel Psellos', *Revue des Études Byzantines*, 35: 73–97.

Gouillard, J. (1967), 'Le Synodikon de l'Orthodoxie: Édition et commentaire', *Travaux et Mémoires*, 2: 1–316.

Kaldellis, A. (1999), *The Argument of Psellos' Chronographia* (Leiden).

Lemerle, P. (1971), *Le Premier Humanisme byzantin* (Paris).

Littlewood, A. R. (1990), 'Michael Psellos and the Witch of Endor', *Jahrbuch der Österreichischen Byzantinistik*, 40: 225–31.

Magdalino, P. (1993), *The Empire of Manuel I Komnenos* (Cambridge).

Maltese, E. V. (1994), 'Michele Psello commentatore di Gregorio di Nazianzo: Note per una lettura dei Theologica', in *SYNDESMOS: Studi in onore di Rosario Anastasi*, ii (Catania), 289–309.

Mango, C. (1980), *Byzantium: The Empire of New Rome* (New York).

O'Meara, D. J. (1998), 'Aspects du travail philosophique de Michel Psellus', in C. F. Collatz *et al.* (eds.), *Dissertatiunculae criticae: Festschrift für Günther Christian Hansen* (Würzburg), 431–9.

Oxford Dictionary of Byzantium (1991), ed. A. P. Kazhdan, A.-M. Talbot, A. Cutler, T. E. Gregory, and N. P. Ševčenko (New York and Oxford).

Podskalsky, G. (1977), *Theologie und Philosophie in Byzanz* (Munich).

Ševčenko, I. (1956), 'The Definition of Philosophy in the Life of Saint Constantine', in M. Halle, H. G. Lunt, H. McLean, and C. H. van Schooneveld (eds.), *For Roman Jakobson* (The Hague), 449–57.

Van den Ven, P. (1902), 'La Vie grecque de S. Jean le Psichaïte', *Le Muséon*, NS 3: 97–125.

7

Psellos' Paraphrasis on Aristotle's *De interpretatione*

KATERINA IERODIAKONOU

There recently has been a lot of interest in Greek commentaries on Aristotle's works. It has become clear that they not only reveal unsuspected subtleties of difficult Aristotelian passages and provide information concerning otherwise unknown doctrines, they also put forward original philosophical views. However, the period usually studied covers only the commentaries from Aspasius and Alexander of Aphrodisias in the second century to Simplicius in the sixth or Stephanus in the seventh century. What I think has not yet been sufficiently acknowledged is that in the East, even after the sixth century, the tradition of commenting on Aristotle's treatises continues uninterrupted until the fifteenth century or even beyond the fall of Constantinople in 1453. In the case of Aristotle's logical works, in particular, the significant number of manuscripts with Byzantine scholia on the *Organon* confirms that Aristotelian logic constitutes a focus of great attention throughout the Byzantine era. Following the tradition of the ancient commentators, but especially that of the Christian commentators of the Alexandrian school, Byzantine scholars such as Photios, Arethas, Michael Psellos, John Italos, Michael of Ephesus, Leo Magentinos, Nikephoros Blemmydes, George Pachymeres, John Pediasimos, Isaak Argyros, Joseph Philagrios, John Chortasmenos, and others produce logical commentaries, paraphrases, compendia, and short treatises on selected logical topics. But in most cases these logical works have not been edited, let alone been closely studied, and so their importance for the development of logical theory in Byzantium has not yet been adequately assessed.

The aim of this chapter is to concentrate on just one of these Byzantine scholiasts, namely Michael Psellos, and even in this case to discuss only one of his many writings on Aristotle's logic, namely his paraphrasis on Aristotle's *De interpretatione*. In analysing Psellos' paraphrasis, I shall attempt to show that his contribution to logic, which comes fairly early in this long Byzantine tradition, is of particular interest for an adequate understanding both of the further developments in Byzantine logic and of the philosophical problems in the Aristotelian work.

The Author

I will begin with a few words about Psellos' interest in, and pursuit of, logical studies. The obvious place to start is his education. Psellos himself says (*Chron.* 3. 3; 6. 37) that his philosophical education was inadequate, and that the scholars of the time did not study in depth the achievements of the ancient philosophers, in particular of Plato and Aristotle. It has been argued, however, that such a statement about the decline and subsequent revival of learning must be treated as nothing but a commonplace.[1] Psellos must have been taught at least basic logic, for it seems that from quite early on a knowledge of the elements of logic in Byzantium was considered as essential for the exposition of Christian dogma and the refutation of heresy.[2] More specifically, Psellos must have learnt Aristotle's logic through the ancient commentators and the Christian tradition; that is to say, through the commentaries of Philoponus, and the works of John of Damascus, Photios, and Arethas. After all, Psellos belonged to the same circle of students as men like John Xiphilinos, who was known for his interest in Aristotle and his mastery of logic, as is attested by Psellos' own letters to him (Sathas v. 446–7) and his funeral oration on him (Sathas iv. 428–9).

The influence of such an education in logic becomes clear when we consider Psellos' philosophical position. For Psellos himself stressed that the mind is capable of grasping truth through reason as well as through revelation, and he tried to bring together Christianity and the ancient philosophical tradition, claiming that the logical pursuit of truth cannot bring one into conflict with Christian doctrine (Sathas v. 447). On the contrary, he pointed out that reasoning is an important part of human nature (*Phil. min. I*, op. 3, 49: ἀνθρωπικώτερον), though it has its limitations due to the inscrutability of God's essence and our limited intellectual power (Sathas v. 326, 414). This is the reason why Psellos cautiously avoided any suggestion that mere logic might resolve deep theological issues, although he often advocated the use of logic (Sathas iv. 462; v. 55). Thus, even if Psellos understandably has a reputation as someone who was primarily interested in advancing the study of Plato, influenced by Plotinus, Porphyry, Iamblichus, Proclus, and Olympiodorus, it is also reasonable to consider him as an Aristotelian scholar; for he never neglected the study of Aristotle, and in particular of Aristotle's logical writings.

Moreover, it seems that Psellos himself taught Aristotle's logic as a necessary preparation for dealing with more philosophical issues, in particular,

---

[1] Browning (1975: 6).   [2] Roueché (1974: 64).

Plato's metaphysics (Sathas v. 475). Quite generally, according to the educational system of Psellos' time, a course of the advanced level included philosophy and the *quadrivium*, and it standardly started with a study of Porphyry's *Isagoge*, Aristotle's *Categories*, the *De interpretatione*, and the *Prior Analytics* 1. 1–7.[3] That means, of course, that there must have been a need for easily digestible commentaries on these logical works; and especially for someone like Psellos who often stressed how important logic is for those who study philosophy (Sathas iv. 428–9; v. 445), it must have seemed highly reasonable to write for his students his own scholia on the *Organon*. In fact, the numerous logical writings which are attributed to him by our sources prove the degree to which Psellos was engaged in promoting a knowledge of Aristotle's logic.

First, we learn directly from him, in the proemium of his unedited commentary on the *Physics*, that he has written a paraphrasis on the *Organon* for teaching purposes.[4] The same fact can also be inferred from a letter to Xiphilinos (*Phil. min. I*, op. 5), in which Psellos stresses the difficulties in compiling for his students a clear synopsis of Aristotle's *Organon*, which seems to be what Xiphilinos has asked him to do.[5] Psellos' synopsis, however, still waits to be recovered from the surviving manuscripts.[6] Second, Psellos seems to be the author of further logical works, this time either on specific books of Aristotle's *Organon* or on select logical topics.[7] For example, the seventeenth-century list of Psellos' works by Leo Allatius, which also includes Psellos' logical works (*PG* 122. 521–2), mentions two commentaries on the *Categories*;[8] but, again, these works have not yet been identified among the texts which have come down to us. Moreover, the same list includes Psellos' works on the *Prior Analytics*, which unfortunately are also unknown; on the

---

[3] For instance, cf. Tatakis (1949: 164).

[4] Zervos (1920: 98 n. 3).

[5] Psellos' letter has the following informative title: Εἰς τὸν δρουγγάριον τῆς βίγλης κῦριν Κωνσταντῖνον τὸν Ξιφιλῖνον, ἀξιώσαντα αὐτὸν μεταβαλεῖν τὸ τοῦ Ἀριστοτέλους λογικὸν ῞Οργανον ἀπὸ τοῦ ἀσαφοῦς ἐπὶ τὸ σαφές.

[6] There is no doubt that Psellos' synopsis of the *Organon* is not the treatise Σύνοψις εἰς τὴν Ἀριστοτέλους Λογικήν (cf. Benakis 1958–9). But could we identify Psellos' synopsis with the treatise Διδασκαλία σύντομος καὶ σαφεστάτη περὶ τῶν δέκα κατηγοριῶν καὶ τῶν προτάσεων καὶ τῶν συλλογισμῶν περὶ ὧν τις προδιδαχθεὶς εἰς πᾶσαν μὲν καὶ ἄλλην ἐπιστήμην καὶ τέχνην, ἐξαιρέτως δὲ εἰς τὴν ῥητορείαν, εὐκόλως ἐμπορεύσεται (*Phil. min. I*, op. 52), which is ascribed to Psellos in many manuscripts? Duffy (1992 edn.: p. xxxvi) considers it as a spurious work, because its style is not characteristic of Psellos. I agree with Duffy's view, and I intend to support it, in what follows, with specific arguments arising from the second part of this work which presents a summary of Aristotle's *De interpretatione*.

[7] Small treatises by Psellos discussing select topics of Aristotle's *Organon* are, for instance, the Περὶ τῆς μίξεως τῶν προτάσεων καὶ περὶ εὐπορίας προτάσεων σύντομος ἔφοδος (*Phil. min. I*, op. 10), and the Σύντομος παράδοσις τῶν δεκατριῶν παραλογισμῶν (*Phil. min. I*, op. 14).

[8] The titles of the two commentaries on Aristotle's *Categories*, which are attributed to Psellos by Allatius, are the following: (i) Ἐξήγησις εἰς τὰς Κατηγορίας τοῦ Ἀριστοτέλους (incipit: Τῶν πραγμάτων, τὰ μὲν κοινωνεῖ), and (ii) Εἰς τὴν Πορφυρίου Εἰσαγωγὴν καί τινα τῶν Ἀριστοτέλους Κατηγοριῶν (incipit: Πολλοὶ μὲν πολλαχῶς τῶν ἀρχαίων).

other hand, we do find in several manuscripts an unpublished commentary and an unpublished paraphrasis on the *Prior Analytics*, and there is good evidence to suggest that they both were written by Psellos.[9]

Focusing now on Psellos' writings on the *De interpretatione*, they must have been considered from early on as standard works of reference; in a fourteenth-century catalogue of the commentators on Aristotle's works, probably written by John Pediasimos,[10] Psellos together with Ammonius and Magentinos are said to be the only commentators on the *De interpretatione* (Stephanus, *in De interp.* v.).[11] In fact, it seems plausible to assume that Psellos must have produced either more than one commentary on this Aristotelian logical treatise, or different versions of the same commentary, a practice which is not at all unusual already in late antiquity and throughout the Byzantine era. It is, therefore, not surprising that in Allatius' list, again, we find four different works, all commenting on Aristotle's *De interpretatione*.[12] It should be pointed out, though, that the incipits of these works do not coincide with any of the incipits of Psellos' surviving writings, and so we are once more in the situation of not having, so far, discovered or identified any of these works.

But if none of these works which Allatius in his extensive catalogue attributes to Psellos coincides with the text of our paraphrasis, is there enough evidence to show that Psellos is really its author? It is, indeed, the case that no doubt about Psellos' authorship is expressed in the manuscript tradition, in the editions, in the translations, and in the relevant secondary literature. On the contrary, all scribes, editors, translators, and modern scholars unanimously attribute it to the famous Byzantine scholar of the eleventh century. Also, among the works which certainly belong to Psellos,[13] there is a scholium on Aristotle's *De interpretatione* which closely resembles the paraphrasis both in content and in style. However, since this scholium is very short and not to be found verbatim in the paraphrasis, little can be inferred from it. There is, though, indirect evidence of Psellos' authorship in the text of the paraphrasis itself; for there is a passage in the paraphrasis in which the author, after referring by name to Ammonius and Philoponus, mentions the view of a philosopher who was appointed by the most literate

---

[9] Ierodiakonou (forthcoming).

[10] Benakis 1987: 362.

[11] It is interesting to note that Psellos' comments on the *De interpretatione* are praised in a short poem by the 12th-cent. author John Tzetzes for their clarity. Indeed, Tzetzes compares Psellos to a pearl diver who brings to the surface the precious thought which is hidden, like a pearl in its shell, by the obscurity of Aristotle's text. See Duffy (1998: 441–5).

[12] The four works on the *De interpretatione*, which Allatius attributes to Psellos, are: (i) Ἐξήγησις εἰς τὸ Περὶ ἑρμηνείας Ἀριστοτέλους (incipit: Ὁ σκοπὸς τοῦ Περὶ ἑρμηνείας ἐστὶ διαλαβεῖν περὶ προτάσεων), (ii) Ἐξήγησις εἰς τὸ Περὶ ἑρμηνείας Ἀριστοτέλους (incipit: Θέσθαι νῦν ἀντὶ τοῦ ὁρίσασθαι), (iii) Σύνοψις καὶ μετάφρασις σαφεστάτη τῆς διδασκαλίας τοῦ Περὶ ἑρμηνείας (incipit: Διαλαμβάνει περὶ προτάσεων), and (iv) Εἰς τὸ Περὶ ἑρμηνείας ἔκδοσις ἐπίτομος (incipit: Τὰ εἴδη τοῦ λόγου πέντε τόν ἀριθμόν).

[13] *Phil. min. I*, op. 15: Τοῦ Ψελλοῦ περὶ προτάσεων ὀφειλουσῶν ἀλλήλαις συναληθεύειν.

king as the ὕπατος τῶν φιλοσόφων,[14] and we do know that Psellos was appointed by Constantine Monomachos (1042–55) as the first ὕπατος τῶν φιλοσόφων.[15] But if the philosopher referred to here is Psellos, and Psellos himself is the author of the paraphrasis, why would he present his own views in this circuitous way? It seems that Psellos avoids here referring to himself, because he is consistent in concealing deliberately, throughout the paraphrasis, his identity as its author; and this for reasons which will be discussed shortly.

Finally, before I turn to the analysis of the text, a brief remark concerning its date: assuming that Psellos wrote this work on Aristotle's *De interpretatione*, and that he was appointed as the first ὕπατος τῶν φιλοσόφων in the year 1045, we here have a *terminus post quem* for the date of the paraphrasis.[16]

The Text

Psellos' paraphrasis was first edited by Aldus Manutius in Venice in 1503 and published again in 1520, together with Ammonius' and Leo Magentinos' commentaries on the *De interpretatione*. The same text was also translated into Latin and edited twice, first by Severinus Boetius in Venice in 1541, and then by Conrad Gresner in Basel in 1542. As to the manuscript tradition of the paraphrasis, Wartelle in his catalogue lists thirty-six manuscripts from various libraries which preserve, according to him, Psellos' comments on the *De interpretatione* under different headings, such as paraphrasis, metaphrasis, expositio, scholia, commentaria. However, this catalogue is not reliable, and it also has proved in many cases to be incomplete. A closer look at the catalogues of the particular libraries, as well as the study of some of the manuscripts themselves, show that only twenty-six of these manuscripts, dating from the twelfth to the sixteenth century, preserve the paraphrasis published in the Aldine edition;[17] most of the other manuscripts preserve the

---

[14] *in De interp.* 28. 42: ὅν καὶ φιλοσόφων ὕπατον βασιλέων τις θήσει φιλολογώτατος.

[15] For instance, see Fuchs (1926: 29).

[16] As has already been pointed out, although the second part of the Διδασκαλία σύντομος also presents a summary of Aristotle's *De interpretatione*, there are good reasons to believe that its author is not the same as the author of the paraphrasis. First, the fact that there are no comments in Διδασκαλία σύντομος on ch. 14 of Aristotle's *De interpretatione* (23ᵃ27–24ᵇ9) suggests that the author considers it as not genuine, whereas the author of the paraphrasis explicitly attributes this chapter to Aristotle. Second, in Διδασκαλία σύντομος there is none of the particular characteristics which distinguish the paraphrasis from the other commentaries on the *De interpretatione*, characteristics which are discussed in the following sections of this paper. Third, one notices substantial differences between the two works in the way the material is presented, in the form of the examples used, and in some interpretations, like for instance in the explanation of the term ἐκ μεταθέσεως. Therefore, if Psellos is indeed the author of the paraphrasis, Διδασκαλία σύντομος probably is not his work.

[17] The manuscripts which preserve Psellos' paraphrasis are: Ambrosianus 194 (= C 97 sup.), saec. XV; 255 (= D 82 sup.), saec. XIII; Baroccianus gr. 117, saec. XVI; Breslau, Magdalenaeus

second part of the spurious Διδασκαλία σύντομος, which also includes a summary of Aristotle's *De interpretatione*.

Now let me briefly describe the text as printed in the Aldine, by presenting its division into an introduction and five parts, which Psellos calls 'τμήματα'. The introduction covers chapter 1 of the standard division of Aristotle's text (*De interp.* 16ᵃ1–18); the first part covers chapters 2–6 (*De interp.* 16ᵃ19–17ᵃ37);[18] the second part covers chapters 7–9 and part of 10 (*De interp.* 17ᵃ38–19ᵇ19); the third part covers the rest of 10 and chapter 11 (*De interp.* 19ᵇ19–21ᵃ34); the fourth part covers chapters 12 and 13 (*De interp.* 21ᵃ35–23ᵃ26); and finally, the fifth part covers chapter 14 (*De interp.* 23ᵃ27–24ᵇ9).[19] Although it is not at all clear how old this division underlying Psellos' paraphrasis actually is, there is no doubt that it is exactly the same as the division found in Ammonius' commentary, with the difference that Ammonius refers to the five parts as 'κεφάλαια'; the other surviving commentaries, that is to say Stephanus' commentary and the anonymous' commentary published by Tarán, also divide their text into five 'τμήματα'. However, for two reasons nothing conclusive can be said about the precise origin of Psellos' division; first, he himself is not strict in always using the same terms, since he also uses 'κεφάλαιον' (*in De interp.* 35. 29) and 'σύνταγμα' (*in De interp.* 27. 5–6) instead of 'τμῆμα'; and second, the divisions of the paraphrasis which are to be found in the manuscript tradition, but also in its Latin translations, slightly differ from the division in the Aldine edition.[20]

Unfortunately, the Aldine edition suffers from a great number of misreadings, false readings, displacements and unnecessary additions:

1. There are misreadings of single words which greatly change the meaning; for instance, there are at least four cases (*in De interp.* 4. 27; 6. 9; 26–7; 8. 3) in which the Aldine edition has ἀπόφασις instead of ἀπόφανσις.

2. There are false readings of sentences which make Psellos' point unintelligible. For instance, the sentence 'οὐ μὴν εἴ τις οὐ δίκαιος ἄνθρωπος,

---

1442, saec. XIV; Hierosolyminatus S. Sepulchri 150, saec. XIV; 107, saec. XIII (?); Laurentianus gr. 10.26, saec. XII; 71.19, saec. XIV; 71.32, saec. XIV; 71.35, saec. XIII; 85.1, saec. XIV; Acquisti 175, saec. XIII; Marcianus gr. Z 599, saec XIV–XV; Mosquensis Bibl. Synod. 455, saec. XV–XVI; Mutinensis 189 (= F 11), saec. XIV; Neapolitanus 334 (= E 12), saec. XV (?); Oxford, Magdalen College 15, saec. XV; Parisinus gr. 1918, saec. XIV; 1919, saec. XV; 1973, saec. XIV; 2136, saec. XVI; Vaticanus gr. 1693, saec. XIV; 1035, (?); Vindobolensis Phil. gr. 139, saec. XIV; 300, saec. XIV; Yale, Philipps 6445, saec. XIII (?).

[18] The first part of Psellos' paraphrasis is subdivided into four subparts under the headings: περὶ ὀνόματος, περὶ ῥήματος, περὶ λόγου, περὶ καταφάσεως καὶ ἀποφάνσεως.

[19] It should be noted that Psellos does not regard ch. 14 as spurious; rather he thinks that it was written by Aristotle as an exercise designed to guide the student to the correct doctrine (*in De interp.* 35. 28–9: τοῦτο γοῦν μοι μόνον τῶν ὅλων τοῦ Περὶ ἑρμηνείας τμημάτων γυμνασίου λόγον ἐπέχον ἐκδίδοται). This view is similar, but not identical, to Ammonius' claim that ch. 14 was composed either by Aristotle himself, writing an exercise for those who study this logical work, or by someone later than Aristotle (*in De interp.* 251. 25–252. 10).

[20] e.g., in the manuscript Baroccianus gr. 117 the fifth part is further subdivided into six subparts, which are called 'ἐπιχειρήματα', and in the Latin translations the second and fourth parts are further subdivided.

ἤδη καὶ ἄνθρωπος οὐ δίκαιός ἐστιν' (*in De interp*. 18. 25), should read 'οὐ μήν εἴ τις δίκαιος ἄνθρωπος οὐκ ἔστιν, ἤδη καὶ ἄνθρωπος οὐ δίκαιός ἐστιν'.[21]

3. There are parts of the text that have been placed in the wrong order. For instance, the eight lines which present the sixteen sentences resulting from the permutations of the four quantifiers (*in De interp*. 11. 16–24) should appear earlier in the text (*in De interp*. 11. 1), since they seem to have been misplaced due to a rearrangement of pages in the manuscript tradition.[22]

4. There are whole parts of the Aldine text which certainly do not belong to Psellos' work. For instance, towards the end of the paraphrasis,[23] there is a sentence which is a redundant repetition of a bit of text some lines above, and does not read well after the preceding sentence which explicitly marks the end of this part of the paraphrasis; most probably, this sentence must have been a scholium in the margin of a manuscript, and it was later added to the main text of the paraphrasis by a not particularly careful editor or scribe. But what immediately follows this sentence in the Aldine (*in De interp*. 27. 7–28. 7) is even more disturbing; for it is a long passage from Ammonius' commentary (*in De interp*. 210. 17–212. 23), with an introducing sentence in the place of a lemma,[24] as if Psellos himself cites Ammonius in his paraphrasis. However, a closer look at the manuscripts proves that it is only an unfortunate addition by an editor or copyist.[25] Moreover, there is a long passage in the Aldine (*in De interp*. 19. 23–20. 4), presenting an interpretation of Aristotle which is actually in conflict with the interpretation offered earlier in the text; this passage, in fact, proves to be a part of Magentinos' commentary (*in De interp*. 22. 8–42). Hence, it should also be regarded as an unfortunate addition by an editor, for there are no traces of this passage in the extant manuscripts. In general, such additions to Psellos' original paraphrasis make clear that the editor must have had in front of him a manuscript with Aristotle's *De interpretatione* in the centre, and in the margins the commentaries of Psellos, Ammonius, and Magentinos, as well as brief scholia by anonymous scholiasts. After all, it is not by chance that Psellos' work on Aristotle's *De interpretatione* was edited by Aldus Manutius together with Ammonius' and Magentinos' commentaries on the same logical work.

---

[21] This is actually a reading which we find in the MS tradition; see e.g. Baroccianus gr. 117, fo. 80ᵛ.

[22] See e.g. Baroccianus gr. 117, fo. 67.

[23] *in De interp*. 26. 51–27. 7: δεῖ δὲ ὑμᾶς εἰδέναι ὡς ὁ Πλάτων πολλὰς τάξεις ἐν τῷ Σοφιστῇ τοῦ μὴ ὄντος παραδέδωκε, καὶ ἐν μὲν σημαινόμενον τοῦ μὴ ὄντος τὸ ὑπὲρ τὰ ὄντα . . . καὶ τέλος ὁμοῦ τε ἐκείνῳ καὶ ἡμῖν τὸ τρίτον τοῦ Περὶ ἑρμηνείας εἴληφε σύνταγμα. εἰσὶ δὲ καὶ ἄλλα ἕτερα σημαινόμενα δύο τοῦ μὴ ὄντος· μὴ ὂν γὰρ λέγεται καὶ ἅπαν τὸ αἰσθητὸν καὶ ἡ στέρησις.

[24] *in De interp*. 27. 7–8: Καὶ ἄλλως ἀπὸ φωνῆς Ἀμμωνίου φιλοσόφου ἀπὸ τοῦ ἀληθὲς δέ ἐστιν εἰπεῖν κατὰ τοῦ τινὸς καὶ ἁπλῶς.

[25] See e.g. Baroccianus gr. 117; Laurentianus 10. 26.

A Commentary or a Paraphrasis?

Leaving the issue of the authorship of the paraphrasis and the various deficiencies of the Aldine edition, let us next focus on Psellos' text itself, and let us here start from its title which in most manucripts is the following:[26] Μιχαήλου Ψελλοῦ παράφρασις εἰς τὸ Περὶ ἑρμηνείας. However, Psellos himself nowhere calls this work a παράφρασις, but he uses instead the terms 'ὑπόμνημα' (*in De interp.* 8. 55; 10. 27; 15. 53; cf. 39. 31: 'ὑπομνηματισμός'), 'σύγγραμμα' (*in De interp.* 28. 36), and 'σύνταγμα' (*in De interp.* 35. 31–2), which are also used to refer to Aristotle's logical treatise. But, then, why is this work called a 'παράφρασις'? Is there a difference between a paraphrasis and a commentary?

At the beginning of his paraphrasis on the *Posterior Analytics*, the fourth-century commentator Themistius (*in An. post.* 1. 2–16) compares his scholia on Aristotle to those written by previous commentators, and states that he decided to produce works which are much shorter, so that the students can learn and remember them more easily. He also stresses that, in this way, he has really innovated as to the form of scholia on Aristotle's logical treatises.[27] Approximately ten centuries later, the commentator Sophonias (*in De an.* 1. 4–3. 9) undertakes to distinguish the way Alexander of Aphrodisias, Ammonius, Simplicius, and Philoponus compiled their commentaries from that of the innovative writings of Themistius, who was then followed, according to Sophonias, among others by Psellos in his logical works.[28] Sophonias actually enumerates the main differences between the two groups of writings:

1. The size of the scholia in the first group is considerably larger than that of those in the second group.

2. The commentators of the first group interpret the Aristotelian text section by section, whereas the commentators of the second group tend to present and discuss it in a continuous flow, as if they were Aristotle himself.

3. The commentators of the first group aim at providing a scholarly understanding of Aristotle's works, while the members of the second group are interested in the use of their writings for more elementary teaching purposes; hence, they often add many useful rules and examples to ease the study of Aristotle's thought.

It is exactly because of these differences that the commentators of the second group should be considered, according to Sophonias, as writing paraphrases rather than commentaries.[29]

But could we apply in the case of Psellos' work on the *De interpretatione* Sophonias' observations concerning the characteristic features of a para-

---

[26] There is, however, a variant of this title; namely, Ambrosianus 194 and the Oxford manuscript of Magdalen College 15 have περίφρασις instead of παράφρασις.

[27] Themistius, *in An. post.* 1. 14: τὸν τύπον κοινούμεθα τῆς συγγραφῆς.

[28] Sophonias, *in De an.* 1. 21: καὶ Ψελλὸς ὕστερον μιμησάμενος ἐν τῇ λογικῇ.

[29] Ibid. 1. 19–20: οὐκ ἐξηγηταὶ μᾶλλον ἤ παραφρασταί.

phrasis? The first characteristic is clearly present, for we only need to compare the size of Psellos' work to Ammonius' commentary on the same Aristotelian treatise. That is to say, the 272 pages of Ammonius' edited scholia in the series *Commentaria in Aristotelem Graeca* certainly outnumber by far the 39 pages of the Aldine edition of Psellos' text, which correspond to approximately 90 pages of the *CAG* series.[30]

Concerning next the continuous flow of a paraphrasis, it must be pointed out that the lemmata which interrupt Psellos' text in the Aldine edition were probably not part of Psellos' original work; they are not to be found in all manuscripts and they also seem to be redundant, since Aristotle's views are incorporated in the main text of the paraphrasis. Of course, we cannot be certain as to who added these lemmata and when, though we may note that they preserve a text which does not always coincide with our standard edition of Aristotle's work.

But there is another more interesting aspect of Sophonias' second characteristic, which certainly applies to Psellos' work on the *De interpretatione*. For at the very end of his paraphrasis,[31] Psellos himself states that he pretends throughout this text to be Aristotle himself. And this is why the alleged author of the paraphrasis uses the first person to talk about the doctrines which he discusses in works like the *De anima* (*in De interp.* 1. 24–5), the *Categories*, the *Topics*, and the *Physics* (*in De interp.* 35. 30–2). Moreover, the obvious anachronism notwithstanding, it is supposed to be Aristotle himself who refers in this text (*in De interp.* 28. 34–41) to Ammonius' commentary on the *De interpretatione* and, most probably, to Philoponus' commentary on the *Prior Analytics*.[32] But although there are many more indications in the paraphrasis which show that Psellos tries to maintain the fiction that Aristotle is its author,[33] there are three obvious lapses: once the name of Aristotle occurs in an example, namely Πλάτων φιλοσοφεῖ καὶ Σωκράτης διαλέγεται καὶ Ἀριστοτέλης τεχνολογεῖ (*in De interp.* 6. 7–8); Aristotle's view on names is twice presented in the third person as the doctrine of the Philosopher (*in De interp.* 2. 14; 17); and finally, when the views of Plato and

---

[30] The extract from Ammonius' commentary which the editor carelessly added to Psellos' paraphrasis gives us an idea as to the length of Psellos' work; that is to say, it is thanks to this extract that we may estimate the 39 pp. of the Aldine edn. of Psellos' text to correspond to approximately 90 pp. of the series *Commentaria in Aristotelem Graeca*.

[31] *in De interp.* 39. 28–31: οὕτω μὲν οὖν ἐγὼ ἐν τῷ λογίῳ τούτῳ θεάτρῳ τοῦ Ἀριστοτέλους πρόσωπον ἐμαυτῷ περιθέμενος, τὸν ἐκείνου περὶ τῶν ἀποφαντικῶν λόγων ἐξωρχησάμην ὑπομνηματισμόν. It is interesting to compare the above text with the following: Sophonias, *in De an.* 1. 11–12: αὐτὸν γὰρ ὑποδύντες Ἀριστοτέλην καὶ τῷ τῆς αὐταγγελίας προσχρησάμενοι προσωπείῳ.

[32] There is no reason to assume, as has been done by Busse in his edn. of Ammonius' commentary (*in De interp.* xv.), that this passage implies the existence of a commentary by Philoponus on the *De interpretatione*; for Philoponus himself discusses the issue which is in question here, namely the notion of the ἐνδεχόμενον, in his surviving commentary on the *Prior Analytics* (*in An. pr.* 42. 35–6; 59. 6–7), and the other available evidence is quite meagre.

[33] See e.g. *in De interp.* 3. 11, 4. 28, 30, 31, 32.

Aristotle on non-being are put forward, Psellos does not manage to avoid referring to Aristotle by name (*in De interp.* 27. 5). In general, though, Psellos presents the logical issues of the *De interpretatione* from Aristotle's perspective, that is to say, as if it were Aristotle himself who, some centuries after completing his work, revises it, either by expanding the elliptic points or by explaining the difficult issues on the basis of the commentators' interpretations.[34] It is obviously this characteristic, then, which explains why, as we have previously said, Psellos deliberately conceals his own identity in this paraphrasis.

Finally, there is no doubt that the third feature, which Sophonias regards as characteristic of a paraphrasis, applies to Psellos' work. For the mere reading of this treatise soon makes it obvious that it has not been written for scholars interested in clarifying the difficult points of Aristotle's thought, but for the teaching of students with little background in logical matters.[35] In fact, the practical aim of Psellos' paraphrasis as a textbook for use in logic courses is attested, as Sophonias rightly expects, by the large number of references to theorems or rules. In the 39 pages of the Aldine edition we find the term '*κανών*' occurring nineteen times;[36] this does not mean, of course, that Psellos discusses nineteen rules, for there are only four, nor that he invents new logical rules, for he simply formulates them on the basis of material already presented by Aristotle.[37] To the use of rules, as indicative of the practical aim of Psellos' paraphrasis, we should also add the use of the imperative, the use of the second person, and the use of verbs referring to the teaching process.[38] In addition, Psellos often presents the Aristotelian doctrines in a question–answer form, which he clearly considers as helpful to the students; in fact, he uses it so much that in a single page we find eight different questions.[39]

---

[34] See e.g. *in De interp.* 8. 55–9. 2, 10. 43–5, 15. 52–3, 28. 17–18, 30. 14.

[35] There is, however, an exception to the rule that Psellos just tries to cover the same ground as Aristotle in a more accessible form, without attention to the details of the *De interpretatione*. For there is one place (*in De interp.* 23. 7–25), in which Psellos proposes a change of the standard text, even though this change is not particularly good. The standard edition of Aristotle's text reads as follows: *De interp.* 20ᵃ35–6: ὁ δ' εἰπὼν οὐκ ἄνθρωπος οὐδὲν μᾶλλον τοῦ ἄνθρωπος ἀλλὰ καὶ ἧττον ἠλήθευκέ τι ἤ ἔψευσται, ἐὰν μή τι προστεθῇ. Psellos' reading deletes τι, exactly as it happens in the relevant lemma of Ammonius' commentatry (*in De interp.* 188. 20), and proposes to have a fullstop after ἠλήθευκε. In other words, Psellos understands the text not as saying that the indefinite name 'not-man' does no more say something true or false than the name 'man', but as saying that 'not-man' does no more say something true than 'man', and says something false if something else is added to it.

[36] *in De interp.* 21. 11, 41, 42, 22. 5, 11, 31, 41, 23. 30, 37, 25. 31, 26. 4, 4, 12, 18, 36, 45, 28. 13, 29. 49, 36. 47.

[37] Psellos' simple rule (*in De interp.* 21. 11), for instance, that in contradictory assertions the subject and the predicate should always be the same, should certainly not be considered as his own logical innovation.

[38] e.g. νόησον σοι (*in De interp.* 12. 39, 15. 9, 12, 53, 17. 37, 19. 5, 21. 26, 34. 28), σκεπτέον σοι (*in De interp.* 36. 1), μέμνησθε (*in De interp.* 31. 37), προτίθεμαί σοι διδάξαι (*in De interp.* 20. 53), διδάξαμεν ὑμᾶς (*in De interp.* 31. 30).

[39] *in De interp.* 10. 2–5, 11. 24–5, 42, 43, 16. 40, 42, 18. 8, 17, 21, 27, 26. 43, 44, 45, 31. 12, 15, 22, 28, 29, 36, 39, 52, 39. 4.

Moreover, Psellos reorganizes the Aristotelian material, constructing diagrams which are easily memorized and learnt by the students. There are several occasions in the paraphrasis on which Psellos discusses a difficult logical issue, either by explicitly referring to a diagram or by giving directions as to how to construct one. Just to give a sense of the importance of diagrams in this work, the term '*διάγραμμα*' is used thirteen times,[40] but we also find the term '*σχῆμα*'[41] and various phrases implying the use of a diagram, like '*αἱ διαγώνιοι προτάσεις*' and '*αἱ κατὰ διάμετρον προτάσεις*'.[42] However, there are no such diagrams in the Aldine edition, although they are in great abundance in the manuscript tradition of Psellos' paraphrasis.[43] In fact, the omission of diagrams from the Aldine edition is yet another of its important deficiencies, as Psellos' text often becomes unintelligible without them. Since we know so little about the history of diagrams in logical texts, it would be hasty to speculate here about the origins of Psellos' logical diagrams. It may be suggested, though, that most of these diagrams are either identical with or quite similar to diagrams which are to be found in the works of previous commentators, for example in Philoponus' commentaries.[44]

Psellos does not only use rules and diagrams to make Aristotle's text more accessible to the students of logic; he also adds, for the same purpose, a considerable number of examples. In particular, Psellos understandably uses Aristotle's standard examples, such as *Κάλιππος*[45] and *Σωκράτης λευκός ἐστιν*.[46] Moreover, he uses either Stoic examples already modified by the ancient commentators, such as *εἰ ἥλιός ἐστιν, ἡμέρα ἐστίν;*[47] or versions of the commentators' own examples, such as *Αἴας ἐμονομάχησεν Ἕκτορι*[48] and *εἰ ὁ θεὸς δίκαιος, τὰ ἐκεῖθεν δικαιότερα.*[49] However, it is Psellos' own examples which are more interesting. For instance, in Psellos' example *Πλάτων φιλοσοφεῖ καὶ Σωκράτης διαλέγεται καὶ 'Αριστοτέλης τεχνολογεῖ* (*in De interp*. 6. 7–8), we should note the use of the verb *τεχνολογῶ* which is not to be found in the ancient commentators,[50] but most importantly Psellos' own understanding of the distinct character of Socrates', Plato's, and Aristotle's philosophy. Also, Psellos twice uses as an example for a mythical animal (*in De interp*. 3. 44, 26. 49), instead of the more standard *τραγέλαφος*, the unusual word *μυρμηκολέων*, i.e. ant-lion, which presumably comes from the Old Testament.[51] To this same Judaeo-Christian

---

[40] Ibid. 19. 3, 10, 30, 20. 24–5, 34–5, 30. 27–8, 50, 31. 14, 32, 33, 32. 13, 35, 35. 8.
[41] Ibid. 34. 42.
[42] Ibid. 10. 4, 11. 13, 16, 13. 29, 20. 20, 22, 26, 35, 30. 49.
[43] See e.g. Baroccianus gr. 117, fos. 63ᵛ, 68, 77, 79ᵛ, 81ᵛ, 82ᵛ, 100, 115ᵛ, 117ᵛ.
[44] See e. g. Philoponus, *in An. pr*. 377.
[45] *in De interp*. 2. 28 = *De interp*. 16ᵃ21.
[46] Ibid. 3. 24–5 = *De interp*. 17ᵇ28.
[47] Ibid. 6. 6–7 = Philoponus, *in An. pr*. 171. 3; 242. 33.
[48] *in De interp*. 7. 2; 8. 28 = Ammonius, *in De interp*. 73. 11–12.
[49] *in De interp*. 7. 3–4; 19–20 = Philoponus, *in An. pr*. 243. 26.
[50] Psellos often uses the verb *τεχνολογῶ*, see e.g. *in De interp*. 16. 21; 23. 29.
[51] Job 4: 11; *Physiologus* A 20; Neilos of Ankyra, *De monastica exercitatione* 49; Germanos of Constantinople, *Orationes* I.

tradition, after all, belong some other examples by Psellos, such as δεῦρο ἀναστάς (*in De interp.* 5. 46) and ἐὰν μὲν ἀρετὴν ἕλωμαι, ψυχῆς σωτηρία μοι προσγενήσεται (*in De interp.* 15. 24–5).

Psellos' Sources

Having thus established that Psellos' work on the *De interpretatione* is rightly called a παράφρασις, let me now turn to its content. More specifically, the study of Psellos' examples introduces us to the next issue with which we should deal in more detail, namely the issue of the influences on Psellos' paraphrasis. The first thing to note is that the stylistic convention followed by Psellos, namely pretending that Aristotle is the author, proves to be quite confusing; that is to say, the first person is here used not only when we are informed about Aristotle's doctrines, but also when the commentators' interpretations as well as Psellos' own views are presented. In addition, the results of an inquiry into Psellos' influences are inevitably limited, since only few of the many commentaries written on the *De interpetatione* are still extant.

Nevertheless, there are indeed many cases in which we can detect Psellos adopting the scholia of the previous commentators. For instance, the view expressed in Psellos' work that a sentence (λόγος) is a product (ἀποτέλεσμα) of our natural capacity to produce vocal sound, and thus by nature, and not its instrument (ὄργανον), which fulfils its function by convention (*in De interp.* 5. 22–35), is supported by the same arguments in Ammonius (*in De interp.* 62. 21–2), in the anonymous commentary (*in De interp.* 16. 1–19), and in Stephanus (*in De interp.* 15. 9–10). Also, when the issue arises of whether the indefinite negative assertion is similar to the universal negative or to the particular negative (*in De interp.* 11. 24–12. 1), Psellos sides with the second view which is already argued for in the same way in Ammonius' commentary (*in De interp.* 111. 10–11). But does this mean that Psellos' paraphrasis heavily depends on the preceding commentaries, and in particular on Ammonius' scholia? Although this is what is generally believed about Psellos' work on the *De interpretatione*, as well as about his other writings on Aristotle, I shall attempt to challenge this view and argue in favour of two theses: first, that Psellos is influenced not only by the Aristotelian commentators, but by other ancient sources among which the Greek grammarians are predominant; and second, that Psellos incorporates in this paraphrasis his own views, some of which may originate in his aim to reconcile the Christian tradition with the ancient philosophers.

There are specific points in Psellos' paraphrasis, on which the influence of the Greek grammarians is noticeable;[52] of these I shall here present only

---

[52] Psellos was taught grammar by the Byzantine grammarian Niketas, in whose funeral oration Psellos often stresses that learning grammar is really basic for all science (Sathas

three, namely his views on the definition of a name, on the tenses of a verb, and on the natural priority of a verb over a name.

The definition of a name

Psellos defines a name (τὸ ὄνομα)[53] as something composite of matter and form, that is, composed of simple vocal sound (ἁπλῆ φωνή) and a certain articulation (ἀπήχησις), that is, a pronunciation according to language and linguistic expression (λεκτικὴ ἐκφώνησις). Now in Ammonius' commentary,[54] we find a remark which closely resembles Psellos' definition, namely that names and verbs are not simply vocal sounds (ἁπλῶς φωναί), but vocal sounds shaped and formed by linguistic imagination (λεκτικὴ φαντασία). It should be noted that, similar though they may be, these two texts partly use different terminology. More specifically, Psellos uses the term 'ἀπήχησις', which is not to be found in Ammonius' commentary. On the other hand, this same term seems to be a standard term used by the Greek grammarians in their introductory discussions about vocal sound. Thus, at the very beginning of his *Ars grammatica*,[55] Dionysius Thrax defines pitch (τόνος) as pronunciation of vocal sound (ἀπήχησις φωνῆς). And also in the scholia on the same work, the term 'ἀπήχησις' is used and defined either as 'ἦχος' (*Schol. in D. Th.* 22. 18), or as 'ὁ ἦχος καὶ ἡ προφορὰ καὶ ἡ ἐκφώνησις' (*Schol. in D. Th.* 309. 43–310. 1).

The tenses of a verb

Psellos points out that, though he accepts to follow Aristotle in calling the tenses of a verb 'cases' (πτώσεις), since they may be said to be derived (πεπτωκέναι) from the present tense, as the genitive and the dative are derived from the nominative, he actually believes that they should be considered as transformations (παρασχηματισμοί).[56] That is to say, Psellos is aware of a distinction similar to the modern distinction between the declension of a name and the conjugation of a verb, but he accepts on this occasion

---

v. 87–96). It should also be noted that Psellos is the author of a treatise with the title Στίχοι πολιτικοὶ περὶ τῆς γραμματικῆς (J. Boissonade, *Analecta Graeca III* (Paris, 1831), 200–28), a small work of 483 verses on grammar.

[53] *in De interp.* 2. 3–5: τὸ γὰρ ὄνομα ἐπεὶ σύνθετόν ἐστιν ἀπό τε τῆς ἁπλῆς φωνῆς συγκείμενον καὶ τῆς ποιᾶς ἀπηχήσεως, ἤτοι τῆς διαλεκτικῆς καὶ λεκτικῆς ἐκφωνήσεως, ἐξ ὕλης καὶ εἴδους συντεθειμένον ἐστίν.

[54] Ammonius, *in De interp.* 22. 33–23. 1: οὐχ ἁπλῶς φωναὶ τὰ ὀνόματα καὶ τὰ ῥήματα, ἀλλὰ τοιῶσδε μορφωθεῖσαι καὶ διαπλασθεῖσαι ὑπὸ τῆς λεκτικῆς φαντασίας.

[55] Dionysius Thrax, *Ars gram.* 6. 15–7. 2: Τόνος ἐστὶν ἀπήχησις φωνῆς ἐναρμονίου ἢ κατὰ ἀνάτασιν ἐν τῇ ὀξείᾳ, ἢ κατὰ ὁμαλισμὸν ἐν τῇ βαρείᾳ, ἢ κατὰ περίκλασιν ἐν τῇ περισπωμένῃ.

[56] *in De interp.* 3. 49–51: πτώσεις δέ, διὰ τὸ πεπτωκέναι τοῦ ἐνεστῶτος, ὥσπερ ἡ γενικὴ καὶ δοτικὴ καὶ τἆλλα, πτώσεις, διὰ τὸ πεπτωκέναι τῆς εὐθείας· καταχρηστικώτερον γάρ μοι εἴρηται τὸ πτώσεις ἐπὶ τοῦ ῥήματος ἀντὶ τοῦ παρασχηματισμοῦ.

to use a common term in both cases. Ammonius, on the other hand, claims that the tenses of a verb are formed from the present tense κατὰ παρασχηματισμόν (*in De interp.* 52. 24), but he makes no comment as to the suitability of the term 'πτώσεις'. In the *Ars grammatica* of Dionysius Thrax,[57] however, the very definition of a verb states that it is an ἄπτωτος λέξις, clearly implying that a verb is conjugated and not declined, and thus its tenses should not be regarded as πτώσεις. Also, Apollonius Dyscolus[58] defines a verb using the term 'μετασχηματισμοί' to refer to the transformations of a verb resulting in its tenses.

The natural priority of a verb over a name

At the very beginning of his paraphrasis,[59] Psellos advocates a rather unusual view, namely that a verb is more perfect than a name. He even repeats it later on, when he claims that he will first discuss names, although verbs are more perfect,[60] but also when he stresses that in an assertion the verb is the most important part.[61]

The view that a verb is more perfect than a name is indeed strange, as it contradicts the standard doctrine found in the commentaries on Aristotle's *De interpretatione*. For according to Ammonius[62] and Stephanus,[63] a name indicates substance (οὐσία), and is thus prior to a verb indicating activity (ἐνέργεια) and affection (πάθος). In addition, there are some grammarians who express exactly the same view, like for example Theodosios of Alexandria[64] and his commentator George Choiro-

---

[57] Dionysius Thrax, *Ars gram.* 46. 4–5: 'Ρῆμά ἐστι λέξις ἄπτωτος, ἐπιδεκτικὴ χρόνων τε καὶ προσώπων καὶ ἀριθμῶν, ἐνέργειαν ἢ πάθος παριστᾶσα.

[58] *Scholia in D. Th.* 71. 24–7: 'Ρῆμά ἐστι μέρος λόγου (ἄπτωτον) ἐν ἰδίοις μετασχηματισμοῖς διαφόρων χρόνων ἐπιδεκτικὸν μετ' ἐνεργείας ἢ πάθους (ἢ οὐδετέρου), προσώπων τε καὶ ἀριθμῶν παραστατικόν, ὅτε καὶ τὰ τῆς ψυχῆς διαθέσεις δηλοῖ.

[59] *in De interp.* 1. 5–7: ἤγουν πρώτως μὲν τὸ ὄνομα ὡς ἀτελέστερον τοῦ ῥήματος, καθὸ τὸ μὲν ὑπόκειται καὶ μεταλαμβάνει, τὸ δὲ κατηγορεῖται καὶ μεταδίδωσιν.

[60] *in De interp.* 4. 35–6: ὅτι ἐπὶ μὲν τοῦ ὀνόματος καὶ τοῦ ῥήματος τῇ ἀπὸ τῶν ἀτελεστέρων ἐχρησάμην προόδῳ ἐπὶ τὰ τελεώτερα.

[61] *in De interp.* 6. 21–2 (see also, *in De interp.* 17. 44–5): καὶ προηγουμένως μὲν περὶ τοῦ ῥήματος τεχνολογῆσαι, ὡς τὸ κῦρος ἐν ταῖς προτάσεσιν ἔχοντος.

[62] Ammonius, *in De interp.* 29. 31–30. 3:Ὅτι μὲν εἰκότως προτετίμηται τὸ ὄνομα τοῦ ῥήματος ἐν τῇ διδασκαλίᾳ, φανερόν· τὰ μὲν γὰρ ὀνόματα τὰς ὑπάρξεις σημαίνουσι τῶν πραγμάτων τὰ δὲ ῥήματα τὰς ἐνεργείας ἢ τὰ πάθη, προηγοῦνται δὲ τῶν ἐνεργειῶν καὶ τῶν παθῶν αἱ ὑπάρξεις.

[63] Stephanus, *in De interp.* 3. 9–12: καὶ ὅτι μὲν τὸ ὄνομα τῆς ὑπάρξεως καὶ τῆς οὐσίας ἐστὶν σημαντικόν, τὸ δὲ ῥῆμα τῆς οὐσίας ἐνέργειαν σημαίνει, προτερεύει δὲ ἡ οὐσία τῆς ἐνεργείας, εἰκότως καὶ τὸ ὄνομα τοῦ ῥήματος προταχθήσεται.

[64] Theodosios, *Gramm.* 17. 31–18. 16: Προτέτακται δὲ τὸ ὄνομα τοῦ ῥήματος, ὅτι τὸ ὄνομα κατ' οὐσιῶν λέγεται, τὸ δὲ ῥῆμα κατὰ πραγμάτων, Κυριώτεραι δέ εἰσιν αἱ οὐσίαι τῶν πραγμάτων... Πρὸ τοῦ ῥήματος δὲ ἐξ ἀνάγκης κεῖται τὸ ὄνομα.Ἐπειδὴ τὸ ἐνεργεῖν τε καὶ πάσχειν τῆς οὐσίας ἐστί, καθ' ἣν ἡ θέσις τῶν ὀνομάτων ἐστίν· ἐξ ὧν ὀνομάτων δηλαδὴ ἡ ἰδιότης τοῦ ῥήματος γεννᾶται. Τοῦτο δέ ἐστιν ἡ ἐνέργειακαὶ τὸ πάθος. Ἔνεστι τοιγαροῦν συννοουμένη ἐν αὐτοῖς ῥήμασιν ἡ εὐθεῖα, ἧς ἄνευ οὐχ οἷά τέ ἐστιν ἡ οὐσία δηλωθῆναι, ἐν μὲν τῷ πρώτῳ καὶ δευτέρῳ προσώπῳ διωρισμένη, ἐν δὲ τῷ τρίτῳ προσώπῳ ἀδιόριστος.

boskos,[65] as well as John Charax who is quoted by Sophronios.[66] These grammarians not only use the commentators' argument of the priority of a substance over an activity, they also add two further arguments: first, that a name is prior to a verb, because whenever the name is abolished (συναναιρεῖν), the verb is abolished too, but whenever the verb is abolished, the name is not abolished; second, that a name is prior to a verb, because the name does not introduce, or make us think of, a verb along with it (συνεισφέρειν, συννοεῖν), whereas the verb does introduce, or makes us think of, a name along with it.

There is evidence, however, that not all grammarians accepted the standard doctrine; in fact, it seems that some of them advocated a view similar to the one discussed in Psellos' paraphrasis. That is to say, some grammarians insisted that a verb is by nature prior (φύσει προγενέστερον) to a name, even if names should be discussed first and then verbs, simply because verbs make their appearance as long as there are substances signified by names.[67] But what kind of arguments did they use to support their unusual view that a verb is by nature prior to a name? It seems that the last argument used by their opponents, namely that a name does not make us think of a verb along with it, whereas a verb does make us think of a name along with it, must have been right at the centre of this debate. The grammarians advocating the natural priority of a verb over a name also used it, but for the opposite purpose. That

[65] George Choiroboskos, *Schol. in Theod. Can. verb.* 2. 22–3. 10 (see also, *Schol. in Theod. Can. nom.* 105. 2–21): Τούτων οὕτως ἐχόντων ἐμάθομεν ἐν τοῖς προλαβοῦσιν, ὅτι ὀκτώ εἰσι τὰ μέρη τοῦ λόγου, ὄνομα ῥῆμα μετοχὴ ἄρθρον ἀντωνυμία πρόθεσις ἐπίρρημα σύνδεσμος, καὶ ὅτι προτέτακται τὸ ὄνομα τοῦ ῥήματος, καθὸ τὸ μὲν ὄνομα οὐσίας ἐστὶ σημαντικόν, τὸ δὲ ῥῆμα συμβεβηκότος, <αἱ δὲ οὐσίαι προτερεύουσι τῶν συμβεβηκότων> · καὶ γὰρ ὁ Σωκράτης προτερεύει τοῦ γράφειν αὐτὸν καὶ τοῦ τύπτειν· εἰκότως οὖν καὶ τὸ ὄνομα ὡς σημαντικὸν ὂν τῆς οὐσίας προτερεύει τοῦ ῥήματος σημαντικοῦ ὄντος τοῦ συμβεβηκότος ... Κατὰ δεύτερον δὲ λόγον προτερεύει τὸ ὄνομα τοῦ ῥήματος, ὅτι μὲν τὸ ὄνομα συναναιρεῖ, τὸ δὲ ῥῆμα συναναιρεῖται · καὶ γὰρ ἀναιρουμένου Σωκράτους συναναιρεῖται καὶ τὸ γράφειν αὐτὸν καὶ τὸ τύπτειν· τὰ δὲ συναναιροῦντα προτερεύουσι τῶν συναναιρουμένων ... Κατὰ τρίτον δὲ λόγον προτερεύει τὸ ὄνομα τοῦ ῥήματος, ὅτι μὲν τὸ ὄνομα συνεισφέρεται, τὸ δὲ ῥῆμα συνεισφέρει · καὶ γὰρ ἐάν τις εἴπῃ τύπτει ἢ γράφει, πάντως συνεισφέρει καὶ τὴν οὐσίαν, ἤγουν τὸν τύπτοντα καὶ τὸν γράφοντα · τὰ δὲ συνεισφερόμενα προτερεύουσι τῶν συνεισφερόντων ... τὸ δὲ συνεισφέρεται δεῖ νοεῖν ἀντὶ τοῦ συννοεῖται.

[66] Sophronios, *Excer. ex Ioan. Char* 376. 34–377. 2: Προτέτακται δὲ τοῦ ῥήματος φύσει τὸ ὄνομα · φύσει δὲ λέγω οὐχὶ αὐτῶν τῶν λέξεων· κατὰ τοῦτο γὰρ μέρη ὄντα ἅμα ἐστίν· ἀλλὰ τῶν πραγμάτων ὧν εἰσι κατηγορικά · τὸ γὰρ ὄνομα οὐσίαν σημαίνει, τὸ δὲ ῥῆμα συμβεβηκός · δῆλον δὲ ὅτι δεύτερον τὸ συμβεβηκὸς τοῦ ᾧ συμβέβηκεν· ἔτι δὲ καὶ ὅτι συναναιρεῖ.

[67] *Schol. in D. Th.* 216. 8–13: Περὶ δὲ τῆς τάξεως ἄξιον ζητῆσαι, τί δή ποτε τῶν ἁπάντων προέταξε τὸ ὄνομα τοῦ ῥήματος προγενεστέρου ὄντος τῇ φύσει · ἀεὶ γὰρ τὰ πράγματα τῶν οὐσιῶν προγενέστερά εἰσιν. Καὶ τοῦ μὲν ῥήματος ὅτι δικαίως τὸ ὄνομα <προ>τέτακται, ἀποχρήσει εἰς ἀπολογίαν, ὅτι εἰ καὶ προτέτακται τῇ φύσει τὸ ῥῆμα, ἀλλ' οὖν γε διὰ τῶν οὐσιῶν τὰ πράγματα φαίνεται. *Schol. in D. Th.* 244. 5–7: Τὸ ῥῆμα ἀναγκαίως μετὰ τὸ ὄνομα κατετάγη · τῇ φύσει μὲν γὰρ πρωτεύει, διὰ δὲ τὸ δίχα τῆς οὐσίας μὴ φαίνεσθαι συγκεχωρήκαμεν τὸ ὄνομα προτάττεσθαι. Sophronios, *Excer. ex Ioan. Char.* 409. 6–9: Ἤδη ἀποδειχθέντος, ὡς τῶν ὀκτὼ τοῦ λόγου μερῶν προτέτακται τοὔνομα, δευτέραν δὲ τάξιν ἀναγκαίως εἴληφε τὸ ῥῆμα, ὅπου γε καὶ προταγῆναι τοῦ ὀνόματος αὐτὸ τινες ἠξίουν, διαλαβόντες περὶ τοῦ ὀνόματος σὺν θεῷ ἔλθωμεν ἐπὶ τὸ ῥῆμα.

is to say, the grammarians who stressed that a verb is by nature prior to a name strongly believed that a verb is perfect (τέλειον), exactly because it does make us think of a name along with it, whereas a name does not make us think of a verb along with it.[68]

To come back to Psellos' paraphrasis, the argument which Psellos gives in order to support the thesis that a name is less perfect (ἀτελέστερον) than a verb, may be found in his interpretation of Aristotle's text which states that, when uttered just by itself, a verb is a name and signifies something.[69] Commenting on this passage, Psellos clarifies the difference between a name and a verb, by arguing that a name indicates only substance, whereas a verb both indicates substance and refers back to something.[70] On the other hand, according to Ammonius, the difference between a name and a verb lies in the fact that a name indicates substance, whereas a verb does not indicate substance, but only refers to something.[71] Hence, what distinguishes Psellos' thesis from the commentators' view is exactly what the second group of the grammarians claim against their opponents; namely, that a verb also indicates substance, or in other words, that a verb makes us think of a name along with it. After all, we still have the tendency to understand a verb as a function with a place-holder for a name. And there is no doubt that, according to some Greek grammarians as well as according to Psellos, this is what makes a verb perfect and prior by nature to a name.

How Original is Psellos' Paraphrasis?

Is it true that Psellos' work on Aristotle's *De interpretatione* is a mere compilation of views expressed by previous commentators as well as by other ancient sources, like for example the Greek grammarians? It is now time to defend my second thesis, namely that the paraphrasis also presents Psellos'

---

[68] Sophronios, *Excer. ex Ioan. Char.* 377. 2–8: Ἀποροῦσι δέ τινες λέγοντες, πῶς τὸ ῥῆμα μονομερῆ λόγον ποιοῦν τέλειον, ὡς ἐν τῷ "γράφω", οὐ προτάσσεται τοῦ ὀνόματος · εἰ γάρ τινι ἐρωτήσαντί σε γράφοντα "τί ποιεῖς;" ἀποκρίνοιο "γράφω", τέλειον λόγον ἐρεῖς. Λέγομεν δέ, ὅτι καὶ οὕτω συνεισφέρεται ὄνομα τὸ σημαῖνον τὴν οὐσίαν, ἀφ' ἧς ἡ ἐνέργεια· ἡ ἀντωνυμία δὲ δήλην τὴν οὐσίαν σημαίνει, καὶ κατὰ τοῦτο μᾶλλον τὸ ὄνομα τὴν πρώτην εἴληφεν τάξιν.

[69] *De interp.* 16ᵇ19–20: αὐτὰ μὲν οὖν καθ' αὑτὰ λεγόμενα τὰ ῥήματα ὀνόματά ἐστι καὶ σημαίνει τι.

[70] *in De interp.* 3. 51–4. 6: δεῖ δὲ καὶ τοῦτο εἰδέναι, ὡς τῶν διαλεκτικῶν φωνῶν, τῶν ὀνομάτων καὶ ῥημάτων φημί, τὸ μὲν ὄνομα ὕπαρξιν δηλοῖ μόνην, τὸ δὲ ῥῆμα μετὰ τῆς ὑπάρξεως καὶ ἀναφοράν. ἀλλ' ἐν μὲν αὐτοτελεῖ προτάσει τῇ λεγούσῃ Σωκράτης περιπατεῖ, τὸ περιπατεῖ ἀναφορικὸν μὲν μᾶλλον νενόηται ῥῆμα · ὑπαρκτικὸν δὲ ἧττον· καὶ δεῖ ἀπὸ τοῦ μᾶλλον τὸ ὅλον ὀνομάζειν ἀναφορικόν· ὅτε δὲ καθ' αὑτὸ τὸ ῥῆμα χωρὶς τῆς πρὸς τὸ ὄνομα συνθέσεως ἐκφωνήσω, ὑπαρκτικὸν νενόηται μᾶλλον ἢ ἀναφορικόν· ἐπεὶ οὖν τότε ὕπαρξιν μᾶλλον δηλοῖ, ὑπάρξεως δὲ δηλωτικὰ καὶ τὰ ὀνόματα, ὄνομα ἂν τηνικαῦτα καὶ τὸ ῥῆμα κλητέον· σημαίνει γάρ τι.

[71] Ammonius, *in De interp.* 50. 23–5: καὶ δεῖ τὰς μὲν φωνὰς τὰς σημαινούσας αὐτῶν τὰς ὑπάρξεις ὀνόματα καλεῖν, τὰς δὲ τὴν ἀναφορὰν τὴν πρὸς τὰ ὑποκείμενα δηλούσας ῥήματα.

own views, or at least some views that are not to be found in the surviving Aristotelian commentaries. In fact, we can detect throughout Psellos' work different degrees of independent thinking on his part; sometimes he gives a slightly different argument to support an established interpretation, sometimes he makes a small but interesting addition to the doctrines of the ancient commentators, sometimes he considerably diverges from what is generally accepted. In what follows, I shall present three examples, each of which illustrates one of the above cases.

A different argument supporting an established interpretation

Right at the beginning of the first part of his paraphrasis,[72] Psellos ventures to discuss the views of Plato and Aristotle on names, trying to establish that there is in fact no disagreement between the two ancient philosophers. This is not, of course, the first time that a commentator attempts to reconcile Plato's and Aristotle's doctrines about names; for there are similar passages also at the beginning of the two complete surviving commentaries on the *De interpretatione*. In particular, Ammonius (*in De interp.* 34. 10–40. 30) argues that to say that names are 'by nature' (φύσει), the view usually attributed to Plato, can be understood in two ways: first, that names are products of nature, that is to say that a fitting name had been given by nature to each thing; second, that names fit the nature of the things named by them, like paintings strive to copy as well as possible the form of their subject. Similarly, to say that names are 'by imposition' (θέσει), the view usually attributed to Aristotle, can also be understood in two ways: first, that it is possible for any man to name any thing with whatever name he likes; second, that names are given by the wise man alone, and that he is the only one who has knowledge of the nature of things and thus is in a position to give a name appropriate to this nature. Now, according to Ammonius, the second sense of 'by nature' coincides with the second sense of 'by imposition'; for what has been imposed by the name-giver, as being appropriate to the thing for which it stands, may be regarded on the one hand as 'by nature', but on the other hand also as 'by imposition', since it has been imposed by someone. And we find exactly the same strategy of reconciling Plato and Aristotle in Stephanus' commentary (*in De interp.* 9. 7–10. 13).

---

[72] *in De interp.* 2. 12–21: Ἔστιν οὖν τὸ ὄνομα φωνὴ σημαίνουσά τι ὑποκείμενον καὶ σύμβολον ἐκείνου τυγχάνουσα · οὐ κατὰ φύσιν δέ, ἀλλὰ κατὰ συνθήκην, ἤτοι θέσιν· καὶ οὐκ ἐναντιοῦται τῷ Πλάτωνι ὁ Φιλόσοφος, κατὰ φύσιν τὰ ὀνόματα λέγοντι, κατὰ θέσιν οὗτος διδάσκων αὐτά · ὁ μὲν Πλάτων, ἐπεὶ ἐν τῷ Κρατύλῳ ἐπιστήμονα τὸν ὀνοματοθέτην εἰσάγει, ἐπιστημόνως αὐτὸν καταναγκάζει καὶ ταῖς ὀνοματοθεσίαις χρῆσθαι, ὥστε ἡμμένας εἶναι τῆς φύσεως · καὶ διὰ τοῦτο κατὰ φύσιν τίθησι τὰ ὀνόματα ὁ δὲ Φιλόσοφος τοῦτο μὲν οὐκ ἀποπέμπεται, εἰ χρὴ διαιτᾶν ἀνδράσι σοφοῖς· διδάσκει δέ, ὡς ὁποῖά ποτ' ἂν εἴη τὰ ὀνόματα, ἐξ ἐπινοίας συντεθειμένα τυγχάνει · πᾶν δὲ τὸ ἀπὸ ἐπινοίας συντεθέν καὶ περατωθὲν τῶν κατὰ συνθήκην οὐ τῶν κατὰ φύσιν ἐστίν· οὐδὲν οὖν κωλύει τὸ αὐτὸ καὶ κατὰ συνθήκην καὶ κατὰ φύσιν λέγειν, πρὸς ἄλλο καὶ ἄλλο ἐκλαμβανομένων ἡμῶν καὶ τὰ ὀνόματα καὶ τὰ ῥήματα.

Psellos does not have a different view on the subject; he, too, states that the two ancient philosophers are in full agreement as to the understanding of the nature of names. His argument, however, does not copy Ammonius' reasoning in the way Stephanus does; that is to say, he does not make the distinction of the two senses of 'by nature' and 'by imposition'. He uses a different method to reconcile Plato's and Aristotle's doctrines, a method based on the observation that something is relative now to one thing and now to another (πρὸς ἄλλο καὶ ἄλλο). Thus, Plato and Aristotle are in perfect agreement, according to Psellos, for a name is 'by nature' (κατὰ φύσιν) relative to the nature of the thing it is a name of, or respectively to the knowledge of this nature the wise person has, who actually gave it the name; at the same time, though, a name is also 'by imposition' (κατὰ θέσιν), or 'by convention' (κατὰ συνθήκην), relative to the conventional way of thinking about the object, or the ordinary notion, ordinary people have of the thing named, for instance a notion corresponding to the characteristic appearance of the thing named. This is, in fact, a method which Psellos uses elsewhere in his paraphrasis, in order to avoid inconsistencies and contradictions. For example, vocal sound is said to be both genus and matter, because relative to the vocal sound of names and verbs it is their genus, whereas relative to names and verbs it is their matter (*in De interp.* 2. 9–12); and the number ten is said to be both more and less, because relative to five it is more, whereas relative to twenty it is less (*in De interp.* 8. 35–7).[73]

But it is important to note that even the method πρὸς ἄλλο καὶ ἄλλο certainly is not unknown to the ancient commentators. Ammonius, for instance, uses it to discuss the cases in which there may be no contradiction between an affirmation and its negation (*in De interp.* 85. 8); also, before him Porphyry uses it to establish that something may be both a genus and a species (*in Cat.* 83. 33), and after him Philoponus uses it to argue that logic may be both an instrument and a part of philosophy (*in An. pr.* 8. 34). Thus, Psellos does not invent a new method and does not argue for an original thesis; on the contrary, we have here just a case in which a known strategy is used to prove an already established thesis. However, even if we cannot say that Psellos breaks new ground on the issue of bridging the gap between Plato's and Aristotle's doctrines about names, there is at least no doubt that he does not simply copy the surviving ancient commentaries.

An interesting addition to the ancient commentaries

At the beginning of the third part of his work on the *De interpretatione* (*in De interp.* 17. 35–19. 18), Psellos discusses the passage in which Aristotle talks about two sets of contradictory pairs of assertions (*De interp.* 19ᵇ19–30); namely, the affirmation (A) 'Man is just' and its negation (B) 'Man is not

---

[73] See also, *in De interp.* 8. 37–9: κατ' ἄλλο καὶ ἄλλο.

just', as well as the affirmation (E) 'Man is not-just' and its negation (F) 'Man is not not-just'. Following the tradition of the ancient commentators, and in particular Ammonius (*in De interp.* 160. 33–165. 3), Psellos calls the assertion (E) 'Man is not-just' an 'affirmation by transposition' (κατάφασις ἐκ μεταθέσεως), and the assertion (F) 'Man is not not-just' a 'negation by transposition' (ἀπόφασις ἐκ μεταθέσεως). Also, both Ammonius and Psellos envisage a diagram with two columns; in the first column the simple affirmation and the negation by transposition, for if the first holds the second also holds, in the second column the simple negation and the affirmation by transposition, for if the second holds the first also does:[74]

(A) Man is just.   (B) Man is not just.
(F) Man is not not-just. (E) Man is not-just.

Furthermore, Ammonius and Psellos take here the opportunity to introduce a third set of contradictory pairs of assertions, namely the affirmation (C) 'Man is unjust' and its negation (D) 'Man is not unjust', which they both call respectively a 'privative affirmation' (στερητική κατάφασις) and a 'privative negation' (στερητική ἀπόφασις). They even add them to the two columns of the diagram; the privative negation in the first column between the simple affirmation and the negation by transposition, and the privative affirmation in the second column between the simple negation and the affirmation by transposition:

(A) Man is just.   (B) Man is not just.
(D) Man is not unjust.   (C) Man is unjust.
(F) Man is not not-just. (E) Man is not-just.

By constructing this diagram, Ammonius and Psellos aim to understand better the way all these assertions are logically related. More specifically, they aim to understand better the passage in Aristotle's text which states that from the four initial assertions the last two are related to the simple assertions in the way privations are, while the other two are not.[75] Thus, in their attempt to decode this obscure Aristotelian remark, which they both call a 'riddle' (αἴνιγμα), Ammonius and Psellos claim that the first part of this difficult passage suggests the following logical relation: assertions by transposition stand in the same relation (τὸν αὐτὸν λόγον) to simple assertions as do privative assertions; in other words, F is logically related to A as D is, and E is logically related to B as C is. As to the last part of Aristotle's passage, Ammonius and Psellos take it to mean that simple assertions do not stand in

---

[74] It is interesting to note that, on the basis of this diagram, Ammonius (*in De interp.* 161. 9–32) and Psellos (*in De interp.* 17. 48–18. 15) explain the use of the terms 'κατάφασις ἐκ μεταθέσεως' and 'ἀπόφασις ἐκ μεταθέσεως'; that is to say, the negation by transposition is thus called, because it is placed in the diagram under the simple affirmation, whereas the affirmation by transposition is thus called, because it is placed in the diagram under the simple affirmation.

negation.

[75] *De interp.* 19^b23–4: ὧν τὰ μὲν δύο πρὸς τὴν κατάφασιν καὶ ἀπόφασιν ἕξει κατὰ τὸ στοιχοῦν ὡς αἱ στερήσεις, τὰ δὲ δύο οὔ.

the same relation to assertions by transposition as do privative assertions; in other words, A is not logically related to F as D is, and B is not logically related to E as C is.

In what follows, both Ammonius and Psellos attempt to explain the reasons which bring about these logical relations: negations by transposition as well as privative negations are both of a greater extension ($\dot{\epsilon}\pi\grave{\iota}\ \pi\lambda\acute{\epsilon}ov$) than simple affirmations, and privative negations are of a greater extension than negations by transposition; on the other hand, affirmations by transposition as well as privative affirmations are both of a lesser extension ($\dot{\epsilon}\pi$' $\acute{\epsilon}\lambda\alpha\tau\tau ov$) than simple negations, and privative negations are of a lesser extension than negations by transposition. But what does it mean to say that some assertions are of a greater or lesser extension than others? Ammonius and Psellos clarify this as follows: the negation by transposition 'X is not not-just' holds for the cases in which the simple affirmation 'X is just' holds, but also in another case, namely the case in which X is not a man, like for example in the case of a dog; and as to the privative negation 'X is not unjust', it holds in the cases in which the simple affirmation holds, in the case in which X is not a man, but also in the case in which a man is neither just nor unjust, like for example in the case of a newborn child. Conversely, although the simple negation 'X is not just' holds in the case of a man who is not just, in the cases of X not being a man, and in the cases of a man being neither just nor unjust, the affirmation by transposition 'X is not-just' holds only in the first two of these cases; and as to the privative affirmation 'X is unjust', it holds only in the first case.

All these remarks are found both in Ammonius' commentary and in Psellos' paraphrasis; but there is a further clarification in Psellos' work, which is not to be found elsewhere. For in order to make intuitively clear to his students the logical relations among the various assertions, Psellos decides to work out in detail the particular logistics of these relations. That is to say, he gives number 1 to assertion (A), because it holds only in one case; number 2 to assertion (F), because it holds in the same case as (A), plus the case in which X is not a man; number 3 to assertion (D), because it holds in the same cases as (F), plus the case in which a man is neither just nor unjust. Conversely, he gives number 3 to assertion (B), number 2 to assertion (E), and number 1 to assertion (C). Hence, he tries to justify Aristotle's claim by pointing out that (F) stands in the same way to (A) as (D), because 2 is more than 1 and 3 is more than 1; also, (E) stands in the same way to (B) as (C), because 2 is less than 3 and 1 is less than 3. Turning next to the second part of the Aristotelian passage, he says that (A) does not stand to (F) as (D) does, because 1 is less than 2 but 3 is more than 2; also, B does not stand to (E) as (C) does, because 3 is more than 2 but 1 is less than 2. To make these complicated relations among such assertions more accessible to the student, he even gives particular directions how to draw a more elaborated version of the diagram, containing now all the relevant information.

Psellos' idea to simplify as much as possible the way of grasping the logical relations among these different assertions is, in principle, helpful. Ammonius also produces (*in De interp.* 162. 9–16), for the same reasons, an arithmetical example; if the number of all beings is 1,000, he says, the simple affirmation holds in 400 cases, whereas the negation by transposition holds in 600 cases. However, this is a rather crude and not particularly illuminating way of representing the complicated relations between these assertions, especially if we add privative assertions. Psellos' more elaborate attempt to illustrate in arithmetical detail the logical relations among the various assertions was certainly not the last one. For example, in Leo Magentinos' commentary (*in De interp.* 22. 7–8), we find a different version of the same project; in particular, what Magentinos desperately tries to prove is that the arithmetical ratios which represent the logical relations of the various assertions either are exactly the same, or have something in common. Leaving aside the analysis of this later work, it is still important in this context to point out that Magentinos' text makes little sense if it is studied in isolation from Psellos' similar views.

A considerable diversion from the generally accepted views

Commenting on Aristotle's phrase that 'every' (πᾶς) does not signify the universal but that it is taken universally,[76] Psellos' text differs from that of the previous commentators in a significant point. Stephanus' comments on the subject,[77] which closely follow the corresponding passage in Ammonius' commentary (*in De interp.* 100. 30–101. 9), suggest that 'every' does not indicate something universal; it rather indicates that the assertion about the thing signified by the universal term 'man' is made universally, that is to say, it is made about every item of which the universal term can be predicated. Psellos, on the other hand, points out that 'every' indicates neither the universal nature which is 'before the many' (πρὸ τῶν πολλῶν), nor the universal nature which is 'in the many' (ἐν τοῖς πολλοῖς), but every individual.[78]

---

[76] *De interp.* 17ᵇ11–12: τὸ γὰρ πᾶς οὐ τὸ καθόλου σημαίνει ἀλλ' ὅτι καθόλου.

[77] Stephanus, *in De interp.* 28. 38–29. 8: ἐλλειπῶς αὐτῷ τὰ τῆς φράσεως εἴρηται· τὸ δὲ ὅλον τοῦτό ἐστιν· ὁ πᾶς προσδιορισμὸς ἢ ὁ οὐδεὶς οὐ σημαίνει [γὰρ] καθολικήν τινα φύσιν ὥσπερ ἄνθρωπος, ἀλλὰ τὴν τοιάνδε σχέσιν σημαίνει τοῦ κατηγορουμένου πρὸς τὸ ὑποκείμενον. οἷον πᾶς ἄνθρωπος βαδίζει ἐν τούτῳ σημαίνει μοι τὸ πᾶς ὅτι καθόλου ὄντος τοῦ ὑποκειμένου ἤγουν τοῦ ἀνθρώπου τὸ βαδίζειν πᾶσιν τοῖς ὑπὸ τὸν ἄνθρωπον οὖσιν ἀτόμοις ὑπάρχει. ἔστι τοίνυν τὸ ὅλον τοῦτο ὅτι τὸ πᾶς οὐ σημαίνει τινα καθολικὴν φύσιν ὡς τὸ ἄνθρωπος, ἀλλ' ὅτι καθόλου ὄντος τοῦ ὑποκειμένου σημαίνει τὸ κατηγορούμενον ὑπάρχειν πᾶσι τοῖς ὑπὸ τὸ ὑποκείμενον τελοῦσιν.

[78] *in De interp.* 10. 19–27: ὁ κατὰ μὲν τοὺς Πλατωνικοὺς οὕτω νοητέον, ὅτι οὐ μερικὴν οὖσαν τὴν ἄνθρωπος φωνὴν προστεθὲν τὸ πᾶς καθόλου ἐποίησεν, ἀλλὰ καθόλου τυγχάνουσαν ἐσήμανεν αὐτὴν ὅτι καθόλου· καθ' ἡμᾶς δὲ οὕτως. ὅτι οὐ χρὴ κατὰ τὸν Πλάτωνα τὸν πᾶς προσδιορισμὸν τοῦ διωρισμένου ποσοῦ τυγχάνοντα καὶ ἐπὶ πλήθους λεγόμενον, τῇ τοῦ ἀνθρώπου προσάπτειν ἰδέᾳ τῇ ἑνιαίᾳ καὶ μοναδικῇ· πῶς γὰρ ἂν πρόσρημα πλήθους σημαντικὸν ἑνικὴν σημανεῖ φύσιν; διὰ ταῦτα τοιγαροῦν τὸ πᾶς οὐ

But what does Psellos have in mind when he brings into the discussion the distinction between a universal nature 'before the many' and 'in the many'? There is no doubt that the technical terminology in this passage refers to a subject which was much discussed by Aristotle's commentators both in antiquity as well as in medieval times; namely, the problem of whether or not universals exist independently of individuals. For after Porphyry's well-known presentation of the problem of universals (*Isag.* 1. 9–14), every commentator writing on his work discusses the same issue.[79] In particular, Ammonius (*in Porph. Isag.* 39. 9–10) accepts all three kinds of universals, namely the universals πρὸ τῶν πολλῶν, or what would later be called *universalia ante res*, and are generally identified with the Platonic Ideas, the universals ἐν τοῖς πολλοῖς, or *universalia in rebus*, which represent Aristotle's notion of the ἔνυλον εἶδος, and the universals ἐπὶ τοῖς πολλοῖς, or *universalia post res*, which are universal concepts acquired by our mind through abstraction from the characteristics of the particulars.

It has been argued that Ammonius' attempt to reconcile the views of the ancient philosophers on the issue of universals is followed in Byzantium by scholars like, for instance, Photios, John Italos, and Nikephoros Blemmydes.[80] It is not my task, here, to comment on the extremely complicated issue of universals in Byzantium, but I think it does not do justice to our sources to claim that, in general, Byzantine scholars always accept the view propounded by the Neoplatonic commentators. For it seems to me that Psellos may provide us with a case in which a Byzantine scholar simply does not follow the Neoplatonic doctrine on the problem of universals. That is to say, the above passage from his paraphrasis implies that Psellos does not believe in the universal nature πρὸ τῶν πολλῶν or in the universal nature ἐν τοῖς πολλοῖς, but he claims that all there is are the individuals; in other words, Psellos rejects here not only the Platonic Ideas, but also the Aristotelian doctrine of immanent universals. However, in order to be sure of fully comprehending Psellos' own thesis, we would also need to closely analyse his other works on the subject, and in particular his brief treatise Περὶ τῶν ἰδεῶν, ἅς ὁ Πλάτων λέγει (*Phil. min. II*, op. 33), in which he adopts the view that universals are God's thoughts. Is it then that Psellos believes that, apart from God's Ideas, there are no other universals but only individuals? At this point, I should suspend judgement; the text in Psellos' paraphrasis is very brief and is not supposed to be discussing the problem of universals.

τὴν καθόλου φύσιν ἐκείνην σημαίνει τὴν πρὸ τῶν πολλῶν, ἀλλὰ μὴν οὐδὲ τὴν ἐν τοῖς πολλοῖς, ἀλλ᾿ αὐτὰ τὰ σύμπαντα ἄτομα · ἅ καὶ αὐτὰ εἰκότως καθόλου λέγοιτ ᾿ ἄν τοῖς καθέκαστον παραβαλλόμενα · διὰ τοῦτο τὸ πᾶς οὐ μίαν μοναδικὴν φύσιν δηλοῖ, ἀλλὰ τὰ ὑπ᾿ ἐκείνην τὴν φύσιν ἄτομα.

[79] Elias, *in Porph. Isag.* 45. 26–7; David, *in Porph. Isag.* 113. 11–12; Olympiodorus, *Prol.* 19. 30–1.

[80] Benakis (1978–9).

Nevertheless, it becomes clear that Psellos objects in his paraphrasis to what is regarded as the Aristotelian view, and maybe presents his own understanding of the subject. That is to say, Psellos does not always follow the ancient commentators in their attempt to bridge the gap between the doctrines of the ancient philosophers, but he decides to distance himself from the work both of Plato and of Aristotle. In this respect, he is not aiming to interpret the Aristotelian text; instead, he uses a particular point in Aristotle's work as an opportunity to hint at his own views on the subject.

To conclude, this brief study of some of the features of Psellos' work on Aristotle's *De interpretatione* gives us a taste of yet another phase in the long tradition of commentaries on Aristotle's logic, that of the Byzantine scholia. Moreover, investigating the form and content of these late commentaries helps us trace the general changes which the commentator's art has undergone during a period of at least ten centuries. Early on, Alexander of Aphrodisias takes a scholarly approach, since he writes for readers who are quite knowledgeable about logical matters; he is interested in illuminating the subtleties of the Aristotelian text, in responding to its critics, and in incorporating the further logical developments in order to present Aristotle's logic as the best logical system. Later on, Ammonius no doubt preserves the scholarly approach, but being a Neoplatonist he often attempts to reconcile the Platonic and Aristotelian doctrines; this takes him some distance from Aristotle, although it is still the Aristotelian text which he tries to interpret as closely as possible. By the time Psellos composes his paraphrasis, however, there is certainly a stress on the teaching purpose of commentaries, which greatly influences their characteristics; most importantly, it seems that the distance from the Aristotelian text becomes such that it does permit interpretations which are no longer close to Aristotle's views. It may be said, therefore, that during this last phase the commentaries on Aristotle's *Organon* are also used as the place where Byzantine scholars present their own ideas, a practice which later becomes more conspicuous in the Western tradition. And it is exactly these ideas that deserve to be brought to light, by closely examining the logical works of Psellos as well as of the other Byzantine commentators on Aristotle's logic.

BIBLIOGRAPHY

A. TEXTS

Allatius, Leo, *De Psellis et eorum scriptis*, ed. J.-P. Migne (*PG* 122; Paris).

Ammonius, *In Aristotelis De interpretatione commentarius*, ed. A. Busse (*CAG* 4/5; Berlin, 1897).

—— *In Porphyrii Isagogen*, ed. A. Busse (*CAG* 4/3; Berlin, 1891).

Anonymus, *In Aristotelis De interpretatione commentarius*, ed. L. Tarán (Meisenheim am Glan, 1978).

Aristotle, *Categoriae et De interpretatione*, ed. L. Minio-Paluello (Oxford, 1949).

—— *Analytica priora et posteriora*, ed. W. D. Ross and L. Minio-Paluello (Oxford, 1964).

David, *In Porphyrii Isagogen commentarium*, ed. A. Busse (*CAG* 18/1; Berlin, 1900).

Dionysius Thrax, *Ars grammatica*, ed. G. Uhlig (Leipzig, 1883).

Elias, *In Porphyrii Isagogen et Aristotelis Categorias commentaria*, ed. A. Busse (*CAG* 18/1; Berlin, 1900).

George Choiroboskos, *Scholia in Theodosii Canones nominales*, ed. A. Hilgard (Leipzig, 1894).

—— *Scholia in Theodosii Canones verbales*, ed. A. Hilgard (Leipzig, 1894).

Leo Magentinos, *In Aristotelis De interpretatione commentarius*, ed. A. Manutius (Venice, 1503).

Michael Psellos, *Chronographie*, ed. É. Renauld, i (Paris, 1926).

—— *Historia byzantina et alia opuscula*, in Μεσαιωνικὴ Βιβλιοθήκη, iv, ed. K. N. Sathas (Paris, 1874).

—— *Miscellanea*, in Μεσαιωνικὴ Βιβλιοθήκη, v, ed. K. N. Sathas (Paris, 1876).

—— *Philosophica minora I*, ed. J. M. Duffy (Stuttgart and Leipzig, 1992).

—— *Philosophica minora II*, ed. D. J. O'Meara (Leipzig, 1989).

Olympiodorus, *Prolegomena et in Categorias commentarium*, ed. A. Busse (*CAG* 12/1; Berlin, 1902).

Philoponus, *In Aristotelis Analytica priora*, ed. M. Wallies (*CAG* 13/2–3; Berlin, 1905).

Porphyry, *Isagoge*, ed. A. Busse (*CAG* 4/1; Berlin, 1887).

Scholia in Dionysii Thracis Artem grammaticam, ed. A. Hilgard (Leipzig, 1901).

Sophonias, *In Aristotelis De anima paraphrasis*, ed. M. Hayduck (*CAG* 23/1; Berlin, 1883).

Sophronios, *Excerpta ex Ioannis Characis*, ed. A. Hilgard (Leipzig, 1894).

Stephanus, *In Aristotelis De interpretatione commentarium*, ed. M. Hayduck (*CAG* 18/3; Berlin, 1885).

Themistius, *Analyticorum posteriorum paraphrasis*, ed. M. Wallies (*CAG* 5/1; Berlin, 1900).

Theodosios of Alexandria, *Grammatica*, ed. C. Goettling (Leipzig, 1822).

B. SECONDARY LITERATURE

Benakis, L. (1958–9), 'Η Σύνοψις εἰς τὴν Ἀριστοτέλους Λογικήν καὶ ὁ Μιχαὴλ Ψελλός', Ἑλληνικά, 16: 222–6.

—— (1978–9), 'Τὸ πρόβλημα τῶν γενικῶν ἰδεῶν καὶ ὁ ἐννοιολογικὸς ρεαλισμὸς τῶν Βυζαντινῶν', Φιλοσοφία, 8–9: 311–40.

—— (1987), 'Grundbibliographie zum Aristoteles-Studium in Byzanz', in J. Wiesner (ed.), *Aristoteles. Werk und Wirkung II* (Berlin and New York), 352–79.

Browning, R. (1975), 'Enlightenment and Repression in Byzantium in the Eleventh and Twelfth Centuries', *Past and Present*, 69: 3–23.

Duffy, J. M. (1998), 'Tzetzes on Psellos', in C. F. Collatz, J. Dummer, J. Kollesch, and M.-L. Werlitz, *Dissertatiunculae criticae: Festschrift für Günter Christian Hansen* (Würzburg), 441–5.

Fuchs, F. (1926), *Die Höheren Schulen von Konstantinopel im Mittelalter* (Berlin).

Ierodiakonou, K. (forthcoming), 'Michael Psellos' Scholia on the *Prior Analytics*', in R. Bodéüs and L. Dorion (eds.), *L'Organon d'Aristote et ses commentateurs*.

Roueché, M. (1974), 'Byzantine Philosophical Texts of the Seventh Century', *Jahrbuch der Österreichischen Byzantinistik*, 23: 61–76.

Tatakis, B. N. (1949), *La Philosophie byzantine* (Paris).

Wartelle, A. (1963), *Inventaire des Manuscripts Grecs d'Aristote* (Paris), with R. D. Argyropoulos and I. Caras, *Supplement* (Paris, 1980).

Zervos, C. (1920), *Michel Psellos: Un philosophe néoplatonicien du XIe siècle* (Paris).

8

'To Every Argument there is a Counter-Argument': Theodore Metochites' Defence of Scepticism (*Semeiosis* 61)

BÖRJE BYDÉN

I

The ontological and epistemological framework of the cogitations set forth in Theodore Metochites' *Semeioseis gnomikai* (*c*.1326)[1] could be described as a rough-hewn Platonist torso with a somewhat mismatched Christian head. On the pattern of the simile of the Divided Line (in Plato's *Republic*), spatio-temporal things are conceived of as somehow flawed representations of the entities of a higher order, which alone are really real and which alone can be truly known. I do not propose to discuss here the ontological status ascribed to these higher-order entities within this framework. What I wish to call attention to is the fact that Metochites, in a number of chapters of the

This chapter was written and first presented in autumn and winter 1997. Since then a major study of Sceptical and anti-Sceptical ideas in 14th-cent. Byzantium has appeared, by Demetracopoulos (1999*a*), including a new critical edn. of Nicholas Kabasilas Chamaetos' *On the Criterion*. The conclusions arrived at by Demetracopoulos are in pretty close agreement with those argued here concerning most of those questions discussed in both places. Demetracopoulos' work is, however, more extensive in bulk as well as in scope, and it contains detailed discussions of a good many points which are only briefly touched upon here. I have added references to some of those discussions in notes. I have also signalled one or two points of some importance where Demetracopoulos and I seem to take divergent views. I would like to express my sincere thanks to those who have read and commented on various drafts of this chapter: the Greek Seminar at Göteborg University in autumn 1997; Beata Agrell; Monika Asztalos; John Demetracopoulos; the anonymous reader of Oxford University Press; Karin Hult; Kimmo Järvinen.

[1] Since the first (and so far only) printed edn., this work has commonly been referred to as the *Miscellanea philosophica et historica*. There are, however, good indications that the author himself entitled it Σημειώσεις γνωμῶν or γνωμικαί. See edn. by Agapitos *et al.* (1996: 21 n. 46).

Semeioseis as well as in other works, emphasizes very strongly the epistemological distinction between the theories of natural philosophy, which, he thinks, are always open to question, and the axioms and theorems of the mathematical sciences, which, he thinks, are not. Metochites opted for a fourfold division of theoretical philosophy, adding logic to the standard Neoplatonic–Aristotelian scheme of natural philosophy, mathematics, and theology or metaphysics.[2] I cannot go into the reasons for the inclusion of logic as a part of philosophy here, but I shall come back to the question of how Metochites envisaged the relation between theology on the one hand and the dichotomy of mathematics and natural philosophy on the other.

The awareness of the imperfections of the material world which Metochites' work reflects may be conspicuous for its depth; yet it is far from being unique in medieval Greek thought.[3] Nor is the pessimistic conclusion at which Metochites arrives concerning our possibilities of ever really knowing anything about the fleeting phenomena of that world. What *is* slightly out of the ordinary is, however, that in chapters 29 (fos. 54^v–56^r = 195–202 MK) and 61 (fos. 110^r–13^v = 370–7 MK) of the *Semeioseis gnomikai* he connects this broadly sceptical outlook with ancient Scepticism. This is the subject I would like to discuss in the present chapter. The first part of it will focus on the relevant Metochites texts. In the second part I shall attempt to situate these in their historical and intellectual context. Let us begin with a summary of *Semeiosis* 61.[4]

The starting-point of this essay is an amplification of a sentence which was probably known to Metochites from Gregory of Nazianzus' *Carmina moralia* (10. 977; 33. 12), but which most of us, I think, would more easily recognize as one of the ancient Sceptical 'slogans': to every argument another argument is opposed.[5] Metochites affirms the truth of this sentence, and he suggests that the Sceptical philosophers (in Metochites' parlance: the 'Ephectics')

---

[2] *Stoicheiosis astronomike* 1. 2, fo. 12^r: τινὲς δέ, καὶ μάλιστα Χρύσιππος καὶ οἱ ἀπὸ τῆς Στοᾶς, καὶ τέταρτον ἕτερον εἶδος τοῦ θεωρητικοῦ προστιθέασι τὸ λογικόν, ὃ τὰς δεικτικὰς μεθόδους ποικίλας καὶ πανστρόφους ἐξετάζει καὶ ἀνευρίσκει καὶ τεχνολογεῖ, θεωρητὸν πάντως ὑποκείμενον ἔχον καὶ αὐτό, ὡς εἴ τι καὶ ἄλλο τῶν ὄντων, καὶ πολλῆς χρῇζον τῆς ἐρεύνης καὶ διευκρινήσεως, ὡς ἄρα τοῦτο καὶ μαρτύρεται τὰ πολλὰ τοῦ Ἀριστοτέλους περὶ τούτου συντάγματα καὶ Θεοφράστου καὶ Χρυσίππου καὶ τῶν ἀπὸ τῆς Στοᾶς. εἰ γὰρ καὶ ὀργανικὴν ἔχει τὴν χρείαν, καὶ ὑπηρετικὴν εἰς τὰς ἁπάσας καθάπαξ θεωρίας, ἀλλ' οὖν καὶ αὐτὸ θεωρητόν ἐστι καθ' ἑαυτό, καὶ τὴν τῆς φιλοσοφίας καθόλου περὶ πάντα πολυπραγμοσύνην εἰς ἑαυτὸ σὺν τοῖς ἄλλοις ἀναγκάζει καὶ ἐφέλκεται.

[3] Metochites himself admits that his views on these matters are commonplace: *Eth.* 10, 84. 5–15 P. Cf. below, n. 55.

[4] The text of *Sem.* 61 is edited as an appendix to this chapter. In the summary, numbers in brackets refer to lines of this edn.

[5] Cf. Sextus Empiricus, *PH* 1. 202–5; Diogenes Laertius 9. 74–6. The relative fame of this 'slogan', as well as such ones as 'we determine nothing' and 'nothing more', even in Byzantine times, can be gauged from the fact that they are entered and explained in the *Suda* (s.v. οὐδὲν μᾶλλον (3: 578. 9–29 A)).

should therefore not be dismissed as mere controversialists but deserve serious attention (1–13). In fact, he says, the Sceptics often have a valid point,

and many things are indeed of such a nature as to be ambiguous and to leave room for contrary opinions and arguments, so that [people] of course also debate [them] vehemently; and to be wholly convinced, or indeed to disbelieve both [opinions], is not easy, but whichever one embraces, it is again possible to feel worries about the [arguments] on the other side, and to waver and be at a loss. The absence of confidence and certitude is great on these subjects, a condition of ignorance and non-apprehension prevailing of necessity. (13–21)

Metochites then goes on to add credentials on the Sceptics' behalf. Apparently, he says, no less respectable a philosopher than Plato laid the foundations of their non-apprehension doctrine, namely, in those dialogues in which a series of propositions are reviewed and demonstrated false. The only conclusion ever reached in them is indeed the Sceptical view that there is no irrefutable opinion among men (22–42). Similarly Socrates, who introduced Plato to philosophy, spent his whole life convicting those who were held in esteem on account of their knowledge of really having no knowledge at all (least of all of the fact that they did not). All his efforts were directed towards revealing ignorance, on the assumption that the value of what men regard as knowledge is only apparent (43–58). This, Metochites explains, was the source of Scepticism and a sort of preparation for the universal war which the Sceptics have since waged against all human claims to knowledge and all sorts of doctrines. In many people's view their struggle has been successful, and many have espoused their cause, even up to the present moment, seeing that nothing is stable in being or in knowledge and that every kind of philosophical enquiry tends to fall into severe difficulties (59–73).

The sole exception, Metochites continues, is the knowledge of God and things divine, obtained through inspiration from above. It cannot be obtained through deduction, for even on theological matters conclusions drawn in this manner are vulnerable, and theologians are often seen to dispute over dogmas arrived at by means of demonstration. Only revelation stands the test (73–86). In contrast, all human views on matters pertaining to natural philosophy, ethics, and arts can be and are in fact often and with reason contradicted. Thus philosophers contradict each other as well as themselves. So do doctors and orators of every kind, and, on the whole, practitioners of every art, albeit more seldom the greater the mechanical component of the art (87–117). In sum, Metochites concludes, there are few things in the world that do not give rise to much uncertainty and doubt and that do not give occasion to a sceptical attitude, that is, to arguing on both sides and asserting universal ignorance (118–24).

So far *Semeiosis* 61. The issues I wish to discuss in this part of the chapter are the following. First, what view on knowledge and being is Metochites here referring to as 'Scepticism'? Second, Metochites seems to think that this view is justified within certain theoretical domains. Which ones and why these? Thirdly I will touch on the question of Metochites' sources. These three questions open out into the wider one to which the second part of the chapter will be devoted, namely, that of the historical and intellectual context into which Metochites' account of Scepticism should be fitted.[6]

To begin, then, with the nature of the view that Metochites calls Scepticism, it is evident that he does not maintain a clear-cut distinction, such as a Sceptic of Sextus Empiricus' stamp would insist on, between Scepticism in a strict and proper sense and a position better characterized as negative dogmatism. Strict Scepticism according to Sextus (*PH* 1. 1–14) means withholding assent to any philosophical opinion, whether positive or negative, including the view that nothing can be known. Metochites rather seems to connect the ancient Sceptics with the view that the nature of things is such as not to allow statements or beliefs about them to be true or false. He also seems to some extent willing to espouse this view himself. Following R. J. Hankinson (1995: 13–17), we may label it 'negative ontological dogmatism'. This being equivalent to the denial of one or both of the laws of non-contradiction and the excluded middle, the label is applicable (for more or less restricted domains) to philosophers like Heraclitus, Anaxagoras, Protagoras, and others.[7] On balance, the conflicting evidence seems to bespeak some such position also for Pyrrho (although caution is called for), who was in that case not a Sceptic in the Sextan strict and proper sense.[8] Granted that (factual) knowledge is some kind of true belief, 'negative epistemological dogmatism' (the view that knowledge is not possible) is a trivial consequence of negative ontological dogmatism. On the other hand, negative epistemological dogmatism does not entail negative ontological dogmatism (unless we also assume a global principle of realism).[9] Thus, the Academic Sceptics, as opposed to Pyrrho himself as well as to the later Pyrrhonists, apparently would not rule out the possibility that some statements about the world might be true and others false ('ontological scepticism'),[10] but if we should trust

---

[6] There is now a discussion of *Sem.* 61 and its context resting on a set of presuppositions that differs from mine in Tambrun-Krasker (1998: 287–9).

[7] At least if we take Aristotle's testimonies in *Met.* 4. 4–8, 1012^{a}24–6 (Heraclitus); 1012^{a}26–8; 1007^{b}25–1008^{a}2 (Anaxagoras); 1007^{b}18–25; 1009^{a}6–15 (Protagoras), at face value.

[8] According to Timo according to Aristocles *apud* Eusebium (*Praep. evan.* 14. 18. 3), Pyrrho argued 'realistically' (see below) from a 'negative dogmatist' thesis about the nature of things to the conclusion that we should suspend judgement on them (the word ἐπέχειν or cognates do not occur). See the discussion of this vexed passage in Bett (1994: 141–3, 166–70).

[9] I understand by 'global realism' in this context the ideal view that any given type of mental/intentional state (e.g. sight, knowledge, ignorance) depends ontologically on a corresponding type of independent object (visible, knowable, unknowable).

[10] So Hankinson (1995: 16), who gives no reference, but may be thinking of Cicero, *Acad.* 2. 73: 'nos, qui veri esse aliquid non negamus, percipi posse negamus'.

Sextus Empiricus they stuck to the dogmatic view that we can never know for certain which is which.[11]

Negative dogmatism involves self-referential paradoxes; Scepticism in the strict and proper sense does not. This point was underlined by Aeneside-mus,[12] the Academic defector[13] and founder of the Pyrrhonist movement, on behalf of which Sextus later applied the Scepticism–dogmatism distinction against a number of competing philosophers. Some of our other evidence for the epistemology of the New Academy (e.g. Cicero, *Acad*. 1. 45, 2. 7, 28) is, however, difficult to square with Sextus' allegations of negative dogmatism, and the incredulous reader might indeed, as Gisela Striker notes, 'be inclined to think that the Pyrrhonists' attempt at demarcating themselves was more a matter of school politics than of differences in content' (1996: 136). However that may be, the two schools sometimes seem to have been lumped together under one heading in non-Sceptical writers of late antiquity: Hippolytus of Rome even thinks fit to make Pyrrho the founder of the Academic school (*Ref*. 1. 23). These writers (among whom I reckon some Neoplatonic com-mentators on Aristotle to which I shall return below) also tend to ignore the consistency claims of Pyrrhonists and (as described by Cicero) Academics alike, with the result that the Sceptics' position is normally described in terms of negative dogmatism (and so refuted as self-contradictory). It may be useful to bear this in mind later as we enquire into the sources for Metochites' account.

I shall call arguments for epistemological positions from premises bearing on the nature of things rather than on the nature of human knowledge itself 'realistic' arguments.[14] That Metochites understood ancient Scepticism as negative dogmatism founded first and foremost on such 'realistic' arguments is well brought out, for example, in a passage of *Semeiosis* 29 (fo. 55^r = 197 MK), where he expresses his approval of the idea (which he ascribes to both the Sceptics and Heraclitus) that it is possible to hold contrary opinions of the same subject. The universal disagreement on all things human, he explains, might be due in part to the fact that we ourselves are 'fickle by nature and flowing in our assumptions', but the chief and principal reason is that the objects that we judge are open to different views, being indeterminate by nature. In sum, then, I would submit that the version of 'scepticism' discussed and defended by Metochites in these texts amounts to the negative dogmatist view that there exist things the nature of which is indeterminate as regards truth and falsity, and of which knowledge is for that reason impossible.

---

[11]   *PH* 1. 3; 1. 226; cf. Aulus Gellius, *Noct. Att*. 11. 5. 8.

[12]   In Photios, *Bibl*. 212, 170^{a}22–38; cf. Sextus Empiricus, *PH* 1. 14–15; 1. 226.

[13]   Assuming the traditional interpretation of Photios, *Bibl*. 212, 169^{b}33 (challenged by De-cleva Caizzi 1992) to be correct. Cf. Demetracopoulos (1999*b*: 360–2).

[14]   The 'global realist' (see n. 9 above) arguing for an epistemological position will be referred exclusively to arguments from ontological premises; but 'partial realists' and 'non-realists' may also avail themselves of such arguments. Such arguments, then, are 'realistic' not in the sense that they presuppose 'realism' but in the sense that they will most typically be used by a 'realist'.

What kind of things? It is clear from numerous passages in which Metochites alludes to the state of flux prevailing in the realms of natural phenomena and human affairs that the domain over which he extends his scepticism (as I will continue to call it for convenience) includes what a modern philosopher describes as '[f]actual knowledge relating to descriptive information regarding the contents of the natural universe and their modes of operation (specifically including man and his works)'.[15] So far an orthodox Platonist might well agree with our Byzantine sceptic. But the Platonist would of course proceed to establish the possibility of knowledge through the introduction of intelligible Forms. Metochites, on the other hand, gives no hint in those texts in which ancient Scepticism is defended (*Sem.* 61 and 29) that there might be some other theoretical domain in which we *can* attain knowledge (at least not by our own efforts: I shall come back shortly to the special case of theology). This is all the more surprising since, as I said at the beginning, the epistemological contrast of natural philosophy and mathematics is a standing theme throughout the *Semeioseis gnomikai.* Chapters 22 and 23 are wholly given over to a comparison of the two branches of knowledge, in which it is maintained that while the principles of natural philosophy leave ample room for divergent views there are in fact no disagreements on mathematical subjects. There is no other reason for this, says Metochites,

than the stability and simplicity of the things that form the subject-matter of this enquiry. For concerning that which is one and always the same and never changing in any way whatsoever ... the correct apprehension too is altogether the same and not in the least of such a nature as to be ambiguous, as is the case with things in the realm of Nature and Becoming, which are ever flowing and changing into the opposite and at the same time force the accounts of them to change with them, and make possible opposite views about them. This, however, is not the case with the objects of the science of mathematics ... (*Sem.* 22, fo. 44^{r-v} = 161–2 MK).[16]

In *Semeiosis* 61, mathematics is left out of account. Why? The simplest answer seems to be to refer to rhetorical common sense. Assuming that Metochites' principal aim is to drive home the thesis stated in the chapter heading ('The views of the Sceptics seem not to be wholly unreasonable'), why should he even bother to enter into the differentiation between the

---

[15] Rescher (1980: 1).

[16] Cf. *Sem.* 7, fo. 14^{r-v} = 161–2 MK; *Stoicheiosis astronomike* 1. 2, fo. 12^r: τὸ δὲ θεωρητικὸν ὑποδιαιρεῖται εἴς τε τὰ ἀνωτάτω καὶ πρῶτα κατὰ φύσιν, μᾶλλον δὲ ὑπὲρ φύσιν καὶ θεῖα, εἰς αὐτὸ δηλαδὴ τὸ θεολογικόν, καὶ εἰς τὰ τούτων ἑξῆς, ἃ καὶ αὐτὰ διχῇ τέμνεται, εἴς τε τὰ μετὰ τῆς ὕλης πρῶτον ὁρώμενα χειραγωγούσης δι' αἰσθήσεως εἰς τοὺς ἐπιλογισμοὺς καὶ τὰ συμπεράσματα τῆς διανοίας, εἶτα κατ' αὐτὴν δὴ τὴν διάνοιαν τῆς ὕλης ἀποτεμνόμενα καὶ ἐλευθερούμενα καὶ χωριζόμενα ἄφθαρτά πως καὶ ἀεὶ ὡσαύτως ἔχοντα καὶ μένοντα τὸν τρόπον τοῦτον τῇ διανοίᾳ καὶ τοῖς κατ' αὐτὴν ἐντὸς κριτηρίοις καὶ ταμείοις ἀμετάβλητα, καθ' ἃ οὐσιοῦται εἴδη ὄντως ἐπιστητὰ μόνα καὶ δευτέραν εἰληχότα τάξιν, μετὰ τὰ πρῶτα καὶ ὑπὲρ ἐπιστήμην ὄντα καὶ διάνοιαν ἁπλᾶ καὶ ἀσυλλόγιστα καὶ μόνον νοητὰ θεῖα, ἃ δὴ δεύτερα εἴδη καὶ κατὰ καιρὸν ἐξ ἀφαιρέσεως οὕτω πως καλοῦσιν οἱ μαθηματικοί, ἔτι δὲ καὶ εἰς τὰ κατὰ φύσιν διοικούμενα καὶ μετὰ τῆς ὕλης ἀχώριστα αἰεὶ καὶ ῥέοντα καὶ μεταβάλλοντα διόλου καὶ ὑπὸ γένεσιν ὄντα καὶ φθοράν.

realms of opinion and science, which would only complicate things and place restrictions on the thesis? If this explanation is right, that is, if mathematics is left out of *Sem.* 61 for purely rhetorical reasons, then it seems that, apart from the fact that the ancient Sceptics are mentioned, Metochites' defence of Scepticism really comes down to a restatement of one of the basic assumptions of his standard Christian Platonism (what we might label its 'Heraclitean element'). The crux of the matter is then what made Metochites associate this specifically with the Sceptics.

Theology, now that's another thing. It could well be argued that the reservations that Metochites expresses on this point should be seen as the kind of clarifications called for in order to prevent his defence of Scepticism from becoming an offence against Orthodoxy. In contrast to the case of mathematics, then, the argument would go, he could not have left that out even if he had wanted to. The question as to the relation between Metochites' scepticism and his views on theology is undoubtedly one of particular concern. As is well known, the revival of interest in ancient Scepticism in the Renaissance was to a large extent bound up with the attempts of Catholic thinkers like Erasmus and Montaigne to meet the challenge of Reformation with more or less well-reasoned versions of Sceptical Fideism.[17] The classic Sceptical approach to religion is the one delineated by Sextus Empiricus. The premisses are that there is a multitude of different views on the gods and that there is no criterion by which we are enabled to choose between them. The practical conclusion is, in Sextus' words, to 'follow without doctrinal belief the common course of life and ... say that there are gods, and ... reverence gods and ascribe to them foreknowledge'.[18] This approach is sometimes referred to as 'Conformist Fideism'.[19]

Does Metochites share it? He does point out that there are divergent views on theological questions too. But the conclusion he draws is not that we should refrain from doctrinal belief. The reason is not too hard to guess. In this domain, we must assume, we have to do with Truth *par excellence*. And truth is essentially one and simple (cf. *Sem.* 61. 103–4). Within the realm of divinities, therefore, it is not the indeterminate nature of the entities themselves which gives rise to different views: the root of the differentiation must lie in the nature of the beholders.[20] So the 'realistic' argument pattern must be abandoned. Inasmuch, then, as (*a*) Metochites' negative epistemological dogmatism depends on the ontological premiss that the relevant objects are in themselves indeterminate as to truth and falsity, and (*b*) divine objects are not

---

[17] The subject of Scepticism and Fideism is extensively treated in Penelhum (1983*a*, 1983*b*).

[18] *PH* 3. 2 (tr. Mates 1996: 173).

[19] The term is introduced by Penelhum (1983*a*: 15).

[20] Metochites elsewhere describes the objects of theology as 'simple and non-deducible and only intelligible, above scientific knowledge and discursive thought' (*Stoicheiosis astronomike* 1. 2, fo. 12ʳ: τὰ πρῶτα καὶ ὑπὲρ ἐπιστήμην ὄντα καὶ διάνοιαν ἁπλᾶ καὶ ἀσυλλόγιστα καὶ μόνον νοητὰ θεῖα; see above, n. 16, for context).

indeterminate as to truth and falsity, it follows that (*c*) theology falls outside the scope of Metochites' negative epistemological dogmatism. Factual knowledge of God and his workings is accessible to whomever so wishes, embodied in Holy Writ and in the writings of the Fathers. At the same time, it is clear that Metochites does embrace a form of Fideism, in the sense that he discards the possibility of establishing theological truths by scientific proof (in this respect he seems to come quite close to the positions adopted later, in the Hesychast debate, by Barlaam of Calabria and Nikephoros Gregoras).[21] Scientific knowledge of God's nature (the 'what' and the 'wherefore') is not to be sought: the truth about God and his workings and the certitude that comes with the apprehension of that truth are not attainable except through divine revelation. Something along those lines, I think, must be Metochites' position. I also take it to be fairly normal in Orthodox Christianity.[22]

Turning now to the sources for Metochites' knowledge of ancient Scepticism, I should state to begin with that I cannot find anything in his account that could only derive from the single self-declared Sceptical source surviving in Greek, in the fourteenth century as in the twenty-first, namely, Sextus Empiricus.[23] Moreover, Metochites keeps silent on a number of features of Scepticism emphasized in Sextus (such as the ethical goal and the dissociation from negative dogmatism), and he subscribes to a view opposed to that of Sextus concerning the relatedness of Plato and the Sceptics (and we might add Heraclitus and the Sceptics).[24] Considering the fact that only one of the Greek Sextus MSS surviving today dates from before Metochites' death (Laur. gr. 85, 19: see below, n. 64), the chances are, I conclude, that Metochites had not read Sextus. Nor have I found any clear indications of his

---

[21] It is, Metochites implies, here and elsewhere, the reliance on discursive thought which is to blame for heterodoxy. Cf. *Eth.* 7, 70. 18–72. 15 P; *Stoicheiosis astronomike* 1.2, fo. 12ᵛ: τὸ μὲν θεολογικὸν τοῖς πάλαι τῶν Ἑλλήνων φιλοσόφοις ἐκ τῶν οἴκοθεν αὐτοῖς λογισμῶν σπουδασθέν, καὶ μὴ ἐκ προλήψεων καὶ θέσεων ἐνθέων, ὡς εἰπεῖν, καὶ τὸ πεφυκὸς καὶ προσῆκον ἐχουσῶν—ἢ καὶ μετὰ προλήψεων ἴσως καὶ θέσεων ἐστιν οἷς ἀλλοτριωτάτων καὶ παντάπασιν ἀποξενωμένων τῶν δικαίων τῆς θείας φύσεως, εὐέλεγκτόν ἐστι κατ' αὐτοὺς καὶ δῆλον ἀτευκτοῦν καθάπαξ τοῖς γε δὴ σώφροσι καὶ νοῦν ἔχουσι τοῦ προτεθειμένου σκοποῦ. ἡμῖν δὲ τοῖς ἀπ' αὐτοῦ τοῦ Θεοῦ καὶ θείων ἀνδρῶν δι' αὐτοῦ καὶ τῆς ἐξ αὐτοῦ φωταυγείας καὶ ἐπιλάμψεως μυσταγωγηθέντων καὶ τελεσθέντων τὰ θεῖα διδαχθεῖσι καὶ διαδεξαμένοις τὰς περὶ τῶν θείων ἀσφαλεῖς καθόλου πρώτας ἀρχὰς καὶ ὑποθέσεις τε καὶ προλήψεις οὐ μόνον ἐστιν ἐκεῖθεν ἔπειθ' οὕτω ῥᾳδίως τε ἅμα καὶ ἀπλανῶς ἐπιτυγχάνειν τῆς θεολογικῆς σοφίας καὶ θεωρίας, ἀλλὰ καὶ ἀκινδύνως εὖ μάλα· ὡς τό γε ἀποτυγχάνειν ἐν τοῖς τοιούτοις, καὶ τῆς ἀληθείας καὶ τῶν ὄντων ἔκτοπα καὶ φρονεῖν καὶ τίθεσθαι καὶ λέγειν, πρᾶγμα πάντων ἐπικινδυνότατον.

[22] It should be noted in this connection that the equipollence slogan which provides the starting-point of *Semeiosis* 61 was used by Gregory of Nazianzus with precisely the application of discursive thought to theological problems in mind: 'Reasoning is of little avail for the knowledge of God: for every argument is opposed by an argument' (*Carm. mor.* 10. 976–7).

[23] Metochites' description of the Sceptics' attitude in the final clause of the chapter bears some superficial resemblance to *PH* 1. 8, but certainly not enough to warrant any conclusions about his dependence on it.

[24] Sextus vigorously repudiates the philosophy of Plato in *PH* 1. 221–5, and that of Heraclitus in *PH* 1. 210–12.

having been familiar with the *Life of Pyrrho* by Diogenes Laertius (9. 61–108) or the summary of Aenesidemus' *Pyrrhonian Discourses* in Photios' *Bibliotheca*.

The *loci classici* for discussions of the epistemological implications of negative ontological dogmatism are in Plato's *Theaetetus* and Aristotle's *Metaphysics* 4. These discussions are brought into the context of Scepticism in some of the Neoplatonic prolegomena to Aristotle. The first of ten questions addressed in the introductions to the Neoplatonic commentaries on the *Categories* has to do with the different principles on which the different philosophical schools have been named, among them the Ephectics, who are said to derive their name from the way they have of judging things (or rather of *not* judging things: *epechein*).[25] Some commentators avail themselves of the chance to refute the Sceptical 'non-apprehension' slogan (Sextus Empiricus, *PH* 1. 200) with a two-part argument claimed to originate from Plato (it is found also in Aristocles, *apud* Eusebium, *Praep. evan.* 14. 18. 11. 4–5 and 12. 5–7, and variants of it recur here and there in Sextus Empiricus);[26] a couple of them also indulge in a few crumbs of doxography.[27]

The refutation of the non-apprehension slogan ascribed to Plato turns, for its first part, on a self-referential paradox: if the Sceptic claims to know that nothing can be known, he must admit that there is knowledge.[28] On the other hand (this is the second part), if he does not claim to know it, why should we believe it?[29] The argument for non-apprehension ascribed by Ammonius and Olympiodorus to the Sceptics runs as follows. Apprehension implies correspondence between the knower and the known. Correspondence between the knower and the known implies that either the known is not changing or the knower is able to adapt to the known when the known is changing. But

[25] ἀπὸ τοῦ τρόπου τῆς ἐν τῷ φιλοσοφεῖν διακρίσεως, Ammonius, *in Cat.* 2. 8–9; cf. Olympiodorus, *Proleg.* 3. 30–2; Philoponus, *in Cat.* 2. 3–4; Simplicius, *in Cat.* 4. 4–5; Elias [?David], *in Cat.* 109. 24. Cf. [Herennius], *in Met.* 518. 9 M: ἀπὸ τοῦ τρόπου τῆς διαλέξεως.

[26] Sextus Empiricus, *PH* 1. 122; 2. 85; 185; *M* 7. 440; 8. 463–5.

[27] Ammonius, *in Cat.* 2. 17–3. 8; Olympiodorus, *Proleg.* 4. 20–5. 6. The argument for non-apprehension also appears as one of four arguments against the existence of philosophy reported and refuted by David, *Proleg.* 3. 32–4. 35; those who 'attempt to refute the existence of philosophy' are identified at 8. 25 as 'the Pyrrhonians,' and refuted over again with the 'Platonic *peritrope*' (see n. 28). I am grateful to Prof. D. J. O'Meara for the reference to David.

[28] As Elias [?David] suggests (*in Cat.* 109. 32), this argument, which is relevant only to a negative dogmatist position on knowledge, probably derives from the *peritrope* against Protagoras in Plato's *Theaetetus* (170 A–171 C). The argument, as one may recall, is as follows: (1) If it seems to someone that *p*, then *p* (= Socrates' interpretation of Protagoras' thesis). (2) It seems to someone that it is not the case that (1). ∴ It is not the case that (1). Like the first part of Aristocles' and the Neoplatonists' argument against the Sceptics, then, this is a semantic paradox.

[29] This part of the argument, which seems to be designed to take the edge off 'strict' Pyrrhonian Scepticism, is not a semantic paradox: (1) No statement is known to be true. (2) (1) is a statement. ∴ (1) is not known to be true. (1) may well be true without being known to be true. The point is rather that if (1) is not known to be true it cannot be asserted with good reason, and therefore does not deserve to be taken seriously (needless to say, from the Sceptic's own viewpoint this is irrelevant, since no Pyrrhonian Sceptic would ever hope to attain more than an equipollence of reasons pro and contra any statement).

the known is constantly changing and the knower is unable to follow it. Therefore there can be no apprehension. To this Ammonius and Olympiodorus reply that while it is true that everything is in flux, as Heraclitus and Cratylus agreed, it is not the case that the human soul is unable to move along with it.[30] Plato has proved, Ammonius avers, that the souls of good people are more than capable of keeping in pace with the changes of things: they anticipate them. The Neoplatonists' disapproval of the assumption that the subject of knowledge is somehow destined to be outrun by the object is not to be found in Metochites. But the 'realistic' argument (see above) ascribed to the Sceptics in these introductions and the language in which it is couched do have much in common with Metochites' account.[31]

So I am convinced that one or other of the commentators has had an influence on the latter. But there are elements in it that do not originate from these texts. Metochites' favourable attitude is one such element. As Ilsetraut Hadot notes (Simplicius, *Commentaire*, tr. 1990: 60), the Sceptics have a rougher handling than all other philosophical schools in these introductions, including the Epicureans and the Cynics. Indeed most ancient Greek authors commenting on Scepticism are hostile.[32] But I am thinking in particular of the connection made between Scepticism and the Socratic dialogues of Plato. This connection may at first sight seem fairly commonplace. The notion that Plato was involved in Scepticism was obviously taken seriously enough in late antiquity to provoke response from Platonists and Sceptics alike: thus Elias [?David] (*in Cat.* 110. 12–30) refutes an argument to that conclusion from the use of adverbs and phrases signalling doubt or hesitation.[33] In the anonymous sixth-century *Prolegomena to the Philosophy of Plato* this argument as well as another four to the same conclusion are rehearsed and refuted (10. 1–11. 25). One of these arguments is indeed the proposition, appearing also in *Sem.* 61. 29–31, that Plato is arguing on both sides of the question in some of his dialogues. Unlike Metochites, however, the anonymous prolegomenist concludes that Plato always opts for the true opinion in the end. Similarly

[30] David only concedes that particulars are in flux, while philosophy, of course, is all about universals (*Proleg.* 4. 21–4). He also does not mention Heraclitus and Cratylus in this context.

[31] Similarly, in Hippolytus, *Ref.* 1. 23, the Academic or Pyrrhonian philosophers are said to have introduced non-apprehension of all things, on the ground that neither among intelligibles nor among sensibles is there anything true: 'for the whole of being [they say] is flowing and changing and never remaining in the same place' (8–10 M).

[32] This goes for Numenius and Aristocles *apud* Eusebium (*Praep. evan.* 14. 5–9; 17–21), for Epictetus (1. 5, 1. 27, 2. 20), for Galen, *De optima doctrina*, for the Stoic fragment preserved in Clement of Alexandria (*Strom.* 8. 5. 15. 2–16. 3 = *SVF* ii. 121), as well as for a number of less important testimonia (such as Hermias 15; Agathias 2. 29, 78. 6–79. 30 K). The three exceptions are Sextus Empiricus, Diogenes Laertius (who takes an impartial attitude even if he was not a Sceptic himself), and Plutarch, notably in his *Adversus Colotem*.

[33] We may for our present purposes disregard the anonymous Middle Platonic commentary on the *Theaetetus* (*CPF* 3. 9) partially surviving in a papyrus fragment (PBerol inv. 9782) discovered in 1901, although the discussion in it of the claim that 'Plato was an Academic' is probably historically related to that of the 6th-cent. Neoplatonic prolegomenist. On the whole question of 'Plato Scepticus', see Annas (1992).

Sextus Empiricus attempts to show 'in opposition to Menodotus and Aene-sidemus'[34] that the man who wrote the Socratic dialogues was not an 'apore-tic' but a dogmatist (*PH* 1. 221–2).

The long and the short of it is that there are no surviving ancient Greek sources (pro- or anti-Sceptical) who endorse the view that Plato was a Sceptic (although Diogenes Laertius admits that 'he passes judgement on the things that he apprehends and refutes what is false, but he suspends judgement on the things that are unclear', 3. 52).[35] Nor are there ones holding Plato respon-sible for the views of the New Academy (although Numenius suggests that Plato's mode of presentation, 'inbetween the plain and the concealed', was at the root of the later disagreements over his doctrines: in Eusebius, *Praep. evan.* 14. 5. 7. 1–8).[36] Furthermore, the extant Greek evidence for the fact that the Academic Sceptics claimed Platonic provenance for their views is rather less substantial than one might expect. The most explicit source is Plutarch, and even he does not impute the claim directly to the Academics themselves: 'So far was Arcesilaus from cherishing any reputation for novelty or laying claim to any ancient doctrine as his own, that the sophists of the day accused him of foisting his own views about the suspension of judgement and the impossibility of infallible apprehension on Socrates, Plato, Parmenides, and Heraclitus'.[37] In addition, the so-called Lamprias catalogue of Plutarch's works contains one item (63) 'On the Academy Being One since Plato', which

---

[34] Or, if Natorp's emendation is preferred to that of the standard text, 'in accordance with Menodotus and Aenesidemus'.

[35] Cf. also 9. 71–2, where Plato, Homer, the Seven Sages, Archilochus, Euripides, Xenopha-nes, Zeno of Elea, Democritus, Empedocles, Heraclitus, and Hippocrates are all mentioned as being according to some people Sceptics *avant la lettre*.

[36] To be sure, the Homeric travesty of Aristo of Chius describing Arcesilaus as 'Plato in front, Pyrrho in back, and Diodorus in the middle' is repeated in both Sextus (*PH* 1. 234), Diogenes Laertius (4. 33), and Numenius (in Eusebius, *Praep. evan.* 14. 5. 13). None of them, however, interprets it as meaning that the Scepticism of the New Academy derived from Plato, or even that Arcesilaus claimed that it did. Numenius sees in Arcesilaus the instigator of what he condemns as the 'secession of the Academy from the doctrines of Plato', and takes the 'Plato in front' of Aristo's verse as referring to the fact that Arcesilaus 'adorned some nonsensical babble with the stylistic Forcefulness (δεινότης) of Plato' (Eusebius, *Praep. evan.* 14. 5. 14). Sextus construes the same verse as suggesting that Arcesilaus was a Platonist (as Sextus understands the term: i.e. a dogmatist) in disguise (*PH* 1. 234). Diogenes Laertius makes no other inferences from Aristo's verse than the rather bland one that 'he seems to have admired Plato and possessed his books' (4. 32). (Contrast the interpretation of modern scholars, e.g. Glucker 1978: 35–6: '[The teachings of Arcesilaus] were officially expounded as Platonic; they appeared to Aristo to be identical with those of Pyrrho; while their central core consisted of dialectical arguments learnt at the school of Megara. Thus we find that . . . Arcesilaus himself did lay a claim to being a Platonist first and foremost.') Besides that, Diogenes, too, states that Arcesilaus 'was the first to change the doctrine received from Plato and to make it more eristic through questions and answers' (4. 28). Note also the bewildering account in Socrates Scholasticus (*PG* 67. 297c–300a = 2. 35. 7–9, 150. 20–151. 2 H): 'For because of the sophists, who were then mocking philosophy, [Aristotle] wrote this [i.e. the *Categories*] as an exercise for the young, setting dialectic against the sophists with the help of sophisms. Now the ephectic philosophers, who expound the [doctrines] of Plato and Plotinus, refute the crafty (τεχνικῶς) statements of Aristotle. But Aetius had not had an ephectic teacher and abided in the sophisms of the *Categories*.'

[37] *Adv. Col.* 1121 f–1122 a, tr. Einarson and De Lacy.

probably indicates that Plutarch subscribed to Philo of Larissa's view of the history of the Academy as marked by continuity. The Lamprias catalogue may have been available to Metochites in Marc. gr. 481.[38]

The idea that the Scepticism of Arcesilaus' Academy was inherited from Socrates and Plato is so familiar to us because it is brought up time and again by Philo's Roman sympathizer, Cicero.[39] Strange to say, Metochites' account of the origins of Scepticism bears closer resemblance to some of Cicero's statements on the issue than to any Greek sources that I have been able to trace. There is of course a difference in that Metochites does not suggest (as Cicero did in his *Academica*) that Plato was a Sceptic through and through: his general idea of the latter's philosophical constitution seems to be that he combined Socratic and Pythagorean elements, much like Numenius and Proclus thought.[40] Metochites' rather more modest venture in *Sem.* 61 is, as we have seen, to point to the aporetic character of some of Plato's dialogues and assert as a historical fact that the Sceptics drew inspiration from these texts. He also connects these traits in Plato with the influence of Socratic *elenchos*. Well, even if they have no strict parallels in the surviving ancient Greek literature, these ideas can of course be said to be quite reasonable. No doubt Metochites was widely read in Plato's and, which is perhaps no less important in this connection, in Xenophon's Socratic writings.[41] It should by no means be excluded that he was himself capable of perceiving (perhaps even of exaggerating) the similarities between Socratic dialectic and the methods of the Sceptics. Still it is hard to rid oneself of the supposition that the idea of a historical doctrinal link between Socrates, Plato, and the New Academy must have come to him from somewhere.

Cicero is, however, a highly doubtful source. It is most unlikely that Metochites knew enough Latin to read the originals.[42] The one Ciceronian work that we may presume him to have studied is the *Somnium Scipionis*, which was translated along with Macrobius' commentary by Maximos Pla-

---

[38] On the Marcianus, see Irigoin (1987: p. cccv).

[39] *Acad.* 1. 46 (Plato), *Acad.* 2. 74 (Plato and Socrates); *De oratore* 3. 67 (Plato's Socrates); *De fin.* 2. 2, *De nat. deor.* 1. 11 (Socrates).

[40] Numenius in Eusebius, *Praep. evan.* 14. 5. 9; Proclus, *in Tim.* 1. 7. 17–8. 9 D. Cf. Dicaearchus in Plutarch, *Quaest. conv.* 8. 2, 719 A; Aristotle, *Met.* 1. 6, 987^{a}32–^{b}7.

[41] Note also the pseudo-Xenophontic letter to Aeschines in Eusebius, *Praep. evan.* 14. 12 (the letter is also found in Stobaeus 2. 1. 29, 2. 10. 17–11. 21 W-H).

[42] Very few Byzantine scholars of the Early Palaeologan period (1259–1328) are known to have had even a working knowledge of Latin. If Metochites had had one, we would surely have been told so either by himself or by the historiographers responsible for his biography, and it would surely have been put to use in diplomatic and other political missions. I should point out in this connection that the chances that Cicero's own Greek sources should have been available in the early 14th cent. are infinitesimal. As Nigel Wilson puts it, 'it is clear that after 1204 Byzantine scholars rarely if ever show direct acquaintance with literature that we cannot read today' (1983: 218). Cicero's source for the continuity view of the history of the Academy is probably Philo of Larissa (Cicero, *Acad.* 1. 13). There is no evidence that any work by Philo survived the end of antiquity (the latest sources of fragments and testimonies noted by Mette (1986–7), are Stobaeus and Augustine, none of whom drew directly on a work by Philo).

noudes (d. *c*.1305). But neither of these makes any reference to Scepticism. For all we know, there might have been other translations, which were lost at an early stage of transmission; there is also the possibility that Metochites had discussed these ideas with Planoudes or some other Greek Latinist, or with Greek-speaking Westerners residing in Constantinople. Speculation is as far as we will get by this route. The alternative is to assume that Metochites produced his own account of the origins of Scepticism from inferences which he made, on the strength of his reading in Plato's dialogues, from the ancient Greek sources on Scepticism that he knew; inferences which do not always seem to be warranted by (or even compatible with) the sources themselves. The latter are likely to include either David's prolegomena to the study of philosophy or Ammonius' or Olympiodorus' prolegomena to the study of Aristotle, and maybe also Hippolytus' *Philosophumena* (*Ref.* 1. 23), whose picture of the Academics/Pyrrhonians is rather similar to that of the Ephectics/Pyrrhonians in the Neoplatonic commentators. In order to perceive the similarities between Socratic dialectic and Sceptical (primarily Academic) method Metochites must have read some sufficiently detailed account of the latter: the testimonies in Eusebius, *Praeparatio evangelica* 14 (notably Numenius, but Aristocles is also relevant) are strong candidates. Another likely influence is Plutarch, *Adversus Colotem*. Metochites greatly admired Plutarch, and the latter's authority should have made it easier for him to take a sympathetic attitude towards the Sceptics in spite of the majority view. Plutarch's *Moralia* were collected in the famous editions of Planoudes around the turn of the thirteenth century. *Adversus Colotem* is not, however, included in the edition of 1296 (Cod. Paris. gr. 1671 (A)). The oldest surviving manuscript of it is in fact Paris. gr. 1672 (E), dated to the beginning of the second half of the fourteenth century, but the exemplar of this manuscript was apparently produced soon after Planoudes' death in 1305.[43] Perhaps Metochites had also read some books of Diogenes Laertius (3–4, 9). Also, considering the fact that he connected the Sceptics with Heraclitean negative dogmatism, it seems reasonable to assume that not only book 4 of Aristotle's *Metaphysics*,[44] but also the descriptions of Heraclitus' doctrines in Plato

---

[43] On these Palaeologan MS edns. of the *Moralia* see Irigoin (1987: pp. cclxxi–cclxxxiv). On Metochites, Planoudes, and Plutarch, see Tartaglia (1987: 345–6) and Ševčenko (1975: 41–2 and nn. 170–7). On Planoudes and the Chora monastery see Wendel (1940: 406–10), but note also the divergent view of Constantinides (1982: 68–70). References to a number of essays in *Sem.* 71 (fos. 143ᵛ–150ʳ = 463–81 MK) make it clear that Metochites was extensively read in the *Moralia*. To the indications of his use of Planoudes' edn. adduced by Tartaglia (1987: 345–6) could be added his praise of the spurious *De Homero*, which is found in no other Plutarch MSS of an early enough date than the Planoudean (Kindstrand 1990: p. v).

[44] The ancient commentators connect Aristotle's criticism here with Scepticism, in a looser or a stricter sense. Asclepius (*in Met.* 222. 11–13) explains that it is directed 'against the so-called Ephectics, and [Aristotle] proves that non-apprehension is not the case'; cf. Philoponus, *in An. post.*, 141. 8–11; Olympiodorus, *in Meteor.* 118. 22–6. Syrianus, however (*in Met.* 73. 16–17), correctly distinguishes between 'those who were later to be called Ephectics' and 'those who supplied these arguments before Aristotle'.

(*Theaetetus*, *Cratylus*, and note *Phaedo* 90 B–D) have conditioned Metochites' view of Scepticism. From this, lastly, it is but a small step to extending the connection also to the 'Heraclitean element' looming large in a number of those Platonizing Jewish and Christian authors that made up Metochites' favourite reading. Indeed, the connection was already established, only awaiting discovery, in such passages as Philo of Alexandria, *De ebrietate* 166–205, and those verses by Gregory of Nazianzus (*Carm. mor.* 10. 976–7) to which Metochites probably owed the very opening phrase of *Semeiosis* 61.[45]

II

Let us now proceed to take a look at the *fortuna* of ancient Scepticism in middle and late Byzantium. As is well known, Photios read and summarized a now lost text of Aenesidemus (*Bibl.* 212). While dissociating himself from Aenesidemus' overall enterprise, the learned patriarch acknowledges the value of the work for students of dialectic (he states that Plato has proved the Sceptics' efforts to be futile: I suppose he is thinking of the Neoplatonic introductions to the *Categories*). Photios' summary is rightly held to belong with the primary evidence on Pyrrhonian Scepticism.[46] But apart from it the whole period right up to the beginning of the fourteenth century shows only very superficial and fragmentary knowledge of the ancient Sceptics. The most substantial information to be found is in the *Suda*, which reproduces (second-hand) an amount of material from Diogenes Laertius' *Life of Pyrrho* (9. 61–108).[47] The eleventh- or twelfth-century historian George Kedrenos devotes the thirteenth and last item of a digression on the doctrines of the ancient philosophers to Sextus and Pyrrho (*PG* 121. 320B–C): like most of his doxographical material it is (in part) culled from Hippolytus' *Philosophumena* (*Ref.* 1. 23).[48] It is significant that not even in the vast and varied output of

---

[45] It is very likely that Metochites was familiar with the *De ebrietate*, as is argued by Demetracopoulos (1999a: 97) on the basis of a parallel in *Sem.* 31 (cited as ch. 29 by Demetracopoulos). If so, he also no doubt recognized and relished the sceptical mood of the paraphrase of Aenesidemus' modes in *De ebr.* 166–205. On Metochites' view of Philo as a 'true adherent of Plato' and a 'dogmatic' (i.e. theoretical) as well as ethical philosopher, see *Sem.* 16 (fos. 31ᵛ–32ʳ = 116–18 MK). It is not necessary to assume that Metochites realized that Philo's arguments were actually borrowed from the works of a Pyrrhonian Sceptic, but the conclusion in *De ebr.* 205 with its recommendation of τὸ ἐπέχειν as the safest course in view of the liability of things to turn into their opposites can hardly have failed to strike him as being pretty much in the vein of ancient Scepticism as he conceived of it. As for Gregory of Nazianzus, Ševčenko asserted that 'Metochites knew all of Gregory, especially his poetry', and substantiated this claim, at least to some extent, in a note (1975: 38 and n. 149). Demetracopoulos argues (1999a: 137–46) that Gregory drew directly on Sextus' *Outlines of Pyrrhonism* for two of his theological discourses (*Or.* 28 and 29).

[46] On its value as a source see Janáček (1976) and Demetracopoulos (1999b); cf. Treadgold (1980: 86–7, 92–3, 183).

[47] The two most substantial entries are ο 802 οὐδὲν μᾶλλον (3: 578. 9–29 A) and π 3241 Πυρρώνειοι (4: 278. 15–32 A). See also n. 64.

[48] The source for the additional information (or whatever word is the most appropriate) is unknown: cf. Podskalsky (1976: 511 and n. 4).

Michael Psellos do we find more than one or two passing references to the Sceptics. A caveat should perhaps be entered: some material of interest might have been transmitted among the scholia on Gregory of Nazianzus. Among the few edited ones we do find older items like a table of contents of Sextus' *Outlines of Pyrrhonism* made by Cosmas of Jerusalem in the early eighth century.[49]

When Metochites says in *Semeiosis* 61 that the Sceptics should not be dismissed as mere controversialists, we may infer that this is the attitude he expects from most of his readers. It is indeed an attitude we encounter in a number of twelfth- and thirteenth-century authors. The Greek Fathers set the example. In the same manner as the man who fixes his attention on Chrysippus, Aristotle, or Plato will become a logician, a scientist, or a philosopher, so the man who studies Pyrrho will become an eristic, according to Clement of Alexandria (*Strom.* 7. 101). Similarly Gregory of Nazianzus (*Or.* 21. 12) castigates 'the Sextuses and the Pyrrhos and the practice of arguing to opposites' which, he claims, 'like a vile and malignant disease have infected the churches'.[50] This cliché of the Sceptics as epitomes of contentiousness accounts for a very large proportion of the allusions to them in middle and late Byzantine authors.[51] In the two centuries preceding Metochites' *Semeioseis* there are no signs, so far as I have been able to find, that ancient Scepticism was ever conceived of as having had more on the agenda than the perverse cultivation of argument for argument's sake.[52]

This is the background against which Metochites' attempted vindication of ancient Scepticism must be seen. A number of scholars from Rodolphe Guilland onwards have spoken of a fourteenth-century 'revival of Scepticism' drawing its most zealous supporters from among the medical profession. However, Guilland's view loses much of its persuasive power as soon as it is realized that the most important part of the evidence consists in a blatant misconstruction of *Semeiosis* 61 as an onslaught on the partisans of such a Neosceptical movement. The mistake was corrected by Hans-Georg Beck half a century ago, but has nevertheless continued to hold the field among historians.[53]

---

[49] *PG* 38. 555–6; re-edited in Mutschmann (1958: pp. xx–xxiii). This Cosmas may have been identical with Cosmas the Melode, who was the fosterbrother of John of Damascus, or with Cosmas, the teacher of John and his fosterbrother (Lefherz 1958: 157–8).

[50] Tr. Annas and Barnes 1985: 18. The same attitude is expressed in non-Christian authors of the period: Himerius, *Or.* 48. 275.

[51] e.g. Nicholas of Methone, George Tornikes, John Bekkos, Neilos Kabasilas, Nikephoros Gregoras (on Gregoras, see below). See Podskalsky (1976: 512 n. 5) for exact references. Add to the list there Gregory Palamas, *Syngr. II* 326. 2–5 and 479. 16–18, as well as Elias of Crete (early 12th century), *In Gregorii Nazianzeni Orationem 32, PG* 36. 901D–902A.

[52] Note, however, Michael Italikos (d. 1157), *Letter* 18, 158. 13 G; this seems to evidence a curiosity about ancient Scepticism, if nothing more.

[53] Guilland (1926: 206–7): transmitted in Nicol (1969: 43), Schmitt (1983: 235), Schrenk (1989a: 455–6; 1989b: 254–6), Dellis (1991–2: 316–17). Correction in Beck (1952: 104–5); cf. Tatakis (1949: 254). Tambrun-Krasker (1998: 286–7) first reports the view of Guilland, then,

In sum, then, the picture seems quite clear. There is nothing to suggest that ancient Scepticism ever attracted the interest of Byzantine intellectuals between Photios and Metochites. We are thus confronted with the task of explaining why Metochites says in *Sem.* 61 that 'many people from that time and *up to this moment* have taken on this [sc. the Sceptical] cause' (68–9). My suggestion is that Metochites does not have in mind here, as it might first seem, some obscure acquaintances of his who had expressed in confidence their allegiance to ancient Scepticism, but rather writers of all periods (not least Christians) who have shared the broadly sceptical outlook on the domains of natural phenomena and human affairs which is in fact part of the common Platonic heritage (the 'Heraclitean element', if you like), but which Metochites connects, as we have seen, with ancient Scepticism.[54] The statement would then be comparable to what Metochites says concerning the very same 'broad scepticism' in another work, the *Ethikos* (I paraphrase): 'there is nothing new in it, which has not been said before and which is not indeed the view of most people' (*Eth.* 10. 84. 5–15 P: cf. n. 3, above).[55]

A few comments have to be made at this stage on the singular compilation transmitted under the fanciful title of Herennius, *Commentary on the Metaphysics*, and drawing on works by Alexander of Aphrodisias, Proclus, Damascius, and George Pachymeres, among others.[56] As E. Heitz showed (1889: 1168–70), the individual chapters of Ps.-Herennius have all been cut more or less in a piece from known sources, with the seeming exception of chapter 3, 'On Knowledge'. Now it is precisely this chapter which matters to us. Lawrence Schrenk suggested that it could be an early fourteenth-century work composed in answer to what he called the 'renaissance of scepticism in the medical profession' (1989b: 255–6). The chapter begins with the remark

adding that '[c]urieusement, B. Tatakis propose une interprétation totalement inverse', quotes the passage cited of Tatakis without comments.

[54] Cf. Demetracopoulos (1999a: 84–5). However, the notion that Metochites is thinking 'not of a philosophical but of a theological' view, namely Fideism (1999a: 85), seems to me mistaken: ll. 70–4 refer unambiguously, I think, to the domains of nature and society. Views akin to Metochites' 'scepticism' in contemporary writers are discussed in Demetracopoulos (1999a: 88–93). It may be added that according to George Pachymeres, *Hist.* 5. 2, 439. 12–15, Nikephoros Blemmydes in *c.*1268 referred to Heraclitus and Cratylus for his own view that Θεοῦ μὲν τὸ εὐσταθὲς καὶ ἀκίνητον, ἀνθρώπων δὲ τὸ μηδὲν ἐν μηδενὶ ἐπὶ τοῦ αὐτοῦ κἂν βραχὺ μένειν. The fact that Pachymeres quotes the statement, seemingly with approval, may suggest that the link between 'the Heraclitean element' of Platonism and a Christian view of the secular world was commonly recognized by the intellectuals of the period.

[55] Cf. *Sem.* 7 (fo. 13^{v} = 59 MK), where a number of Oriental peoples are said to hold Pythagoras in great honour, having 'much in common with him in their philosophical approach, and this has been a fact from his own days *right up to this moment*'. What Metochites alludes to here can scarcely be anything like a living tradition of Pythagoreanism in the East, but rather recent developments in mathematics and astronomy, of which he was well aware.

[56] On the sources of the compilation (apart from ch. 3, ss. 5–7) and the method of the compiler see Heitz (1889). The best text of the passages discussed below is also found in Heitz (1889: 1181–3). The Herennius meant by the author of the title is probably the one mentioned by Porphyry, *V. Plot.* 3. 24–30, as one of Plotinus' fellow students.

that most arguments of the Academic or Ephectic philosophers are directed against the evidence of sense-perception (on the basis of which the intellect operates). The author promises to review some such arguments which he has copied down and subsequently refute them to the best of his ability. What follows then is a free quotation of Philo of Alexandria's paraphrase of Aenesidemus' Modes (*De ebrietate* 167–202), with an interpolated section (3. 5, 522. 30–523. 15 M) that was identified by Schrenk (1989*b*) as a new Greek fragment of Galen's *De experientia medica* (19. 3), a work of which two other fragments have come down in the original, but which is preserved as a whole only in a ninth-century Arabic translation from the Syriac.[57]

The fragment deals with the cosmological problem of whether the world has had a beginning or not. In Ps.-Herennius 3 it is inserted between the last two Philo excerpts so as to form an illustration of the argument in Philo corresponding to the tenth Mode in Sextus Empiricus, 'depending on persuasions and customs and laws and beliefs in myth and dogmatic suppositions'.[58] In this way it comes to exemplify the kind of never-ending debate between philosophers of different schools that Philo calls to mind on questions like whether the universe is infinite or finite, whether the world has had a beginning or not, and whether it is governed by spontaneous change or divine providence (*Ebr.* 198–9). In its original context, on the other hand, the passage is part of an Empiricist doctor's attempt to refute an argument turning on the sorites paradox, brought against him by a Dogmatist, by showing that the paradox has no bearing on reality but rather proves how preposterous it is to rely on reason alone. There are other examples, says the Empiricist, of 'things which by the argument of the logos ... are quite unknown';[59] and he goes on to relate the aporia of whether bodies mix by way of interpenetration or juxtaposition, and after that our cosmological problem. The Empiricist's concern here is to call attention to the limitations of reason, not to illustrate the equipollence of opposed views: it is the method of repeated observation that he is out to defend, rather than suspension of judgement. But in spite of the difference between the original context and that in Ps.-Herennius 3, the graft serves its new purpose well. An antinomical problem like the cosmological one formulated by Galen's Empiricist is of course liable to be one to which all kinds of solutions have been offered and none universally accepted. Indeed, this particular problem *is* one of those mentioned in the passage of Philo preceding the Galen fragment in Ps.-Herennius 3.[60]

---

[57] See Walzer (1932: 449–52).
[58] *PH* 1. 145, tr. Annas and Barnes (1994: 108).
[59] Tr. Walzer, in Frede (1985: 80).
[60] Note also that the contradictions implied by the concept of movement mentioned in *De exp. med.* 19. 1 seem to have been one of the items discussed in Aenesidemus' work (Photios, *Bibl.* 212. 170[b]9), even though it is left out of account in Philo's version of the Modes.

Another surprise comes in the next section of the chapter (Ps.-Herennius 3. 6), where the refutation of the Sceptical position is carried out in the form of a *cogito*, put together, as Schrenk was also able to show (1989*a*), from chapters 10. 10 and 15. 12 of Maximos Planoudes' Greek translation of St Augustine's *De trinitate*. Reverberations of Planoudes, *Trin.* 15. 12. 74–7 can be found also in the introduction to the chapter (3. 1). I would surmise that the mention of Academics there is also due to Augustine's influence.

Now that the sources of the Sceptical and anti-Sceptical arguments in Ps.-Herennius 3 have all been tracked down thanks to Schrenk's efforts, we can also see, I think, that these arguments have all been elicited from original contexts in which ancient Scepticism is not the matter at issue, but Sceptical or anti-Sceptical arguments are rehearsed for some independent reason (neither Philo nor Galen even mentions Sceptics or Scepticism in these works), and that these arguments have then been brought to bear on the question of Scepticism by means of editorial touches. This goes to show that Ps.-Herennius 3 is not just a slapdash collection of any old material on Scepticism that its author found ready to hand, but the product of active search and perceptive selection. It seems evident that the author, whatever his shortcomings,[61] must have been seriously concerned about the problems posed by Scepticism.

It is therefore to be regretted that Ps.-Herennius 3 is of doubtful value as a witness to the interest in Scepticism in early fourteenth-century Byzantium. As to the compilation as a whole, there is no evidence for a date before the mid-fifteenth century.[62] Cross-references to other chapters at the beginning and end of chapter 3 indicate that this chapter was probably written especially for the compilation, but the compiler may have added them to pre-existing material. As regards Schrenk's thesis that chapter 3 should be dated in the early fourteenth century, there is precious little substance in it. The two arguments to support it that I am able to discern in Schrenk's two papers on Ps.-Herennius are both false: an erroneous dating of the oldest MS and the

---

[61] Ch. 5 (excerpts from Proclus, *in Parm.*) was judged severely, chs. 1–2 (excerpts from George Pachymeres, *Philosophia*) more mildly, by Heitz (1889: 1176); ch. 3 he even considered to possess certain merits (1889: 1183).

[62] Westerink (1986: pp. cxi–cxiv), who seems to have assumed that Ps.-Herennius 3 was composed for the occasion of the compilation, suggested, on the grounds that the Damascius and Proclus excerpts of Ps.-Herennius 5–9 have been copied from MSS belonging to Bessarion's library, 'que le Ps.-Herennius a été composé à Rome avant l'an 1468, lorsque la bibliothèque de Bessarion fut transportée à Venise' (1986: p. cxiii). The Philo excerpts of Ps.-Herennius 3, however, are according to Wendland (1897: p. xxix) dependent on a MS of the UF family, whereas the Philo MS in Bessarion's library suggested by Westerink as a possible source (Marc. gr. 40) is the 'exemplum potissimum' of the H family (Cohn 1896: p. xi). As to the excerpts of Planoudes' translation of Augustine, I can only say that none of the following obvious errors in Ps.-Herennius 3 are noted in the apparatus of Papathomopoulos *et al.* (1995): οὕτω Plan. 15. 12. 45: οὕτε [Her.] 524. 15 M ‖ μὴ ζῶντα Plan. 10. 10. 14: ζῶντα [Her.] 524. 20–1 M ‖ ὡς Plan. 10. 10. 20: ὢν [Her.] 524. 23 M. (However, the printed Planoudes text (10. 10. 15) and [Herennius] (524. 22 M) agree on τὸν νοῦν : τὸν νοοῦντα ci. Heitz (1889: 1183): *id quod intellegit* Augustine; perhaps Planoudes wrote τὸ νοοῦν.) If these erroneous readings are indeed absent from the Planoudean tradition, this suggests a few links between the Planoudes text used by the author of Ps.-Herennius 3 and our oldest MSS of the latter text.

traditional misconstruction of Metochites' *Semeiosis* 61 as an attack on creeping Pyrrhonist perversion among the doctors of Constantinople.[63]

The oldest MSS of Ps.-Herennius are in fact dated in the latter half of the sixteenth century. This marks the approximate *terminus ante quem* for Ps.-Herennius 3, while the *post quem* is set by Planoudes' translation of the *De trinitate* in 1281. Pending further corroboration of Westerink's (1986: pp. cxi–cxiv) hypothesis of a date before 1468 for the whole compilation (see n. 62), nothing more definite can be said with confidence.

Little by little, the dossier of Scepticism continues to swell throughout the fourteenth century.[64] The works of the leading theologians involved in the

---

[63] Schrenk suggests, on the one hand, that Codex B. O. Z. Cim. 142, containing the whole of Ps.-Herennius, should be dated to the 14th cent. (1989*b*: 251 n. 7), but, on the other hand, that the compilation as we know it was made 'perhaps as late as the sixteenth century', probably by the well-known forger Andreas Darmarios (1989*b*: 256). He refers to Hahn (1900: 1324) for a tentative dating of the Warsaw MS to the 13th cent. (1989*b* 251 n. 7), but Hahn in fact only reproduced erroneously a MS description in a list by a librarian of the Zamoyski library, printed in Foerster (1898: 571), where this dating obviously refers to another MS. Foerster later (1900: 440–4) made his own description of B.O.Z. Cimelia 142 in which he stated that it was copied in a 16th-cent. hand; not, however, that of Darmarios. He also discussed Heitz's hypothesis (1889: 1186–7) that the compilation may have been the work of Darmarios. After a brief review of the MS material (he mentions 19 MSS besides the Varsoviensis: cf. Schrenk 1989*b*: 251 n. 7; 1989*a*: 451) he concludes that '[v]on Seiten des Alters der Handschriften also steht der Vermuthung von Heitz nichts im Wege' (1900: 441). It may be added that the fabulous 'Beast of Tarentum' held by Schrenk to be a possible 'key to pinpointing more exactly the origin of the third chapter' (1989*b*: 252–3 n. 14) is unlikely to take us very far in the right direction. Clearly, τοῦ θηρὸς Ταράντου in Ps.-Herennius (519. 11 M) is only a misspelt variant of θηρίον, ὃ καλεῖται τάρανδρος in Philo (*Ebr.* 174, 203. 20 W). In fact Wendland in his apparatus criticus to this passage in Philo reports (*mutatis mutandis*) τάρανδος as the reading *both* of Ps.-Herennius (based on Codd. Ambros. P 143 sup. and Ambros. R 117 sup. (1897: p. xxviii)) *and* of a number of Philo MSS. Indeed, Foerster (1900: 446) reported ταράνδου as the reading also of Cod. Cim. 142.

[64] Let me briefly sum up the hard (or at least semi-resistant) facts about the transmission of ancient works on Scepticism in the 14th cent. Regarding Sextus Empiricus, first, we know that a Latin translation of the *Outlines of Pyrrhonism* was made in the early 14th cent. The translator may have been Nicholas of Rhegium (Schmitt 1983: 243 n. 6). On Nicholas see Weiss ([1950] 1977: 125–37). Leaving aside the 5 fos. of an original 9th/10th-cent. MS now divided between Codd. Paris. suppl. gr. 1156, Vat. gr. 738, and Vindob. theol. gr. 179 (see Eleuteri 1985: 435–6), the oldest Greek MS of the *Outlines* (Monac. gr. 439) dates from after 1376 (Mutschmann 1958: p. viii and n. 1). *M* 7–11 (*Adversus dogmaticos*) as well as a few pages of *M* 1 are preserved in a 13th/14th-cent. MS (Laur. gr. 85, 19) (Mutschmann 1914: pp. vi–x). *M* 5 (*Adversus astrologos*) is extant in a MS dated around 1342 (Laur. gr. 9, 32) (Mau 1961: p. xiii). The rest of the Sextus tradition belongs to the 15th and later centuries. In contrast, all the three best Diogenes Laertius MSS date from between the 12th and the early 14th cents. Diogenes' *Life of Plato* (book 3) has also been transmitted in a number of Plato MSS, three of which (probably) date from the 14th cent. (Long 1964: p. xx). The Byzantine testimonies to Diogenes are rather numerous; excerpts from the *Life of Pyrrho* (9. 61–108) are found in the *Magnum excerptum*, preserved in two 12th-cent. MSS (ed. Markovich 1999: ii). As to the other sources, four MSS of books 14 and 15 of Eusebius' *Praeparatio evangelica* belong to the 13th and 14th cent. (Mras [1950] 1982: pp. xiii–li). Over and above the three old MSS of Photios' *Bibliotheca* (10th–13th cent.), it should be noted that extracts from *Bibl.* 212 (and seven other codices) are found in Cod. Paris. suppl. gr. 256, fos. 239–47, which may have originated in the school of Nikephoros Gregoras (Diller 1962: 392–3). The rest of the tradition belongs to the 15th cent. and later (see Martini 1911: especially p. 108). On the transmission of Plutarch, *Adv. Col.*, see above, n. 43.

Hesychast debate contain scattered references to Sceptical philosophers and doctrines (if the expression is allowed). In Gregory Palamas' works we find the traditional patristic cliché as well as one or two passages which seem to suggest familiarity with authentic Sceptical arguments.[65] The pièce de résistance among the relevant documents, however, is a work entitled *Against the Statements Made on the Criterion of Truth, Whether it Exists, by the Accursed Pyrrho*, by Nicholas Kabasilas Chamaetos, the influential theologian and supporter of Palamas.[66] This opuscule (89 lines in the new edition) consists of a series of refutations, more or less sophistical, of Sceptical arguments against the existence of a criterion of truth.[67]

There are two things to be noted as regards Kabasilas' sources. First, the *On the Criterion* is the first work in the period after iconoclasm whose dependence on Sextus Empiricus (the *PH*, quite possibly *M* 7 too) is manifest. Given the obvious fact that Kabasilas did not belong in the small select ranks of a philosophical avant-garde, this may indicate that the *Outlines of Pyrrhonism* (and quite possibly the *Adversus dogmaticos* too) was in circulation, on a modest scale at least, in the middle of the fourteenth century (and thus before the earliest extant Greek MS was copied). Second, at one point (lines 70–4), Kabasilas introduces as an example of things of which we have certain knowledge the fact that we exist (for if we did not we would not be capable of doubting our existence). It seems probable that this idea is owed, directly or indirectly, to Planoudes' translation of the *De trinitate*.[68] If so, we have

---

[65] In his first and second letters to Barlaam, *Syngr.* 1. 258. 4–14; 1. 292. 1–25. Palamas could be drawing either on Diogenes Laertius, 9. 90, or, more probably, on Sextus Empiricus, *M* 8. 329–34. Examples of the traditional cliché are found in *Syngr.* 2. 326. 2–5 and 2. 479. 16–18. In addition, it is worth noticing that the 'equipollence slogan', in the version found in Gregory of Nazianzus and (slightly modified) in Metochites, is put to repeated use in Palamas' first *Triad in Defence of the Holy Hesychasts*. The pagan philosophers have proved the truth of the slogan, says Palamas, 'by incessantly refuting each other and being refuted in turn, each through apparently stronger arguments' (*Triad.* 1. 1. 1, 9. 19–24 M; cf. *Triad.* 1. 2, quaestio, 71. 5–7 M; *Triad.* 13. 13, 137. 27–8 M).

[66] The new edn. in Demetracopoulos (1999a: 13–20) supersedes that of Radermacher (1899).

[67] The first refutation, however, sets out to prove that the negation of the existence of knowledge is self-contradictory: it is in effect identical with the two-part argument ascribed to Plato by the Neoplatonic commentators on Aristotle (see nn. 29–30, above). There is a telling difference in that Kabasilas in the course of his argument maintains that also claiming *not* to know that there is no knowledge implies that there is knowledge (18. 13–14 D; 12–13 R).

[68] φανερὸν δὲ ὅτι ψεῦδος λαμβάνει καὶ ἀσυλλόγιστός ἐστι · ψεῦδος γάρ ἐστιν ὅτι, εἰ ἐπεκρίθη ἡ διαφωνία ἡ περὶ τοῦ κριτηρίου, ἐγινώσκομεν ἂν τὸ κριτήριον πρότερον. τοῦτο δὲ οὐκ ἔστιν ἀναγκαῖον. οὔτε γὰρ ἀδύνατον, πρὸ τοῦ λυθῆναι τὴν περί τινων λόγων διαφωνίαν, πρότερον ἡμᾶς βεβαίως εἰδέναι περὶ τοῦ πράγματος· γινώσκομεν γὰρ βεβαίως ὅτι ἐσμέν· εἰ δέ τις περὶ τούτου ἀμφιβάλλει (δυνατὸν γὰρ τοῦτο φῆς εἶναι· παντὶ γὰρ λόγῳ ἴσον ἀντικεῖσθαι λόγον), λύσομεν τὴν ἀμφιβολίαν, εἴ γε καὶ τοῦτο δοίης, ὅτι εἴ. εἰ γὰρ μὴ εἴ, οὐδέ τι λέγεις, καὶ οὐκ ἔστιν οὐδεμία περὶ οὐδενὸς ἀμφιβολία. πρῶτον μὲν οὖν οὐκ ἔστιν ἀδύνατον πρὸ τοῦ λῦσαι τὴν διαφωνίαν εἰδέναι τὸ βέβαιον, περὶ οὗ ἡ διαφωνία (19. 66–20. 76 D; 77–91 R). Cf. [Herennius] 3. 6, 524. 3–4, 24–8 M (≈ Planoudes, *Trin.* 10. 10. 36–45) (quoted from Heitz 1889: 1182–3): εἰ γὰρ εἴπω ὅτι ἀληθῶς καὶ βεβαίως γινώσκω ὅτι ζῶ, τί πρὸς ταῦτα φήσει ὁ ἐφεκτικός;... Περὶ πολλῶν μὲν πραγμάτων ἠμφισβήτησαν οἱ ἄνθρωποι καὶ ἄλλος μὲν τοῦτο, ἕτερος δὲ ἐκεῖνο ἐδόξασεν· εἶναι δὲ ἑαυτὸν καὶ ζῆν καὶ νοεῖν καὶ μεμνῆσθαι καὶ θέλειν καὶ λογίζεσθαι καὶ

evidence that Augustine's arguments against Scepticism were paid attention to in Byzantium as early as the early 1350s or thereabouts. Ps.-Herennius 3 might thus fit into place as another product of the intellectual concerns of that time.[69]

So, it might seem reasonable to assume that the mere existence of a refutation of Sceptical arguments dating from the middle of the fourteenth century implies that some other scholars or philosophers as well must have taken an interest in or even propounded such arguments at the time.[70] But considering the quantitative (and qualitative) limitations of Kabasilas' work, as well as the absence in it of any hints at a definite polemical context, one has to admit that it gives no clear indication about the width and depth of this interest. Indeed, there have been attempts to explain the emergence of the work in a way which does not presuppose any contemporary interest in ancient Scepticism. Jean Boivin and later Ihor Ševčenko drew attention to a letter from Gregory Palamas to John Gabras in which one of the followers of the anti-Palamite Gregory Akindynos is described as an eristic, through the mouth of whom 'the words of the evil objection flowed, the one which [the Akindynites] had learned from Pyrrho's Ephectic [school] and maliciously applied to things divine' (*Syngr. II* 326. 2–5). Boivin compared this with a passage in Nikephoros Gregoras' *Byzantine History* and suggested that some of Palamas' opponents were labelled (indeed, labelled themselves) Ephectics on account of their reluctance to make positive statements on theological issues.[71] I shall come back to this. Ševčenko went a step further. As he explained,

[i]n the light of the passage from Palamas' letter, the refutation of 'Pyrrhon' by Cabasilas may be seen as a piece of Palamite polemics against opponents who maintained that no one could behold the 'essential energies' of the Divinity and in that sense they suspended judgment. In this refutation, Cabasilas proceeded by syllogisms. The adversaries had to be crushed with their own weapons. (1954: 51)

One cannot help feeling, however, that if the adversaries aimed at were really only nominally associated with Scepticism, as Ševčenko suggests, the procedure chosen by Kabasilas was remarkably beside the point. It is one thing to

κρίνειν οὐδεὶς ἀμφιβάλλει· ὁπότε καὶ εἰ διστάζει, καὶ ἔστι καὶ ζῇ καὶ νοεῖ ...Somewhat more remote parallels are found in ?Chrysippus *apud* Clementem, *Strom.* 8. 5. 15. 7–9 = *SVF* ii. 121; Sextus Empiricus, *M* 9. 198; Oenomaus of Gadara *apud* Eusebium, *Praep. evan.* 7. 7 (on the latter see Lloyd 1964: 198–200).

[69] There is even a case to be made (admittedly weak) for the possibility that Kabasilas drew on Ps.-Herennius 3 rather than directly on the *De trinitate*: the wording in the relevant part of Kabasilas' work is never so close to Planoudes' translation as it is in 20. 70–1 D (γινώσκομεν γὰρ βεβαίως ὅτι ἐσμέν) to [Herennius], 524. 3–4 M (βεβαίως γινώσκω ὅτι ζῶ). But this may of course be accidental.

[70] This type of argument ('ex elencho ad respondentem', as we may dub it) is familiar from the history of Byzantine Platonism, where there is a 12th-cent. analogue in Nicholas of Methone, *Refutation of Proclus*.

[71] In a note included in the Bonn edn. of Nikephoros Gregoras, *Hist.* 1275 S (reprinted in *PG* 148. 957 n. 75).

call someone who is a negative dogmatist in respect of a certain class of entities a Sceptic, as Metochites did; it is another thing to try to refute that person's views by overthrowing genuinely Sceptical arguments.

What we need, I suppose, is some evidence to suggest that there may have been more than a nominal connection between some of these adversaries and the arguments of the ancient Sceptics. John Dellis has argued that there was. According to him, Kabasilas' aim was to refute the negative theology raised against the Palamites by Barlaam of Calabria (and Nikephoros Gregoras), which, he implies, rests on arguments drawn from the ancient Sceptics (1991– 2: 321–3). However, the most precise indication that Dellis offers of Bar- laam's dependence on Sceptical arguments is the fact that he 'championed a certain form of agnosticism'. True enough: but it seems to me that we must distinguish carefully between the sense in which Barlaam (as well as the Cappadocian Fathers, Ps.-Dionysius, Maximus the Confessor *et al.*) could be said to represent a form of 'agnosticism', and the senses in which a strict Sceptic and a negative dogmatist on theological matters could be said to do it. 'Agnosticism' in the sense that it is considered impossible to have scientific knowledge of God's nature, so as, for example, to demonstrate (in the Aristotelian sense) the truth of Trinitarian or Christological tenets, is more or less ubiquitous in the Orthodox tradition, and there is no need to suppose that Barlaam had recourse to the Sceptics for arguments in favour of that;[72] whereas I very much doubt that 'agnosticism' in the negative dogmatist sense that it is considered impossible to have factual knowledge about God and his workings, or in the Sceptical sense that it is left open even whether it is possible or not to have factual knowledge about God and his workings, is attributable to Barlaam.[73] Dellis offers no examples of Sceptical arguments being used by Barlaam. I doubt that Kabasilas found any. Perhaps then we should look in another direction.

The main target of Kabasilas' pro-Palamite polemic in the 1350s was Nikephoros Gregoras. A couple of excerpts from *M* 6. 7–10 in the margin of a page in the commonplace-book (Heidelb. Pal. gr. 129) of the famous historian and polymath seem to suggest that he had actually studied parts of the works of Sextus Empiricus.[74] Gregoras being also the intellectual heir to Theodore Metochites, it might seem promising to look for expressions of a benevolent attitude towards Scepticism or even of Sceptical influence in Gregoras' work. Alas, as far as direct references are concerned, the reward

---

[72] See the outline of 'die theologische Methodenfrage in der griechischen Patristik' in Pods- kalsky (1977: 88–106).

[73] He affirms the truth of the Nicene Creed and the Bible as axiomatic (Podskalsky 1977: 129– 30). Furthermore, for all his emphasis on the indemonstrability of Trinitarian dogma, he does acknowledge a cosmological proof of God's existence (Podskalsky 1977: 142 n. 621).

[74] Many of the excerpts contained in the Heidelbergensis are apparently copied from other florilegia (Biedl 1948: 103–4); this is possibly the case with the Sextus extracts as well, which exhibit at least one important deviation from the rest of the tradition as we know it (see Eleuteri 1985: 433).

is rather slight.[75] The passage of the *Byzantine History* that made Boivin recall Palamas' letter to John Gabras describes the civil and ecclesiastical strife following on the death of Andronikos III in 1341.[76] Gregoras deplores the fact that the theologians then, unlike the philosophers of ancient Athens, were unwilling to set aside their internal conflicts for times of outer peace. 'Sublime theology', he complains, was 'thrashed in the streets by the camp of the "felons" [*palamnaioi*: a pun on Palamas' name] and the Pharisees, although there might have been some Maccabees to resist them, as well as those who took an Ephectic position on account of the times' (*Hist.* 14. 8. 4, 722. 5–21 S). It is quite clear, as Jan Louis van Dieten has pointed out (Nikephoros Gregoras, *Rhomäische Geschichte 3*, tr. van Dieten 1988: 331 n. 331), that the people to whom Gregoras is referring as Sceptics are such as for tactical reasons 'withheld' their disapproval of Palamas' doctrines (and not, it should be noted, all those who refused to accept them), and that one of the most prominent members of this group was Gregoras himself. I do not think, however, that this reference can be put straight on a par with the one in Palamas' letter to John Gabras. In the latter the names of Pyrrho and the Sceptics are used in the derogatory sense that had been authorized by Clement of Alexandria and Gregory of Nazianzus. This is obviously not the case in the Gregoras passage, where the word 'Ephectic' is used in its radical sense of 'one who practises *epoche*, who suspends his judgement'.

This connotation is the dominating one in a few allusions to the Sceptics in Gregoras' letters too. It is interesting to note that some of these occur in a context which is pervaded by precisely the broadly sceptical outlook on natural and social phenomena that Metochites associated with the Sceptics. This is the case, for example, in *Letter* 148 to Demetrios Kabasilas (dated by Leone '1330–2, post 1351').[77] The letter opens in a mood and a turn of phrase

---

[75] To begin with, we should discard without further ado the mention of Sextus and Pyrrho in a quotation of Gregory of Nazianzus (*Or.* 21. 12) in the record Gregoras left of his speech at the Church Council of 1351 (*Hist.* 19. 1. 6, 930. 5–6 S), because it is wholly accidental to Gregoras' purposes there. Contrast the view of Guilland (1926: 206), who has again been all too much relied on by later scholars.

[76] See the discussion in Nikephoros Gregoras, *Rhomäische Geschichte 3*, tr. van Dieten 1988 331–2 n. 331.

[77] Cf. also *Letter* 30 to Andronikos Zarides (dated 1322–early 1326). Gregoras opens the letter (30. 1–11) by suggesting that Plato's dialogues show that he did not adhere strictly to a single unified philosophical system. An example is Socrates' *epoche* on the question of Archelaus of Macedonia's happiness (*Gorgias* 470 D–E). I take it that Gregoras means to suggest that, even though Plato is known to be a dogmatic philosopher, there are sceptical features in some of his dialogues (although the *Gorgias* is admittedly not the most appropriate example of that). Gregoras then makes various rhetorical uses of the equipollence argument. Among the ancient examples enumerated by Gregoras we find the antithesis of Pyrrho and Plato, who 'both practised philosophy, one, however, with a view to showing that reality is subject to non-apprehension, the other in order that he should on the contrary remain innocent of defeatism. And as being in a halfway house between the two, Anaxagoras and Protagoras declared [the one] that things are both in this state and not in this state, [the other] that things are to each man such as they appear to him' (30. 45–50 L). I assume that the statement on Plato's motives for doing philosophy alludes to *Phaedo* 90 B–D, and conclude that τῆς ἀπονοίας, in p. 47 probably means

that are strongly suggestive of a Metochitean *Semeiosis*. How strange, Gregoras exclaims, that one and the same thing will appear fortunate to some, and unfortunate to others, and indeed sometimes blissful and sometimes not to one and the same person. Wise was he who said that for each man the measure of the matters of life is his own mind.[78] Then, almost like an echo of *Semeiosis* 61, Gregoras goes on:

> It is because of this, I think, that the Sceptical philosophers have also been left very great space for not determining in any way anything that is and not stating what is the quality of this thing and what is the destiny of that thing..., or travelling on what path one might get lucky through skill, rather than hope to attain skill by luck. (148. 14–18 L)[79]

If we compare Gregoras' references to the Sceptics to those of earlier Byzantine authors, it is clear that Gregoras too restricts himself to using them as a cliché. However, the main connotation is not now that of perverse fondness of argument, as in those writers taking their cue from Clement and Gregory of Nazianzus, but of non-commitment, and the attitude is vaguely sympathetic. It seems safe enough to assume that Gregoras' idea of Scepticism has evolved on the basis of his association with Metochites. The exact relation between the evidence of a critical interest in ancient Scepticism on the part of the Palamites (especially Nicholas Kabasilas Chamaetos) and the rather sparse and innocuous expressions of a sympathetic attitude that we find in Gregoras is harder to ascertain. On the one hand, Kabasilas' attempt to refute the Sceptics remains unexplained if, as Ševčenko suggested, the names of the latter were only used as a classicist figure of speech for the real adversaries. On the other hand, there is no direct evidence that Sceptical ideas or arguments were seriously entertained by anyone in the late thirteenth and fourteenth centuries. However, as is well known, the resuscitation of works and authors who had long been out of use was a distinguished feature of this era. If Gregoras was prepared, on occasion, to style himself an Ephectic, perhaps that was enough to prompt a bit of Sextus scholarship on the part of his enemies; the refutation of Sceptical arguments that resulted

---

'despondency' or 'defeatism' rather than 'madness'. It is true, as Demetracopoulos points out (1999*a*: 100), that the expression in this context must denote non-apprehension (although not necessarily specifically Pyrrho's doctrines). Still I feel hesitant to view it as Demetracopoulos does as a clear disapproval of the ἀπόνοια of Pyrrhonism, considering that the immediate context is opaque (*Plato* refused to give in to what *he* thought was defeatism), and that the general context is one of rhetorical oppositions. After all, earlier in the same letter Socrates, taken as a representative of Plato's views, is said to have practised *epoche* in the *Gorgias* (30. 8 L).

[78] Who? Leone suggests Protagoras, but it could as well be Anaxagoras who is meant: cf. Aristotle, *Met.* 4. 5, 1009^{b}26–8. To my mind, however, this device of praising an author while identifying him only by quoting his words rather suggests that Gregoras is thinking of one of his contemporaries: there is nothing quite similar to the quotation in the *Semeioseis gnomikai*, but there might be in one of Metochites' orations or poems, which are largely unedited.

[79] τίνα τρίβον ὁδεύσας τέχνῃ τύχην εὕροι τις ἂν κτλ., apparently alluding to Plato, *Gorg.* 448 *c* 5–7 (cf. Aristotle, *Met.* 1. 1, 981^{a}3–5).

may have been earnestly intended to be just that, whereas the side-effect of suspicion cast on Gregoras would certainly have been considered as a bonus.[80]

I have argued in this paper that the knowledge of ancient Scepticism in the three or four centuries preceding the publication of Theodore Metochites' *Semeioseis gnomikai* (*c*.1326) was all but restricted to a handful of passages in the Church Fathers, where 'Pyrrho', 'Sextus', and 'Scepticism' are used as bywords for vile and destructive contentiousness. In *Semeioseis* 29 and 61, Metochites attempts a partial vindication of Scepticism, which he construes as negative dogmatism with regard to the realms of natural phenomena and human affairs, and which he traces back to Socrates and Plato. He fails to discuss the epistemological status of mathematics in connection with Scepticism, whereas in other contexts he is often at pains to emphasize the certainty of mathematical knowledge. He does, however, reject the application of negative dogmatism—as well as scientific proof—to the revealed truths of religion, siding with the Orthodox Christian tradition. I think it should be appreciated as one of the ironies of fate that *Semeiosis* 61 is introduced by a sentence by Gregory of Nazianzus, whose stigmatization of the Sceptics as wicked and dangerous mischief-makers set the tone for centuries in the Greek-speaking world. Metochites does not manifest a deeper understanding of Scepticism or show himself familiar with its central texts, such as Sextus Empiricus. His view of it seems to be based on various sources, among which the Neoplatonic introductions to Aristotle are perhaps the most important. It seems likely that his sympathy for Scepticism was strengthened by his great familiarity with and admiration for Plutarch. But essentially it rested on his

---

[80] Demetracopoulos (1999*a*: 88–109) is more positive about the influence of ancient Scepticism on Gregoras. The most important evidence in favour of his assessment is a passage in Gregoras' *Scholia on Synesius, On Dreams* (628–9). Gregoras there enumerates five factors to illustrate the point that 'the adequate representation of the things is impeded in many ways'. These are (1) different temperament; (2) different way of life; (3) different food (or nurture: τροφή); (4) different time; (5) different movement of the things represented. It is perfectly clear from the further explanation Gregoras gives of the last factor, for which he draws on Aristotle, *Div. somn.* 2. 464^{b}7–16, that it is intended as a paraphrase of the last sentence of the lemma (*De ins*. 17. 181. 19–20 T): (1) corresponds to 'different in nature'; (2) to 'different in custom'; (3) and (4) to 'different in experiences'. That is to say that the main determinant of Gregoras' list of factors is the Synesius text itself. Of course, this does not exclude the possibility that some account of the Sceptical Modes was at the back of Gregoras' mind when he drew up the list: (1) may be said to bracket together Modes 1 and 2 in the Sextan order; (2) may be said to correspond to Mode 10; (3) and (4) may be compared to Mode 4; and (5) to Mode 5. If Gregoras did associate Synesius' datives of respect with some such account, then, he may very well have had, as Demetracopoulos argues (1999*a*: 96–9), Philo, *Ebr*. 166–205, in mind. All the Modes mentioned are in fact found in Philo, including Mode 2 (*pace* Demetracopoulos (1999*a*: 98–9): *Ebr*. 176–7, and cf. 171): there is consequently no need to assume that Gregoras had recourse to Sextus Empiricus or Diogenes Laertius in order to supplement his scholion, as Demetracopoulos suggests (ibid.). There is also no need to assume that Gregoras recognized that the Philo passage was a paraphrase of the Sceptical Modes (which presupposes knowledge of some other account). In conclusion, it remains a striking fact that neither Metochites nor Gregoras ever refers to any work by Sextus, and that there is not one sure trace of Sextan influence in either writer's œuvre.

failure to distinguish between the positions adopted by the ancient Sceptics and the 'broad scepticism' (or negative dogmatism) regarding human knowledge (founded on sense-experience and/or reason) espoused by many writers in the Orthodox tradition.

No evidence confirms the idea of a Sceptical movement in early fourteenth-century Byzantium. Especially, there is no sufficient ground for assuming that the chapter on Scepticism found in Ps.-Herennius, *Commentary on the Metaphysics* and including excerpts from Philo of Alexandria, Galen, and Augustine, belongs to this period. Nikephoros Gregoras, the friend and disciple of Metochites, makes occasional reference to Scepticism, of which he seems to conceive along the same lines as his teacher. One of Gregoras' fiercest opponents in the Hesychast struggle, Nicholas Kabasilas Chamaetos, composed a short refutation of the Sceptical arguments against a criterion of truth, in which he draws on Sextus Empiricus. I have suggested that Gregoras' sympathy for Scepticism may have been an incentive for Kabasilas to set about the study which resulted in this pamphlet; but I have argued that it makes little sense to assume that the pamphlet was aimed at Gregoras or any other anti-Palamites.

NOTE ON THE EDITION

For this edition of Theodore Metochites, *Semeioseis gnomikai*, chapter 61, microfilm copies of the following MSS have been collated:

M (Marc. gr. 532 [coll. 887]), fos. 154^v–158^r.

P (Par. gr. 2003), fos. 111^r–113^v.

E (Esc. gr. 248 [*olim* Y.I.9]), fos. 293^v–295^v.

On **P** see Agapitos *et al.* (1996: 17–20); Arco Magrì (1982: 56–64). On **M** see Agapitos *et al.* (1996: 16–17). On **E** see Agapitos *et al.* (1996: 20–2); Arco Magrì (1982: 56).

The relationship between the MSS of the *Semeioseis gnomikai* is discussed in Agapitos *et al.* (1996: 22–3), and will receive a definitive treatment in Karin Hult's edition of *Semeioseis* 1–26 and 71 (forthcoming). It may be summarized as follows:

P and **M** are independent. **E** is an apograph of **M**. All the other known MSS descend from **P**.

Both **P** and **M** were probably copied from the author's original MS. **M** was probably copied before the author made the additions to his own MS that are reproduced in **P**. **M** should then be dated 1326–March 1332 (and probably before May 1328), while **P** will have been executed no earlier than 1330 (whether before March 1332 or not is less certain: the identification by Ševčenko of Metochites' hand in some of the marginal notes found in **P** is called into question by Agapitos *et al.* [1996, 19–20]). **E** is dated 1539–42. **M** is in part illegible, owing to water damage; **E** is then the only witness of this branch. In this edition, however, no readings of **E** have been noted in the apparatus, since **E** has no readings relevant to the chapter which satisfy the following three conditions: the text is illegible in **M**; **E** goes against **P**; **E** is not obviously wrong.

I am grateful to Karin Hult for letting me profit from her work on the text and tradition of the *Semeioseis* in advance of the publication of her edition. Thanks are also due to Kimmo Järvinen for valuable comment.

"Ότι οὐκ ἔξω λόγου παντάπασι δόξειεν ἂν εἶναι τὰ τῶν
Ἐφεκτικῶν ἐναντιουμένων πρὸς πᾶσαν κατάληψιν, καὶ ὅτι
Πλάτων καὶ Σωκράτης ἀρχὰς εἰς τοῦτ᾽ ἔδωκαν

"Λόγῳ παντὶ λόγος παλαίει," λόγος ἐστὶν εὖ εἰρημένος πρότερον· οὐκοῦν δὴ
5   καὶ γνώμη τε γνώμῃ πάσῃ καὶ δόξα δόξῃ καὶ κρίσις κρίσει. ὅτε δὲ τοῦθ᾽
οὕτως ἔχει, μήποτε προσμαρτυρία τις ἐντεῦθεν ἐπὶ τοῖς Ἐφεκτικοῖς
κληθεῖσι τῶν κατὰ φιλοσοφίαν ὡς οὐ μόνον ἐριστικῶς ἀλλ᾽ οὐδὲ
παντάπασιν ἀκαίρως ἡ σπουδὴ σφίσιν ἔχει, καὶ τοίνυν οὐδ᾽ ὀστρακιστέον
ἐξ Ἑλλήνων τελείως τὸ δόγμα, οὐδ᾽ ἀπορριπτέον ἀνεπιστρόφως πάντῃ, οὐδ᾽
10   ἡγητέον εὐπεριφρόνητον καθάπαξ, ὡς ἂν ἀμέλει φιλονεικίας ἔργον ὄν, καὶ
ἀνήνυτος εἴτουν ἀνόνητός τις αὐθάδεια κατὰ τῶν ὄντων καὶ λέσχη, καί τις
ἀφρονεστάτη πρόθεσις, "τύπτειν ἀέρα," καὶ "λίθους ἕψειν," καὶ τἄλλ᾽ ὅσα
ταῖς παροιμίαις μελαγχολώντων, ὡς εἰπεῖν, ἔργα. καὶ γὰρ δὴ ταῖς
ἀληθείαις πολλὰ τῶν παρ᾽ αὐτοῖς λεγομένων ὁρᾶν ἔστιν ὡς οὐκ ἔξω τοῦ
15   καιροῦ, καὶ πολλά γε τῶν ὄντων ἐπαμφοτερίζειν πέφυκε καὶ χώραν διδόναι
ταῖς ἐναντίαις δόξαις καὶ λόγοις, ὥστε καὶ πάνυ τοι κατεπιχειρεῖν
ἀκμαστικῶς, καὶ οὐ σφόδρα πείθεσθαι μήτε μὴν ἀμφοτέρωθεν ἀπιστεῖν
ῥάδιον, ἀλλ᾽ ὅ τι ἂν τις προσεῖτο, μάλ᾽ ἔστιν αὖθις ἐκ τῶν ἐπὶ θάτερα
δυσχεραίνειν καί σείεσθαι καὶ ἀπόρως ἔχειν, καὶ μεγάλη τις ἐνταῦθα
20   πίστεως καὶ βεβαιότητος ἐρημία, καὶ ἀμαθίας, ἀνάγκη, καὶ ἀκαταληψίας
κρατοῦσα διάθεσις.

Δοκεῖ μέν γε καὶ ὄντως ὁ πάντα σοφὸς αὐτὸς Πλάτων, καὶ πλεῖστον
ἐνευδοκιμήσας καὶ τοῖς πρὸ αὐτοῦ τῶν σοφῶν καὶ ὅσοι μετ᾽ αὐτὸν
ἐπιγνώσει καὶ περινοίᾳ τῶν ὄντων, καὶ ἀδόλως κομιδῇ φιλοσοφήσας καὶ
25   μετὰ σεμνοῦ τοῦ ἤθους καὶ σχήματος, καὶ πλεῖστον πεφροντικὼς ἀληθείας
καὶ τοῦ κατὰ φιλοσοφίαν προσήκοντος ἀξιωματικοῦ καὶ ἀλλοτρίου
παντάπασι σοφιστείας ἁπάσης καὶ ἁπλοϊκοῦ, αὐτὸς δὴ μάλιστα δοῦναι
τὰς ἀρχὰς τοῖς ἐφεκτικῶς φιλοσοφήσασι καὶ τῇ συνηγορίᾳ τῆς
ἀκαταληψίας, τοῖς μακροῖς ἐκείνοις λόγοις καὶ συχνοῖς τοῖς περὶ ὁτουοῦν
30   ἑκάστοτε μηδὲν περαίνουσιν ἀλλ᾽ ὅσ᾽ ἂν καὶ προτείνοιντο ταῖς διαλέξεσι
πάντ᾽ ἀπελέγχουσιν ἄπορα καὶ τῆς ἀληθείας ἔξω. οὐδὲν γὰρ ἄλλ᾽ ἢ τὸ τῶν
Ἐφεκτικῶν ἐν τούτοις, ὡς οὐδὲν ἄρ᾽ ἀσφαλὲς ἐν ἀνθρώποις τῶν δοκούντων
τε καὶ λεγομένων ἑκάστοις περὶ ἑκάστων ὡς μάλα τοι σαφῶς ληπτῶν, οὐδ᾽
ἄσειστον λόγοις ἐναντίοις καὶ κραταιὸν μετ᾽ ἀληθείας ἀνόσου παντάπασι
35   καὶ ἀτρέπτου, ἀλλὰ καὶ τὰ φαινόμενα κομιδῇ τρανῶς εἰρῆσθαι καὶ οἷς
ἔστιν ἀπολυπραγμονήτως καὶ ἀβασανίστως τῶν λεγόντων ἕπεσθαι
πονοῦσιν ἐπ᾽ αὐτούς, καὶ πολυπραγμονοῦσι καὶ βασανίζουσι τά τε
λεγόμενα καὶ τοὺς λέγοντας μετὰ μεγίστου τοῦ θάρρους καὶ τῆς
πεποιθήσεως ὡς ἠκριβωκότας εὖ μάλα, καὶ μηδὲν ἔτι περαιτέρω καὶ
40   πλέον ὂν φανήσεται πειρωμένοις καὶ προσέχουσι τοῖς λόγοις τὸν νοῦν·

---

2   καὶ ὅτι καὶ **M**
4   cf. Gr.Naz., *Carm. mor.* 10.977; 33.12; S.E., *PH* 1.202; D.L., 9.74
5   γνώμῃ γνώμη τε **P**   8   ἐξοστρακιστέον **P**
12   τύπτειν ἀέρα cf. *CPG* 2:111–12 ann. 17 λίθους ἕψειν cf. *CPG* 1:430.1
20   ἠρεμία codd.: correxi

κόμπος τὸ πᾶν καὶ μακρὸς λῆρος καὶ ἀμαθία σὺν θράσει, καὶ πάντ' ἐν
ἀκαταληψίᾳ, καὶ πάντ' ἐλέγχεται.

Τὰ δ' αὐτὰ καὶ ὁ καθηγητὴς αὐτῷ πάσης τῆς σοφίας καὶ τῆς ἀκριβείας
τοῦ ἤθους καὶ τῶν ἀγαθῶν, ὡς αὐτός φησι, πάντων, Σωκράτης, διὰ παντὸς
45 περιιὼν ἐφιλοσόφει τοῦ βίου, καὶ διέτριβεν 'Αθήνησι κατελέγχων ἅπαντας,
ὡς μηδὲν ὁτιοῦν εἰδότας ἄξιον λόγου καὶ τοῖς νοῦν ἔχουσιν εὖ μάλα πιστὸν
τοὺς ἐφ' ἑκάστοις μέγα φρονοῦντας οἷς προσεῖχον καὶ σπουδάζειν ἠξίουν
καὶ πίστιν ἀναμφήριστον πραττομένους τῶν προστυγχανόντων περὶ ὧν
φασι καὶ σεμνύνονται, καὶ τοῦτ' αὐτὸ μάλιστ' ἀγνοοῦντας καὶ πρώτως, ὡς
50 οὐδ' ἴσασιν ὅτι καί ἀγνοοῦσι, καί, λίαν ἐπισφαλέστατα καὶ ἀμαθέστατ'
ἔχοντας, δοκοῦντας πλουτεῖν καθ' ἑαυτῶν ἐν ἄκρᾳ πενίᾳ, καὶ ἀνενδεῶς
ὁτουοῦν ἔχειν, μάλιστ' ὄντας ἐν χρείᾳ, καὶ μάλ' ἐρρῶσθαι, δυστυχῶς
ἔχοντας μάλα τοι καὶ νοσοῦντας, καὶ ἀνίατα, καθότι μηδὲ νοσεῖν οἴονται,
μηδὲ ζητοῦσι τοὺς ἰωμένους. καὶ σχεδὸν ὁ πᾶς αὐτῷ βίος κινδυνεύει καὶ
55 πόνος εἶναι βάσανος ἁπάντων καὶ τῆς ἀμαθίας ἔλεγχος, ὡς μηδὲν ἄρα ποτ'
ἐν ἀνθρώποις ὂν καταλήψεως ὑγιές, ἀλλ' ἅπαντα κενῶς σπουδαζόμενα καὶ
δοκοῦντα τιμῆς ἄξια, μικρά τε καὶ μείζω, καὶ ὅσα τῶν ἀξιολογωτέρων
ἀνύσαι, καὶ ὅσα δευτέρας τύχης τινὸς καὶ τάξεως.

Καὶ ταῦτ' εἰσὶν ὄντως, ἧπερ εἴρηται, τῶν ἐφεκτικῶν λόγων τοῖς ὕστερον
60 ἀρχαί· ταῦθ' ὥσπερ δή τινες προαγῶνες πρὸς τὸν σκοπὸν σφίσι καὶ μελέται
τινὲς εἰς τὴν πρόθεσιν γυμναστικαὶ καλλίστας ἐλπίδας πρὸς τὴν μάχην
ὑπανοίγουσαι τοῖς ἀνδράσιν ἔδοξαν· ἐντεῦθεν ἄρ' ὡς ἀπό τινων
εὐδιοικήτων καὶ γεννικῶν προοιμίων καὶ παρασκευῆς ἀξιολόγου πρὸς
τὴν μάχην ὥρμηνται· ἐντεῦθεν ἄρ' ἀπό τινων τόπων ἐπικαιροτάτων μετ'
65 ἀσφαλείας κατέδραμον ἅπασαν ἀνθρωπίνην γνωστικὴν εὕρεσιν, καὶ τὸν
παγκόσμιον κατὰ πάσης τῆς σοφίας καὶ λόγων ἁπάντων καὶ δογμάτων
ἁπάντων ἀπηρυθρίασαν ἄρασθαι πόλεμον. καὶ πολλοῖς οὐ μάτην δοκοῦσι
πονεῖν· καὶ πολλοὶ γὰρ ἐξ ἐκείνου μέχρι καὶ νῦν προσήκαντο τὴν σπουδὴν
ταύτην, καὶ προσέχειν ἀξιοῦσι τὸν νοῦν, ὡς ἀληθῶς πάντ' ἄνω καὶ κάτω
70 φερόμενα καθορῶντες, καὶ μηδὲν ὅ τί ποθ' ἑστὸς ἐν μονῇ τινος οὐσίας καὶ
γνώσεως ἄτρεπτον, καὶ πᾶσαν ζήτησιν περὶ τῶν ὄντων καὶ τῶν ἐν βίῳ
πάντων πολλῷ περιπίπτουσαν τῷ πλάνῳ καὶ δυσοδίᾳ καὶ δυσχερείᾳ
χρῆσθαι καὶ ἀνύτειν ἐπιτυχῶς καθάπαξ πρὸς ἀσφαλῆ τὴν εὕρεσιν, ἄνευ δὴ
τῆς περὶ Θεοῦ καὶ τῶν θείων μόνης σοφίας, ἄνωθεν πάντως ἐξ ἐπινοίας
75 τινὸς θεοφορήτου· ἢ πόθεν ἄλλοθεν, καὶ ποίας τῶν συλλογιστικῶν τρόπων
καὶ τῶν δείξεων ἀνάγκης; ἐπεὶ καὶ περὶ τούτου τοῦ μέρους πάνθ' ὅσα σοφίᾳ
τινὶ χειραγωγούσῃ δι' ἀποδείξεων οἱ πρότερον ἐκεῖνοι τῇ ματαίᾳ γνώσει
θαρροῦντες φθέγγονται οὐκ ἄσειστα οὔτ' ἀθῶα πάσης ἐπηρείας οὐδ' ἀζήμια
παντάπασιν εἶναι δοκεῖ, καὶ πολλὰ πολλοῖς ἐλέγχοις εὐθύνεται, καὶ πολλοὶ
80 πρὸς ἀλλήλους, νέοι πρὸς τοὺς φθάσαντας καὶ ἡλικιῶται πρὸς ἀλλήλους,
ἀντιταττόμενοι καταπολιορκοῦσι καὶ καταστρέφουσι τἀλλήλων, καὶ
πάντα δόγματα καταστρέφουσι, καὶ οὐδὲν ἐῶσιν ἀνεπιτίμητον ἀληθέσιν
ἀποδείξεσι τῶν ηὑρημένων καὶ δεδομένων ἀνθρωπίνῃ, καθὼς ἔφην, σοφίᾳ·
μόνα δὲ τὰ πάσης ἐπέκεινα σοφίας ἐκ Θεοῦ πάντως εἰλημμένα παρ' ἡμῖν

---

^{58} ἀνύσαι codd. : corr. Müller ^{60} προάγωνες codd. : corr. Müller
^{68} καὶ μέχρι νῦν **P** ^{70} ἑστὼς codd. : correxi ^{83} εὑρημένων **P**

85 περὶ αὐτοῦ Θεοῦ καὶ τῶν θείων περιγίνεται τῷ κράτει τῆς ἀληθείας τίμια
καὶ πάσης αἰδοῦς καὶ ἀσφαλείας πάσης δόγματα.

Τὰ δ' ἄλλα πάνθ' ὅσ' ἄνθρωποι σοφίζονται περὶ τῶν ἐν φύσει, περὶ τῶν
κατὰ τεχνικήν τιν' ἄσκησιν ἐκ φυσικῶν αὖθις λόγων ἐξ ἐμπειρίας, περὶ τῶν
κατὰ τὸν βίον πρακτέων καὶ ἄττα προσήκειν ἀξιώσειέ τις καὶ λυσιτελεῖν
90 ἀνθρώποις, πάνθ' ὁμοῦ ταῦτα καὶ τοὺς ἐναντίους ἐπιδέχονται λόγους, ὅπως
ἂν ἀμέλει καὶ νοοῖντο καὶ λέγοιντο, καὶ πλεῖστοι δὴ περὶ τῶν αὐτῶν
τἀναντία πείθοντες οὐκ ἔξω κατ' ἀμφότερα τοῦ καιροῦ σπουδάζοντες
ὁρῶνται. καὶ τοῦθ' ὁρᾶν ἔστιν εὖ μάλ' ἐπὶ τῶν φιλοσοφησάντων καὶ
διατριψάντων φιλοπονώτατα περὶ τὴν τῶν ὄντων ἔρευναν καὶ θεωρίαν, μὴ
95 μόνον ἀλλήλοις περὶ τὰ πλεῖστα διατεινομένων τἀναντιώτατα καὶ λόγων
ἑκατέρωθεν εὐπορούντων, ἀλλ' ἔστιν οὗ καὶ ἑαυτοῖς καὶ περιπιπτόντων οἷς
ἐν ἄλλοις φθάσαντες εἰρήκεσαν. καὶ δῆλόν γε ὡς τοῦτ' ἔστιν ὃ καὶ τὰς
διαφορὰς τῶν αἱρέσεων κατὰ φιλοσοφίαν καὶ τὰς ἀκηρύκτους καὶ
ἀσπόνδους μάχας ἐδημιούργησε καὶ κατεστήσατο παλαίσματα περὶ τὸν
100 βίον καὶ τὰ θέατρα φιλοσοφίας, ὥσπερ δὴ καὶ μονομάχων καὶ
παγκρατιαστῶν τῶν περὶ τὴν ἀλήθειαν τῶν ὄντων ἑνοειδῆ γε οὖσαν, ὡς
αὐτοί φασιν, ἀδόλως πονούντων, καὶ μέντοι καὶ πάντων ἐπιτυχῶς ἔχειν
τὴν περὶ πάντων ἀλήθειαν οἰομένων, καὶ οἰομένων γε τὰ πλεῖστον
ἀλλήλων διεστῶτα, καὶ πολλάκις μάλιστ' ἀλλήλων μαχιμώτατα. καὶ
105 τοῦθ' ὁρᾶν ἔστιν ἐπὶ τῶν ἰατρικῶν περὶ τῶν αὐτῶν ἀλλήλοις
ἀντιστατούντων καὶ πάντων ἀξιούντων σφίσιν ἑκάστοις πείθεσθαι ὡς
μόνοις ἱκανῶς τοῦ καιρίου καὶ λυσιτελοῦς ἔχουσιν, ἀλλὰ καὶ ἑαυτοῖς
στασιαζόντων, εἴ τις προσέχει τὸν νοῦν, καὶ περὶ ὧν ἄρα χθὲς καὶ πρὸ
τρίτης, μᾶλλον δὲ καὶ πρὸ δυοῖν ἴσως ἢ τριῶν ὡρῶν, ἄλλως ἐφιλοσόφουν
110 τἀναντί' ἑκάστοτε νῦν γε εἶναι τιθεμένων καὶ σπουδαζόντων· καὶ τοῦθ'
ὁρᾶν ἔστιν ἔτι κατὰ πάσης τεχνικῆς ἀσκήσεως ὡσαύτως, εἰ καὶ ἧττον
ὡς ἀληθῶς ἐπὶ τῶν βαναύσων μάλιστ' ἢ τῶν ἐλλογιμωτέρων· καὶ τοῦθ' ὁρᾶν
ἔστιν ἐπὶ βουλευτικῶν λόγων ἐπιεικῶς—καὶ τεχνολογεῖται διάφορα
πολλοῖς καὶ στωμύλλεται, καὶ τἀναντί' αὖθις τοῖς πράγμασιν ἀπαντᾷ—
115 καὶ τοῦτ' ἐπὶ πάσης δικαστικῆς κρίσεως, καὶ ψέγειν ἄττα δὴ καὶ
οὕστινας ἂν ἀμέλει προτιθεμένων καὶ τοὐναντίον ἐπαινεῖν ἀξιοῦν καὶ
θαυμάζειν.

Καὶ πάντ' ἐν εὐρίποις, καὶ πάντα λόγων ἐφ' ἑκάτερα καὶ λεγόντων
τυγχάνειν οἷά τ' ἐστί, καὶ πάντ' αὖθις εὐέλεγκτα δείκνυσθαι, καὶ οὐδέν
120 ἐστι τῶν ὄντων σχεδόν, καὶ περὶ ἃ πάντως οἱ λόγοι, ὃ μὴ οὕτω καὶ
πολλῆς ἀσαφείας αἴτιον καὶ ἀπιστίας περὶ πᾶσαν γνώμην, καὶ
τοῖς Ἐφεκτικοῖς ἀφορμὴν τῇ γνώμῃ δίδωσιν, εἴτουν ταῖς ἀντιθετικαῖς
καὶ μαχίμοις ἐνστάσεσι καὶ συνηγορίαις τῇ κατὰ πάντων ἁπλῶς ἀμαθίᾳ.

---

[100] τὰ om P   [108] προσέχοι P   [109] προτρίτης P
[115] ἄττα P   [118] cf. Pl., *Phaedo* 90 c4–6.

BIBLIOGRAPHY

A. Texts

Agathias, *Historiarum libri 5*, ed. R. Keydell (*Corpus fontium historiae Byzantinae* 2; Berlin, 1967).

Ammonius, *in Cat.*, ed. A. Busse (CAG 4/4; Berlin, 1895).

Aristotle, *Metaphysics*, ed. W. D. Ross, 2 vols. (Oxford, 1924).

[Aristotle], *De mirabilibus auscultationibus*, ed. O. Apelt (Leipzig, 1888).

Asclepius, *in Met.*, ed. M. Hayduck (CAG 6/2; Berlin, 1888).

CAG = Commentaria in Aristotelem Graeca, 23 vols. (Berlin, 1882–1909).

Cicero, *Academica*, ed. J. S. Reid (London, 1885).

—— *De finibus bonorum et malorum*, ed. L. D. Reynolds (Oxford, 1998).

—— *De natura deorum*, ed. A. S. Pease, 2 vols. (Cambridge, Mass., 1958).

—— *De oratore*, ed. K. F. Kumaniecki (Leipzig, 1969).

Clement of Alexandria, *Stromateis 7–8*, ed. O. Stählin and L. Früchtel, in *Clemens Alexandrinus*, iii, 2nd edn. (Berlin, 1970).

CPF 3 = Corpus dei papiri filosofici greci e latini, iii (Florence, 1995).

CPG = Corpus paroemiographorum Graecorum, i, ed. E. L. von Leutsch and F. G. Schneidewin (Göttingen, 1839; repr. Hildesheim, 1958); ii, ed. E. L. von Leutsch (Göttingen, 1851; repr. Hildesheim, 1958).

Damascius, *Traité des premiers principes*, ed. L. G. Westerink, i (Paris, 1986).

David, *Prolegomena*, ed. A. Busse (CAG 18/2; Berlin, 1904).

Diogenes Laertius, *Vitae philosophorum*, ed. H. S. Long, 2 vols. (Oxford, 1964).

Elias [?David], *in Cat.*, ed. A. Busse (CAG 18/1; Berlin, 1900).

Epictetus, *Entretiens*, ed. J. Souilhé, 4 vols. (Paris, 1948–65).

Eusebius, *Die Praeparatio Evangelica*, i. *Einleitung, die Bücher 1 bis 10*, in *Eusebius Werke*, viii, ed. K. Mras (Berlin, 1982).

—— *La Préparation évangélique: Livres 14–15*, ed. E. des Places (*Sources chrétiennes*, 338; Paris, 1987).

Galen, *On Medical Experience*, ed. (from the Arabic version) R. Walzer (London, New York, and Toronto, 1944).

—— *On Medical Experience*, tr. R. Walzer and M. Frede, in *Galen, Three Treatises on the Nature of Science: On the Sects for Beginners, An Outline of Empiricism, On Medical Experience* (Indianapolis, 1985), 49–106.

—— *De optima doctrina*, ed. I. Marquardt, in *Claudii Galeni Pergameni scripta minora*, i (Leipzig, 1884), 82–92.

Gellius, *Noctes Atticae*, ed. P. K. Marshall, 2nd edn. (Oxford, 1990).

George Kedrenos, *Historiarum compendium*, ed. J.-P. Migne (*PG* 121–2. 368; Paris, 1889–94).

George Pachymeres, *Relations historiques: Livres 1–6*, ed. A. Failler, 2 vols. (Corpus fontium historiae Byzantinae, 24; Paris, 1984).

Gregory of Nazianzus, *Carmina moralia*, ed. J.-P. Migne (*PG* 37. 521–968; Paris, 1862).

—— *Or. 21*, ed. J. Mossay (Sources chrétiennes, 270; Paris, 1980).

Gregory Palamas, *Triads 1–3* (*Défense de saints hésychastes*), ed. J. Meyendorff, 2nd edn. (Louvain, 1973).

Gregory Palamas, *Syngrammata*, i, ed. B. Bobrinsky, P. Papaevangelou, J. Meyendorff, and P. Christou (Thessalonica, 1962); ii, ed. G. Mantzarides, N. Matsoukas, and B. Pseutonkas (Thessalonica, 1966).

[Herennius], *in Met.*, ed. A. Mai, in *Classici auctores e Vaticanis codicibus editi*, ix (Rome, 1837), 513–93.

Hermias, *Satire des philosophes païens*, ed. R. P. C. Hanson and D. Joussot (Sources chrétiennes, 388; Paris, 1993).

Himerius, *Declamationes et orationes*, ed. A. Colonna (Rome, 1951).

Hippolytus of Rome, *Refutatio omnium haeresium*, ed. M. Marcovich (Berlin and New York, 1986).

Maximos Planoudes, *Αὐγουστίνου Περὶ τριάδος βιβλία* 15 *ἅπερ ἐκ τῆς Λατίνων διαλέκτου εἰς τὴν Ἑλλάδα μετήνεγκε Μάξιμος ὁ Πλανούδης*, ed. M. Papathomopoulos, I. Tsavari, and G. Rigotti, 2 vols. (Athens, 1995).

Michael Italikos, *Lettres et discours*, ed. P. Gautier (Archives de l'orient chrétien, 14; Paris, 1972).

Nikephoros Gregoras, *Historia byzantina* (Corpus scriptorum historiae Byzantinae, 19/1–2, ed. L. Schopen; Bonn, 1829–30).

Nikephoros Gregoras, *Rhomäische Geschichte 3*, tr. J. L. van Dieten (Bibliothek der griechischen Literatur, 24; Stuttgart, 1988).

——*Epistulae*, ed. P. A. M. Leone, 2 vols. (Matino, 1982–3).

——*Scholia on Synesius, On Dreams*, ed. J.-P. Migne (*PG* 149. 521–612).

Nicholas Kabasilas Chamaetos, *Κατὰ τῶν λεγομένων περὶ τοῦ κριτηρίου τῆς ἀληθείας, εἰ ἔστι, παρὰ Πύρρωνος τοῦ καταράτου*, ed. J. Demetracopoulos (Athens, 1999), 13–20; previous edn. by L. Radermacher, in *Natalicia Regis Augustissimi Guilelmi II Imperatoris Germanorum ab Universitate Fridericia Guilelmia Rhenana* (Bonn, 1899), 5–12.

——*Contra Gregorae ineptias*, ed. A. Garzya (1954), 521–32.

Olympiodorus, *Prolegomena*, ed. A. Busse (CAG 12/1; Berlin, 1902).

——*in Meteor.*, ed. W. Stuve (CAG 12/2; Berlin, 1900).

PG = Patrologiae cursus completus. Series Graeca, ed. J.-P. Migne, 161 vols. (Paris, 1857–66).

Philo of Alexandria, *Opera*, ed. L. Cohn, i (Berlin, 1896).

——*De ebrietate*, ed. P. Wendland, in *Philonis Alexandrini opera quae supersunt*, ii (Berlin, 1897), 179–214.

Philoponus, *in Cat.*, ed. A. Busse (CAG 13/1; Berlin, 1898).

——*in An. post. 1*, ed. M. Wallies (CAG 13/3; Berlin, 1909).

Photios, *Bibliothèque*, ed. R. Henry, 8 vols. (Paris, 1959–77).

Plato, *Opera*, ed. J. Burnet, 5 vols. (Oxford, 1900–7).

Plutarch, *Adversus Colotem*, ed. M. Pohlenz (Leipzig, 1952).

——*Quaestiones convivales*, ed. C. Hubert (Leipzig, 1971).

[Plutarch], *De Homero*, ed. J. F. Kindstrand (Leipzig, 1990).

Porphyry, *Vita Plotini*, in *Plotini opera*, i, ed. P. Henry and H.-R. Schwyzer (Paris and Brussels, 1951), 1–41.

Proclus, *in Tim.*, ed. E. Diehl, 3 vols. (Leipzig, 1903–6).

Prolégomènes à la philosophie de Platon, ed. L. G. Westerink (Paris, 1990).

Sextus Empiricus, *Pyrrhoniae Hypotyposes*, in *Sexti Empirici opera*, i, ed. H. Mutschmann and J. Mau, 2nd edn. (Leipzig, 1958).

—— *Outlines of Scepticism*, tr. J. Annas and J. Barnes (Cambridge, 1994).

—— *The Skeptic Way: Sextus Empiricus's Outlines of Pyrrhonism*, tr. B. Mates (New York and Oxford, 1996).

—— *Adversus Mathematicos* 1–6, in *Sexti Empirici opera*, iii, ed. J. Mau (Leipzig, 1961); *Adversus Mathematicos* 7–11, in *Sexti Empirici opera*, ii, ed. H. Mutschmann (Leipzig, 1914).

Simplicius, *in Cat.*, ed. C. Kalbfleisch (CAG 8; Berlin, 1907).

—— *Commentaire sur les Catégories*, tr. I. Hadot *et al.*, fasc. 1: *Introduction, première partie* (*Philosophia antiqua*, 50; Leiden, 1990).

Socrates Scholasticus, *Historia ecclesiastica*, ed. G. C. Hansen (Berlin, 1995); previous edn. by J.-P. Migne (*PG* 67; Paris, 1865).

Stobaeus, *Anthologium*, ed. K. Wachsmuth and O. Hense, 4 vols. (Berlin, 1889–1912).

Suidae lexicon, ed. A. Adler, 5 vols. (Leipzig, 1928–38).

SVF = *Stoicorum veterum fragmenta*, ed. J. von Arnim, 3 vols. (Leipzig and Berlin, 1905–23).

Synesius, *De insomniis*, ed. N. Terzaghi (Rome, 1944).

Syrianus, *in Met.*, ed. W. Kroll (CAG 6/1; Berlin, 1902).

Theodore Metochites, Σημειώσεις γνωμικαί (*Miscellanea philosophica et historica*), quoted from Cod. Paris. gr. 2003, with parallel references to the edn. by C. G. Müller and T. Kiessling (Leipzig, 1821; repr. Amsterdam, 1966).

—— *Miscellanea 8 and 93. Theodoros Metochites on Philosophic Irony and Greek History*, ed. and tr. P. A. Agapitos *et al.* (Nicosia and Göteborg, 1996).

—— 'Αστρονομικὴ κατ' ἐπιτομὴν στοιχείωσις, quoted from Cod. Vat. gr. 182.

—— 'Ηθικὸς ἢ Περὶ παιδείας, ed. I. Polemis (Athens, 1995).

B. SECONDARY LITERATURE

Annas, J. (1992), 'Plato the Sceptic', in J. C. Klagge and N. D. Smith (eds.), *Methods of Interpreting Plato and his Dialogues, Oxford Studies in Ancient Philosophy*, suppl. vol., pp. 43–72.

—— and Barnes, J. (1985), *The Modes of Scepticism: Ancient Texts and Modern Interpretation* (Cambridge).

Arco Magrì, M. (1982), 'Per una tradizione manoscritta dei *Miscellanea* di Teodoro Metochita', *Jahrbuch der Österreichischen Byzantinistik*, 32/4: 49–64.

Beck, H.-G. (1952), *Theodoros Metochites: Die Krise des byzantinischen Weltbildes im 14. Jahrhundert* (Munich).

Bett, R. (1994), 'Aristocles on Timon on Pyrrho: The Text, its Logic, and its Credibility', *Oxford Studies in Ancient Philosophy*, 12: 137–81.

Biedl, A. (1948), 'Der Heidelberger cod. Pal. gr. 129: Die Notizensammlung eines byzantinischen Gelehrten', *Würzburger Jahrbücher für die Altertumswissenschaft*, 3: 100–5.

Burnyeat, M. (1983), *The Skeptical Tradition* (Berkeley, Calif.).

Constantinides, C. N. (1982), *Higher Education in Byzantium in the Thirteenth and Early Fourteenth Centuries (1204–ca.1310)* (Nicosia).

Decleva Caizzi, F. (1992), 'Aenesidemus and the Academy', *Classical Quarterly*, 42: 176–89.

216　　*Börje Bydén*

Dellis, J. (1991–2), ῾Ή κριτικὴ τοῦ Νικολάου Καβάσιλα στὴ θεωρία τοῦ Πυρρωνισμοῦ᾽, Φιλοσοφία, 21–2: 313–36.

Demetracopoulos, J. (1999*a*), Νικολάου Καβάσιλα Κατὰ Πύρρωνος. Πλατωνικὸς φιλοσκεπτικισμὸς καί ἀριστοτελικὸς ἀντισκεπτικισμὸς στὴ βυζαντινή διανόηση τοῦ 14ου αἰῶνα (Athens).

——(1999*b*), ῾Ό κώδικας 212 τῆς Μυριοβίβλου τοῦ Φωτίου: Αἰνησιδήμου Πυρρώνειοι λόγοι᾽, Βυζαντιακά, 19: 349–99.

Diller, A. (1962), 'Photius' *Bibliotheca* in Byzantine Literature', *Dumbarton Oaks Papers*, 16: 389–99.

Eleuteri, P. (1985), 'Note su alcuni manoscritti di Sesto Empirico', *Orpheus*, 6/2: 432–6.

Elter, A. (1899), 'Analecta ad historiam litterarum Graecarum. 1. De Sexto Empirico', in *Natalicia Regis Augustissimi Guilelmi II Imperatoris Germanorum ab Universitate Fridericia Guilelmia Rhenana* (Bonn), 11–28.

Foerster, R. (1898), 'Zur Handschriftenkunde und Geschichte der Philologie. 5. Eine griechische Handschrift in Russisch-Polen und das Anthologion des Orion', *Rheinisches Museum*, 53: 547–74.

——(1900), 'Zur Handschriftenkunde und Geschichte der Philologie. 6. Handschriften der Zamoyski'schen Bibliothek', *Rheinisches Museum*, 55: 434–59.

Foerster, R. (1901), 'Zu Herennios' Metaphysik. Erklärung', *Wochenschrift für klassische Philologie*, 18/8: 221–2.

Garzya, A. (1954), 'Un opuscule inédit de Nicolas Cabasilas', *Byzantion*, 24: 521–32.

Glucker, J. (1978), *Antiochus and the Late Academy* (*Hypomnemata*, 56; Göttingen).

Guilland, R. (1926), *Essai sur Nicéphore Gregoras: L'Homme et l'œuvre* (Paris).

Hahn, V. (1900), 'Griechische und lateinische Handschriften der gräflich Zamoyskischen Bibliothek in Warschau', *Wochenschrift für klassische Philologie*, 17/48: 1323–7.

Hankinson, R. J. (1995), *The Sceptics* (London and New York).

Heitz, E. (1889), 'Die angebliche Metaphysik des Herennios', *Sitzungsberichte der Königl. Preussischen Akademie der Wissenschaften zu Berlin*, 2: 1167–90.

Irigoin, J. (1987), 'Histoire du texte des "Œuvres morales" de Plutarque', in *Plutarque, Œuvres morales*, i/1 (Paris), pp. ccxxvii–cccxxiv.

Janáček, K. (1976), 'Zur Interpretation des Photios-Abschnittes über Ainesidemos', *Eirene*, 14: 93–100.

Lefherz, F. (1958), *Studien zu Gregor von Nazianz: Mythologie, Überlieferung, Scholiasten* (Bonn).

Lloyd, A. C. (1964), 'Nosce Teipsum and Conscientia', *Archiv für Geschichte der Philosophie*, 46: 188–200.

Long, A. A., and Sedley, D. N. (1987), *The Hellenistic Philosophers*, 2 vols. (Cambridge).

Markovich, M. ed. (1999), *Diogenes Laertius Vitae philosophorum*, 2 vols. (Stuttgart and Leipzig).

Martini, E. (1911), 'Textgeschichte der Bibliotheke des Patriarchen Photios von Konstantinopel. 1. Die Handschriften, Ausgaben und Übertragungen', *Abhandlungen der philologisch-historischen Klasse der Königl. Sächsischen Gesellschaft der Wissenschaften*, 286 (Leipzig).

Mette, H.-J. (1986–7), 'Philon von Larisa und Antiochos von Askalon', *Lustrum*, 28–9: 9–63.

Nicol, D. M. (1969), 'The Byzantine Church and Hellenic Learning in the Fourteenth Century', in G. J. Cuming (ed.), *The Church and Academic Learning* (Studies in Church History, 5; Leiden), 23–57.

Penelhum, T. (1983*a*), *God and Skepticism: A Study in Skepticism and Fideism.* (Philosophical Studies Series in Philosophy, 28; Dordrecht).

—— (1983b), 'Skepticism and Fideism', in Burnyeat (1983: 287–318).

Podskalsky, G. (1976), 'Nikolaos von Methone und die Proklosrenaissance in Byzanz (11./12. Jh)', *Orientalia Christiana Periodica*, 42: 509–23.

—— (1977), *Theologie und Philosophie in Byzanz: Der Streit um die theologische Methodik in der spätbyzantinischen Geistesgeschichte (14./15. Jh)* (Byzantinisches Archiv, 15; Munich).

Rescher, N. (1980), *Scepticism: A Critical Reappraisal* (Oxford).

Schmitt, C. B. (1983), 'The Rediscovery of Ancient Skepticism in Modern Times', in Burnyeat (1983: 225–51).

Schrenk, L. P. (1989*a*), 'Augustine's *De Trinitate* in Byzantine Skepticism', *Greek, Roman and Byzantine Studies*, 30: 451–6.

—— (1989b), 'Byzantine Evidence for Galen's *On Medical Experience*', *Byzantinische Zeitschrift*, 82: 251–7.

Ševčenko, I. (1954), 'Nicolaus Cabasilas' Correspondence and the Treatment of Late Byzantine Literary Texts', *Byzantinische Zeitschrift*, 47: 49–59.

—— (1975), 'Theodore Metochites, the Chora, and the Intellectual Trends of his Time', in P. A. Underwood (ed.), *The Kariye Djami*, iv. *Studies in the Art of the Kariye Djami and its Intellectual Background* (London), 17–91.

Striker, G. (1996), 'On the Difference between the Pyrrhonists and the Academics', in *Essays on Hellenistic Epistemology and Ethics* (Cambridge), 135–49.

Tambrun-Krasker, B. (1998), 'Le Prologue du "Traité des Lois" de Pléthon et le regain d'intérêt pour le scepticisme aux XIVe et XVe siècles', in J.-D. Dubois and B. Roussel (eds.), *Entrer en matière: Les Prologues* (Paris).

Tartaglia, L. (1987), 'Il *Saggio su Plutarco* di Teodoro Metochita', in *Talariskos: Studia graeca Antonio Garzya sexagenario a discipulis oblata* (Naples), 339–62.

Tatakis, B. N. (1949), 'La Philosophie byzantine', in É. Bréhier (ed.), *Histoire de la philosophie* (fascicule supplémentaire, 2; Paris).

Treadgold, W. T. (1980), *The Nature of the Bibliotheca of Photius* (Washington, DC).

Walzer, R. (1932), 'Galens Schrift über die medizinische Erfahrung (vorläufiger Bericht)', *Sitzungsberichte der Preussischen Akademie der Wissenschaften, Philosophisch-historische Klasse*, 449–68.

Weiss, R. (1977), *Medieval and Humanist Greek: Collected Essays* (Padua).

Wendel, C. (1940), 'Planudea', *Byzantinische Zeitschrift*, 40: 406–45.

Wilson, N. G. (1983), *Scholars of Byzantium* (London).

9

The Anti-Logical Movement in the Fourteenth Century

Katerina Ierodiakonou

The debate among Byzantine philosophers and theologians about the proper attitude towards ancient logic is just one episode in the turbulent history of the reception of ancient philosophy in Byzantine thought, but it certainly raises one of the most complicated and intriguing issues in the study of the intellectual life in Byzantium. For there are many Byzantine authors who explicitly praise and themselves make use of, to a lesser or greater extent, the ancient logical traditions; yet, at the same time, there are also many others who fiercely reject the logical doctrines of pagan philosophers and their use, especially in theology. What I am particularly interested in, here, is to examine how the Byzantine attitude towards ancient logic differs from one author to another and from one period to another, what exactly the arguments presented in favour and against relying on these ancient theories are, and to what extent ancient logic, or some more developed form of it, actually is used by Byzantine thinkers.

There is no doubt that ancient logic, and more specifically Aristotle's syllogistic, was taught extensively throughout the Byzantine era as a preliminary to more theoretical studies. This is amply attested not only by biographical information concerning the logical education of eminent Byzantine figures, but also by the substantial number of surviving Byzantine manuscripts of Aristotle's logical writings, in particular Aristotle's *Prior Analytics*, and of the related Byzantine scholia, paraphrases, and logical treatises. In fact, the predominance in Byzantium of Aristotle's logic is so undisputed that, even when Byzantine scholars suggest changes in Aristotelian syllogistic, or attempt to incorporate into it other ancient logical traditions, they consider these alterations only as minor improvements on the Aristotelian system. Nevertheless, Byzantine authors are not all unanimous as to the importance of the study of Aristotle's logic, and more generally, as to the importance of any kind of logical training. There is plenty of evidence that, in different periods of Byzantine history, some Byzantine philosophers and theologians stress that, when it comes to theology, we should not rely on logical arguments, whereas others insist that we should avail ourselves of logic either in the exposition of Christian dogmas or even in the attempt to prove their truth.

This certainly is a vast topic and, of course, I do not intend to discuss here all the periods of the history of this debate about the significance and use of logical or logically trained reasoning. Instead, I shall focus on the fourteenth century, and I shall try to present the different attitudes towards logic espoused by the Byzantine authors of the time. I choose this period because in the fourteenth century all the various attitudes to the topic have their famous advocates, and because by this time most views have been articulated in a clear and relatively sophisticated way. There are, though, many authors of the fourteenth century who are concerned about this issue and investigate the implications of the various positions in their philosophical and theological treatises. For this reason, I have decided to limit my topic yet further and to present only an exposition of the views on logic of three fourteenth century Byzantine scholars who played a particularly important role in the debate, namely Nikephoros Gregoras (1290/3–1358/61), Barlaam of Calabria (c.1290–1348), and Gregory Palamas (c.1296–1359). Even in the case of these three authors, however, I shall concentrate on some of their writings only; after all, many of them are still unedited. Hence, the texts I mainly draw my evidence from are Gregoras' *Florentios* and *Antirrhetika I*, Barlaam's first and second letters to Palamas, Palamas' first letter to Gregory Akindynos and his first and second letters to Barlaam.

It is true that these specific texts, as well as the intellectual milieu of the fourteenth century, have been discussed extensively on different occasions in modern times. Nevertheless, when modern scholars comment on the disputes between Gregoras, Barlaam, and Palamas, they rarely focus on the controversy over the importance and use of ancient logical theories; rather, their attention is principally drawn by the theological issues arising from the Hesychast debate, in which these Byzantine thinkers were protagonists.[1] By contrast, I shall put aside the theological issues involved here, as well as their impact on the attempts to bring about the Union of the Churches. Nor will I examine the political background of these disputes; it may seem surprising for us, and also extremely interesting, that at the time discussions on logic were sometimes held in front of the emperor and had important consequences for the relations between the Byzantine state and the Latin West, but this is not my topic. My own aim is to study what these Byzantine authors claim concerning the significance of Aristotelian syllogistic, why and how they

---

[1] The Hesychast debate was the second stage in the controversy between Gregoras, Barlaam, and Palamas; it concerned, briefly stated, the method of prayer and contemplation of the Byzantine monks, who were claiming to be able to achieve communion with God through inner quietude and silence (ἡσυχία). See e.g. Tafrali (1913: 170–203); Meyendorff (1964: 134–56); Christoforides (1993).

defend such claims, and what use, if any, they actually make of Aristotle's logic.

To start with, let us first examine Nikephoros Gregoras' position on the importance and use of ancient logic, drawing our evidence mainly from two of his works; namely, the dialogue *Florentios*, written around 1330 against Barlaam, and the *Antirrhetika I*, written before 1347 against Palamas.

Gregoras in these works claims that logic is just a word-play for mediocre minds, since Aristotelian syllogisms are nothing more than instruments which actually prove inadequate to help us reach the transcendental reality of theological truths; and he even compares Aristotelian syllogisms to the rudder of a ship which someone keeps at home, imagining himself thus to be a captain, or with the plectrum of a lyre, which makes someone think he is a musician.[2] For, according to Gregoras, the kind of knowledge we acquire through logic is not knowledge of the real things; rather, logic may only provide us with knowledge of the sensible objects which are mere images of reality and not reality itself (*Antirrh. I* 2. 4. 291. 14: εἰκόνα ἐκείνου καὶ οὐκ ἐκεῖνο), just like the myths of the poets which are never true but only fiction (*Flor.* 965–7: ἰνδάλματα τῆς ἀληθείας). After all, Gregoras points out, Aristotle himself suggested that the conclusions derived from his two main types of syllogisms, namely the dialectical and the demonstrative syllogisms, are subject to doubt; on the one hand, dialectical syllogisms have premises which may be true, but they may also be false, since they are nothing more than probable or commonly held beliefs, and on the other hand, demonstrative syllogisms are based on principles which are not themselves demonstrated, but are formulated on the basis of an inductive reasoning which has as its starting-point the observation of sensible objects, that is, mere images and not the real things.[3]

---

[2] *Flor.* 932–41 (cf. *Corresp.* 197. 24–30): Ἀλλὰ ταῦτα μέν, Νικαγόρας φησί, τὰ τῶν συλλογισμῶν δηλαδή, χαμερποὺς διανοίας ἐπίκτητα ἐπεφύκει καὶ νόθα ἐγκαλλωπίσματα · ὄργανα γάρ τινα ταῦτα πεφύκασιν ἄλλου χάριν οἰκονομούμενα οἱ δ᾽ Ἰταλοὶ καὶ ὅσοι κατ᾽ἐκείνους τῶν τῆς παιδείας προθύρων ἄκρῳ δακτύλῳ γενόμενοι καὶ μηδόλως ἐπὶ νοῦν ἀναβιβασάμενοι ὅτου χάριν τὰ τῆς τέχνης προπαιδεύεσθαι χρή, τούτοις μόνοις ἐνέμειναν, οἰηθέντες ἐντεῦθεν ἔχειν τὸ πᾶν, ὥσπερ ἂν εἴ τις ἐνόμιζεν ἄριστος εἶναι νεὼς κυβερνήτης, ὅτι πηδάλιον οἴκοι ἐκτήσατο ἢ ὅτι πλῆκτον μουσικός.

[3] *Antirrh. I* 2. 4. 289. 22–291. 11 (cf. *Flor.* 978–92): Δυοῖν ὄντοιν συλλογισμοῖν, οἷς τῶν ἀγωνιζομένων οἱ πλείους κέχρηνται, ποτέρῳ τούτων δίδως σαυτόν; Οἶσθα γὰρ ἐκ τοῦ Περιπάτου νῦν ἀνατέλλων, ὡς Ἀριστοτέλης ἐν τῷ πρώτῳ τῆς Ἀποδεικτικῆς, μὴ εἶναι τὸν διαλεκτικὸν συλλογισμὸν ἐπιστήμην φησί. Πῶς γὰρ ἂν εἴη ἐπιστήμη ἡ τὴν ἰσχὺν ὁμοίαν ἐφ᾽ ἑκάτερα κεκτημένη, ἐπί τε τὴν τοῦ ψεύδους δηλαδὴ καὶ τῆς ἀληθείας ἀνατροπήν;... Ἔπειτα, οὐδ᾽ ἥν ἐπιστημονικὴν εἶναι φησιν ἀπόδειξιν, οὐδ᾽ αὐτῇ γε δήπουθεν ἀναμφισβητήτῳ δίδωσι κεχρῆσθαι, ἄτε ἐπαγωγικοῖς τισι κόμμασι προβαλλούσῃ τῷ νῷ τὰ μερικὰ καὶ καθέκαστα καὶ τοῦτο ποιούσῃ γε ἐμπειρίαν καὶ καθόλου συναθροισμὸν εἰς εἴδη τινὰ νοητά, τῶν ἔξωθεν εἰδώλων καὶ τύπων καθάπερ ἐν βιβλίῳ τῇ φαντασίᾳ. Εἴδωλα γὰρ καὶ ψευδῆ λαμβάνων ἐντεῦθεν ὁ νοῦς, πῶς ἂν ἔχοι πορεύεσθαι πρὸς ἀλήθειαν; ὡς κινδυνεύειν σοι τὸν μετέωρον ἐκεῖνον καὶ θεωρητικὸν νοῦν φαντασίαν εἶναι καὶ ἀνοηταίνοντα νοῦν.

Therefore, Gregoras concludes, a purified and true intellect (*Antirrh. I* 2. 4. 293. 6: ὁ καθαρὸς καὶ ἀληθὴς νοῦς) in the state of grace has no need of Aristotle's syllogisms. For there is no doubt that the logician uses deceitful methods (*Flor.* 964–5: μεθόδους ἀπατηλάς) and sophisms (*Antirrh. I* 2. 4. 287. 12: σοφίσματα), in order to charm (*Antirrh. I* 2. 3. 285. 28: σαγήνη) those who are uninitiated, and to confuse them (*Antirrh. I* 2. 4. 287. 12: σύγχυσις), and at worst to lead them to blasphemous conclusions (*Antirrh. I* 2. 3. 283. 6: βλάσφημα). In addition, Gregoras uses a powerful and elaborate metaphor to illustrate his anti-logical position: as Ikaros was mistaken to think that with his wings he would be able to fly close to the sun, in the same way those who believe that they may use logic as an instrument to find out something about God and his attributes are dangerously deluded.[4]

Gregoras is consistent, throughout his work, in adopting a negative attitude towards Aristotelian syllogistic. And it is worthwhile to underline that this particular stance on the importance and use of ancient logic comes from someone who enthusiastically studied and promoted the study of ancient philosophical theories, of astronomy and mathematics;[5] indeed, from someone who is rightly regarded as one of the most important representatives of the Byzantine Renaissance and a forerunner of the Renaissance in the West.[6] However, Gregoras' rejection of logic in a way does not come as a surprise; for he believed that, by criticizing the use of logic, he was criticizing the Latin theologians who extensively used Aristotle's syllogisms. Thus, when the papal legates visited Constantinople in 1334 to negotiate the Union of the Churches, Gregoras addressed in a public speech the issue of the harmful consequences brought about by the use of Aristotelian syllogistic, in the hope of persuading the Byzantines not to take part in discussions with the Latin theologians.[7] And it has been interestingly suggested that the fact that Gre-

---

[4] *Antirrh. I* 2. 3. 281. 1–14 (cf. *Corresp.* 189. 1–8): Ἀλλὰ τά τε ἄλλα διαπορθμεύουσι ταῖς ἡμῶν ἀκοαῖς τὸν μακρὸν δαλιχεύοντες χρόνον οἱ μῦθοι, καὶ δὴ καὶ Ἰκάρου τινὸς ὑπομνήματα ἔχομεν ἐξ αὐτῶν, ὡς ἐπιθυμήσειεν ὁ μάταιος πτερῶν, ἐπεὶ μὴ ἐβούλετο μήτε γῆν ἐκεῖνος ἔτι πατεῖν, ὁ δὲ καὶ φύσεως ὑπερόρια διὰ θράσους πλεονεξίαν ἤδη ἐπόθει· καὶ ἦν ταῦτα ἐφόδια τἀνδρὶ σφαλερὰ καὶ πρόσω, ἢ ὥστε καὶ σωφρονοῦντος εἶναι δοκεῖν. Τῆς ὁμοίας τοίνυν κακοβουλίας εἶναι δοκῶ μοι καί, ὅπερ ὁ βαρυδαίμων οὗτος ἐργάζεται τήμερον... Πτερὰ γὰρ καὶ αὐτὸς συλλογιστικῶν δῆθεν ἀποδείξεων κηροπλαστήσας μηδαμῆ μήτ' αὐτῷ μήτε τῇ ὑποθέσει προσήκοντα τετόλμηκεν ἐφίπτασθαι τῷ πελάγει τῆς ἀψαύστου θεολογίας ὁ ἀναιδής, οὐκ εἰδώς, ὡς ὑψωθήσεται μὲν ὁ μάταιος καὶ τῶν θείων τῆς ἐκκλησίας πραγμάτων καὶ θρόνων τρανῶς κατορχήσεται τρόποις ἀρρήτοις συγχωροῦντος θεοῦ καὶ θήσει τὸν θρόνον αὐτοῦ ὡς ἐπὶ νεφελῶν κατὰ τὸν αὐτοῦ πατέρα διάβολον.

[5] Guilland (1926: 77–89, 194–227, 271–85).

[6] Tatakis (1949: 256); Guilland (1926: 295).

[7] This event is powerfully narrated by Gregoras himself, who in his voluminous history undertook to describe in detail the troublesome years of the history of Byzantium between 1204 and 1359. *Hist.* 507. 19–508. 3: ἄλλως τε καὶ τοῖς διαλεγομένοις ὄργανον εἶναι νομίζεται τὸν συλλογισμὸν εἰς τὴν τοῦ προκειμένου κατασκευήν, καθάπερ τὴν σκαπάνην τῷ σκαπανεῖ καὶ τὴν κώπην τῷ πλέοντι. ὃ καὶ παρ' αὐτοῖς δὲ τοῖς Ἰταλοῖς, εἴπερ ἄλλο τι, σπουδαζόμενον ἴσμεν, ἐνταυθοῖ δὲ χώραν οὐκ ἔχειν εὑρίσκομεν τὸν συλλογισμόν, οὔτε τὸν κατ' ἐπιστήμην

goras rejected Aristotle's logic, always stressing its systematic use by his contemporary Latins, had such an effect on the Byzantine attitude towards Aristotle that, in their disputes about Aristotelianism and Platonism, Byzantine scholars after Gregoras conceived of Aristotle's philosophy mainly through the filter of Western scholasticism, rather than by consulting directly the evidence found in the ancient tradition.[8]

There is, however, a further reason which seems to have prompted Gregoras' strong opposition to Aristotelian syllogistic; namely, Gregoras wished to follow in this matter the early Church Fathers, who dismissed logical studies following a tradition to be found among Neoplatonists. For instance, such an attitude towards logic can be found in Gregory of Nazianzus' thirty-second *Oratio*,[9] in which he characterizes nearly all ancient philosophical traditions as epidemic diseases, which have managed to infect even the members of the Christian Church. In particular, Gregory claims that those who depend on Aristotle's methods, or for that matter on Chrysippus' syllogisms, in order to acquire true knowledge are really mediocre minds; they can only be saved if they realize how weak logical demonstrations are in comparison to God's grace.[10]

In fact, this distinction between the knowledge we acquire through logic and the true knowledge which is based on God's grace reminds us of the Neoplatonist doctrine of dialectic as a form of knowledge of the principles of reality which goes beyond what can be captured in discursive reasoning. Indeed, Plotinus stresses in his treatise on dialectic (*Enn.* 1. 3. 4–5), a distinction between dialectic (διαλεκτική) and logic (τὴν λεγομένην λογικὴν πραγματείαν); according to this distinction, dialectic is not an instrument (ὄργανον) which deals with isolated theorems or statements and the logical relations between them, but it is the most valuable part of philosophy (φιλοσοφίας μέρος τὸ τίμιον), since it is concerned with real being (περὶ τὸ ὂν καὶ τὸ τιμιώτατον), whereas logic simply deals with sentences and syllogisms (περὶ προτάσεων καὶ συλλογισμῶν), and therefore is superficial in the sense that its scope merely is what we say about things and easily leads to preoccupation with petty precisions of speech. And, of course, there are more Plotinean passages, for instance about the inadequacy of discourse in understanding reality, which seem to have influenced, on this particular

καὶ ἀποδεικτικήν, οὔτε μὴν τὸν κατὰ τὴν διαλεκτικὴν τέχνην, περί τε θεοῦ καὶ τῶν τῆς θείας καὶ ζωαρχικῆς τριάδος τῆς ζητήσεως οὔσης.

[8] Tatakis (1949: 257–8).

[9] Gregoras repeatedly refers to Gregory of Nazianzus' doctrines and discusses his negative attitude towards logic; see e.g. *Hist.* 508. 12, 510. 21–2, 511. 20, 513. 4, 518. 14.

[10] *PG* 36. 201B (cf. *PG* 36. 204B–C): Ὁ δὲ ὀλίγος ἐστὶ τὴν διάνοιαν, καὶ πένης τὴν γλῶτταν, καὶ οὐκ οἶδε λόγων στροφάς, ῥήσεις τε σοφῶν καὶ αἰνίγματα, καὶ τὰς Πύρρωνος ἐνστάσεις, ἢ ἐφέξεις, ἢ ἀντιθέσεις, καὶ τῶν Χρυσίππου συλλογισμῶν τὰς διαλύσεις, ἢ τῶν Ἀριστοτέλους τεχνῶν τὴν κακοτεχνίαν, ἢ τῆς Πλάτωνος εὐγλωττίας τὰ γοητεύματα, οἳ κακῶς εἰς τὴν Ἐκκλησίαν ἡμῶν εἰσέφησαν, ὥσπερ Αἰγυπτιακαί τινες μάστιγες. Ἔχει καὶ οὗτος ὅθεν σωθῇ. Καὶ διὰ τίνων ῥημάτων; Οὐδὲν τῆς χάριτος πλουσιώτερον.

topic, the early Church Fathers as well as Gregoras. For example, in *Ennead* 5. 5. 1 Plotinus talks about the true intellect (τὸν ἀληθῆ νοῦν) which has true knowledge, since it would be impossible for the intellect not to be intelligent, that is to lack understanding; and this true knowledge of the intellect cannot be acquired, according to Plotinus, through logical demonstrations or sense-perception, for what is thus known is simply a mere image of reality and not reality itself (εἴδωλόν ἐστι καὶ οὐκ αὐτὸ τὸπρᾶγμα).[11]

Yet Plotinus, and much more so his student Porphyry, did accept for logic a propaedeutic role,[12] which Gregoras never recognizes; as far as he is concerned, logical studies should be altogether dismissed, and logical theory should be regarded as completely useless. Many of his contemporaries, however, including Barlaam and Palamas, adopt a more complex attitude towards logic; for they both believe that logic is indeed useful, though it has its limitations, but they come to express quite different views as to the limits of the use of logic.

There seems to have been a long tradition in Byzantium of philosophers and theologians who were in agreement concerning the use of logic in defending Christian dogmas either against the pagans or against the heretics. As the fifth-century historian Socrates tellingly reports in his *Historia ecclesiastica*, the Christians adopted right from the beginning an eclectic attitude towards Greek *paideia*; that is to say, they rejected certain aspects of pagan philosophy and appropriated others, like for example logic. And he even specifies the reason why the Christians should study and use logic, employing the following vivid illustration: one should always try to use the same weapons as one's enemy, because in this way it becomes much easier to destroy the enemy.[13] In fact, the positive attitude towards ancient logical theories is often made explicit in the works of eminent Byzantine thinkers. For instance, during the ninth century, it can be found in the letters and philosophical writings of Photios, who underlines the importance of the role of logic in the search for true knowledge.[14] Later on, in the eleventh and twelfth century,

---

[11] The obvious influence of this text on Gregoras' work becomes even more evident, when one notices the similarities in the specific wording which Plotinus uses and Gregoras faithfully adopts. See e.g. εἰδώλων καὶ τύπων (*Antirrh. I* 2. 4. 291. 8 = *Enn.* 5. 5. 1. 17–18); ἀνοηταίνοντα νοῦν (*Antirrh. I* 2. 4. 291. 11 = *Enn.* 5. 5. 1. 3); ἀληθὴς νοῦς (*Antirrh. I* 2. 4. 293. 6 = *Enn.* 5. 5. 1. 1).

[12] See e.g. *Enn.* 1. 3. 4. 18–23.

[13] PG 67. 420ʙ–421ʙ: Ἡ Ἑλληνικὴ παίδευσις, οὔτε παρὰ τοῦ Χριστοῦ, οὔτε παρὰ τῶν αὐτοῦ μαθητῶν, ἤ ὡς θεόπνευστος ἐδέχθη, ἤ ὡς ἐπιβλαβὴς ἐξεβλήθη, Καὶ τοῦτο, ὡς ἡγοῦμαι, οὐκ ἀπρονοήτως ἐποίησαν, Πολλοὶ γὰρτῶν παρ' Ἕλλησι φιλοσοφησάντων, οὐ μακρὰν τοῦ γνῶναι τὸν Θεὸν ἐγένοντο. Καὶ γὰρ καὶ πρὸς τοὺς ἀπρονοησίαν εἰσάγοντας, οἶον Ἐπικουρίους, ἤ ἄλλως ἐριστικούς, μετὰ τῆς λογικῆς ἐπιστήμης γενναίως ἀπήντησαν, τὴν ἀμαθίαν αὐτῶν ἀνατρέποντες · καὶ διὰ τούτων τῶν λόγων, χρειώδεις μὲν τοῖς τὴν εὐσέβειαν ἀγαπῶσι κατέστησαν... Οὐ μὴν τέχνην διδάσκουσι λογικήν, πρὸς τὸ δύνασθαι ἀπαντᾶν τοῖς βουλομένοις τῇ ἀληθείᾳ προσπολεμεῖν. Σφόδρα δὲ καταπολεμοῦνται οἱ πολέμιοι, ὅταν τοῖς αὐτῶν ὅπλοις χρώμεθα κατ' αὐτῶν.

[14] See e.g. *Ep.* 290. 64–71: οἴκοι μὲν γὰρ μένοντι ἡ χαρίεσσα τῶν ἡδονῶν περιεπλέκετο τέρψις, τῶν μανθανόντων ὁρῶντι τὸν πόνον, τὴν σπουδὴν τῶν ἐπερωτώντων, τὴν τριβὴν

Michael Psellos[15] and his pupil John Italos[16] repeatedly advocate the systematic use of logic—to such a degree that Italos' pupil Eustratios of Nicaea considered it appropriate to state that even Christ had argued with the help of Aristotelian syllogisms.[17]

In a similar spirit Gregory Palamas points out that we should make use of Aristotle's logic in order to rebut the ancient philosophers, just as we use the poison which we take from the snakes to produce medical drugs against their own bites.[18] And Barlaam of Calabria also claims that he uses an argument *ad impossibile* in order to refute the Latin theologians, who should therefore accept that their reasoning is untenable, since by their own logical standards it ends up in absurdities.[19] However, the most interesting issue with regard to the use of logic, which both Barlaam and Palamas extensively discuss in their writings, is not how to use logic for defending the Christian dogmas against the views of the pagans and the heretics; what is mainly at issue between them is whether logical methods can actually be used to prove Christian dogmas, that is, whether logic is of any help in our attempt to acquire knowledge of God and of his attributes. This specific question constitutes part of a more general and quite controversial problem, which has been raised again and again throughout the centuries both in the East and in the West, namely the problem of the relation in Christianity between faith and reason. And on this particular issue Palamas and Barlaam advocate very different views.

But before we look closer at Barlaam's and Palamas' conflicting positions on the use of Aristotle's logic in theology, some brief preliminary remarks are

τῶν προσδιαλεγομένων, δι' ὧν ἡ πρὸς τὸ μὴ 'ρᾶστα παράγεσθαι καταρτίζεται γνώμη, τῶν ταῖς μαθηματικαῖς σχολαῖς λεπτυνομένων τὴν διάνοιαν, τῶν ταῖς λογικαῖς μεθόδοις ἰχνευόντων τὸ ἀληθές, τῶν τοῖς θείοις λογίοις ἰθυνομένων τὸν νοῦν πρὸς εὐσέβειαν, ὁ τῶν ἄλλων ἁπάντων ὑπάρχει πόνων ὁ καρπός.

[15] See e.g. Sathas v. 447: τὸ γὰρ συλλογίζεσθαι, ἀδελφέ, οὔτε δόγμα ἐστὶ τῆς ἐκκλησίας ἀλλότριον, οὔτε θέσις τις τῶν κατὰ φιλοσοφίας παράδοξος, ἀλλ' ἢ μόνον ὄργανον ἀληθείας καὶ ζητουμένου πράγματος εὕρεσις.

[16] e.g. in the part of the *Synodikon* which anathematizes Italos, the fifth article (209–13) makes clear Italos' interest in using logic for theological purposes: Τοῖς μὴ πίστει καθαρᾷ καὶ ἁπλῇ καὶ ὁλοψύχῳ καρδίᾳ τὰ τοῦ Σωτῆρος ἡμῶν καὶ Θεοῦ καὶ τῆς ἀχράντου αὐτὸν τεκούσης δεσποίνης ἡμῶν καὶ θεοτόκου καὶ τῶν λοιπῶν ἁγίων ἐξαίσια θαύματα δεχομένοις, ἀλλὰ πειρωμένοις ἀποδείξεσι καὶ λόγοις σοφιστικοῖς ὡς ἀδύνατα διαβάλλειν, ἢ κατὰ τὸ δοκοῦν αὐτοῖς παρερμηνεύειν καὶ κατὰ τὴν ἰδίαν γνώμην συνιστᾶν, ἀνάθεμα.

[17] The last two of Eustratios' twenty-four propositions, which are edited by Joannou (1952: 34), clearly show his strong conviction for the propriety of using Aristotle's syllogistic in theology: κγ΄. Ὅτι ὁ ἀναιρῶν τῆς τέχνης τὸν λόγον καὶ τῆς ἐπιστήμης τὴν ἐπιχείρησιν, ὁδῷ προβαίνων μάτην ἐρεῖ καὶ τοῦ Θεοῦ γενέσθαι τὴν σάρκωσιν. κδ΄. Ὅτι πανταχοῦ τῶν ἱερῶν καὶ θείων λογίων ὁ Χριστὸς συλλογίζεται ἀριστοτελικῶς.

[18] *Ep. Bar. B'* §37. 281. 15–19: Εἰ δὲ τῶν ἐν ταύτῃ [i.e. ἐν ἀποδείξει] τι χρήσιμον ἡμῖν, θαυμαστὸν οὐδέν· καὶ παρὰ τῶν ὄφεων γὰρ ἔστι τι χρηστὸν φάρμακον ἡμῖν, ἀλλ' ἀνελοῦσι καὶ διελοῦσι καὶ συσκευασαμένοις καὶ χρησαμένοις σὺν λόγῳ κατὰ τῶν ἐκείνων δηγμάτων.

[19] *EG I* 63–6: χρῶμαι γὰρ αὐτῇ παρακατιὼν κατὰ τὴν δι' ἀδυνάτου λεγομένην δεῖξιν· ἀπάγων τὴν ἐκείνων θέσιν εἰς τοιοῦτον τ' ἀδύνατον. δεῖ γὰρ τὰς τῶν προσδιαλεγομένων θέσεις εἰς τοιαῦτα ἀπάγειν, ἃ καὶ αὐτοῖς ὁμολογεῖται εἶναι ἀδύνατα.

needed to set up the context of their controversy.[20] First, both Barlaam and Palamas know logic well. Barlaam comes to Greece from the humanist milieu of Italy, where Aristotle's syllogistic is studied with great diligence, and often accuses his contemporaries in Constantinople of ignorance in logical theory.[21] Palamas, on the other hand, was taught logic by no other than Theodore Metochites, and he is reported to have been admired for his logical competence when he was young.[22]

Second, the controversy starts with Palamas' objections to Barlaam's treatises against the papal legates, namely the Dominican bishops Francesco da Camerino and Richard of England, who came to Constantinople in 1334 to discuss the issue of the *filioque*.[23] In his *Antilatin Treatises*,[24] Barlaam argues that the syllogisms used by the Latins are neither demonstrative nor dialectical; they are not demonstrative, because nothing can be demonstrated about God, while they are not dialectical, because their premises are disputed by the theologians of the Eastern Church.[25] Therefore, Barlaam concludes, it may be possible to produce commonly accepted dialectical syllogisms about God's attributes, but we cannot have certain knowledge of God. Palamas wishes to challenge this general claim, since it could easily lead to relativism and the different theological schools would thus have no way to demonstrate the truth of their doctrines.[26] According to Palamas,

---

[20] For detailed information about the historical events which led to the first episode in the Palamas–Barlaam controversy, see e.g. Meyendorff 1953; Sinkewicz 1980.

[21] See e.g. Tafrali (1913: 174–7); Schirò (1959: 7–9); Polemis (1964: 51–2).

[22] See e.g. Christou (1959: 108); Meyendorff (1953: 98–9; 1964: 28–9).

[23] For a precise chronology of the papal legates' visit to Constantinople, cf. Sinkewicz (1980).

[24] Barlaam's twenty-one *Antilatin Treatises*, which were presented before the Imperial Court and the Patriarchal Synod in the first half of 1335 (cf. Sinkewicz 1980: 489–94), have survived in many MSS (cf. Meyendorff 1953: 103 n. 3; Sinkewicz 1982: 184 n. 12), but unfortunately they are still unedited. Any references to them here are based not on the close reading of the MSS, but on scattered evidence about them found in the secondary literature. They are numbered here according to their order in the MS tradition, which is given by Sinkewicz (1981: 187–9) in his inventory of Barlaam's works.

[25] It is interesting to see how Barlaam himself describes the aim and method of his treatises against the Latins. *EG I* 920–30: ὁρῶν ἔγωγε ὡς ἀδύνατόν ἐστιν ἕκαστον τῶν ὑπ' αὐτῶν γινομένων συλλογισμῶν προχειρισάμενον ἀνασκευάσαι, ἐπ' ἄπειρον γὰρ ἂν συνέβη τοὺς λόγους γενέσθαι, ἐσκεψάμην πῶς ἂν εἴη ἑνὶ λόγῳ ἅπαντας ἀνασκευάσαι (καὶ δεῖξαι ὄντας σοφίσματα). ἑώρων οὖν δυνατὸν ὂν τούτου τυχεῖν, εἴ τις οἷός τ' εἴη δεῖξαι τοὺς ἐκείνων συλλογισμοὺς μήτε διαλεκτικοὺς ὄντας μήτε ἀποδεικτικούς. ἀλλὰ τὸ μὲν μὴ εἶναι αὐτοὺς διαλεκτικοὺς προχειρότατον ἦν μοι δεῖξαι δηλώσαντι μόνον ὡς ἃ λαμβάνουσιν ἐπίσης ἡμῖν ἀμφισβητεῖται τῷ συμπεράσματι. τὸ δὲ μὴ εἶναι ἀποδεικτικοὺς ἀδύνατον ὅλως ἦν ἐξελέγξαι συγχωρήσαντι δυνατὸν εἶναι ἀποδεικτικῶς ἐπὶ τῶν θείωνσυλλογίσασθαι.

[26] It is important to note the characteristic title which Palamas gave to his own treatises against the Latin theologians: Λόγοι ἀποδεικτικοὶ δύο περὶ τῆς ἐκπορεύσεως τοῦ Ἁγίου Πνεύματος. These two treatises, which are usually referred to as *Apodictic Treatises*, were most probably written during the second half of 1335 (cf. Sinkewicz 1980: 494–8), i.e. before Palamas and Barlaam started their correspondence; they deal mainly with the theological issue of the *filioque*, rather than with the use of logical demonstrations in theology (cf. Meyendorff 1964: 44; Podskalsky 1977: 150–1). It seems that Akindynos had already objected to the use of 'ἀποδεικτικός' in their title, and Palamas attempts to respond to him on this issue in his first letter (cf. *Ep. Ak. A'* §13. 217. 8–11).

logical demonstrations should indeed be used to prove the Christian dogmas about God's attributes, so that there would be really solid grounds on which to rebut the Latin theses, like for instance the thesis about the procession of the Holy Spirit.[27] It therefore becomes clear how the Palamas–Barlaam dispute, having grown out of an important theological issue, soon turned into a question concerning the use of Aristotelian logic in theology.

Third, there is a parallel discussion at the same time in the West, developing around Thomas Aquinas' thesis that sacred theology is a demonstrative science based on principles which are not self-evident, but revealed by God. Although Aquinas' *Summa contra Gentiles* and *Summa Theologica* were only later translated into Greek by Demetrios and Prochoros Kydones, Barlaam is probably well-informed about these works and often expresses his disapproval of what he regards as Aquinas' exaggerated rationalism.[28]

Fourth, since this chapter is only concerned with Barlaam's and Palamas' views on the method which should be followed for acquiring some understanding of God's essence and of his attributes, the texts I draw my evidence from, in what follows, belong to the early stages of the Barlaam–Palamas controversy. That is to say, I mainly focus on the letters which Barlaam and Palamas exchanged directly or through their common friend Gregory Akindynos; they all date from the period 1336–7,[29] when the interlocutors were still on reasonably good terms with each other.[30]

---

[27] *Ep. Ak. A'* §8. 211. 26–212. 11: Τί μεν γάρ ἐστι θεός, οὐδεὶς πώποτε τῶν εὖ φρονούντων οὔτ᾽ εἶπεν οὔτ᾽ ἐζήτησεν, οὔτ᾽ ἐνενόησεν. Ὅτι δὲ ἔστι θεὸς καὶ ὅτι εἷς ἐστι καὶ ὅτι οὐχ ἕν ἐστι καὶ ὅτι τὴν τριάδα οὐχ ὑπερβέβηκε καὶ πολλ᾽ ἕτερα τῶν περὶ αὐτὸν θεωρουμένων, ἔστι ζητῆσαί τε καὶ ἀποδεῖξαι. Εἰ γὰρ μὴ ταῦτα, οὐδὲ μαθεῖν ὅλως ἔστι τι περὶ θεοῦ. Εἰ δὲ μανθάνομεν καὶ ζητοῦμεν καὶ τοῦτο παρὰ τῶν εὖ εἰδότων καὶ ἐπισταμένων, τὰ μὲν ἄρα τοῦ θεοῦ γινώσκεται, τὰ δὲ ζητεῖται, ἔστι δ᾽ ἃ καὶ ἀποδείκνυται, ἕτερα δέ εἰσιν ἀπερινόητα πάντῃ καὶ ἀνεξερεύνητα · τρόπος γεννήσεως, ἐκπορεύσεως, τελείας ἅμα καὶ ἀνεκφοιτήτου προελεύσεως, ἀδιαιρέτου τε ἅμα καὶ τελείας διαιρέσεως, καὶ τ᾽ ἄλλων ὧν διὰ πίστεως ἐπιστημόνως ἔχομεν.

[28] There is no doubt that Barlaam criticizes Aquinas in some of his *Antilatin Treatises*, as for instance in his *Antilatin Treatise 16*: Πρὸς τοὺς πρέσβεις. Κοινὴ ἀνασκευὴ πάντων τῶν συλλογισμῶν, οὓς ἐκτίθενται οἱ Λατῖνοι περὶ τῆς ἐκπορεύσεως τοῦ ἁγίου πνεύματος (cf. Sinkewicz 1982: 194–5). It is also the case that his *Antilatin Treatise 13* has the title: Κατὰ Θωμᾶ λέγοντος ὅτι κατὰ μόνα τὰ πρός τι διαφέρουσιν ἀλλήλων τὰ θεῖα πρόσωπα (cf. Sinkewicz 1981: 188). However, modern scholars disagree about the extent of Barlaam's knowledge of Aquinas' works; that is to say, Schirò (1959: 10–13) and Podskalsky (1977: 140) claim that Barlaam seems to have known Aquinas' writings well, whereas Sinkewicz compares some of Barlaam's discussions of Aquinas' views with Aquinas' own texts, and concludes (1982: 195 n. 56) that Barlaam's knowledge of the *Summa Theologica* and the *Summa contra Gentiles* was minimal and restricted to what was provided for him by his Latin opponents.

[29] For a more precise chronology of these letters, see e.g. Meyendorff (1953: 104); Sinkewicz (1980; 1982: 183–8).

[30] e.g. in his first letter to Akindynos, Palamas shows great respect for Barlaam's zeal for knowledge. *Ep. Ak. A'* §4 206. 10–16: Σὺ δὲ ἐρωτήσας μετὰ τῆς γιγνομένης ἐπιεικείας τε ὁμοῦ καὶ παρρησίας, μᾶλλον δὲ φιλομαθείας, μάθε καὶ δίδαξον ἡμᾶς διὰ γραμμάτων τήν τε δόξαν τοῦ ἀνδρὸς καὶ τὸν σκοπὸν τῶν γεγραμμένων οὕτω. Τὸν μὲν οὖν εἰσόμεθα καὶ μεθ᾽ ἡδονῆς δήπου· τί γάρ ποτ᾽ ἂν ἄλλο προσδόκιμον ἡμῖν εἴη παρ᾽ ἀνδρὸς ἀκριβοῦς εὐσεβείας πόθῳ τὴν ἐνεγκοῦσαν ἀπολιπόντος; And Barlaam ends his second letter to

Let us turn now to the specific views propounded by Barlaam and Palamas on the topic of the use of Aristotelian syllogisms in theology; they are, briefly stated, the following: Both Barlaam and Palamas follow Pseudo-Dionysius, when they claim that it is not possible to contemplate God himself or his essence through logical reasoning.[31] However, they offer different interpretations of Pseudo-Dionysius' position in this matter, when they attempt to specify the degree and the way in which Aristotle's syllogistic may help us to understand at least something about God's attributes.[32] Barlaam claims that we have demonstrative science neither of God himself nor of his attributes, but that we can know God's attributes by using dialectical syllogisms, which are based on the doctrines of scripture and the divinely inspired theories of ancient philosophers about the created world. Thus, according to Barlaam, although dialectical syllogisms do not give us knowledge of God's essence, they are indispensable in preparing the soul in its effort to grasp God through intuition in contemplation, on the condition that they are grounded in the appropriate premisses, for instance those provided by divinely inspired ancient philosophers.[33] Palamas, on the other hand, agrees that neither demonstrative nor dialectical syllogisms yield any knowledge of God himself, but he insists that we can acquire knowledge of God's attributes through demonstrative syllogisms, and not through dialectical ones; moreover, he makes clear that these demonstrative syllogisms are based only on the revealed wisdom of the Christian Fathers. Palamas, therefore, underlines that it is faith and grace, not the rationality of pagan philosophy, which plays the significant role in our attempt to grasp God himself who transcends

---

Palamas, by expressing the hope that their disagreement can easily be resolved. *EG III* 791–6: τί ἔτι διαφερόμεθα, ὦ θεσπέσιε δέσποτα; ὑπὲρ τίνος λοιπὸν ὁ θερμὸς ζῆλος καὶ ἡ ἐξ αὐτοῦ μάχη; καὶ γὰρ τἀμὰ αὐτὰ ταῦτά ἐστιν, ὅτι οὐχ ὑπὲρ τὴν ἐμὴν μόνον, ἀλλ' ἁπλῶς καὶ ὑπὲρ πᾶσαν ἀπόδειξίν ἐστι τὰ θεῖα, οὐκοῦν συμφωνοῦμεν· ἀγαπᾶν ἄρ' ἀλλήλους μόνον χρὴ ὡς ταῦτα περὶ τῶν αὐτῶν φρονοῦντας, οὐ φιλονεικεῖν.

[31] Both Palamas and Barlaam often refer in their letters to Pseudo-Dionysius' doctrines. See e.g. Palamas, *Ep. Ak. A'* §11. 215. 3–6; *Ep. Bar. A'* §18. 235. 2–3; §22. 237. 19–20; *Ep. Bar. B'* §10. 265. 27–266. 1; §11. 266. 16–17; §20. 271. 26–8; 272. 1–5; §22. 273. 12–13; §31. 278. 10–11; §45. 285. 12–19; Barlaam, *EG I* 49–50, 232–3, 370–2, 440–3, 780–1; *EG III* 176–8, 309–11, 350–2, 478–81. For instance, the following passage from Pseudo-Dionysius' treatise *De divinis nominibus* is at the centre of the Palamas–Barlaam debate, *PG* 3. 872A: καὶ διὰ γνώσεως ὁ Θεὸς γινώσκεται, καὶ διὰ ἀγνωσίας, καὶ ἔστιν αὐτοῦ νόησις, καὶ λόγος, καὶ ἐπιστήμη, καὶ ἐπαφή, καὶ αἴσθησις, καὶ δόξα, καὶ φαντασία, καὶ ὄνομα, καὶ ἄλλα πάντα, καὶ οὔτε νοεῖται, οὔτε λέγεται, οὔτε ὀνομάζεται.

[32] Modern scholars have diverging views as to whether Palamas' or Barlaam's interpretation of Pseudo-Dionysius' writings is in agreement with the true spirit of his doctrines. See e.g. Meyendorff (1964: 132–3, 204–5); Giagazoglou (1994: 48–52).

[33] *EG III* 263–72 (cf. *EG I* 826–45; *EG III* 245–6): θαυμασίους δὲ καὶ πεφωτισμένους παρὰ θεοῦ προσεῖπον τοὺς φιλοσόφους, οὐχ ἁπλῶς, ἀλλὰ κατ' αὐτὸ τοῦτο τὸ ὀρθῶς διορίσασθαι, τίς μὲν ὁ φυσικὸς καὶ δοξαστικός, τίς δ' ὁ μαθηματικὸς καὶ ἀποδεικτικός, τίς δ' ὁ ὑπὲρ τούτους καὶ θεολόγος · ὅτι οὐχ ὁ δι' ἀποδείξεως τὰ ὄντα μεταδιώκων, ἀλλ' ὁ διὰ νοεροῦ φωτὸς τοῖς πρώτοις ἐντετυχηκὼς νοητοῖς. οὐ μήν, ἀλλὰ καὶ ἐν οἷς ἂν ἢ περὶ θεοῦ ἢ περὶ τῶν αὐτοῦ προόδων ἢ περὶ προνοίας ἢ περὶ ἀρετῶν ἢ περὶ ἄλλου του τῶν τοιούτων ὀρθῶς ἀπεφήναντο, οὐκ ἔχω ὅπως οὐ θεῖον φωτισμὸν αἴτιον τοῦ τοιούτου ἡγήσομαι.

rationality.[34] It is only later that Palamas further develops his views on the knowledge of God, and introduces a twofold epistemological theory, according to which we contemplate God himself through illumination, but understand God's activities with reason.

To better understand these two opposing attitudes towards the use of Aristotelian syllogisms, let us look closer at the arguments Barlaam and Palamas actually use to support them. And let us first examine at least some of Palamas' arguments, since the whole controversy starts with his objections to Barlaam's writings against the Latins:[35]

1. According to Aristotle (e.g. *Top.* A1 100^{a}27–100^{b}23), the premisses of demonstrative syllogisms are true, whereas those of dialectical syllogisms are only generally accepted, and thus they are merely probable. Christian theology uses demonstrative syllogisms, because the principles on which theological arguments are based are necessary and unchangeable, being revealed by God.[36]

2. According to Aristotle again (e.g. *An. post.* A2 71^{b}16–25), demonstrative syllogisms are the only kind of syllogisms through which we acquire certain knowledge. Therefore, demonstrative syllogisms are superior to dialectical syllogisms and more fitting in the realm of Christian theology; if theology is said to use only dialectical and not demonstrative syllogisms, it becomes nothing more than a form of persuasive argumentation (πιθανολογία).[37]

3. According to Aristotle again (e.g. *An. post.* A33 88^{b}30–2), demonstrative syllogisms are only about universals, because it is only about universals that we can acquire certain knowledge. Now, although syllogisms about God

---

[34] *Ep. Bar. A'* §54. 256. 26–257. 5 (cf. §35. 245. 28–246. 13; §42. 249. 14–250. 4): Ὑπὲρ ἀπόδειξιν μὲν γὰρ λέγειν σε τὸ θεῖον καὶ ἡμεῖς συγχωρήσομεν, οὐχ ἕως μέντοι κατ' Ἀριστοτέλην τοῦτο λέγεις, ὡς νῦν τοῦτο φῇς λέγειν· χαμερπὴς γάρ, ὦ τάν, ἡ περὶ τῶν θείων τοῦ ἀνδρὸς δόξα καὶ ὡς εἰπεῖν ἄδοξος· πῶς γὰρ οὔ, ὅς, ἵνα κατὰ τὸ ἀποστολικὸν εἴπω, γνοὺς τὸν θεόν, οὐχ ὡς θεὸν ἐδόξασεν ἢ ἐσεβάσθη, ματαιωθεὶς δ' ἐ τοῖς οἰκείοις διαλογισμοῖς, δαίμοσι μὲν ἐπεφήμισε τὸ θεῖον, κτίσμασι δ' ἐστιν οἷς προσεμαρτύρησε τὸ ἀγέννητον, ψυχῶν δὲ τῶν ἡμετέρων, τό γε εἰς αὐτὸν ἧκον, ἀπεσύλησε τὸ ἀθάνατον· Ὁ γὰρ θύραθεν νοῦς οὐδὲν πρὸς ἡμᾶς· ὁ δὲ δυνάμει τούτου χωρὶς καὶ κατ' ἐκεῖνον αὖθις οὐδέν.
[35] Meyendorff (1953: 108 n. 3) and Sinkewicz (1980: 499; 1982: 238) claim that, when Palamas raised his objections against Barlaam's views, he had read only one of Barlaam's *Antilatin Treatises*, namely *Antilatin Treatise 5*: Πρὸς τοὺς ἀντιλογικοὺς τῶν Λατίνων, ὅτι ἀδύνατόν ἐστιν αὐτοῖς πρὸς Γραικοὺς διαλεγομένους διὰ συλλογισμῶν ἀποδεῖξαι ὅτι οὐ μόνος ὁ πατὴρ ἀρχή καὶ πηγή ἐστι θεότητος.
[36] *Ep. Ak. A'* §13. 217. 28–218. 4: Τίνι δώσομεν τὸ εὐσεβές; Ἆρα τῷ ἑδραίῳ, τῷ ἀμετακινήτῳ, τῷ ἐν μηδενὶ πτυρομένῳ κατὰ τὸν ἀπόστολον, ἢ τῷ καὶ οἴκοθεν ἀεὶ σαλευομένῳ; Καὶ ὁ μὲν ἐξ ἀληθῶν καὶ οἰκείων ἀεὶ τῷ προκειμένῳ, ὁ δὲ οὐ μόνον ἐξ ἐνδόξων, ἃ οὐ πάντως ἀληθῆ, ἀλλ' ἔστιν ὅτε καὶ ἐκ παντάπασι ψευδῶν, πάντως δὲ καὶ τῷ προκειμένῳ ἀλλοτρίων. Τίνι τούτων πιστεύεις δεικνύντι σοι περὶ τῶν θείων;
[37] *Ep. Bar. B'* §20. 271. 21–8 (cf. *Ep. Ak. A'* §9. 213. 2–10; §13. 218. 6–11): Εἰ δὲ καὶ τὴν τελείαν καὶ βεβαίαν δεῖξιν ἀπόδειξις δηλοῖ, μεθ' ἣν οὐκ ἔστιν ἀληθείας εὕρεσις τελεωτέρα, καθάπερ ἐπὶ τῶν δικαστηρίων ἡ ἀπόφασις, τί τελεώτερον καὶ βεβαιότερον τῶν πατρικῶν ἀποδείξεων ἡμῖν, ὥστε τοῦθ' ἡμῖν κυρίως ἀπόδειξις, διὸ καὶ ὁ ἱερὸς καὶ θεῖος Ἱερόθεος ὑπὲρ τοὺς πολλοὺς μαρτυρεῖται τῶν ἱερῶν διδασκάλων οὐ "καθαρότητι νοῦ μόνον καὶ ταῖς ἄλλαις ἱεραλογίαις, ἀλλὰ καὶ τῇ τῶν ἀποδείξεων ἀκριβείᾳ".

are obviously about a singular reality, they should be regarded as demonstrative syllogisms; for syllogisms about God are even more secure than syllogisms about universals, since in the case of syllogisms about universals there is a greater degree of uncertainty due to the fact that they involve impressions of all the individuals falling under the universal, and it is difficult, if not impossible, to grasp and compare all the underlying individual subjects.[38]

4. According to Aristotle again (e.g. *An. post.* A8 75^{b}24–6), there is no demonstration of perishable things, because nothing holds of them eternally and necessarily, but only at some time and in some way. Now, since everything in the created world is perishable, demonstrative syllogisms, strictly speaking, cannot be about created beings, but only about the creator himself, who is eternal and imperishable.[39]

5. The Christian Fathers regard their own arguments as demonstrations and, on many occasions, express their disapproval of the use of dialectic in trying to prove statements about God.[40]

6. Palamas gives a specific example of a demonstrative syllogism, which is based on two quotations from Pseudo-Dionysius' *De divinis nominibus* (*PG* 3. 641D and 645B), and concerns the procession of the Holy Spirit:[41]

> The Holy Spirit is by nature from God.
> What is by nature from God has its source in God, i.e. possesses its being from the source of divinity.
> Only the Father is the source of divinity.
> Therefore, the Holy Spirit is only from the Father.

---

[38] *Ep. Ak. A'* § 9.212. 22–213. 2 (cf. *Ep. Bar. A'* §27. 240. 19–26): Λεγόντων οὖν ἡμῶν ὅτι ὁ θεὸς τέλειος, ὁ τέλειος εἷς, καὶ τ' ἄλλα συνείρειν διανοουμένων συμφώνως τοῖς πατράσιν, ὅπως εἷς ὁ τέλειος, εἴ τις τῶν ἀνεπιστημόνων τούτων ἀποδεικτικῶν προσίσταιτο λέγων ἐπὶ τῶν μοναδικῶν ἀπόδειξιν μὴ εἶναι, παρ' ἡμῶν εὐθὺς ἀκούσεται ὡς καθόλου μὲν οὐκ ἔστι · πῶς γὰρ ἐπὶ τῶν μὴ καθόλου; Ἀψευδὴς δὲ οὐδὲν ἧττον ἀπόδειξίς ἐστι, καὶ γὰρ ἀναγκαία καὶ ἐπὶ τῶν μοναδικῶν καὶ ἀνεξαπάτητος μᾶλλον αὕτη ἡ ἀπόδειξις. Ἐπὶ γὰρ τῶν καθόλου γένοιτ' ἂν μᾶλλον ἡ ἀπάτη, διὰ τῆς φαντασίας θηρωμένης τῆς τοιαύτης ἀποδείξεως, δυσξυμβλήτων τε καὶ δυσπεριλήπτων ὄντων πάντων τῶν ὑποκειμένων. Οὐ μὴν ἀλλὰ καὶ ἐφ' ὧν τὸ κοινὸν ἀνώνυμον, τὸν αὐτὸν τρόπον γένοιτ' ἂν ἀπόδειξις καὶ ἐπί τινος εἴδους τοῦ καθόλου καὶ ἐφ 'ἑνὸς ἑκάστου γε τῶν μερικῶν ἀποδείξεις γίνονται, καθόλου μὲν οὐ · πῶς γάρ; Ἀψευδεῖς δὲ καὶ ἀναγκαίαι.

[39] *Ep. Bar. B'* §56. 292. 16–25: Ἔτι, τὸ ἀναγκαῖον δεῖ ἔχειν τὰς προτάσεις, ἐπεὶ καὶ ἡ κυρίως ἀπόδειξις κατ' Ἀριστοτέλην ἐπὶ τῶν ἀναγκαίων τε καὶ ἀϊδίων, τουτέστι τῶν ἀεὶ ὄντων, ἃ δὴ κἀκ τῶν ἀεὶ ὄντων λαμβάνουσι τὰς ἀποδείξεις · τοιαῦτα γὰρ τὰ ὄντως ἀναγκαῖα · τὸ δ' ἀεὶ ὂν ἄναρχόν ἐστι καὶ ἀτελεύτητον· ὃ γὰρ ἦν ὅτε οὐκ ἦν καὶ ἔσται ὅτε οὐκ ἔσται, πῶς ἀεὶ ὄν; Πῶς δ' ἀναγκαῖον εἶναι; Τοιοῦτον δὲ τῶν ὄντων καὶ κτιστῶν οὐδέν. Οὐδὲν ἀπόδειξις ἄρ' ἐπ' οὐδενός ἐστιν, ἐπεὶ καὶ Ἀριστοτέλης ἐπὶ λέξεώς φησι, "τῶν φθαρτῶν ἀπόδειξις οὐκ ἔστι", καὶ τὸ συμπέρασμα τῆς ἀποδείξεως δεῖ εἶναι ἄφθαρτον καὶ ἀΐδιον.

[40] *Ep. Ak. A'* §8. 211. 14–20 (cf. *Ep. Ak. A'* §9. 213. 10–13; *Ep. Bar. A'* §31. 243. 10–26): Αἵ τε γὰρ ἐπιγραφαὶ τῶν πατρικῶν φωνῶν ἑῶσι τοῦτο παραδέξασθαι. Κἄν τις φιλονεικότερον ἐνίσταιτα καὶ τὰς ἐπιγραφὰς ὡς παρεγγράπτους παραγράφηται, ἡμεῖς καὶ αὐτὰς δείξομεν αὐτῷ τοῦτο μαρτυρούσας τὰς φωνάς· "εἷς πατήρ, εἷς υἱός, ἓν πνεῦμα ἅγιον, ὥστε κατὰ τοσοῦτον τοῦτο ἐκείνοις ἥνωται, καθόσον ἔχει μονὰς πρὸς μονάδα τὴν οἰκειότητα · καὶ οὐκ ἐντεῦθεν" φησὶ "μόνον ἡ τῆς κοινωνίας ἀπόδειξις".

In general, Palamas advocates that we can indeed have demonstrative syllogisms which prove certain attributes of God, like for instance his existence, his being one, creator, and cause of everything, or his being the sole source of the Holy Spirit.

To bridge the gap between himself and Palamas, Barlaam suggests at first that their dispute boils down to nothing more than a terminological difference.[42] In particular, Barlaam claims that the problem arises from their different use of the term 'demonstration' (ἀπόδειξις), which has actually two senses; it often has a wide sense which covers every kind of proof used by public speakers, speechwriters and philosophers, but it also has a narrow sense, which in fact is the sense Aristotle is concerned with in the *Posterior Analytics*. On Barlaam's view, although 'demonstration' in the first sense may be used for syllogisms about God's attributes, it can never be used for such syllogisms in the second sense.[43] However, in addition to this attempt at reconciliation, Barlaam produces further arguments in order to support his thesis that syllogisms about God's attributes are dialectical, and not demonstrative in the narrow sense; some of the arguments used by Barlaam are the following:

1. According to Aristotle (e.g. *An. post.* A2 71^{b}19–22), first principles cannot be demonstrated, because the premisses of demonstrative syllogisms need to be prior by nature to their conclusions. Since there are no premisses prior by nature to divine truths, for truths about God are absolutely primary, syllogisms about God's attributes cannot be demonstrative.[44]

2. According to Aristotle (e.g. *An. post.* A2 71^{b}19–22), the premisses of demonstrative syllogisms refer to the causes of their conclusions. Since no

[41] *Ep. Ak.* Α΄ §11. 215. 3–12: Αὐτίκα Διονυσίου τοῦ μεγαλοφυεστάτου θεοφάντορος θεολογοῦντος ὅτι "μόνη πηγὴ τῆς ὑπερουσίου θεότητος ὁ πατήρ", καὶ ἔστι "πηγαία θεότης ὁ πατήρ, ὁ δὲ υἱὸς καὶ τὸ πνεῦμα τῆς θεογόνου θεότητος οἷον ἄνθη καὶ ὑπερούσια φῶτα", εἴ τις τὸ ὑπερούσιον πνεῦμα φύσει ἐρεῖ ἐκ τοῦ θεοῦ, τὸ δὲ φύσει ὂν ἐκ τοῦ θεοῦ πηγάζεσθαι ἐκ τοῦ θεοῦ, τουτέστιν ἐκ τῆς πηγαίας θεότητος τὸ εἶναι ἔχειν, πηγαία δὲ θεότης μόνος ὁ πατήρ, εἶτα συμπεραίνει ὡς ἐκ μόνου τοῦ πατρός ἐστι τὸ πνεῦμα, τίς λόγος μὴ οὐκ εὐσεβῶς ἅμα καὶ ἀποδεικτικῶς καὶ ἀναμφιλέκτως ἔχειν οἴεσθαι τοῦτον τὸν συλλογισμόν,

[42] *EG I* 309–10 (cf. *EG I* 283–4): τίς δὲ ἡ διαφωνία; πράγματος μὲν ὡς οἶμαι, οὐδενός, περὶ μόνην δὲ τὴν λέξιν αὐτὴν ὁρῶ οὖσαν.

[43] *EG I* 311–1 (cf. Akindynos, *Ep. Pal.* 5. 42–63): διττὸν γάρ ἐστι τὸ τῆς ἀποδείξεως ὄνομα · κοινῶς τε καὶ ἰδίως λεγόμενον. τὸ μὲν γὰρ ἐπὶ πάσης ἁπλῶς ἡστινοσοῦν δείξεως λέγεται, ὅταν ἐξ ἀληθῶν τε καὶ γνωριμωτάτων καὶ ἀναμφισβητήτων δεικνύηται, καθὸ σημαινόμενον καὶ ῥήτορες καὶ λογογράφοι καὶ φιλόσοφοι καὶ πάντες ἁπλῶς τὸ "ἀποδέδεικται καὶ ἀποδείξομεν" καὶ τὰ τοιαῦτα τῶν ῥημάτων ἑκάστοτε λέγουσιν ἐφ' ὧνοίονται ἀληθέστατα δείκνυσθαι. ἰδίως δὲ λέγεται ἀπόδειξις ἐπὶ τοῦ ἀποδεικτικοῦ συλλογισμοῦ, τοῦ ἀντιδιαστελλομένου πρὸς τἆλλα τοῦ συλλογισμοῦ εἴδη.

[44] *EG I* 349–58: πρῶτον μὲν γὰρ οὐδεὶς ἀποδεικτικὸς συλλογισμὸς ἐπιχειρεῖ πρώτην ἀρχὴν καὶ ἀξίωμα δεικνύναι · ὁ γὰρ τοῦτο ποιῶν οὐ μόνον οὐκ ἐπιτυγχάνει τοῦ ἀποδεικτικῶς συλλογίζεσθαι, ἀλλὰ καὶ λίαν ἀμαθὴς καὶ ἀπαίδευτος περὶ τὰ τοιαῦτα κρίνεται τὸ ὑπὲρ ἀπόδειξιν ἀποδείξεως δεῖσθαι νομίζων. According to Schirò (1959: 14–15), Podskalsky (1977: 131–2), and Sinkewicz (1982: 189–90), this and the next two arguments were first used by Barlaam in his *Antilatin Treatise 5*.

human being is able to refer to the causes of any reality in the Trinity, syllogisms about God's attributes cannot be demonstrative.[45]

3. According to Aristotle (e.g. *An. post.* A2 71^{b}22–3), the premisses of demonstrative syllogisms are homogeneous with their conclusions; that is to say, the premisses are about things in the same genus as the subject of the conclusion. Since God is not in the same genus as the things created by him, and since we only have knowledge of premisses about things created by God, no statement about God can be demonstrated.[46]

4. The obvious fact that there is considerable disagreement about God's attributes between the theologians of the East and the West, as well as the fact that there are so many different interpretations of Scripture, shows that theological syllogisms are dialectical and not demonstrative.[47]

5. Palamas' allegedly demonstrative syllogism of the theological truth that the Holy Spirit is only from the Father is flawed, at least for two reasons: first, it begs the question, because the conclusion is essentially the same as one of the premisses, namely that only the Father is the source of divinity; and second, no demonstrative syllogism can prove that an attribute belongs to only one thing.[48]

Therefore, Barlaam concludes, demonstrative syllogisms are used only for things which can be securely grasped by reason, and not for things concerning God.

Now the end of the Barlaam–Palamas controversy is well-known; Barlaam was condemned by the Ecumenical Synod of 1341 and returned to Italy, whereas Palamas became archbishop of Thessaloniki and after his death was declared a saint.[49] But I am not that concerned, here, with the outcome of this

---

[45] *Antilatin Treatise 5*, Par. gr. 1278, fo. 77^v 12–16 (quoted in Sinkewicz 1982: 190 n. 34): ἔτι, τῶν ἀποδεικνυμένων πάντων αἴτιά ἐστιν οἱ ὅροι καὶ τὰ ἀξιώματα, ἐξ ὧν ἀπεδείχθησαν, τῶν δὲ ἐν τῇ τριάδι ζητουμένων, οὐδένα ὅρον ἢ ἀξίωμα, ὅσα ἄνθρωποι νοοῦσιν, οἷον τ' εἶναι αἴτιον.

[46] *Antilatin Treatise 5*, Par. gr. 1278, fo. 77^v 17–22 (quoted in Sinkewicz 1982: 190 n. 35): ἔτι, ἕκαστον τῶν ἀποδεικτικῶν ἀνάγκη ἀποδεδεῖχθαι ἔκ τινος ἀρχῆς, ἢ καὶ ὁμογενῆς ἔσται αὐτῷ τῷ δεικνυμένῳ, καὶ καθολικωτέρα περιέχουσα καὶ ἄλλα πολλὰ ὁμογενῆ τῷ συμπεράσματι, τοῦτο δὲ ἐν τοῖς περὶ θεοῦ ἀμήχανόν ἐστιν εὑρεῖν.

[47] *EG I* 403–11 (cf. *EG I* 619–28): ἔτι ὁ ἀποδεικτικὸς συλλογισμὸς πᾶσιν ἁπλῶς δοκεῖ εἶναι ἀληθής, καὶ ἀμφισβήτησίς τις περὶ αὐτοῦ οὐδεμία συνίσταται, οὗτος δέ, πρῶτον μὲν τοῖς μὴ τριάδα σεβομένοις ἀλλὰ μονοπρόσωπον θεόν, ἀμφισβητηθήσεται, ὡς περὶ δύο προσώπων, πατρὸς καὶ πνεύματος, διαλεγόμενος. ἔπειτα οὐδὲ πᾶσι τοῖς τρισυπόστατον εἰδόσι τὸν θεὸν ὁμολογηθήσεται, οἱ γὰρ λατῖνοι οὐδὲν κωλύειν φασὶ καὶ μόνην πηγὴν τῆς ὑπερουσίου θεότητος τὸν πατέρα εἰρῆσθαι, καὶ ἐκ πατρὸς δι' υἱοῦ τὸ πνεῦμα τὸ ἅγιον ἐκπορεύεσθαι, ὡς ἀνώτερον αὐτοὶ ἐνεδειξάμεθα.

[48] *EG I* 500–7 (cf. *EG I* 359–85): ἀλλὰ μὴν καὶ τὸ συναγαγεῖν "τὸ μόνον" αὐτόθεν, ἐκ τοῦ εἰρῆσθαι ὁ παρὰ τοῦ πατρὸς ἐκπορεύεται, ὃ σὺ φῂς ἀποδεικτικώτατον εἶναι, οὐ μόνον ἀποτυγχάνει τοῦ ἀποδεικτικὸν εἶναι, ἀλλ', ἤδη, πρὸς τῷ ἀσυλλόγιστον εἶναι, καὶ τὸ ἐν ἀρχῇ αἰτεῖται · τὸ μέν, ὅτι οὐκ ἴσμεν πᾶν τὸ ὑπάρχον τινὶ καὶ μόνῳ ὑπάρχον, ὥστε οὐκ ἀνάγκη εἰ ὑπάρχει τῷ πατρὶ προβολέα εἶναι τοῦ ἁγίου πνεύματος καὶ μόνῳ ὑπάρχειν· τὸ δέ, ὅτι ἐπὶ πασῶν τῶν ἀποδεικτικῶν ἐπιστημῶν οὐδεὶς συλλογισμὸς δείκνυσι τί μόνῳ ὑπάρχον αὐτόθεν.

[49] See e.g. the anathemas against Barlaam and the eulogies on Palamas in the *Synodikon* (572–751). Also, in his encomium of Palamas, the Patriarch Philotheos ends his narration of the

public debate; for the purposes of this chapter, I believe that it is preferable to put it aside, since the secondary literature on it has been greatly influenced by the theological preferences of modern scholars. What I am more interested in is the use Palamas and Barlaam made of Aristotelian syllogistic, and their understanding of Aristotle's logical theory; that is to say, the central issue is whether the dispute between Barlaam and Palamas partly rests on a misinterpretation of ancient logic, perhaps even a careless reading of the Aristotelian texts. In fact, Palamas stresses in places that Barlaam gets Aristotle wrong;[50] but is he right?

The study of Barlaam's writings makes clear, I think, that his use of ancient logic is grounded in a firm understanding of Aristotle's logical theories. Indeed, when Barlaam claims that there can be no demonstrative syllogisms about God's attributes, he is well aware of the fact that, according to Aristotle's *Metaphysics* (E1 1025^{b}14–16) and his *Posterior Analytics* (A9 76^{a}16–18; A10 76^{a}31–2), first principles cannot be demonstrated. It is dialectic, Aristotle says in his *Topics* (A2 101^{b}2–4), in his *Metaphysics* (Γ3 1005^{a}19–20), and in his *Posterior Analytics* (A11 77^{a}26–35), which concerns itself with first principles and justifies the basic premises from which all sciences start. Moreover, in Aristotle's *Metaphysics* (Γ4 1005^{b}35–6; Γ6 1011^{a}3–4), there is even a specific example of a dialectical proof of a first principle, namely the dialectical proof of the principle of non-contradiction. Hence, following Aristotle's reasoning, Barlaam stresses that it is important in theology to determine of which things demonstration ought to be sought; and for this reason, he rightly accuses Palamas of failing to recognize that our understanding of God's attributes cannot come from demonstrative syllogisms, but only from dialectical ones.[51]

Indeed, Palamas' reasoning has a number of important flaws which are due to misinterpretation of specific aspects of Aristotle's logical theories. For instance, in the third of Palamas' arguments mentioned above, Palamas

---

Palamas–Barlaam controversy with the following passage, which leaves no doubt as to who was thought to be the winner of this debate, at least from the point of view of the Eastern Church. *PG* 151. 600 A: Ἡδ' Ἐκκλησία Χριστοῦ τὸν ἑαυτῆς ἐπιγινώσκει προστάτην Γρηγόριον δηλαδὴ τὸν μέγαν, καὶ κροτεῖ καὶ θαυμάζει, καὶ παντοδαποῖς τισιν ἀνάδει τοῖς τῶν ἐπαίνων στεφάνοις· τί μὲν οὐ λέγουσα τῶν θαυμαστῶν κατ' ἐκείνου, τί δ' οὐ ποιοῦσα; μᾶλλον δὲ πάντα μὲν τὰ βέλτιστα καὶ λέγουσα καὶ ποιοῦσα, ἄξιον δ' ἐκείνου μηδέν τι μηδαμῶς ποιεῖν καὶ λέγειν δοκοῦσα. Οὐ μὴν ἀλλὰ καὶ βασιλεὺς αὐτὸς σύν γε τοὺς καθ' αἷμα προσήκουσι, καὶ δὴ καὶ τοὺς προύχουσι τῶν ἐν τέλει, καὶ διδάσκαλον εὐσεβείας, καὶ κανόνα δογμάτων ἱερῶν καὶ στύλον τῆς ὀρθῆς δόξης, καὶ πρόμαχον Ἐκκλησίας, καὶ βασιλείας εὐσεβοῦς καύχημα, καὶ πᾶν ὅ τι γε τῶν καλλίστων μετὰ μεγάλου τοῦ θαύματος αὐτὸν ἀπεκάλουν.

[50] e.g. Palamas accuses Barlaam of misrepresenting Aristotelian logic, when he advocates that syllogisms about God's attributes are dialectical, since this claim might wrongly suggest that dialectical syllogisms are superior to demonstrative syllogisms. *Ep. Bar. B'* § 17. 269. 23–7: Ἔτι, εἰ διὰ μὲν τοῦ διαλεκτικοῦ συλλογισμοῦ καὶ τὴν τῶν θείων γνῶσιν θηρώμεθα, διὰ δὲ τοῦ ἀποδεικτικοῦ μόνην, ὡς σὺ λέγεις, τὴν τοῦ κόσμου, κρείττων ἂν εἴη ὁ διαλεκτικὸς τοῦ ἀποδεικτικοῦ · τοῦτο δ' ὁ σὸς Ἀριστοτέλης οὐκ ἂν ποτε συγχωρήσειεν.

[51] For Palamas' misconception of specific aspects in Aristotle's logic, see Sinkewicz (1982: 199–202).

assumes that an impression (φαντασία) is involved only in syllogisms about universals and not in syllogisms about God. But this is not an Aristotelian view; for Aristotle (e.g. *De an.* Γ8 432ᵃ8–14) explicitly says that, in order to think something, whatever that may be, we need to depend on impressions. Moreover, in the same argument, Palamas advocates the view that the impressions relied upon in syllogisms about universals are not reliable, because it is difficult to grasp and compare all the underlying individual subjects, that is all the particulars covered by the universal notion. In fact, Palamas elsewhere claims that syllogisms about universals are not reliable, since universals are formed through induction and it is impossible to grasp all the particulars falling under the universal.[52] However, Palamas presupposes here that in induction we need to observe all the particulars involved; and this is certainly not the position Aristotle adopts in his writings (e.g. *An. post.* A31 88ᵃ11–17; B2 90ᵃ28–30).

Similarly, in the fourth of his arguments, Palamas misinterprets Aristotle, when he concludes, on the basis of Aristotle's claim that there is no demonstration of perishable things, that there can be no demonstrative syllogisms about anything other than God. For it is clear that Aristotle talks here about the perishable particulars, and not about their species and genera, which are universals and imperishables. After all, if Palamas does believe that, strictly speaking, demonstrative syllogisms cannot be about created beings, what does that say about mathematical truths? In general, then, Palamas seems to distort Aristotelian logic in order to show that syllogisms about God's attributes are demonstrative. Barlaam, on the other hand, attempts to establish that it is only through dialectical syllogisms that we may acquire knowledge of God's attributes; and he does it by closely following Aristotle's texts.

Having said that, however, another point needs to be made; for the kind of understanding which we acquire through Barlaam's dialectical syllogisms does not correspond to what Aristotle says on this matter. According to Barlaam, the premisses of dialectical syllogisms depend on the doctrines of Scripture and the inspired theories of ancient philosophers about the created world; on the basis of such premisses, Barlaam claims, we do manage to grasp God's attributes. Now in the case of the Aristotelian dialectical proofs of first principles, Aristotle implies that their premisses, even if true, certainly are not explanatory of the conclusion, and hence they do not provide us with real understanding (*An. post.* A13). It is only through demonstration, Aristotle stresses (*An. post.* A2), that we acquire knowledge, since demonstration tells

---

[52] *Ep. Bar. B'* §58. 293. 9–16 (cf. §60. 294. 4–18): Ἔτι, τὰ καθόλου, ἅ εἰσιν ἀρχαὶ τῆς ἀποδείξεως, δι' ἐπαγωγῆς ἔχουσι τὴν πίστιν· ἐπαγωγὴ δέ ἐστιν ἐν τῷ πάντα τὰ μερικὰ ἐπαγαγεῖν καὶ μηδὲν ἀφεῖναι · τὰ δὲ μερικὰ ἀδιεξίτητα · τῶν ἀδυνάτων ἄρ' ἐπαγωγὴν γενέσθαι καὶ τὰ καθόλου ἄρα ἄπιστα καὶ ἀνεπίστητα καὶ ὅτι γε καθόλου. Καὶ οὐ μόνον οὐκ ἐπιστάμεθα αὐτὰ κρεῖττον ἢ κατὰ ἀπόδειξιν, ἀλλ' οὐδὲ δόξαν βεβαίαν ἔχομεν περὶ αὐτῶν· ἐκ δὲ τῶν τοιούτων ἀρχῶν πῶς ἂν γένοιτο ἀπόδειξις, ἥτις ἐστὶν ὑπόληψις ἀμετάπειστος;

us both what is the case and the reason why it is the case; knowing a fact not through its explanation is not, strictly speaking, a case of understanding. In order to get a firm understanding of the first principles, we need, on Aristotle's view (*An. post.* B19), to grasp them through intuition, which does not at all depend on dialectical syllogisms, though dialectical syllogisms may facilitate such an understanding.

To conclude, it may be true that Barlaam defended his views in an arrogant and agressive way, but it seems that he was much closer to Aristotle's text. Palamas constantly accused him of being influenced by the Latins— even calling him Latinohellene (λατινέλλην)—but such accusations only confused matters. It is in fact indicative that, when the theological and political disputes finally faded away, Barlaam's work was re-examined, and his logical views were appreciated by some Byzantine scholars, like Bessarion and Scholarios. And this is what I try to do; namely, to free the discussion of the Byzantine attitudes towards Aristotle's logic from its ideological parameters, in order to better understand the connection between Byzantine thought and ancient philosophy. For it seems that the problem which agitated the fourteenth century, both in the East and in the West, namely the problem of whether, and if so how, to incorporate within Christian theology logical methods still remains a controversial issue.

BIBLIOGRAPHY

A. Texts

Barlaam of Calabria, *Epistole greche. I primordi episodici e dottrinari delle lotte esicaste*, ed. G. Schirò (Palermo, 1954).

Gregory Akindynos, *Letters of Gregory Akindynos*, ed. A. Constantinides-Hero (Washington, DC, 1983).

Gregory of Nazianzus, *Oratio 32: De moderatione in disputando*, ed. J.-P. Migne (*PG* 36; Paris, 1858).

Gregory Palamas, Συγγράμματα, i, ed. P. Christou, B. Bobrinsky, P. Papaevangelou, and J. Meyendorff (Thessaloniki, 1962).

Michael Psellos, *Miscellanea*, in Μεσαιωνικὴ Βιβλιοθήκη, v, ed. K. N. Sathas (Paris, 1876).

Nikephoros Gregoras, *Historia Byzantina*, ed. L. Schopen, i (Bonn, 1829).

—— *Correspondance*, ed. R. Guilland (Paris, 1967).

—— *Fiorenzo o Intorno alla Sapienza*, ed. P. Leone (Naples, 1975).

—— *Antirrhetika I*, ed. H.-V. Beyer (Vienna, 1976).

Philotheos, *Gregorii Palamae Encomium*, ed. J.-P. Migne (*PG* 151; Paris, 1865).

Photios, *Epistulae et Amphilochia III*, ed. B. Laourdas and L. G. Westerink (Leipzig, 1985).

Plotinus, *Opera I–II*, ed. P. Henry and H.-R. Schwyzer (Oxford, 1964, 1977).

Pseudo-Dionysius, *De divinis nominibus*, ed. J.-P. Migne (*PG* 3; Paris, 1857).
Socrates Scholasticus, *Historia ecclesiastica*, ed. J.-P. Migne (*PG* 67; Paris, 1865).

B. SECONDARY LITERATURE

Christoforides, V. (1993), *Οι Ησυχαστικές Έριδες κατά το ΙΔ' Αιώνα* (Thessaloniki).
Christou, P. (1959), *Ὁ Γρηγόριος Παλαμᾶς καί ἡ Θεολογία εἰς τήν Θεσσαλονίκην κατά τόν Δέκατον Τέταρτον Αἰῶνα* (Thessaloniki).
Giagazoglou, S. (1994), *'Η Αποδεικτική Μέθοδος στη Θεολογία του Αγίου Γρηγορίου Παλαμά'*, in K. Voudouris (ed.), *Φιλοσοφία και Ορθοδοξία* (Athens), 45–66.
Gouillard, J. (1967), 'Le Synodikon de l'Orthodoxie: Édition et commentaire', *Travaux et Mémoires*, 2: (1976), 1–136.
Guilland, R. (1976), *Essai sur Nicephore Gregoras: L'Homme et l'œuvre* (Paris).
Joannou, P. (1952), 'Eustrate de Nicée', *Revue des Études Byzantines*, 10: 24–34.
Meyendorff, J. (1953), 'Les Debuts de la controverse hesychaste', *Byzantion*, 23: 87–120.
——(1954–5), 'L'Origine de la controverse Palamite: La Première Lettre de Palamas à Akindynos', *Θεολογία*, 25: 602–13; 26: 77–90.
——(1964), *A Study of Gregory Palamas*, tr. G. Lawrence (Aylesbury).
Podskalsky, G. (1977), *Theologie und Philosophie in Byzanz* (Munich).
Polemis, D. (1964), *"Η πρός τόν Βαρλαάμ διένεξις τοῦ Γρηγορᾶ. 'Η 'Αντιλογία'*, *Ἑλληνικά*, 18: 44–72.
Schirò, G. (1959), *'Ο Βαρλαάμ καί ἡ Φιλοσοφία εἰς τήν Θεσσαλονίκην κατά τόν Δέκατον Τέταρτον Α ἰῶνα* (Thessaloniki).
Sinkewicz, R. E. (1980), 'A New Interpretation for the First Episode in the Controversy between Barlaam the Calabrian and Gregory Palamas', *Journal of Theological Studies*, 31: 489–500.
——(1981), 'The Solutions Addressed to George Lapithes by Barlaam the Calabrian and their Philosophical Context', *Mediaeval Studies*, 43: 151–217.
——(1982), 'The Doctrine of the Knowledge of God in the Early Writings of Barlaam the Calabrian', *Mediaeval Studies*, 44: 181–242.
Tafrali, O. (1913), *Thessalonique au quatorzième siècle* (Paris).
Tatakis, B. N. (1949), *La Philosophie byzantine* (Paris).

10

Byzantine Commentators on the Chaldaean Oracles: Psellos and Plethon

POLYMNIA ATHANASSIADI

The Collection and its Transmission

The Chaldaean Oracles are a divine revelation—or so they were believed to be by their Neoplatonic commentators—of a cosmological and soteriological system and of a set of moral and ritual rules and instructions. What survives of them is a total of some 350 lines in Greek hexameter verse divided into 190 fragments of unequal length, the overwhelming majority of which have reached us through two channels: Proclus and, to a lesser extent, Damascius. In Byzantine times, however, Damascius' testimony as transmitter and interpreter of the Chaldaean material was flatly ignored, while Proclus remained an influential figure as exegete of both Plato and the Oracles.[1] It is true that, unlike Damascius, he had produced a systematic—and voluminous—commentary on the Chaldaean revelation, a commentary which was indeed deemed worthy of a refutation by Procopius of Gaza. Yet this pious act was not enough to prevent the Commentary from traversing the so-called dark ages so as to reach men like Arethas and Psellos. The latter in particular was a confessed admirer of Proclus, whom he proclaimed to be at the pinnacle of all science and wisdom.[2]

Intrigued by the Chaldaean Oracles themselves as much as by Proclus' exegesis, Psellos decided to form his own collection and append to it a systematic commentary for the use of his Christian audience. At the same time he epitomized the Proclean commentary in the form both of selections and of summaries; in the case of the latter one may safely assume (with the

---

[1] On the history and the theology of the Oracles, see Athanassiadi (1999).

[2] Cf. Psellos, *Chron.* 6. 38: προβαίνων εἰς τὸν θαυμασιώτατον Πρόκλον ὡς ἐπὶ λιμένα μέγιστον κατασχών, πᾶσαν ἐκεῖθεν ἐπιστήμην τε καὶ νοήσεων ἀκρίβειαν ἔσπασα.

majority of scholars) that the three versions of the theology of the Oracles produced by Psellos for his own use and for that of his friends and students depend directly on Proclus' treatise, rather than deriving from an epitome or a refutation of it.[3]

Subsequently the Proclean Commentary was lost, leaving Psellos' corpus of forty-two oracles as the only collection of Chaldaean wisdom in the Byzantine world. Indeed this is the very text which Plethon came across as he sought a revelation more ancient than both the Judaeo-Christian and the Islamic. Plethon recognized in the hexameters the message of Zoroaster as transmitted by his pupils, none other than *les mages hellénisés*,[4] and he therefore ignored the traditional title of the collection as well as Psellos' commentary, suppressed six oracles and drastically edited the remaining thirty-six. More importantly however, he rearranged their order according to his own philosophical criterion, appended to each fragment a short exegetical note, which makes clear how substantially his own interpretation departs from that of Psellos, and finally added an overall comment (Βραχεῖά τις διασάφησις τῶν ἐν τοῖς λογίοις τούτοις ἀσαφεστέρως λεγομένων), where he parts company with all his predecessors who had viewed the Oracles apophatically. By contrast Plethon makes them the vehicle for the formulation of a positive theology represented by an only but not transcendent God.

In doing all this, Plethon produced the first critical edition of the Oracles some 450 years before Wilhelm Kroll.[5] And it is amusing to note that Kroll, who pointedly ignored Plethon when producing his own edition of 1894, was led on in his task by the same logic and editorial philosophy as his Byzantine predecessor. Like Plethon's, Kroll's codification of the material that he found in the Neoplatonists and in Psellos, betrays great intellectual curiosity; his purpose, as he himself admits, was to reconstruct the philosophical and theosophical system of the Chaldaeans and not to produce a straightforward

---

[3] Psellos has transmitted 42 fragments, which cover the entire thematic spectrum of the Oracles, though the emphasis is definitely on ritual and eschatology (cf. *Philosophica minora II*, ed. D. J. O'Meara (Leipzig, 1989), 126–52, including the three expositions of the theology of the Oracles). It has been satisfactorily argued that Psellos depends entirely on Proclus, cf. *Les Oracles chaldaïques*, ed. E des Places (Paris, 1971), 154, and, esp., 203 with references. L. G. Westerink's thesis (1940), according to which Psellos had at his disposal only Proclus' refutation by Procopius of Gaza, has been further undermined by the attribution to the Chaldaean Oracles of a doubtful Heraclitean hexameter deriving from Arethas (West 1968), which provides evidence for the availability of the Proclean commentary beyond the Byzantine 'dark age'. Besides, a careful reading of Psellos' own commentary suggests that he had read Proclus, in the original rather than in the refutation of Procopius, with a sympathetic eye and made his own philological and theological comments with a view to the Christian audience that he was addressing. It must also be pointed out that, despite his criticisms, a conscious effort towards a reconciliation of the Christian with the 'Chaldaean' theology alongside an uncommon involvement with the eschatology and the magical aspect of the Oracles are to be detected throughout.

[4] See Bidez and Cumont (1938).

[5] *De oraculis chaldaicis* (Breslau, 1894).

edition. His arbitrary—by the standards of editorial orthodoxy—codification, which descends from the theoretical to the practical, was unquestion-
ingly adopted seventy-five years later by Des Places, who simply inserted in
his edition a few new fragments which had been in the mean time identified as
Chaldaean by Bidez and others.[6] Finally, Kroll's order of the Chaldaean
Oracles became a sacrosanct fossil for the wider world, when in 1989 Ruth
Majercik appended to Des Places' text an English translation and commentary.[7] As I have argued elsewhere (Athanassiadi 1999: 158–9), instead of the
nineteenth-century ideological edition that we have at the moment, we need
one based on the criterion of provenance. Such a text would constitute a
sounder and more objective basis on which to found any future research on
the oracles.

Psellos and Plethon as Readers of the Oracles: Soteriological Concerns and Metaphysical Preoccupations

In comparing the two Byzantine collections of the Oracles, I propose
to concentrate on Plethon's work. This emphasis is dictated by the need
to redress the scholarly balance, as Psellos' recension and especially his
several summaries on Chaldaean theology have been assiduously studied
and, what is more, treated as an objective basis for the reconstruction
of the Chaldaean system. This is the main reason for the confusion in
modern scholarship regarding the theological content and the magical
practices of the Chaldaean Oracles which, in view of the key position that
they hold in Neoplatonism, constitute a text of primary importance for
religious and philosophical studies. We must wake up to the fact that what
Psellos offers is at best a subjective, and often careless, reading of one,
not altogether 'orthodox', source—Proclus. Plethon's work on the other
hand has only recently begun to be considered, thanks to the efforts first of
Michel Tardieu, who has studied and edited the Arabic tradition of the
Plethonian recension, and now of Brigitte Tambrun-Krasker who has produced a critical edition of it with translation and commentary.[8] While I agree
with their general outlook on Plethon's ideological background and with
their perception of some of the differences between his approach and that
of Psellos, I would like to dwell on certain points which may lead to the
clarification of more general issues. Possibly the best way of initiating
the comparison between Psellos and Plethon is to consider briefly the six
oracles (Nos. 107, 149, 150, 159, 206, and 212) that the latter leaves out of his
corpus.

---

[6] Cf. *Les Oracles chaldaïques* (Paris, 1971). For the new fragments, see M. Tardieu in Lewy
(1978: 520–2) and Saffrey (1969).
[7] *The Chaldean Oracles* (Leiden, 1989).
[8] *Oracles Chaldaïques* (Athens, 1995).

No. 107,[9] the second longest oracle in our collection, condemns in naïve and rather prudish language the natural sciences or, in Psellos' words, πᾶσαν ἑλληνικὴν σοφίαν (*PG* 122. 1128C = 130. 1–2). Its simple, analytical diction contrasts sharply with the sophisticated and often deliberately obscure style of the other oracles, and to the expert eye of Plethon it must have appeared of Christian–Byzantine rather than ancient inspiration, not least through its profession of a radical form of cosmic pessimism, which exiled 'the plant of Truth' (ἀληθείης φυτὸν) from earth. As a fully fledged, if old-fashioned, Platonist and a typical Renaissance scholar, Plethon would have considered this as intellectually obscurantist and wrong on metaphysical grounds, and as such he excised it as a forgery.

No. 159,[10] which was hopelessly incomplete in the form in which Plethon discovered it in Psellos, seems to commend violent death by qualifying as 'most pure' the souls of those who suffered such a fate. This proposition flatly contradicts another Chaldaean oracle that Plethon includes in his collection (No. 166/17), while going totally against the grain of both Platonism and popular Greek ethics, in which the souls of βιαιοθάνατοι are deemed to haunt the world of the living. Plethon therefore seems to have excised the oracle for reasons of both form and content. Moreover Psellos' commentary, which Plethon had before his eyes, and which extols the teaching of the oracle by associating it with the Christian martyrs, doubtless added insult to injury.

Of special interest when assessing Plethon's methodology is the exclusion from the collection of No. 212.[11] Tardieu suggests that this was done for metrical reasons, the line being an iambic trimeter,[12] whereas the regular metre of oracular poetry, and especially of the Apollinian responses to theological questions in late antiquity, was the dactylic hexameter. If this is so, Plethon's decision to banish from his collection a saying which is so much in tune with the overall teaching of the Chaldaean Oracles tells

---

[9] The numbering of the Oracles follows the edn. of Des Places. When a second number occurs, it refers to the sequence in Plethon's collection, and therefore reproduces the numbers of the Tambrun-Krasker edn.

Μὴ τὰ πελώρια μέτρα γύης ὑπὸ σὴν φρένα βάλλου·
οὐ γὰρ ἀληθείης φυτὸν ἐν χθονί......
Μηδὲ μέτρει μέτρον ἠελίου κανόνας συναθροίσας·
ἀιδίῳ βουλῇ φέρεται πατρός, οὐχ ἕνεκεν σοῦ.
Μήνης ῥοῖζον ἔασον· ἀεὶ τρέχει ἔργῳ ἀνάγκης.
Ἀστέριον προπόρευμα σέθεν χάριν οὐκ ἐλοχεύθη.
Αἴθριος ὀρνίθων ταρσὸς πλατὺς οὔποτ᾿ ἀληθής,
οὐ θυσιῶν σπλάγχνων τε τομαί· τάδ᾿ ἀθύρματα πάντα,
ἐμπορικῆς ἀπάτης στηρίγματα. Φεῦγε σὺ ταῦτα,
μέλλων εὐσεβίης ἱερὸν παράδεισον ἀνοίγειν,
ἔνθ᾿ ἀρετὴ σοφία τε καὶ εὐνομία συνάγονται.

[10] ...βίη ὅτι σῶμα λιπόντων
ἀνθρώπων ψυχαὶ καθαρώταται../ψυχαὶ ἀρηΐφατοι καθαρώτεραι ἢ ἐπὶ νούσοις
(Arethas' version).

[11] "Ἃ δὴ λέγει νοῦς, τῷ νοεῖν δήπου λέγει.

[12] Tardieu (1987: 153).

us something about his philological rigour, at least on this particular occasion.[13]

Finally Nos. 150, 206, and 149,[14] as well as being metrically incomplete, are straightforward magic injunctions which blatantly contradict Plethon's view of the Chaldaean revelation as a highly spiritual text. Yet Plethon does not excise from his corpus every single 'magical' oracle. As a clue towards elucidating his criterion of selection, I suggest that we consider one of those he does include, No. 147/24. The text provided by Psellos reads as follows:

> Πολλάκις ἢν λέξῃς μοι, ἀθρήσεις πάντα λέοντα
> Οὔτε γὰρ οὐράνιος κυρτὸς τότε φαίνεται ὄγκος,
> ἀστέρες οὐ λάμπουσι, τὸ μήνης φῶς κεκάλυπται,
> χθὼν οὐχ ἕστηκεν· βλέπεται δέ <τὰ> πάντα κεραυνοῖς.

Personally I detect here another Byzantine forgery, but clearly this is not how Plethon viewed the text. Admittedly he had major doubts as regards its state, but he solved them by resorting to drastic emendations, which incidentally create metrical problems.[15] Thus, in Plethon's reconstruction of the text, the oracle reads as follows:

> Πολλάκις ἢν λέξῃς μοι, ἀθρήσεις πάντη λεκτὸν
> Οὔτε γὰρ οὐράνιος κυρτὸς τότε φαίνεται ὄγκος,
> ἀστέρες οὐ λάμπουσι, τὸ μήνης φῶς κεκάλυπται,
> χθὼν οὐχ ἕστηκεν· βλέπεται δέ <τὰ> πάντα κεραυνοί.

Turning from the text to the commentaries on this oracle, we realize that, like his source Proclus, Psellos is engrossed by the technical aspect of the Oracles. One of his main concerns is the reconstruction of the magical ceremonies, which he assumes—clearly following Proclus—to have played a crucial role in the articulation of the system. Spells and magical instruments, astrological and alchemical material, are subjects which fascinate Psellos and he provides literal and often ingenious explanations for them. Conversely Plethon, who cannot possibly banish every reference to τελεταί without ending up with only a few lines of text, interprets all references to them and their paraphernalia as initiation into the mysteries of the mind and as symbols of the spiritual truth. Thus in the passage under discussion the key word

---

[13] It should be pointed out that, on one occasion at least (No. 147/24 discussed below), Plethon succeeds in conveying what he wants at the cost of violating the metre.

[14] Ὀνόματα βάρβαρα μήποτ' ἀλλάξῃς (150)
Ἐνέργει περὶ τὸν ἑκατικὸν στρόφαλον (206)
Ἡνίκα δ' ἐρχόμενον δαίμονα πρόσγειον ἀθρήσεις,
θῦε λίθον μνούζιριν ἐπαυδῶν (149).

[15] A sensible (and metrically possible) emendation—πάντ' ἀχλύοντα—was proposed by Lobeck. For a good discussion of the oracle in connection with Iamblichus and Psellos, see Johnston (1990: 111–33), who does not mention Plethon. A paraphrasis of oracle 147 is to be found in Iamblichus *de myst.* 2. 4, 75. 12–15; the Iamblichan meaning agrees with Plethon's and not Psellos' text and interpretation.

for Psellos is 'lion' which he identifies with the zodiac sign of Leo, while pointing out its well-known solar connections. If, he tells us, during the Chaldaean ceremonies one addresses the leonine source of the stars by its proper name, then one will witness precisely what the oracle describes. The reason for this lies in the fact that when the superior *hegemonikon* (governing part) of the leonine source manifests itself, its overwhelming power conceals the landscape of the heavens from our view, though it by no means eliminates its essence (οὐκ ἀναιρεῖ τὴν οὐσίαν τοῦ οὐρανοῦ (1133C = 134.14)). As opposed to this astrological-magical interpretation of the oracle, Plethon proposes a purely spiritual explanation of the divine words (ἐκ τοῦ θεοῦ λέγει τὸ λόγιον): 'If you insistently address me or invoke me, says God to the initiate, then you will see everywhere what you have addressed, that is me whom you invoked. For nothing else will be visible to you but all things as lightning, that is the fire which leaps everywhere over the world.' As well as providing a topos of Sufi teaching, Plethon's exegesis justifies Chaldaean (and Zoroastrian) pyrolatry: to the believer who has advanced in mystical know-ledge, and has not remained at the spiritually imperfect level of Semele, God manifests himself in his unadulterated form of divine fire. What is interesting in the present case is that, faced with the possibility of introducing a vital teaching of mystical theology, Plethon did not hesitate to break formal philological rules—πάντῃ λεκτόν does not scan. More importantly, how-ever, by asserting that the highest principle may appear to man and be comprehended in its entirety by him, Plethon parts company not only with Psellos, but equally with the original interpreters of the Oracles, the Neopla-tonists themselves, who postulated a negative theology placing the supreme God beyond vision and intellection.

To Plethon's mind however, games with divine apparitions, whether in their undisguised or symbolic form, were dangerous things. As if to empha-size this, he places immediately after the 'theophanic' oracle that we have just considered the austere injunction Μὴ φύσεως καλέσῃς αὔτοπτον ἄγαλμα (101/25), and warns his readers that the goddess Nature is not visible to human eyes; should she be ritually invoked, she will show to the initiate *some* only of the symbols of her status and not her true nature—in other words she will manifest what the Christian Psellos understands and person-alizes as 'a multitude of demons'—φυσικῶν δαιμονίων μόνον πληθύν (1136D = 136. 13). Though the two exegetes seem to be saying the same, the crucial difference in their interpretation is again one of faithfulness to the Neoplatonist approach. Whether following Proclus or of his own accord, Psellos gives as the reason for the demonic apparition of Nature—and therefore the need to leave her uninvoked—the fact that she is not wholly intelligible (οὐκ ἔστι παντάπασι νοητόν: 1136D = 136. 10). Plethon on the other hand concentrates on the verb μὴ καλέσῃς: the reason for his negative injunction is that the spiritual essence of Nature is simply not visible to the human eyes.

Even more revealing for our purposes is the disparity displayed by the two commentators when they interpret No. 90/19.[16] For Psellos the dogs who spring out of the earth are *real*. They are the material demons (ἔνυλοι δαίμονες) who haunt the earth (1140C = 139. 1). Conversely, for Plethon they are illusory apparitions (φαινόμενα ἀνυπόστατα), amounting to no more than the phantoms of the initiate's irrational urges.[17]

From the human point of view the most important aspect of any holy book, or mystic way, is the soteriological. Viewing the collection as a way to salvation, Plethon displays great optimism. Oracles that could be classified as eschatological are considered by him in purely symbolic terms. Thus for the oracle Ψυχῆς ἐξωστῆρες ἀνάπνοοι εὔλυτοι εἰσίν (124/9) he gives as its hidden meaning the following: 'the reasoning which pushes away the soul, that is away from wickedness, and thus allows it to breathe, is easily set free, without difficulty released from the forgetfulness which held it prisoner'. Psellos' literal understanding of the same oracle, while revealing an uncommon preoccupation with death, also betrays a certain amount of wishful thinking: when death as a physical event approaches, the powers which push the soul outside the body are free, that is unconstrained by any natural force; indeed they are eminently able to liberate the soul from its bodily fetters (1144C = 142. 4 ff.).Typically Psellos views the oracle as referring to a primarily physical activity; Plethon on the other hand perceives death in this context as a moral and spiritual state, and consequently uses the oracle as a pretext for a discussion on the freedom of the will.

Another 'eschatological' oracle (162/8) drills an even greater abyss between the two commentators. Psellos' version, which reads as follows, Ἃ ἃ τούσδε χθὼν κατωρύεται ἐς τέκνα μέχρις is critically emended by Plethon to Ἃ ἃ τούσδε χθὼν κατοδύρεται ἐς τέκνα μέχρις. Psellos understands the apocalyptic utterance as a reference to the unbelievers (περὶ τῶν ἀθέων ὁ λόγος), those who deny God's existence. God extends his punishment to their posterity. 'The earth howls over them', that is, their subterranean abode bellows over them and the awful sound is like the roaring of a lion (1145B–C = 143. 13). Against this Christian hell, Plethon dynamically balances a picture of earthly failure: those who, while on earth, do not hasten towards the realm of light where their soul has originated, fail to accomplish their duty towards their own mortal nature (for this is how Plethon understands 'earth' in the present context), but equally they wrong their own children who share in their parents' wickedness by reason of their misguided upbringing.

---

[16] ἐκ δ' ἄρα κόλπων
γαίης θρώσκουσι χθόνιοι κύνες οὔποτ' ἀληθὲς
σῆμα βροτῷ δεικνύντες.

[17] This again is an important point in Sufi teaching which can be driven home in quite dramatic terms: as one advances along the way, one acquires the ability to distance oneself from one's passions, which at times may leap out of oneself in the physical form of the animal whose characteristics are most appropriate to the conquered and thus alienated passion of the devotee.

The Platonic division of humanity into the educated and the uneducated (the πεπαιδευμένοι and the ἀπαίδευτοι) is always present in Plethon's mind. If on the ontological level evil equals non-existence, on the moral level its infinite shades and gradations appear to him as a greater or lesser deficiency in education. Thus, commenting on 161/21 (ποιναὶ μερόπων ἄγκτειραι (Psellos); αἱ ποιναὶ μερόπων ἄγκτειραι (Plethon)), the latter regards misfortune as an eminently educative force in a world in which nothing ever happens at random. An optimist by nature and upbringing, he allegorizes the punitive demons who seize hold of men as the inhibitions which turn man away from wickedness and attach him to the good. Commenting on the same oracular phrase Psellos had talked of the need of purification for all and had concluded with the pessimistic, but historically relevant, remark that 'indeed we see many of those who have lived in piety and purity fall into unexpected misfortunes' (1141A = 139. 25–6). Psellos' sense of the tragic and the absurd in history was certainly not shared by his successor. Indeed, as a commentator of the Chaldaean Oracles, Plethon displays an unexpected *joie de vivre*, when he deliberately turns the call to an ascetic life into an exhortation to a life of terrestrial well-being.[18]

Turning from ethics and eschatology to metaphysics, we discover that Plethon's understanding of the system which he extracts from the thirty-six oracles that he has retained from Psellos' recension, is austerely monistic; it is a vertical emanational construction which pointedly ignores the triadic structures of both Neoplatonist and Christian theology. Besides, as has already been pointed out, the fiery first principle, which pervades all its emanations, is not transcendental. Thus the famous Chaldaean line which concludes the oracle that heads Kroll's collection,

$$ὄφρα μάθῃς τὸ νοητόν, ἐπεὶ νόου ἔξω ὑπάρχει \ (1.10)$$

and which is to be found in Psellos in the metrically maimed form,

$$Μάθε τὸ νοητόν, ἐπεὶ νόου ἔξω ὑπάρχει,$$

appears in Plethon's corpus as follows:

$$Μάνθανε τὸ νοητόν, ἐπεὶ νόου ἔξω ὑπάρχει \ (29).$$

Psellos gives the line its classic apophatic interpretation, that the intelligible transcends intellection (1148D–1149A = 145). Plethon introduces a subtle division between the concepts of actuality and potentiality—ἐνεργείᾳ and δυνάμει. The intelligible, he postulates, has been planted in man; it is outside him ἐνεργείᾳ, not δυνάμει (ἔξω τοῦ σοῦ ὑπάρχει νοῦ ἐνεργείᾳ δηλαδή). It is therefore up to the individual man to activate the innate knowledge of the intelligible.

---

[18] See No. 158/16 and the equivalent commentaries by Psellos (1125 = 127–8) and Plethon for two diametrically opposed interpretations.

Even more optimistic (as requiring less energy on the part of man) is the monistic message dispensed by Plethon's interpretation of No. 88/20:

> Ἡ φύσις πείθει πιστεύειν[19] εἶναι τοὺς δαίμονας ἀγνούς,
> καὶ τὰ κακῆς ὕλης βλαστήματα χρηστὰ καὶ ἐσθλά.

While on this occasion the texts of Psellos and Plethon are virtually the same, their interpretations are typically antithetical. Psellos dispays a much more literal and at the same time gloomier understanding of the text. Starting from a fundamentally dualistic conception of the universe, he stages choruses of evil demons who often *pretend* to be good in order to lead the initiate astray.[20] To this deliberately perverse behaviour on the part of the supernatural, Plethon opposes a profoundly reassuring view: everything for him, even the offspring of the so-called 'evil matter', is essentially good, a point that he argues in extreme Platonic terms when stating that the oracle refers to matter as being evil not in essence, but in view of its position as the very last entity in the order of existence;[21] in this context 'evil' is an emphatic way of speaking, an extreme expression to denote the minimal participation in the good enjoyed by matter. The ultimate message of the oracle according to Plethon is that, if the offspring of the so-called bad matter can be good as deriving from God who is αὐτοαγαθός, far more so are the demons who are both logical and immortal, two characteristics which ensure for them an exalted position in the ladder of being.

A final example of the contrasting preoccupations of the two exegetes concerns No. 79/34 (Πᾶς ἴσχει κόσμος νοεροὺς ἀνοχῆας ἀκαμπεῖς (Psellos); Ὢ πῶς κόσμος ἔχει νοεροὺς ἀνοχῆας ἀκαμπεῖς (Plethon)). Psellos approaches the oracle from a technical point of view and analyses it according to the complicated system of the Chaldaean cosmography that he finds in Proclus, using for this purpose abundant jargon (1132D = 133. 8 ff.). Plethon, on the other hand, who believes in the existence of one pre-eternal and indestructible world, emends the plurality of the worlds in the original (πᾶς κόσμος becomes simply κόσμος). Having established by philological means that we only have *one* world, Plethon then explains the oracle as referring to the emanating capacity of this one world, while interpreting the term ἀκαμπεῖς as an emphatic way of putting across its indestructibility (ἄφθαρτον εἶναι).[22]

---

[19] πιστεύειν del. Plethon.
[20] καὶ πολυειδεῖς προφέρονται μορφαὶ δαιμονιώδεις ... καὶ ἱλαραὶ καὶ χαρίεσσαι πολλάκις φαινόμεναι φαντασίαν τινὸς ἀγαθότητος πρὸς τὸν τελούμενον ὑποκρίνονται. (1137 = 136. 18–22)
[21] ὡς ἐσχάτην ἐν ταῖς οὐσίαις τεταγμένην καὶ τοῦ ἀγαθοῦ ἐπ᾽ ἐλάχιστον μετέχουσαν, τὸ ἐλάχιστον αὐτῆς ἀγαθὸν τῷ κακῷ σημαῖνον.
[22] This message is conveyed even more clearly by Plethon's definitive work on the *Laws*: in the chapter on the 'Eternity of the All' (2.27), he postulates that all species, whether eternal, immortal in time, or mortal, are integrated into one system.

Psellos as the Last of the Neoplatonists

Having looked at individual oracles and the way in which our two commentators analyse them, we may now pass to questions of a more general nature. What in particular drove each of them to the Chaldaean revelation and incited him to produce annotated recensions of it? What do these recensions tell us about their authors?

To begin with Psellos, we notice straightaway that his interest in the Oracles and in Proclus' commentary is unduly vivid for a pillar of the Byzantine establishment. Intellectual—and even spiritual—curiosity is certainly to be detected at the root of his choice, but, to judge from his commentary, which nowhere deviates substantially from Christian orthodoxies, one comes to the conclusion that, if Psellos originally approached the collection in a spirit of unprejudiced enquiry, this must soon have given way to a desire to find in the work confirmation from pagan quarters of the theological and moral infallability of his own faith. Thus Psellos often twists the meaning of the text to meet the dogmatic requirements of Christianity, as for example when he equates the invariably female second principle of the Chaldaean triad—the dynamis—with the Son (1144A–B = 141. 15 ff.); at other times he cannot withhold his joy at the discovery of points of undeniable agreement between the two creeds, as is clear from enthusiastic interjections of the type: Ἡμέτερον καὶ ἀληθὲς τὸ δόγμα! (1145A = 142. 21). However, a closer— and less charitable—examination of the evidence might reveal a hypocritical compliance with the tenets of Christianity on the part of the commentator out of fear. In one instance he describes in great detail—and with obvious relish—a magical instrument, the *strofalos* of Hecate, only to end with the following pietist remark: 'all this is nonsense' (1133B = 134. 2). Another time he lapses into pure apology: 'for my part I do not accept the ceremonies of the Chaldaeans nor do I adhere to their doctrines. All I am doing is offering you some hints of the abstruseness of the system' (1132C = 133. 4–6). Not περιεργασία but φιλομάθεια is his guiding principle as he approaches the Chaldaean revelation.[23]

When it comes to magical practices Psellos is wholly engrossed by his material and is eager to turn the slightest hint into a theory with multiple adaptations. Whether in this task he was guided by Proclus we cannot know. What is certain, however, is that the sheer amount of space that he devotes to the magical aspect of the Oracles betrays a considerable bias in this direction. Another area which fascinates Psellos is the systematic.[24] Though he makes no effort to arrange by subject-matter the oracles that he selects from Proclus' corpus, his interest in classification is obvious. Accordingly his various attempts at a reproduction of the essentials of the system for the sake of a

---

[23] Cf. *Philosophica minora I*, ed. J. M. Duffy, op. 32, 100–1.
[24] See in this regard the meticulous analysis of oracle 158 (1124 = 126–7).

diverse audience are characterized by excessive attention to the logic of the structure, and true delight in the understanding and reproduction of technical jargon.

On the evidence of the commentary, Psellos' Christianity can be said to be of the gloomy variety, his view of the human condition being uncompromisingly pessimistic: his demons are real punitive forces of an avenging God. Thus to the Chaldaean statement that 'the Father does not inspirit fear but infuses persuasion' (14), Psellos retorts that this is only partially true of the Christian God who is both light and fire, consuming the wicked (1144A = 141. 8 ff.).[25] Psellos' playing down of the emanational element in the articulation of the cosmos is also an expression of his pessimism. For him this universe does not hang together according to a mathematical model, and our earth is a tragic place from which providence and grace are often absent, and where packs of demons range freely in a world in which matter is viewed in unambiguously dark colours.

Plethon and the New Spirit

Between Psellos' and Plethon's time the corpus of the Chaldaean Oracles together with Proclus' considerable commentary was lost.[26] What Plethon found was Psellos' recension with its rather garrulous commentary punctuated by the landmarks of Christian theology and by a vivid interest in magic. Plethon proceeded to edit the text massively, and even more importantly to reorganize the fragments according to the requirements of a system, and to substitute in the title the adjective 'Magian' for 'Chaldaean'.

The precise title of the Plethonian recension is $Μαγικὰ\ λόγια\ τῶν\ ἀπὸ$ $Ζωροάστρου\ μάγων$—*Magian Oracles of the Magi Pupils of Zoroaster*. Before proceeding to enquire about the Persian connection, it is worth giving a brief summary of Plethon's carreer. George Gemistos assumed the name Plethon with its obvious associations in 1439 when, at the age of about 80, he travelled to Florence as a participant in the ill-fated Council of Union. On the margin of his eristic activities as a committee member, Plethon delivered a series of lectures on Plato which made a certain impact, influencing the artistic repertory of the Italian Renaissance as much as the directions of classical scholarship. Even more relevantly to our theme, he is reported as having said at the Council that within a few years neither Christianity nor Islam, but a new form of paganism, would be a universal religion.[27]

---

[25] For a different view, Plethon No. 36 with commentary.

[26] For the extraordinary length of the commentary, see. Marinus, *V. Procl.* 26.

[27] George of Trebizond reports the following: 'audivi ego ipsum Florentiae...asserentem unam eandemque religionem uno animo, una mente, una praedicatione universum orbem paucis post annis esse suscepturum. Cumque rogassem Christine an Machumeti? Neutram, inquit, sed non a gentilitate differentem', in Legrand (1903: No. 256, p. 287).

Back in the Peloponnese Plethon spent the rest of his long life defining this paganism. In what survives of his magnum opus, the *Laws* (which incidentally was burnt immediately after his death by the first Ottoman Patriarch of Constantinople, George Gennadios Scholarios), Plethon sets out the principles of a social and religious reform based on a monotheism more perfect, as he postulates, than the laws of Christianity and Islam, since its prophet—Zoroaster—is older and wiser than both Jesus and Muhammad. For Plethon Zoroaster is 'the most remarkable exegete of all divine and otherwise good things',[28] his ἡγεμὼν τῶν λόγων, that is the guide who inspires, reveals and initiates in the mysteries of the beyond. As Plethon's mentor, Zoroaster is followed by a score of mythical and historical figures, the most important among whom are Pythagoras, Plato and their successors (*Legg.* 1. 1. 32). In his *Reply to Scholarios' views on Aristotle*, Plethon is more specific about his spiritual genealogy, pointing out that Plato's philosophy is based on the Pythagorean tradition, but also stating that Pythagoras acquired his wisdom through contact with the Zoroastrian Magi at whose feet he sat in Asia Minor; 'that this was the philosophy espoused by Plato is proven by the still extant oracles of Zoroaster's disciples, which agree on all accounts (πάντῃ καὶ πάντως) with Plato's doctrines'.[29] Thus, without having recourse to the Neoplatonists, Plethon reproduces their fundamental doctrine of the dependence of Plato on Pythagoras, while adding another dimension, that of Zoroastrianism. What may be the background of this fantastic theory?

In a letter to Theodora Palaeologina, Gennadios Scholarios offers the following information on Plethon's spiritual grounding:

the sum total of his apostasy was consummated by a certain Jew with whom he studied because he was an expert on Aristotle. He was a follower of Averroes and of the other Arab and Persian commentators of Aristotle's works, which have been translated by the Jews into their own language. He is also the man who acquainted him with Zoroaster and the rest. With this man, who was ostensibly a Jew but in reality a Hellene, he stayed for a long time not only as his pupil but also in his service being supported by him. He was one of the most influential men at the Court of these barbarians; his name was Elissaeus.[30]

In another letter to the Exarch of the Peloponnese Joseph, who had after Plethon's death sent Gennadios the *Book of Laws*, the patriarch addresses the dead apostate in the following terms: 'How could you deliver yourself to Zoroaster?... You were introduced to him, about whom you knew nothing before, by the polytheist Elissaeus who pretended to be a Jew, and was at the time a man of great influence at the Court of the barbarians. You fled your

---

[28] *Legg.* 1. 1. 30, and for what follows in the text.

[29] *Contra Scholarii pro Aristotele objectiones*, ed. E.V. Maltese (Leipzig, 1988), 5. 4. Plethon has also left a short theogony in prose Ζωροαστρείων τε καὶ Πλατωνικῶν δογμάτων συγκεφαλαίωσις, ed. C. Alexander, in *Traité des Lois* (Paris, 1858), 262–9.

[30] George Scholarios Gennadios, *Œuvres complètes*, iv, ed. L. Petit, M. Jugie, and X. A. Sideridès (Paris, 1935), 152; Bidez and Cumont (1938: O 115, 260).

country and lived with him in order to absorb his wonderful teaching.' Gennadios' information is corroborated by Plethon's laconic statement: 'I have learned about Averroes from the greatest Italian sages and from the Jews'.[31] How are we to interpret this evidence?

A combined reading of the times and the personal circumstances of George Gemistos would yield something like the following. Born around 1360 in Constantinople to a well-to-do and influential family, George had the benefit of an excellent education. His tutor, Demetrios Kydones, was a pupil of the Hesychast Nicholas Kabasilas and the translator of Thomas Aquinas, but also a well-travelled man who understood in depth both East and West, both theology and politics. Gemistos was thus aware of an esoteric tradition in East and West when as a young man he set out for Adrianople where the Ottoman Court had been established since the 1360s. What led him there was clearly the reputation of a wise man, expert in the Arab commentators and also versed in mystical wisdom; his learning need not however have been specifically Kabbalistic, an assumption generally advanced by historians because Elissaeus was a Jew. Things were (and are) much more vague than that, and the mystical syncretism of the various spiritual masters who were influential for a time at a Seljuk or an Ottoman Court could be compounded of the most extraordinary (or even contradictory) ingredients from East and West, from scholastic and popular quarters alike. Elissaeus—a mysterious figure who seems to have been burnt at the stake—appears to have accepted George as his *mürid*, that is as a pupil who had to live with him and serve him on a daily basis, thus slowly progressing along the stations of the spiritual way not least through the virtue of obedience. His teaching would have been heterodox by the standards of any official dogma, since it was an eclectic synthesis borrowing elements and figures from all traditions and reorganizing them according to his own judgement. And Plethon's marked indifference to the ritual aspect of the Chaldaean Oracles may owe something to his master's unconventional attitude towards religious practice. However this may be, Scholarios' information that Elissaeus was eventually burnt alive would tally with the overall picture: spiritual masters who proved too original were condemned by the Islamic establishment to exemplary deaths. Such was indeed the fate of Shihâboddîn Yahyâ Sohrawardî (1155–91), the Iranian mystic, whose influence Henry Corbin detects behind Plethon's theories.

Sohrawardî was an Azerbaidjani, that is a native of the Zoroastrian holy land of Atropatene. His conviction that in Iran the sacred tradition had suffered no break with the coming of Islam led him to regard Zarathustra as the original prophet. Even more interestingly, he turned to Plato, whose Ideas he interpreted for the purposes of his theosophical system in terms of Zoroastrian angelology. An elaborate hierarchy of worlds, intelligences, and corresponding angels unites the one and only God of the Islamic faith with

---

[31] Masai (1956: 60 n. 2).

man who may, thanks to this cosmic and at the same time gnosiological and salvational ladder, ascend and reach the ultimate cause of being. And it is this very 'ladder', this intermediate angelic realm which extends between the Intelligible and the Sensible, between the face of God (to use Islamic vocabulary) and the face of Man, that is the domain of Revelation.

Sohrawardî's sanctioning of the prehistory, as it were, of Iranian religion together with his Platonist leanings may have qualified him for a martyr's death, but at the same time they earned him a rich intellectual progeny, the so-called Platonists of Persia (known as the Ishrâqîyûn), to the study and propagation of whose teaching Henry Corbin devoted his life. Unlike Corbin, I do not believe in a direct influence of Sohrawardî on Plethon, though an indirect knowledge of his writings through oral channels seems to me very probable. Sohrawardî's renown was vast and Elissaeus sounds exactly the type of man to be fascinated by the synthesis of Zarathustra and Plato attempted by the Iranian scholar. Such a man would then serve up to his audience his own brand of the way to salvation—possibly without any reference to his source. Plethon's emphasis on the importance of orality— ἀπὸ φωνῆς—in any theological teaching, 'so that the disciples become wiser in their soul rather than keeping their science in books' (*Contra Schol.* 5. 2) is a characteristic feature of all mystical traditions. Being syncretistic by nature as well as averse to the practice of footnoting and, above all, secretive, distinguishing between an inner (*bâtin*) and an outer (*zahir*) meaning in everything, such traditions make it very difficult for outsiders—and even for insiders—to follow up their intellectual lineage.

Back home from the Court of the Barbarians, Plethon eventually came across Psellos' recension of the Chaldaean Oracles and, remembering not only the words of Elissaeus but also the tradition which attributed Oracles to Zoroaster,[32] he recognized in the hexameters the sage's revelation to mankind *as transmitted by his pupils*. The short concise commentary that he dedicated to the sacred book that would replace the Bible and the Koran, propagates a theology of light which proceeds in strict verticality, and an angelology whose function is soteriological. This scheme contradicts and exposes both the Trinitarian structures of the Christians and the inaccessible unicity of the Koranic God. A strong didactic streak permeates the Plethonian corpus, which systematically ascends from the subjective to the objective—from a psychic to a cosmic level. Once the principles of how the descended soul can embark on its journey of return have been established, the ontological structure of the universe is revealed to the initiate. The gnosis imparted by the Magian revelation is at once theoretical and theophanic-salvational, its purpose being initiatory and ultimately redemptive.

---

[32] Nicholas of Damascus, IIA. 90 fr. 68, 372 (Jacoby). According to Bidez and Cumont (1938: i. 99), the Ζωροάστρου λόγια, which are mentioned by Nicholas of Damascus alongside the Σιβύλλης χρησμοί, are likely to have been composed in Greek at the beginning of our era; cf. Porphyry, *V. Plot.* 16: 'Αποκαλύψεις... Ζωροάστρου.

From Iamblichus onwards the Chaldaean Oracles served the Neoplatonists as the holy book *par excellence*, a text more sacred even than the Orphic and the Platonic writings, and as such it was assiduously commented on by each successive generation of believers. Like them, Psellos viewed the hexameters as a treasure-house of spiritual truths, the holy book of a community into which he would integrate himself at least philosophically if not theologically, as a scholar rather than a fully fledged adept. Indeed the distinction between the two is tenuous, as witnessed by the embarassed tone that often underlies Psellos' statements. But the sincerity of his allegiance should not be called into doubt: the spirit in which he approaches the Oracles as revealed through his commentary testifies to no substantial break with the Neoplatonic trad-ition and it would not be an exaggeration to say that his task as an exegete is in no way different from that of his late antique predecessors who in their attempt to create a religious oecumenism interpreted all theogonies and theologies whether Greek or Oriental in the light of the *Platonic Theology*. Likewise and with similar intentions Psellos viewed the Chaldaean Oracles *sub specie Christianitatis*. In scholastic, if not in essential terms, he is the *direct* descendant of the Neoplatonists.

Plethon on the other hand belongs to a totally different world, a world governed by the spirit of cosmopolitanism in social and especially cultural terms. The oral tradition of an Oriental mysticism—not necessarily narrowly Islamic—which had flourished since the ninth century in the greater Middle East and which had been abundantly fertilized by Neoplatonism, was a primary influence on him and an influence that he succeeded in amalgamating with what one might call for reasons of practical convenience the Florentine Neopaganism. As a commentator on the Oracles, Plethon is the *indirect* heir of the Neoplatonists, the man who appropriated their most sacred text not simply in order to reinterpret it within its own context, but so that he might use it as the companion of a new spiritual way.

BIBLIOGRAPHY

A. TEXTS

De oraculis chaldaicis, ed. W. Kroll (Breslau, 1894).
Les oracles chaldaïques, ed. E. des Places (Paris, 1971).
The Chaldean Oracles: Text, Translation and Commentary, ed. R. Majercik (Leiden, 1989).
George Gemistos Plethon, *Oracles chaldaïques: Recension de Georges Gémiste Pléthon* (with appendix by M. Tardieu reproducing and translating the Arabic version), ed. B. Tambrun-Krasker (Athens, 1995).
—— *Contra Scholarii pro Aristotele objectiones*, ed. E. V. Maltese (Leipzig, 1988).
—— *Traité des Lois*, ed. C. Alexandre (Paris, 1858).

George Gemistos Plethon, Ζωροαστρείων τε καὶ Πλατωνικῶν δογμάτων συγκεφαλαίωσις, ed. C. Alexandre, in *Traité des Lois* (Paris, 1858), 262–9.

George Scholarios Gennadios, *Œuvres complètes*, ed. L. Petit, M. Jugie, and X. A. Sideridès, iv (Paris, 1935).

Michael Psellos, *Chronographie*, ed. É. Renauld, i (Paris, 1926).

——*Philosophica minora I*, ed. J. M. Duffy (Stuttgart and Leipzig, 1992).

——*Philosophica minora II*, ed. D. J. O'Meara (Leipzig, 1989).

B. Secondary Literature

Athanassiadi, P. (1999), 'The Chaldaean Oracles: Theology and Theurgy', in P. Athanassiadi and M. Frede (eds.), *Pagan Monotheism in Late Antiquity* (Oxford), 149–83.

Bidez, J., and Cumont, F. (1938), *Les Mages hellénisés*, i–ii (Paris).

Johnston, S. I. (1990), *Hekate Soteira* (Atlanta).

Legrand, E. (1903), *Bibliographie hellénique XVe–XVIe siècles*, iii (Paris).

Lewy, H. (1978), *Chaldaean Oracles and Theurgy*, 2nd edn. (Paris).

Masai, F. (1956), *Pléthon et le platonisme de Mistra* (Paris).

Saffrey, H. D. (1969), 'Nouveaux oracles chaldaïques dans les scholies du *Paris. gr.* 1853', *Revue de Philologie*, 43: 59–70.

Tardieu, M. (1987), 'Pléthon lecteur des Oracles', *Mêtis*, 2: 141–64.

West, M. L. (1968), 'A Pseudo-Fragment of Heraclitus', *Classical Review*, NS 18: 257–8.

Westerink, L. G. (1940), 'Proclus, Procopius, Psellus', *Mnemosyne*, 10: 275–80.

Plethon and Scholarios on Aristotle

GEORGE KARAMANOLIS

Introduction

The final phase of Byzantine philosophy is marked by the onset of a great controversy over the primacy of the two main ancient authorities in philosophy, namely Plato and Aristotle. The whole controversy, which soon spread widely among Greek intellectuals of the time, marks a clear revival of Byzantine philosophical thought in many senses. In terms of quantity, for instance, we witness a significant rise in the number of philosophical treatises, which are concerned in one way or another with this debate which started in 1439. This is the date when George Gemistos Plethon (1355/60–c.1453) published his short work Περὶ ὧν Ἀριστοτέλης πρὸς Πλάτωνα διαφέρεται (henceforth mentioned as De differentiis) in which he strongly criticized Aristotle's philosophy as being much inferior to Plato's.[1] Four or five years later George Scholarios (1400/5–1472) will respond to Plethon with a long and carefully argued work defending Aristotle against Plethon's criticisms (Κατὰ τῶν Πλήθωνος ἀποριῶν ἐπ' Ἀριστοτέλει; henceforth mentioned as Contra Plethonem).[2] Plethon will reply to Scholarios five or six years later (i.e. 1448/9) now advocating his views in a much more scholarly manner and criticizing further Aristotle's philosophy (Πρὸς τὰς Σχολαρίου περὶ Ἀριστοτέλους ἀντιλήψεις; henceforth mentioned as Contra

In writing this article I have benefited much from discussions I had with Chris Deliso and from his own work on Plethon. I am most grateful to Dr Katerina Ierodiakonou and Prof. Michael Frede who commented on earlier versions of this paper and suggested numerous improvements. Helena Thomaides improved significantly the style of my penultimate draft.

[1] I use the edn. of B. Lagarde, 'Le De Differentiis de Plethon d'après l'autographe de la Marcienne', Byzantion, 43 (1973), 312–43. An English tr. of Plethon's treatise is provided in Woodhouse (1986: 192–214).

[2] Scholarios wrote his work in the last half of 1443 or the first half of 1444; see Woodhouse (1986: 216). I use the edn. of L. Petit, M. Jugie, and X. A. Siderides, Œuvres complètes de Gennade Scholarios, iv (Paris, 1935), 1–118.

Scholarii).[3] Scholarios did not write a direct reply to Plethon's novel treatise but he hardly lost interest in the issue.[4]

With Plethon and Scholarios the scenery for a heated philosophical debate was set.[5] Scholarios' student, Matthew Kamariotes, will write against Plethon, while Theodore Gazes will be equally critical of him.[6] Plethon's views also found support. Michael Apostoles responds to Gazes with a brief treatise in which he criticizes Aristotle's views on substance.[7] This prompted Gazes' cousin, Andronikos Kallistos, to write in defence of Gazes, advocating Aristotle's views against the criticisms of Plethon and Apostoles.[8] The most ardent critic of Plethon, and admittedly the most bitter writer in the whole controversy, will be George Trapezountios (1395–1472/3) who writes a polemical work in which he praises Aristotle and vilifies Plato.[9] Trapezountios was the first in the controversy to write in Latin. His work will open up the discussion to Westerners, and indeed several Italians will take part in it.[10] A thorough reply to Trapezountios will come from Plethon's friend and correspondent Bessarion, who had closely followed the development of this debate. Bessarion criticizes Trapezountios for his hostility to Plato but also attempts to approach the whole issue of the merits of the Platonic and Aristotelian philosophy, and how the two compare, in a scholarly way; he not only shows a far better knowledge of the ancient texts than anyone involved in the controversy that far, but also tries to be fair in his judgement.[11] Though he himself was an ardent Platonist, Bessarion takes an intermediary position between Platonists and Aristotelians, arguing that the ancients used to see the philosophies of Plato and Aristotle as being largely in accord.

Contentious though the spirit may have been to some extent, this controversy strongly revived philosophical discussion among Byzantines. Philosophical topics which had always been regarded as important in Byzantine philosophy, like, for instance, the question of fate and free will,[12] or the

---

[3] I use the edn. of E. V. Maltese, *Georgius Gemistus Plethon Contra Scholarii pro Aristotele objectiones* (Leipzig, 1988).

[4] Scholarios wrote a long letter to Plethon about 1450 in which the tone is rather reconciliatory; printed in his *Opera*, iv. 118–51.

[5] For a short historical account of the Plato–Aristotle controversy see Monfasani (1976: 201–29). Mohler (1942: i. 346–98) gives an account of the main contributions to the controversy.

[6] See below nn. 12 and 13.

[7] See n. 13.

[8] See n. 13.

[9] *Comparationes philosophorum Aristotelis et Platonis* (published in 1458). Before this, Trapezountios wrote a work against Gazes (*c*.1454); see Woodhouse (1986: 365).

[10] See Monfasani (1976: 214–29).

[11] Bessarion responded to Trapezountios in 1469 with his *In calumniatorem Platonis* (ed. Mohler, ii). Bessarion published the last book (6) of this work independently before that date as *De arte et natura* (later appended to his longer work) to respond to Trapezountios on Aristotle's conception of teleology, more precisely, whether nature has a purpose. See Monfasani (1976: 209–11).

[12] The main texts are by Plethon, Περὶ εἱμαρμένης, ed. C. Alexandre (Paris, 1858; repr. Amsterdam 1966), 64–78; Theodore Gazes, Περὶ ἑκουσίου καὶ ἀκουσίου, ed. Mohler, iii. 239–46; Matthew Kamariotes, Λόγοι δύο πρὸς Πλήθωνα περὶ εἱμαρμένης ed. A. S. Reimarus

question of universals[13] become fashionable again, and now they are treated in the framework of the Plato–Aristotle dispute. What interests now is not so much how the views of Plato or Aristotle are to be construed, but which one of these views is right, given a certain construal. In order to construct such an argument, the Byzantines had to go back not only to the texts of Plato and Aristotle, but also to their ancient commentators. So now the Byzantines find themselves engaged in a discussion of their philosophical tradition. As we know, this is the ancient philosophical tradition which Byzantine philosophers inherited from late antiquity and continued in many ways; they were engaged in the exegesis of ancient texts, they were addressing philosophical problems inherited from antiquity, approaching them in ancient philosophical terms, and they also showed their preferences for, or even loyalty to, certain ancient philosophical authorities. But now Byzantine philosophers, like Plethon, Scholarios, Gazes, and Bessarion, to name the most prominent, feel the need to take a clear position towards the ancient philosophical tradition, argue rigorously about the use of specific ancient philosophical sources, and, most especially, try to justify their philosophical predilections.

One may indeed wonder why such a discussion arose at all at the end of the Byzantine era and why, once it arose, it found such fertile ground and went on for decades. One explanation, in my view, for why such a discussion arose so vividly, has to do with the increasing consciousness among Byzantines that the ancient philosophical tradition was not one body of thought, but that it was extraordinarily rich in different, and indeed rival, authorities and schools of thought. The more use they made of ancient philosophical authorities, the more they realized how much these authorities differ on several fundamental issues. Plato and Aristotle were the most prominent among them and had become part of the philosophical curriculum of Platonist schools from the third to the sixth centuries AD, as the several extant Neoplatonist commentaries suggest. This was a tradition which Byzantines largely inherited, and after the revival of learning in the ninth century, they were becoming more and more eager to show their preference for the philosophy of Plato or that of Aristotle and to be committed Platonists or Aristotelians.

Yet it was more complicated than this. From the end of the classical age and until the end of late antiquity there had been propounded many different, often rival, ways to construe the texts of Plato and Aristotle. Being an Aristotelian or a Platonist, most especially, did not indicate a definite

(Leiden, 1721); cf. the correspondence between Bessarion and Plethon, *Epist.* 18–21, ed. Mohler, iii. 455–68. Scholarios also made remarks on the question(s) of fate and determinism in several of his writings. For some references see Turner (1964: esp. 365–72).

[13] See mainly Bessarion, Πρὸς τὰ Πλήθωνος πρὸς Ἀριστοτέλη περὶ οὐσίας (ed. Mohler, iii. 149–50); Theodore Gazes, Πρὸς Πλήθωνα ὑπὲρ Ἀριστοτέλους (ibid. 153–8); Michael Apostoles, Πρὸς τὰς ὑπὲρ Ἀριστοτέλους περὶ οὐσίας κατὰ Πλήθωνος Θεοδώρου τοῦ Γαζῆ ἀντιλήψεις (ibid. 161–9); Andronikos Kallistos, Πρὸς τὰς Μιχαήλου Ἀποστόλου κατὰ Θεόδωρον ἀντιλήψεις (ibid. 170–203).

philosophical position, but rather a whole range of them. This happened because the works of Aristotle and especially of Plato allowed plenty of room for personal interpretation. As a result, we have many varieties of Platonism and of Aristotelianism, that is, varieties of exegetical traditions of the classical authorities, which, when seen with reference to a particular question, amount to quite different philosophical positions. All these varieties, which often strongly contested each other, had claims on counting as orthodox. The Byzantines inherited various forms of Platonism and Aristotelianism, but they largely forgot the polemic between or within schools over alternative interpretations of the two classical philosophers.

Another element which seems to have played a crucial background role was Christianity. The Byzantines were Christians, and to some extent Byzantine philosophy evolved from the Christian philosophy of late antiquity. A party of early Christians considered philosophy helpful for the elucidation and articulation of the Christian dogma. Byzantine philosophers basically continue this Christian philosophical tradition which from its origins and through the centuries appropriated various elements of the ancient philosophical tradition according to its needs. Elements from Platonic, Aristotelian, Stoic, or Neoplatonic philosophy fascinated different Christian thinkers who integrated them into their own treatment of issues about Christian dogma. The early Patristic tradition tended to show a clear preference for Plato's philosophy, while in later Greek Patristic thought (from the eighth century onwards) this changes.[14] Aristotle's philosophy, which often had been met with hostility by the early Fathers, enjoyed a remarkable revival in the eight and ninth centuries and again from the eleventh century onwards. As Byzantine philosophers were Christians, they often were strongly interested in how ancient philosophical views compare to Christian dogma and had views as to which ancient philosophical authority was closer to Christianity. If they did not explicitly express their views on this question, these can be nevertheless detected in their attempts to provide philosophical treatment of questions raised by the Christian faith which inclined more to the one or the other direction or tradition. Accordingly, their philosophical treatises acquire a Platonic, Aristotelian, or even Stoic flavour.

The existence of conflicting tendencies is already manifest in the eleventh century in arguments on how to construe ancient philosophical texts *vis-à-vis* Christian doctrine. To mention the most conspicuous cases, the Aristotelianism of John Italos (*c.*1025–82) or of Eustratios of Nicaea (1050–*c.*1120) was perceived as a philosophical position filled with pagan atheism, and in this spirit was condemned by the official Church.[15] Two centuries later the

---

[14] In the Latin Patristic tradition there is a clear shift in allegiances from Plato in late antiquity and the early Middle Ages to Aristotle in the 13th cent. See Hankins (1996: 360–77). Such a shift is less clear in the Greek Patristic tradition.

[15] The condemnation of Italos and Eustratios is to be found in the *Synodikon*, ed. J. Gouillard (1967: 57–71, with his comments in 188–202). Their philosophical views are discussed by Lloyd (1987); Mercken (1990: 410–19).

question of the value of Aristotle's philosophy and how it compares with Plato's is openly discussed in some detail by Theodore Metochites (1270–1332) and Nikephoros Gregoras (1324–1398).[16] In all these discussions the primary issue is not so much how Aristotle's philosophy compares with Plato's, but rather which philosophy is sound, that is, which philosophical authority comes closer to Christian doctrine. This, as we will see, will be the main point of the entire controversy which started with Plethon and Scholarios. Almost certainly, then, this controversy brought to the surface tendencies which for a long time existed among the Byzantines.

But one still wonders what triggered the discussion in mid-fifteenth century so forcefully as to acquire such dimensions. One factor which clearly played a role is the prominence of one distinct interpretative line of ancient philosophy which by then had been present on the Byzantine philosophical scene for some time. I refer to the Western scholastic tradition of interpreting Aristotle. The first contacts with this tradition go back to the days of Maximos Planoudes (*c*.1255–1305) and especially Demetrios Kydones (1324–98).[17] But, as we will see, Scholarios is much more philosophically committed to scholasticism and sets out to integrate it within the Byzantine philosophical tradition. It was partly the prominence of the scholastic tradition which led Byzantines to reconsider their own stance on ancient philosophy and how, if at all, it differed from the Westerners.

Plethon clearly refers to this tradition in the first lines of his *De differentiis*. Further, it is quite telling that Plethon's *De differentiis* originated in lectures which he gave to Italian intellectuals who were certainly familiar with the scholastic school of thought and perhaps had had enough of it by then. Plethon tells us that his *De differentiis* was written 'for those attached to Plato' (*Contra Scholarii* 24. 28–9). Undoubtedly such a comparison of Plato to Aristotle would be much more significant in a place like Italy where scholasticism had been thriving for more than two centuries. But the prominence of scholasticism is only one important aspect for our understanding of the entire controversy. Clearly we need to closely examine the philosophical motives behind it—and this will be one of my aims in this chapter.

One may ask here why I assume that the motives behind this controversy were solely philosophical. I would answer that I do not. There are still many unanswered questions concerning the origins of the controversy and more generally, concerning the intellectual climate of the time. Furthermore, we know that political concerns permeated almost all theological and intellectual discussions then. So I do think that there are more than philosophical motives involved here. But I want to argue that this controversy *also* has

---

[16] See Theodore Metochites, *Miscellanea philosophica et historica*, ed. C. G. Müller and T. Kiessling (Leipzig, 1821), chs. 3, 9, 25; Ševčenko (1962: 241–3); Nikephoros Gregoras, *Florentios*, 1262–70, ed. P. Leone, *Florenzo o Intorno alla Sapienza* (Naples, 1975). The second part of *Florentios* is nothing else but a criticism of Aristotle's philosophy.

[17] For the history of the reception of Aquinas in Byzantium see Papadopoulos (1974); Podskalsky (1977: 180–220).

philosophical motives and, more generally, a serious philosophical dimension. This dimension has not been appreciated so far, as this debate has been largely approached as a cultural phenomenon.[18] The arguments advanced by the parties involved, for instance, have hardly been studied. Yet most works written in the years of the controversy have philosophical ambitions, some are of philosophical interest, and some even have philosophical merits. If we want to appreciate them justly, we have to study them as philosophical texts. This can be done in two main ways: (*a*) in purely philosophical terms (that is, how good they are and how they recommend their authors as philosophers), and (*b*) from the point of view of the history of philosophy, that is, by researching their sources and their influence.

This latter project is particularly important because the use of philosophical sources is central to the whole controversy, and I will basically focus on this here. I will examine the conception Plethon and Scholarios have of Aristotle's philosophy and the arguments by means of which they attacked or justified Aristotelian philosophy. This will lead me on to investigate how Plethon and Scholarios operate the ancient philosophical sources, and to which they are most indebted. It will emerge, I hope, that, concerned though they were with problems which also preoccupied ancient philosophers, Plethon and Scholarios appear to make very selective reference to, and use of, the relevant ancient sources. On the basis of their use of ancient sources at least, both will appear to be far more complicated than what labels such as 'Platonist' or 'Aristotelian' would capture. I will try to look more closely into one particular argument to which both Plethon and Scholarios assign much weight, namely the argument concerning Aristotle's explanation of how the world came about. The reason why I want to focus on this is that this argument exemplifies the use of various philosophical resources in the controversy. It also may illuminate for us, at least partly, how Scholarios justifies his use of Aristotle's philosophy and to which interpretative tradition Plethon may have objected when he criticized Aristotle's philosophy.

Plethon's Criticism of Aristotle

The publication of the *De differentiis* was a turning-point in Plethon's career. It was the first work which George Gemistos published under the name 'Plethon' (which was meant to allude to Plato), thus intending to manifest his philosophical allegiance and his philosophical aspirations.[19] Until that

---

[18] See for instance Monfasani (1976), Kristeller (1979), and esp. Hankins (1986). Monfasani admits that the lack of scholarly attention to the philosophical arguments precludes the just appreciation of the debate.

[19] Presumably Plethon wanted to become known as a second Plato. Marsilio Ficino refers to him as follows: 'Plethonem quasi alterum Platonem' (*Opera Omnia*, ii. 1537, quoted by Woodhouse 1986: 187).

time, Gemistos had not been inactive in philosophical matters. By then he had written a summary of the doctrines of Zoroaster and Plato and a treatise *On Virtues*.[20] The latter he may have published shortly before his *De differentiis*. Presumably by then he had also written his commentary on the Chaldean Oracles.[21] Yet his *De differentiis* is quite unlike these works in a number of ways: it has a distinctly polemic tenor, it examines several philosophical issues on which Plethon had never expressed himself before, and most importantly, it does not contain traces of a spirit which several of Plethon's contemporaries regarded as one of his characteristics, namely paganism.

Already the formulation of the work's title (Περὶ ὧν Ἀριστοτέλης πρὸς Πλάτωνα διαφέρεται) is indicative of its aim and its scope. To begin with, Plethon does not profess to compare Platonic with Aristotelian philosophy and as part of such an enterprise to discuss Aristotle's differences from Plato. He rather exclusively focuses on Aristotle's differences from Plato, taking Plato as the standard against which he measures Aristotle. Plethon argues that Aristotle differs from Plato in all fundamental philosophical questions, and it is on those that Plethon will focus in his work (*De diff.* 330. 3–6).[22] Aristotle's differences from Plato's views are taken to amount to departures from the truth which Plato's philosophy represents, and as such they are to be criticized. The title's formulation further suggests that Plethon took Aristotle's departures from Plato to constitute a rebellion against his master.[23]

The impression conveyed by the title is confirmed by the treatise. Plethon's criticisms of Aristotle often take the form of merely contrasting the view of the Platonists or of Plato (οἱ περὶ Πλάτωνα) with Aristotle's contradictory view (*De diff.* 326. 31–327. 18, 328. 5–20, 330. 8–331. 15, 342. 28–37). In most cases Plethon gives little argument as to why Aristotle's views are to be criticized. It looks as though it is sufficient for him to prove that Aristotle indeed departed from Plato's views. His main charge against Aristotle is lack of understanding and acumen (ἀμαθία; 324. 28, 334. 17, 342. 28; cf. 327. 12 οὐδὲν διακρίνων); Aristotle, in Plethon's view, did not understand, or misunderstood, Plato's doctrines and came to think that they were in need of amendment and improvement which he aimed to offer with his innovations (καινοποιεῖν, 330. 27; κεκαινολόγηται, 331. 31). As he argues it, Aristotle

---

[20] Ζωροαστρείων τε καὶ Πλατωνικῶν δογμάτων συγκεφαλαίωσις, ed. C. Alexandre, *Traité des Lois*, (Paris, 1858, repr. Amsterdam, 1966), 262–9, Περὶ ἀρετῶν, ed. J. P. Migne (*PG* 160. 866–82).

[21] Μαγικὰ λόγια τῶν ἀπὸ τοῦ Ζωροάστρου Μάγων ἐξηγηθέντα; on this work see Woodhouse (1986: 48–61).

[22] Οὐ γὰρ ἅπαντα ἁπλῶς τὰ Ἀριστοτέλους ἡμῖν διορθοῦν πρόκειται, ἀλλὰ περὶ τῶν μεγίστων μόνων καὶ κυριωτάτων εἰπεῖν, καὶ ὧν μάλιστα πρὸς Πλάτωνα διενηνεγμένος οὐκ ὀλίγῳ τῷ μέσῳ τἀνδρὸς λέλειπται (*De diff.* 330. 3–6; cf. 334. 17–20).

[23] Plethon's title is similar in formulation with the title of one of Numenius' works (mid-2nd cent. AD) written to castigate the sceptical Academy's betrayal of what he takes to be Plato's philosophy entitled Περὶ τῆς τῶν Ἀκαδημαϊκῶν πρὸς Πλάτωνα διαστάσεως (ap. Eusebium, *Praeparatio Evangelica* 14. 4–9; fr. 24–9 Des Places).

innovated in philosophy without any actual philosophical reason (εἰκῇ; *De diff.* 331. 30; cf. 334. 23) and only as a result of his contentious spirit (*De diff.* 334. 23–6, 342. 40) and his desire for vainglory (*Contra Scholarii* 5. 14). This view goes back to antiquity,[24] and, as we will see, Plethon may have been acquainted with one of its sources.

Plethon nevertheless recognizes that Aristotle's teaching is permeated by Plato's doctrines. Indeed, he accuses Aristotle of having drawn heavily on Plato (*Contra Scholarii* 5. 19–20).[25] But since Aristotle eventually distorted Plato's views in one way or other, he is, according to Plethon, a degraded Platonist who preserves a confused picture of the Platonic heritage. This Plethon sees as evident in Aristotle's writings. He claims that whenever Aristotle contradicts Plato he falls into mistakes and self-contradictions. This is, for instance, the case, Plethon argues, with universals, on which Aristotle contradicted his earlier, more Platonic, position (ἀσύμφωνος εἶναι; *De diff.* 325. 16–24). Similar contradictions are allegedly to be detected in Aristotle's views on chance and necessity (*De diff.* 332. 24–5), or on the immortality of the soul (*Contra Scholarii* 26. 25–8). Plethon here uses an ancient technique which we most clearly find in Plutarch, especially in his *On the Contradictions of the Stoics* where Plutarch accuses the Stoics of falling into contradiction just where, and by implication just because, they diverge from Plato.[26]

Plethon's criticism is based on the view we find in several ancient Platonists according to which Plato's philosophy represents the complete truth, a truth revealed to mankind and hence sacrosanct.[27] Such a view, of course, suggests that Plato is committed to certain doctrines and that his philosophy amounts to a complete set of doctrines covering all crucial philosophical issues. We know, however, that Plato's philosophical writings do not lend itself to such a systematization. The reasons why Platonists nevertheless had such a conception of Plato's philosophy cannot be expounded here. The crucial point for us here is that Platonists of this conviction had to construct Plato's doctrines themselves, either by relying on isolated Platonic passages which appealed to them, or by relying on sources other than Plato's texts. Plethon evidently took such a view and followed similar practices. He maintains that

---

[24] Aristotle's ingratitude to Plato was first suggested by Aristotle's student, Aristoxenus, but it was emphasized by Atticus in the 2nd cent. AD, who accused him of contentiousness. The charge was repeated by Origen and Theodore of Cyrrhos. Düring (1957: 318–28, 373–4) has collected the relevant testimonies.

[25] ἀλλὰ ᾿Αριστοτέλης, φοιτητὴς γεγονὼς Πλάτωνι καὶ ἔπειτα ὑπὸ προσχήματι φιλοσοφίας σοφιστικὴν μετελθὼν καὶ κενῆς δόξης ἐρασθεὶς ἐπὶ τῷ ἰδίας ἑαυτοῦ ἀρχηγέτης γενέσθαι, τὰς μὲν ὑπὸ Πλάτωνος συγγεγραμμένας φιλοσοφίας ἀρχὰς ἐκ παμπόλλων ἐτῶν ἐς ἐκεῖνον κατεληλυθυίας ἀνέστρεψέ τε καὶ διέφθειρεν, ἃ δ᾽ ἀπὸ φωνῆς Πλάτωνος διήκουσεν αὐτὸς συγγεγραφὼς ἑαυτοῦ ἐποιήσατο, συχνὰ καὶ ἐν αὐτοῖς ἁμαρτών. (*Contra Scholarii* 5. 14–20)

[26] On Plutarch's method and argument see Boys-Stones (1997).

[27] Cf. Numenius ap. Eus. *Praep. evan.* 9. 7. 1, Atticus ap. *Praep. evan.* 9. 1. 2, Diogenes Laertius 3. 56.

Plato, like the Pythagoreans before him, did not write down all of his doctrines, but only the fundamental principles of philosophy, leaving the rest to be articulated by his students on the basis of those principles and from what they had heard from him (*Contra Scholarii* 4. 10–5. 14). We will see that Plethon attributed to Plato views of later sources, like those of the Stoics, presumably on the grounds that these views had already been anticipated or even outlined by Plato. So we have to treat Plethon's presentation of what he takes to be Plato's philosophy with great caution.

The view that Plethon takes, according to which Plato's philosophy represents the truth, or at least is very close to it, entails that there is no point or room for progress further than Plato. Aristotle's novelties, even in fields like logic or natural science, were not regarded as progress over Plato. Rather, Plethon considers them trivial (*De diff.* 322. 7–8 on Aristotle's science), unsatisfactory, or simply mistaken (*De diff.* 323. 5–6 on Aristotle's logic). Like several ancient Platonists, Plethon seems to believe that Plato's philosophy was not only true but also complete, covering for all serious philosophical issues. Even later discoveries, including Aristotle's, were often thought to be already outlined in Plato. Under this conception of Plato's philosophy, Aristotle's departures from it are assumed to amount to mistakes of various kinds, since they represent departures from the truth. This is why Plethon finds it sufficient criticism of Aristotle's philosophy to show its distance from Plato's.

Before we pass to a closer examination of Plethon's arguments against Aristotle's philosophical views, we have to ask ourselves why Plethon came to criticize Aristotle so fiercely and what he aimed to achieve by this. If he wanted to praise Plato's philosophy, why did he do it in this way? Though never an Aristotelian himself,[28] Plethon was not always so dismissive of Aristotle's views.[29] In the *Book of Laws*, for instance, which he published at the end of his life, Plethon indicates in the prologue that in theology he will follow Zoroaster and Plato, but that in natural philosophy he will follow Aristotle (*Legg.* prol. 4, ed. Alexandre). Why then is Plethon so polemical against Aristotle in the *De differentiis*?

The opening lines of Plethon's *De differentiis* are important in this respect. There he draws a contrast between the ancient philosophical tradition, on the one hand, which, according to him, showed a clear predilection for Plato, and, on the other, the trend of most Westerners, who, following the Arab Averroes, held Aristotle in high esteem (*De diff.* 321. 3–8). So, Plethon seems to suggest, if one wants to stay loyal to the ancients, one has to prefer Plato's philosophy. But such a claim is historically a gross oversimplification. Scholarios will justifiably point out that many ancients preferred Aristotle to

---

[28] Leo Allatius attributes to Plethon an *Explicatio in voces Porphyrii et in decem Categorias Aristotelis* and a commentary on Aristotle's *Analytics*, but this may be a mistake as there are no traces of such works. See Woodhouse (1986: 20).

[29] See, for instance, Plethon's epistle 19 to Bessarion (ed. Mohler, iii. 460–1).

Plato, like the Peripatetics, for instance, but, more significantly, that many Platonists in antiquity had a great respect for Aristotle, like Porphyry, Syrianus, and Simplicius (*Contra Plethonem* 3. 1–34). Indeed, the majority of the Platonist commentators in late antiquity were devoted students of Aristotle,[30] as they maintained that Platonic and Aristotelian philosophy are quite compatible and rather complementary.[31] Scholarios presents Plethon with a dilemma. Either Plethon ignores the ancient philosophical tradition or he deliberately distorts it to fit his own argument, but in either case, Plethon misrepresents the ancients and, more crucially for his argument, ancient Platonism.

Plethon himself was, at least to some extent, aware of such an objection. In his *Contra Scholarii* he concedes to Scholarios one exception among Platonists, namely Simplicius, who admired and studied Aristotle.[32] However, Simplicius was not an exception but rather a typical case among late ancient Platonists. It is difficult to imagine that Plethon did not know of the works of Porphyry, Iamblichus, and other Neoplatonist commentators of Aristotle, who may have preferred Plato to Aristotle, especially in areas like metaphysics, but had also studied Aristotle, especially his logic. Yet Plethon presents the Platonist tradition as united and talks about 'the Platonists' (οἱ περὶ Πλάτωνα), as if there was only one stream of Platonism in antiquity.

Scholarios challenges Plethon's assumed unity of the Platonist tradition even further, when he emphasizes that Plethon represents a specific kind of Platonism, namely that of Proclus (Letter to the Princess of Peloponnese, *Opera*, iv. 153. 23–4). This claim by Scholarios does not only dispute Plethon's correct representation of the Platonist tradition but quite clearly also suggests as a reason Plethon's commitment to a specific party of this tradition. I will return to this claim of Scholarios below.

Plainly the reason why Plethon talks in terms of a unified tradition of Platonism and of ancient philosophy in general was his wish to dissociate the Hellenic–Byzantine philosophical tradition from the Western one as strongly as possible. Plethon separates the two in terms of their preferences for Plato and for Aristotle, respectively. He seems to suggest that the scholastic use of Aristotle resulted from a mistaken construal of his philosophy, on the basis of which scholastics defended the great merit of Aristotle's philosophy. As is well known, they maintained that Aristotle's philosophical views are aligned

---

[30] For a brief survey see the introduction in Sorabji (1990).

[31] Later in the controversy, Aristotelians will insist on this point and allude to ancient Platonists like Porphyry (see e.g. Andronikos Kallistos, ed. Mohler, iii. 170–203). Bessarion will acknowledge the testimony of these ancient sources and will take it into account.

[32] Σιμπλίκιος τοῦτο μόνος ποιεῖ, καὶ δῆλός ἐστι κατὰ τῆς ἐκκλησίας αὐτὸ ποιῶν... καὶ πειρᾶται δὴ Ἀριστοτέλη Πλάτωνί τε καὶ Παρμενίδῃ συνωδὸν ἀποφαίνειν, οὐδ' ὁτιοῦν λέγων πιθανὸν, ὅσα δ' ἄλλοι τὲ τῶν παλαιῶν κατὰ Ἀριστοτέλους καὶ δὴ καὶ Πλωτῖνος, Σιμπλικίου πολὺ ἀμείνων ἀνήρ, συνέγραψε κατά τε ἄλλων αὐτοῦ καὶ τῶν γε κατηγοριῶν, ὅσα Πρόκλος κατά τε ἄλλων καὶ μάλιστα τῆς αὐτοῦ θεολογίας. σὺ δὲ τὸ Σιμπλικίῳ κατὰ τῆς ἐκκλησίας σπουδασθὲν εὐγνωμοσύνην καλεῖς, καίπερ Σιμπλικίου μάλιστα αὐτὸ πεποιηκότος, ὃς καὶ αὐτὸς πρὸς σεαυτὸν πολλάκις ἔσχισαι. (*Contra Scholarii* 1. 20–2. 12).

with the Christian dogma and lend support to Christian theology. But, how, Plethon wonders in the first page of his *De differentiis*, can one claim this, when Aristotle argues for a mortal soul and for a universe without creator, indeed 'inclining towards atheism' (*De diff.* 332. 17–18; *Contra Scholarii* 41. 19–20)? How can there be a stronger contradiction with Christian doctrine?

It is this basic misunderstanding of Aristotle of which Plethon accuses Scholarios when he criticizes him for lack of understanding (ἀμαθία, ἀσυνεσία; e.g. *Contra Scholarii* 21. 30, 25. 17). He argues that Scholarios badly misconstrues the spirit of Aristotle's views (*Contra Scholarii* 6. 26–32, 11. 20–2, 17. 2–9, 20. 6–11, 29. 9–10, 42. 20–1), as he mistakes them for philosophical views which support (συμβαλλόμενον; *Contra Scholarii* 17. 19) Christian doctrine, while Plethon claims that he has done justice to the spirit (διάνοια) of Aristotle's views (*Contra Scholarii* 6. 26–32, 11. 18–20, 20. 23), as he is free from Scholarios' bias.

Plethon seems to identify two distinct points, namely that Aristotle's philosophy is incompatible with Christian doctrine, and that Aristotle's philosophy is bad philosophy. Plethon can do this effectively because he grants the widely shared assumption among both Byzantines and the scholastics that pagan philosophy is to be judged against the ultimate criterion of Christian revelation. According to this view, the philosophy of any ancient author is good or bad to the degree it is close to Christian doctrine. Such an assumption is central to Plethon's argument. He does not claim that the fault of the Western approach lies in its Christian perspective, but rather in a certain philosophical bias which this perspective generated regarding Aristotle's philosophy; if this bias is resolved, then Aristotle's philosophy is left without value. Plethon sets out to resolve this bias by showing that Plato's philosophy is much closer to Christianity than Aristotle's. If this holds, then Aristotle opposition to Plato's views amounts to opposition to Christian doctrines. In this sense, Aristotle's differences from Plato constitute sufficient evidence for Aristotle's opposition to Christianity.

But if this is the case, why, one wonders, does Plethon draw his initial contrast between the ancients who preferred Plato and the moderns who prefer Aristotle? One may say that such an argument would have a strong appeal to the audience for which it was devised, namely to Italian humanists, who would be eager to return to the ancients, but, as we have seen, it was a weak point which Scholarios criticized.

Yet Plethon's point may be more subtle. Scholarios apparently took the reference to the ancients as a reference to pagans only, but Plethon is very likely to have referred also to Christian Platonists. Indeed, in his *Contra Scholarii* he mentions that Cyril of Alexandria had Plato's philosophy and not Aristotle's in mind when he pronounced pagan philosophy as being compatible (συνωδόν) with Christian faith (*Contra Scholarii* 3. 30–4. 7). Plethon seems to refer to the view of early Church Fathers according to which Plato's philosophy was the best element in pagan culture, as it came close to Christian doctrine. This is a view which we find in Justin Martyr, in Clement, in Origen, and, quite clearly, in Eusebius, who tried to legitimize Plato's philosophy within the new faith by arguing that Plato had had intimations of the Christian truth. If Plethon indeed refers to this early Christian position, the traditional view about Plethon according to which he was a pagan, a view which, as we will see, Scholarios repeatedly emphasized, seems to be contradicted. But even if this is so, this does not mean that Scholarios' view was entirely wrong. As often is the case, the means to polemics may come from anywhere, if they enhance its efficiency. As I will argue in the following, Plethon is likely to have drawn on a particular early Christian source in his polemic against Aristotle's philosophy.

Sources of Plethon's Anti-Aristotelian Arguments

Plethon says in his *Contra Scholarii* (24. 24–9) that he wrote the *De differentiis* when he was ill in Florence and was bored at home.[33] Even if we believe this, Plethon could still have had access to books or he could have been under the influence of authors whom he had studied in the past. Besides, Plethon[34] had time to revise his work before its publication when he came back to Mistra. One source which may well have furnished him with anti-Aristotelian arguments and abundant praise for Plato was Eusebius' *Praeparatio evangelica* to which Plethon was probably indebted.

Eusebius (writing early fourth century AD) devotes half a book (*Praep. evan.* 15. 1–16) of this long work to discrediting Aristotle's philosophy. On the one hand, Eusebius aims to to expose the contradictions between pagan philosophers, while, on the other, he means to stress the importance of Plato's philosophy as a philosophy which came closer to Christian truth; in this sense, he argues, Plato had been superior to all other Greek philosophers (11. 1. 3). The reason for Plato's achievement, according to Eusebius, was either the fact that Plato had come into contact with Hebrew wisdom or because he had independent access to the truth (11. 8. 1). Aristotle, on the other hand, according to Eusebius, contradicted Plato's philosophy, and to the extent that this philosophy has such a close proximity to Christian truth, by contradicting Plato, Aristotle also contradicted Christianity.[35] As we have

---

[33] ... οὐ γὰρ οὐδὲ πάνυ σπουδάσασιν ἐκεῖνα συνεγράφη, ἀλλὰ νοσήσασιν ἐν Φλωρεντίᾳ, ὡς καὶ αὐτὸς οἶσθα, καὶ ἔκ τε τῆς οἰκίας ἐν ᾗ ἐσκηνοῦμεν συχνῶν ἡμερῶν οὐ προϊοῦσι, καὶ κατὰ τὸ εἰκὸς ἀλύουσιν, ἅμα δέ τι καὶ τοῖς Πλάτωνι προσκειμένοις χαριζομένοις συνεγράφη. (*Contra Scholarii* 24. 24–9)

[34] Monfasani (1976: 201–2) and Diller (1956: 29) do not distinguish between the text of Plethon's lectures as delivered in Florence and the published text of the *De differentiis*. But Plethon may have taken some time to revise and summarize his lectures. His text looks condensed, polished, and stylistically elaborate. On this scenario, which I find more credible, the *De diff.* was disseminated about 1440/1.

[35] Like Eusebius, Plethon feels the need to give an air of objectiveness to his criticism against Aristotle. He thus says that he will not slander (συκοφαντεῖν) Aristotle but that he will try to be

seen, this is exactly the element on which Plethon's criticism of Aristotle's philosophy relies.

In the *Praeparatio* Eusebius moves to discredit Aristotle's philosophy by quoting selected passages from Platonists who were wholly or partially critical of Aristotle. I suggest that Plethon was familiar with this selection of Platonist objections to Aristotle's philosophy. There is some indirect evidence in support of this hypothesis. Michael Apostoles, who defended Plethon's views against Gazes, when he comes to criticize Aristotle's views on the soul, mentions that ancient Platonists had already strongly criticized them. The Platonists he refers to are Atticus, Plotinus, and Porphyry (*Ad Gazae objectiones*, ed. Mohler, iii. 166).[36] These Platonists in this order are those whom Eusebius quotes in his anti-Aristotelian section (*Praep. evan.* 15. 4–13). Clearly Apostoles relies on Eusebius' selection here.

One reason why Plethon himself is likely to have been inspired by the same selection is that it covers a wide range of fundamental issues in which Aristotle's views diverged from Plato's and includes issues which Plethon highlights, like Aristotle's rejection of the immortality of the soul, of Plato's theory of Forms, and of the divine providence. Eusebius' anti-Aristotelian polemic is carried out pre-eminently through the quotations from the Platonist Atticus (second half of second century AD).[37] Each one of the ten preserved, the prologue apart (fr. 1), focuses on a particular issue in which Aristotle allegedly diverges from Plato's doctrine, such as good life (*eudaimonia*; fr. 2), theology and divine providence (fr. 3), the creation of the world (fr. 4), the fifth element (fr. 5), the nature and constitution of the universe (fr. 6), the immortality of the human soul (fr. 7), the world-soul (fr. 8), and finally Aristotle's criticism of Plato's Forms (fr. 9). Plethon's *De differentiis* is organized in sections in which he exposes Aristotle's departure from Plato's views on a particular crucial issue, such as the first principle and the constitution of the world (Migne I–II), logic (Migne III–VIII), the soul and the intellect (Migne IX–XI), ethics (Migne XII–XIII), the fifth element (Migne XIV), questions on physics including Aristotle's conception of teleology (Migne XV–XVII), causality and determinism (Migne XVIII), motion (Migne XIX), while in the remaining long section (Migne XX) Plethon criticizes Aristotle's rejection of Plato's Forms.

---

fair with him (*De diff.* 321. 14–22; cf. Eus. *Praep. evan.* 14. 1. 13), although Aristotle slandered Plato (*De diff.* 321. 15, 334. 21–4).

[36] . . . ὡς ἄλλοι τε πολλοὶ μαρτυροῦσι, καὶ δὴ καὶ Ἀττικὸς καὶ Πλωτῖνος, ἔτι γε μὴν καὶ Πορφύριος ἐν τοῖς πρὸς Ἀριστοτέλην βιβλίοις ἐντελέχειαν εἶναι φάσκοντα τὴν ψυχήν. ἀλλ' οὐχ οὕτω περὶ ψυχῆς ὁ Πλάτων ἐφιλοσόφησεν οὔτε μὴν τῶν εἰδῶν πέρι καὶ τῶν γενῶν, ἃ δὴ ἀνώτατα τῶν ὄντων ὑπάρχοντα, τερετίσματά τε καὶ λήρους εἰπεῖν Ἀριστοτέλης ἐτόλμησεν. (Michael Apostoles, ed. Mohler, iii. 166. 2–6). The latter sentence is a literal quotation of Atticus ap. Eus. *Praep. evan.* 15. 13. 1.

[37] The numbers of Atticus' fragments are according to the edn. of them by É. des Places, *Atticus Fragments* (Paris, 1977).

As we see, Plethon does not cover all issues which Atticus' critical fragments in Eusebius cover—he leaves out those which are irrelevant in an argument for the contradiction between Aristotle's philosophy and Christian doctrine (that is, the world-soul and the constitution of the universe). Yet Plethon attributes the same special importance to theology and divine providence, the question of good life (*eudaimonia*), the immortality of the soul, and Plato's Forms, which we also find in Atticus' fragments. Furthermore, he stresses the close connection between ethics, psychology, and theology, exactly like Atticus does (Atticus fr. 3. 9–31, fr. 7. 11–28; *Contra Scholarii* 27. 19–20).

Besides, some of Plethon's arguments and his language are strongly reminiscent of Atticus' polemic. Regarding Aristotle's view of man's final end, Plethon criticizes Aristotle for distancing himself as much as Epicurus, arguing that Aristotle foreshadowed Epicurus' view that pleasure should be man's final goal (*De diff.* 329. 24–32; Atticus fr. 3. 49–53).[38] This misrepresentation of Aristotle, who, as we know, agrees with Plato that pleasure cannot be the supreme Good (*Nicomachean Ethics* 10. 2), occurs only in Atticus, who draws this parallelism between Aristotle and Epicurus in order to underline Aristotle's distance from Plato's thought. In his *Contra Scholarii*, Plethon again takes up this parallelism, which in Atticus also concerned divine providence (fr. 3. 53–96), and now criticizes Aristotle for abandoning divine providence like Epicurus (*Contra Scholarii* 45. 9–10) and thus for inclining to atheism (*Contra Scholarii* 45. 22–4; Atticus fr. 3. 96–100). Plethon also repeats Atticus' argument according to which Aristotle had maintained against Plato that virtues are not sufficient for attaining a good life, but that there also are goods other than virtue which contribute to a good life. Like Atticus, Plethon attributes to Plato the Stoic position according to which virtue is necessary and sufficient for a good life (*De diff.* 329. 19–22, *Contra Scholarii* 34. 19–33). Indeed, quite generally, Plethon had a strong sympathy for the Stoic philosophy and Stoic ethics in particular, presumably because he thought that the Stoics preserve Plato's doctrine in several areas and especially in ethics.[39] Further, Plethon accuses Aristotle of being motivated by a contentious spirit against Plato (*De diff.* 321. 15, 334. 21–4, *Contra Scholarii* 40. 20–7), a criticism which occurs prominently in Atticus (fr. 5. 15–30, 6. 72–3, 7. 37–9, 87–9). Finally, Plethon's use of the comparatively rare word τερέτισμα (*De diff.* 340. 37) to characterize a trivial Aristotelian point is probably inspired by Atticus' use of the word to refer to Aristotle's

---

[38] Trapezountios will make the same argument about Plato. See Monfasani (1976: 158); Garin (1973). Trapezountios is probably inspired by Atticus' argument too, which he now turns against Plato. He not only knew the *Praeparatio* well, but he is the first who translated it into Latin. Interestingly, he left out the anti-Aristotelian section of book 15. See Monfasani (1979: 78–9).

[39] Plethon states that he will follow Plato and the Stoics in his ethics on his *Book of Laws* (prol. 1, ed. Alexandre). Plethon's debt to the Stoics becomes clear in his Περὶ εἱμαρμένης (64–78, ed. Alexandre).

supposedly contemptuous rejection of Plato's Forms (fr. 9. 15–16).[40] All these indications strongly suggest that Plethon probably drew on Atticus' excerpts in the *Praeparatio* and was inspired by his polemical spirit against Aristotle.

Plethon may well have used further sources in his anti-Aristotelian work, and I will suggest another one shortly, but he also produced personal arguments in his criticism of Aristotle. An example is Plethon's argument against Aristotle's conception of virtue as a mean (328. 5–329. 8, cf. *Contra Scholarii* 30. 22–3). Plethon contends that if virtue lies in the mean between two extremes, as Aristotle maintained (*Nicomachean Ethics* 2. 6–7), then a person who wants what he ought to and does not want what he ought not to is virtuous. But by this reasoning, Plethon argues, the totally wicked person also achieves the mean, since he wants what he ought not to and does not want what he ought to. The fallacy of Plethon's argument lies in the fact that at the same time he identifies the good with one extreme and with the mean between the two extremes. But, as Scholarios rightly remarks (*Contra Plethonem* 87. 16–17), Aristotle does not say that all extremes are vices and all means are virtues, but only that where virtue lies, this is the mean. Such a bad argument suggests that Plethon did not always study the relevant parts of Aristotle's texts, but he instead relied on doxographical accounts of Aristotle's doctrines or on polemical accounts like those excerpted by Eusebius in his *Praeparatio evangelica*.

Scholarios' Defence of Aristotle

If we now look at Scholarios, he offers us a different prespective on Plethon's motivation in his criticism of Aristotle, which, as he claims, disconcerted him so much that he decided to write a long response to Plethon's treatise. Scholarios argues that Plethon's polemic is neither of mere scholarly importance nor only about Aristotle, but is about ourselves, that is, about us as Christians.[41] Scholarios is not very explicit in his *Contra Plethonem* as to which is Plethon's goal in the *De differentiis*; he disputes that Plethon's real goal was merely to criticize Aristotle because of a philosophical attraction to Plato's philosophy (*Contra Plethonem* 8. 2–3) and claims that he had detected traces of pagan superstition in Plethon's work (*Contra Plethonem* 114. 19–115. 26). Elsewhere, though, Scholarios clearly expresses his concern about the rise of paganism, saying that he takes issue with Plethon because he is concerned about the Christian faith (Letter to Exarch Joseph, *Opera*, iv. 156. 4–7) and not because he was actually interested in defending Aristotle (ibid.), since both Plato and Aristotle fall short of the truth of Christianity (cf.

---

[40] The term is originally Aristotle's (*An. post.* 83ᵃ33), but also occurs in Philoponus (*De aet. mundi* 31. 7 Rabe) in a section critical of Aristotle; cf. n. 36.

[41] ... ἅμα δὲ καὶ οὐχ ὑπὲρ Ἀριστοτέλους μόνον καὶ ἀληθείας, ἀλλὰ καὶ ἡμῶν αὐτῶν ὁ πόλεμος ἔσται. (*Contra Plethonem* 5. 36–6.1)

Letter to Plethon, *Opera*, iv. 121. 27–35).[42] Indeed, in the margin of his manuscript, Scholarios notes next to the title that his work is also 'against pagans, that is, polytheists' (καὶ κατὰ Ἑλλήνων ἤτοι πολυθέων).[43] Exactly because Scholarios perceives Plethon's attack as a thrust against the Christian identity of the Byzantines, he addresses his work to the Emperor Constantine Palaeologos, thus trying to provoke an official response against him. But why does Scholarios understand Plethon's critical work in this way?

Scholarios seems to suggest that it is one thing to be attracted to Plato's philosophy more than Aristotle's and quite another to criticize Aristotle thoroughly. A Christian could also be attracted to Plato's philosophy because of its proximity to Christian doctrine, but this is no reason for him to deny such proximity in Aristotle's philosophy. Scholarios argues that it is not merely Plato's philosophy which inspired Plethon—in his view, Plethon had a very limited understanding of Plato (*Contra Plethonem* 8. 2 and *passim*)—but rather a specific form of Platonism, namely that of Proclus (Letter to the Princess of Peloponnese, *Opera*, iv. 153. 23–4), who was known for his strongly paganistic religious spirit. Hence Scholarios expresses serious doubts whether Plethon's aim was to present Plato's philosophy as being better than Aristotle's on the grounds that it is closer to Christianity. In Scholarios' view, Plethon's aim was to restore paganism, and his attack on Aristotle was a cunning way of attempting this. If Scholarios is not very explicit about this in his *Contra Plethonem*, this is because, as we have seen, there is nothing in Plethon's work under attack to suggest the threat of paganism. Apparently, Scholarios had at his disposal other evidence of Plethon's paganism and knew of his activities, although he did not write anything against him before Plethon had published his *De differentiis*.[44] But whatever other evidence Scholarios had, one still wonders why an attack on Aristotle's philosophy could be taken as equivalent to an attack on the Christian faith. The fact that Scholarios decided to attack Plethon only after the latter had criticized Aristotle is quite telling of Scholarios' perception of Aristotelian philosophy.

Scholarios explicitly argues that Aristotle came closer to Christian doctrines than any other philosopher (*Contra Plethonem* 4. 34–5), and goes as far as to identify Aristotle with Christian truth (95. 4). If we look elsewhere in Scholarios' work, we find this view again. In the Praise he composed of Aristotle, Scholarios claims that Aristotle was the first philosopher to denounce polytheism in favour of monotheism in a clear and unambiguous way (*Opera*, viii. 507. 2–3). The question which arises now is how Scholarios

---

[42] καὶ ἡμεῖς οὐ Πλάτωνι φιλονεικοῦντες, οὐκ Ἀριστοτέλους πεφροντικότες ἰδίᾳ, τῷ δὲ σκοπῷ τοῦ Γεμιστοῦ χαλεπαίνοντες, ζήλῳ τῆς πίστεως περιττὸν ἄλλως εἱλόμεθα πόνον. (Letter to Exarch Joseph, *Opera*, iv. 156. 6–7)

[43] See the apparatus criticus of the edn. of Petit, Jugie, and Siderides, *Opera*, iv. 1.

[44] Scholarios claims (Letter to the Princess of Peloponnese, *Opera*, iv. 152–3) that Plethon was expelled from Constantinople and sent into exile in Mistra, but it is not certain that this was the reason why Plethon moved. See Woodhouse (1986: 29–30).

came to form such a view about Aristotle's philosophy. To answer this we have to have some picture of Scholarios' personality and philosophical education.

Scholarios had an exceptionally good knowledge of philosophical literature.[45] He was one of the few in his age who was familiar with both the Greek exegetical tradition, and also the Latin philosophical tradition from Augustine and Boethius to the scholastics and, most especially, to Thomas Aquinas.[46] Scholarios finds that in this last phase Latin philosophy had surpassed all previous philosophers who wrote in Latin, and he confesses he wished Thomas Aquinas had not belonged to the Western Church.[47] Scholarios indeed shows an unprecedented enthusiasm for scholastic philosophy and a real dedication to it—he spent many years translating, summarizing, and commenting on Aquinas' works.[48] More importantly, Scholarios, unlike previous Byzantine students of Aquinas, also shows a strong philosophical commitment to scholastic philosophy,[49] and his study of Aristotle is largely guided by Aquinas. He quite openly expresses his admiration for the scholastic achievement in his dedicatory letter to the Emperor Constantine Palaeologos which prefaces his commentary on Aristotle's logical works. There Scholarios states that in his Aristotelian commentaries he adopts the scholastic method of writing a philosophical commentary. He justifies this by saying that he considers this method to be a clear advance over the ancient and the Byzantine method of writing commentaries.[50] Indeed, his commentaries on Aristotle's works show a strong influence by Aquinas, and he often prefers to translate Aquinas' commentaries rather than write new ones.

The way Scholarios talks in this letter is indicative of his awareness that he belongs to a certain philosophical tradition, but also of the fact that this tradition has its limits and has to be complemented by the scholastic tradition. The method which Scholarios refers to is that of the *quaestiones disputatae*, which became fashionable with scholastics and especially with

[45] For an account of Scholarios' career and work see Jugie (1941); Turner (1969); Woodhouse (1986: 115–18); and more fully Zisis (1988).

[46] We do not know who taught Scholarios philosophy and who introduced him to scholastic philosophy. He says that he was largely self-taught (Epistle to Constantine Palaeologos, *Opera*, vii. 2. 31–3 10), and this may well be true (see Zisis 1988: 80 ff.). However this is, Scholarios is clearly an exception as regards his philosophical education at this age.

[47] Marginal note by Scholarios on the summary of Aquinas' *Summa Theologica* Ia, IIae cited by Podskalsky (1974: 305). Cf. his commentary on Aquinas' *De ente et essentia*, *Opera*, vi. 177–8, on how Scholarios regarded on Aquinas' place in the orthodox tradition.

[48] Besides Scholarios translated works of Western theologians, like Peter of Spain's *Summulae logicae*, tr. Scholarios, in *Opera*, viii. 283–339.

[49] The question about the impact of scholastic theology on Scholarios' theological views will not concern me here. On this see Podskalsky (1974: 305–23; 1977: 222–6).

[50] Καὶ πρὸς ταῦτα τὰ ζητήματα προχωροῦμεν τῷ λατινικῷ τρόπῳ, τιθέντες τε τὸ πρόβλημα καὶ ἐπιχειροῦντες εἰς τοὐναντίον ἐν τοῖς πλείστοις. εἶτα διοριζόμενοι τἀληθὲς καὶ λύοντες τὰ ἐπιχειρήματα. ὃ δὴ τῶν ἡμετέρων ἐξηγητῶν οὐδείς πω μέχρι τῆς ἡμέρας τῆσδε, ὅσα γε ἐγὼ οἶδα, τυγχάνει τεθαρρηκώς. (Epistle to Constantine Palaeologos, *Opera*, vii. 5. 22–6). I take the ἡμέτεροι ἐξηγηταί to refer to Greek commentators.

Thomas Aquinas. According to this method, the problem has first to be stated, then comes the thesis, there follows an objection or a series of objections to the thesis, contrary arguments in favour of the thesis, a summary of all arguments, and, finally, numbered answers to the objections mentioned. Scholarios thinks that, by adopting this method, he is doing much better than some ancient commentators, like Alexander of Aphrodisias, for instance (*Contra Plethonem* 77. 25–8).[51] However, at no point does Scholarios dismiss the entire ancient Byzantine exegetical tradition. On the contrary, he considers it an invaluable philosophical body of exegesis[52] to which Thomas Aquinas, as Scholarios argues, was much indebted.[53] His view seems to be that the two traditions are compatible and complementary. In fact, he may not have considered them as two different traditions, in the way we, nowadays, do. His formulation in the Letter to the Emperor Constantine suggests that in his view scholastics benefited much from the heritage of the ancient commentators, but moved further into more subtle discussions of the ancient philosophical issues.

The reason why Scholarios is so much attracted by scholastic philosophy is because he shares its orientation of seeking to elucidate questions regarding the Christian dogma, employing methods such as those outlined above and also employing Aristotle's philosophy. The scholastics indeed considered the Aristotelian world-view to be largely compatible with Christian dogma, and this view was more or less clear in their commentaries of Aristotle's works or in their treatment of dogmatic questions by means of the Aristotelian conceptual apparatus. The spirit which underlies Scholarios' defence of Aristotle's philosophy is the same that we find in scholastic attempts to show Aristotle's views to be congruent with Christian doctrines. In fact, Scholarios invokes the authority of the Western wise men (σοφοί; *Contra Plethonem* 6. 35, 7. 30–5), that is, scholastics, in support of his view that Aristotle, although he sometimes falls short of the Christian truth, as is the case with his view of the eternity of the world and of the movement of the stars (*Contra Plethonem* 20. 26–7, 22. 38–9), he came closer to the truth, that is, to Christianity, than any other philosopher including Plato (4. 32–5). In view of this, we should be sceptical towards Scholarios' claims that he did not not really prefer Aristotle to Plato (*Contra Plethonem* 4. 26–31, cf. Letter to Exarch Joseph, cited above), that both have fallen short of the truth (ibid.), and that he was not actually interested in defending Aristotle; such claims simply indicate that Scholarios was so immersed in the scholastic way of thinking that he could not dissociate Aristotle's philosophy from Christian faith.

[51] See also below, p. 278. cf. Epistle to Constantine Palaeologos, *Opera* vii 2. 8–9.

[52] Scholarios' debt to the scholastic tradition has shadowed his equally great debt to the Greek commentators. Tavardon (1977) stresses Scholarios' debt to Porphyry and Simplicius. On this see also below.

[53] Scholarios sometimes realized that Thomas Aquinas had drawn on ancient commentators. In his translation of Thomas' commentary on the *De anima*, Scholarios notes that Aquinas drew on Philoponus (*Opera*, vi. 327). See Zisis (1988: 346) and below, p. 277–8.

Indeed, Scholarios takes Aristotle to be the measure against whom everybody in philosophy, including Plato, should be judged. One should concede to Plato, Scholarios argues, only where Plato does not diverge either from the truth or from Aristotle (*Contra Plethonem* 113. 5–6). Scholarios accepts that in some cases Plato and Aristotle are in accord, like, for instance, on the question of the immortality of the celestial bodies (*Contra Plethonem* 98. 1–20), but this seems to be the exception rather than the rule. For the most part Plato is to be criticized. Scholarios argues that for the best of his views Plato was indebted to Hebrews and to the intellectual tradition of other nations (*Contra Plethonem* 12. 6–7). But Plato, Scholarios continues, did not stay with these truths, but blended them with poetic absurdities and thus rendered them useless (12. 20–2, 14. 12–13).

Scholarios here reverses a well-known apologetic argument, most clearly articulated by Eusebius in his *Praeparatio evangelica*, which, as we have seen, Plethon probably had used as a source of his anti-Aristotelian arguments. Plato's plagiarism of Hebrew wisdom was a central theme among early Christian apologists (Clement, *Stromateis* 1. 81. 4, Eusebius, *Praep. evan.* 1. 11–38) who argue that the proximity of Plato's thought to Christianity is to be explained in terms of Plato's indebtment to Hebrews. In their view, the Greek poetic elements, disturbing though they are, do not destroy the value of Plato's philosophy (Eusebius, *Praep. evan.* 13. 14. 6).[54] Yet for Scholarios this blend of elements is fatal for the value of Plato's philosophy (*Contra Plethonem* 14. 12–34). Aristotle, on the other hand, Scholarios argues, used only his inquisitive mind to establish the truth of the matter and did not hesitate to depart from his master's views whenever he found them unsatisfactory (*Contra Plethonem* 14. 35–6). Also for Scholarios Plato is not systematic and clear enough, but full of obscurity and ambiguity, while Aristotle, in his view, offers what Plato's philosophy lacks, namely a system or at least clearly articulated philosophical positions (*Contra Plethonem* 15. 32–16. 13).

Plethon is quite right in arguing that Scholarios goes against the early Christian tradition of preferring Plato (*Contra Scholarii* 3. 25–4. 9). For Eusebius and his followers Plato was the first who brought philosophy to perfection by distinguishing the three traditional branches of philosophy (*Praep. evan.* 11. 1), while Scholarios attributes this distinction to Aristotle (*Contra Plethonem* 15. 17–27). For Eusebius, as has been seen, Aristotle's philosophy is to be dismissed as being at odds with the Bible (since it is at odds with Plato), whereas Scholarios claims the opposite. But this does not mean that Scholarios goes against Christian tradition *simpliciter*, as Plethon argues, but rather that he goes against this particular Christian tradition. Clearly Scholarios is aware of this tradition, as he explicitly refers to Cyril of Alexandria and Augustine (Letter to Plethon, *Opera*, iv. 139. 33–4), both of

---

[54] George Trapezountios will elaborate on Scholarios' argument against Plato (*Comparatio* 3. 9). See Hankins (1986: ii. 445).

whom, especially Augustine, sympathized with Plato's philosophy. Even Aquinas himself was quite sympathetic to Plato despite his strong preference for Aristotle. Sometimes he criticized Plato's view, but often maintained that the two philosophers were equally close to Christian doctrine (for example, in their views of God).[55] The conclusion which seems to emerge is that, on the one hand, Scholarios' defence of Aristotle's philosophy reflected his debt to scholasticism, but on the other hand his criticisms of Plato target Plethon's arguments in favour of Plato and seem to go against Plethon's tacit use of sources of anti-Aristotelian argument, such as Eusebius' *Praeparatio*.

Plethon and Scholarios on Aristotle's View about the World's Coming into Being

Plethon starts his criticism of Aristotle by first criticizing Aristotle's God. Why does Plethon begin with this? One reason may be the fact that Plato's *Timaeus* was a well-known dialogue among Christian intellectuals in the Greek East and Latin West alike[56] and the Platonic account of the cosmogony was widely thought to be largely compatible with the biblical account of Genesis. Another reason may be Plethon's view that Aristotle's relevant accounts are so clearly incompatible with the Christian account that they make the best starting-point for his attack, as they can justify his criticism for Aristotle's inclination to atheism (*De diff.* 332. 14-18; *Contra Scholarii* 41. 19-20).

The contrast which Plethon draws between Plato's and Aristotle's God concerns both metaphysics and physics. As far as metaphysics is concerned, Plethon argues that Plato's God, as presented in the *Timaeus*, is the king (βασιλεύς) of the universe and also its creator, which means that God, the demiurge, is ontologically different from all other principles of the world, such as its sensible and intelligible components, namely matter and Forms. Quite significantly, Plethon postulates that Plato's God created not only material entities but also the intelligible substance (*De diff.* 321. 22-3).[57] According to him, the Platonic demiurge did not directly create the sensible world, but he first created the intelligible world of Forms; the sensible world was created through this intelligible substance (δι 'ἐκείνης) and not directly from God (*De diff.* 336. 20-5).

Plethon's view is quite interesting. Unlike many ancient Platonists who denied that matter has its origins in, or indeed any connection with, the

[55] See Weisheipl (1974).

[56] The first part of the *Timaeus* was translated and commented by Chalcidius around AD 350. See Waszink (1962 ix–xvii). According to Klibansky (1950:28), 'the first part of the dialogue was studied and quoted throughout the [Latin] Middle Ages, and there was hardly a medieval library of any standing which had not a copy of Chalcidius' version'.

[57] ... τὸν πάντων βασιλέα θεὸν Πλάτων δημιουργὸν τῆς νοητῆς τε καὶ χωριστῆς πάντῃ οὐσίας, καὶ δι' αὐτῆς τοῦ παντὸς τοῦδε τοὐρανοῦ τίθεται. (*De diff.* 321. 23-4).

intelligible realm, thus postulating a fundamental dualism between sensible and intelligible reality, Plethon maintains that matter originated in the intelligible realm, which also was created. He thus postulates a double creation, that is, first of the intelligible and then of the sensible world. This was a rather isolated view among Platonists in antiquity; it was held by Longinus (third century AD; Proclus, *In Timaeum* 1. 322. 18–26), Plotinus' contemporary and Porphyry's teacher. But this is a view which Christians like Origen, for instance, also took, as they maintained that God first created intellects like angels and souls, and then the visible world.

Plethon claims that Aristotle contradicts this picture in many ways. First, Plethon argues, Aristotle's God, the unmoved mover of *Metaphysics* 12, is not the only divine principle, but is an intellect like the other celestial spheres and like these moves eternally and is not subject to corruption (*De diff.* 322. 21–31). But then the status of Aristotle's God, Plethon argues, is not sufficiently elevated because Aristotle's God is not *essentially* distinct from the other eternal entities (*De diff.* 322. 22–323. 4). Indeed, Aristotle parallels his God with a general who sets order in the army (*Met.* 12. 1075^{a}13–15) and Plethon appears to object that on such a view God's only difference from the other officers is his primacy among them. But this is a superficial reading of *Met.* 12; the unmoved mover is not a sphere and does not move intransitively, while it is quite clear from Aristotle's text that its status is different from the moving spheres, since they depend for their existence on the unmoved mover.

Plethon's understanding of the 'creation' of the world according to Aristotle's *Met.* 12 is equally superficial. He argues that Aristotle's God is not the cause of anything which came into being, but is merely responsible for the movement of the worldly entities, that is, their change (*De diff.* 321. 25–7). The fact that Aristotle never talks of God as 'father' or 'creator', but only as the general in the army suggests to him that Aristotle's first principle accounts only for the *movement* and not for the *existence* of anything. The general, Plethon argues, is merely responsible for the order in the army, but he does not bring the army into being (*Contra Scholarii* 13. 23–30, 15. 28–33); so, according to Plethon, the general does not account for the army's being (οὐσία; *Contra Scholarii* 16. 27–32, *De diff.* 342. 17–24). For Plethon, then, Aristotle's God is merely a moving cause and not the efficient cause of the universe, and as such is to be paralleled with the rower who is the moving cause of a boat, and not with the shipbuilder who is the cause of the boat's unity, that is, of its being (*Contra Scholarii* 14. 26–30). Further support for his argument Plethon finds in the fact that Aristotle rejected Plato's Forms. For a Platonist like Plethon, the Forms are the models which God used to create the sensible entities, so in this sense the Forms play a causal role in the creation. Aristotle denied their existence, in Plethon's view there is nothing to account for the existence of the sensible entities, but only for their change (*De diff.* 339. 31–5). Nevertheless, Plethon does not notice that the existence of the celestial spheres in Aristotle's account is based on motion and change. Indeed, the very essence of sensible substances, among which also the celestial spheres are numbered, is to change, and in this sense their very *existence* depends on God, as it is God who accounts for this change.

The fact that Aristotle postulates an eternal universe confirms, in Plethon's view, that Aristotle's God is the moving and not the efficient cause of the universe; to Plethon its eternity means that Aristotle's universe never came into being by God (*De diff*. 322. 17–19; *Contra Scholarii* 8. 1–6).[58] Aristotle, according to Plethon, identified the temporal and the causal sense of creation, and this was his fatal mistake, because on the one hand he was moved to deny the existence of the efficient cause of the universe altogether, while on the other hand he came to criticize Plato's account in the *Timaeus*, where creation is described in temporal terms (*De diff*. 322. 10–19). Plato, on the other hand, Plethon argues, had distinguished between these two senses, as he talks in the *Phaedrus* of the soul as uncreated, in the sense that it is not created in time, while in the *Timaeus* the soul is presented as being created, in the sense that it has an external cause, namely God (*De diff*. 322. 10–17; *Contra Scholarii* 9. 12–25). Here Plethon may well draw on the work of Philoponus who presents the same argument about two senses of 'creation' in Plato with reference to the *Phaedrus* and the *Timaeus* (*De aet. mundi* 195. 7–8 Rabe). Plethon seems to imply that Plato's temporal implications in the *Timaeus* are not to be taken literally, presumably because, as already ancient Platonists had remarked, talk of the temporal beginning of the universe was simply an expository device, and thus Aristotle's objections against the *Timaeus* miss their target. Like many ancient Platonists, Plethon appears to suggest that Plato's account of creation is to be understood in the sense that the world has an external cause who accounts for its being, namely God.

In his response Scholarios tries to elucidate some crucial Aristotelian concepts and terms which, as he argues, Plethon had seriously misunderstood. He nevertheless accepts the limitations of Aristotle's account. He agrees, for instance, that Aristotle's view about the eternity of the world is at odds with the biblical account, and he as a Christian believes that the world had a temporal beginning (*Contra Plethonem* 20. 29–30, 22. 37–23. 20). Scholarios' refutation of Plethon's thesis involves the following three arguments: (*a*) the eternity of Aristotle's universe does not contradict its causal dependence on God; (*b*) by being a moving cause Aristotle's God also is the efficient cause of the universe; and (*c*) Aristotle's God also is a final cause of the universe.

Scholarios argues that the fact that Aristotle's world is eternal does not mean that it does not have a cause that accounts for its existence (*Contra*

---

[58] ... καὶ πάνυ δῆλός ἐστιν Ἀριστοτέλης οὐ τῆς οὐσίας καὶ τοῦ εἶναι τῷ οὐρανῷ τὸν θεὸν αἴτιον, ἀλλὰ μόνης τῆς κινήσεως δοξάζων. καὶ ἡ αἰτία δὲ τοῦ οὕτω αὐτὸν δοξάσαι ὡς κάλλιστα ἡμῖν ἐξεύρηται. ὑπὸ γὰρ τοῦ ἀΐδιον μὲν τὸν οὐρανὸν νομίσαι, τῶν δ' ἀϊδίων οὐσιῶν ἡ δ' ἡντινοῦν γένεσιν μήτε χρονικὴν μήτε κατ' αἰτίαν ἀξιοῦν εἶναι, οὕτω ἠνάγκασται δοξάσαι. (*Contra Scholarii* 8. 1–6; cf. ibid. 16. 27–32).

Plethonem 11. 11–12). Eternal substances also have a *causa essendi*, namely a cause which accounts for their being. Hence, the world, though eternal, does have a cause of its being. Aristotle does not maintain, Scholarios argues, that eternal substances did not come into being, but that they did not come into being through generation (*Contra Plethonem* 19. 35–7). This also is the case with the world's coming into being. Generative processes involve time. But generation is only one way of coming into being.

Scholarios draws a sharp distinction between generation and production. Something can come into being (γίγνεσθαι) without generation (γενέσθαι), and thus something can be 'created' (γινόμενον) but ungenerated (ἀγέννητον; e.g. *Contra Plethonem* 23. 38–9). The Platonic sense of creation (δημιουργεῖν) implies generation, that is, a process involving time but also pre-existing matter (*Contra Plethonem* 38. 15–16). In the same fashion that craftsmen create their artworks from existing matter, the Platonic demiurge created the world from pre-existing matter which was in a state of disorder (*Contra Plethonem*, 19. 30–2, 29. 27–8, 38. 17). Scholarios argues that Aristotle's sense of the world's coming into being is not that of a generation (δημιουργία), which amounts to the transformation (μεταβολή; 24. 1, μετάπλασις; 38. 28) of a material substratum into something else, but a production (ποιεῖν). The produced entity, the universe, comes into being all at once (οὐκ ἐφεξῆς ἀλλ᾽ ὅλον ἅμα; 19. 26). Scholarios argues that in this sense Aristotle's God is a creator (ποιητής) and not merely a craftsman (δημιουργός 38. 33), since his God brings everything into being and does not only transform a material substratum, and thus Aristotle's sense of creation is much closer to Christian doctrine than Plato's.

The terms which Scholarios uses to describe Aristotle's sense of the world's coming into being are significant as they betray his philosophical sources on the issue. Two of the terms he uses have a strong Platonist background, namely the terms προαγωγή and πρόοδος (*Contra Plethonem*, 38. 20–6). Both terms were used by Platonists in late antiquity to describe the procession of immaterial entities from a higher immaterial principle in the intelligible realm. Scholarios refers explicitly to Platonist interpreters of Aristotle who approve of his picture of an eternal world (*Contra Plethonem* 20. 10–13).[59] Who are the Platonists that Scholarios has in mind? The cited passage is quite suggestive in their regard. According to this, Platonists maintained that Aristotle had followed Plato in believing that the universe was eternal but had a cause to account for its being. Such a position, we know, was held by Porphyry and was elaborated later by Simplicius.[60] Their view was the result

---

[59] ᾽Αλλ᾽ οἱ μετὰ ᾽Αριστοτέλη Πλατωνικοί, τῇ τοῦ παντὸς ἀϊδιότητι θέμενοι, καὶ ᾽Αριστοτέλει ἐπαινοῦντες, ὡς δὴ γενναίως αὐτὴν ἀποδεδειχότα, τοῦτο χαρίζονται Πλάτωνι, ὅτι καὶ αὐτὸς ἀΐδιον εἶναι τὸ πᾶν ἐφρόνει, καὶ γενητὸν οὐ κατὰ χρόνον, ἀλλ᾽ κατ᾽ αἰτίαν ἐνόει. (*Contra Plethonem* 20. 10–13).

[60] Porphyry's view is to be found in the remaining fragment of his commentary on the *Timaeus* (ed. A. R. Sodano, *Porphyrii In Platonis Timaeum Commentarionem Fragmenta*, Naples, 1969). On Simplicius' commentary *In de caelo* see Hoffmann (1987).

of a certain interpretation of the *Timaeus* and also of Aristotle's *Met.* 12 and the *De caelo*, which cannot be expounded here. Yet the aim of both Porphyry and Simplicius was to show that Plato's views in the *Timaeus* are largely in accord with Aristotle's views in the *De caelo*. Scholarios, however, fends off their arguments for such an accord.

Scholarios was also indebted to scholastic sources for his argument in defence of Aristotle's account in *Met.* 12. This is suggested by another term which Scholarios uses to indicate the Aristotelian non-generative coming into being of the universe, namely the term ἔγχυσις (infusion; *Contra Plethonem* 24. 1). The term occurs for the first time in the Greek philosophical vocabulary in this sense.[61] It translates the Latin term 'infusio' which Thomas Aquinas often employed to indicate that something came about spontaneously, that is, without generation.[62] The case *par excellence* was the imparting of God's grace. Another such case was the entering of the soul into the body. Yet I do not find Thomas employing the term in his interpretation of the Aristotelian account of the world's coming into being in *De caelo* or in *Met.* 12. Nevertheless, his interpretation is very close to that of Scholarios; Aquinas takes *creatio* to amount to *emanatio*,[63] and Scholarios uses the term to convey a sense of emanation, or as he puts it, a καθόλου ποιεῖν. Scholarios uses the term *infusio* similarly to Thomas when he refers to the soul's entering into the body (*Contra Plethonem* 78. 39–40), but apparently extends its use to cover the world's coming into being.

Scholarios further argues that Aristotle's moving cause in fact amounts to an efficient cause (*Contra Plethonem* 28. 8–9). He first argues that κινεῖν may also mean ποιεῖν and he gives examples of such a meaning from *Met.* 12 (*Contra Plethonem* 28.10–11). Indeed, when Aristotle speaks of a moving cause (τὸ κινοῦν), he refers to an efficient cause. This becomes quite clear at the end of chapter 4 of *Metaphysics* 12 where Aristotle identifies the art of building as the moving cause of a built house and the art of medicine as the moving cause of a cured patient (1070^{b}27–33). These examples show quite clearly that Aristotle's moving causes account for something coming into being. These moving causes are also final causes in the sense that they move something towards ends which constitute the desirable effects. The form of a parent is the moving cause of the child (1070^{b}31) in the sense that the child is

---

[61] The words ἐγχέω, ἔγχυσις, had only the literal meaning 'pour'/'pouring' in the ancient and medieval Greek texts; see LSJ, Stephanus, *Thesaurus Linguae Graecae*, Lampe, *A Patristic Greek Lexicon*, s.v.

[62] The term is explained as follows in *A Lexicon of St Thomas Aquinas* (Baltimore, 1948): 'infusio': the action of infusing some principle or quality or idea into the mind or the soul, especially the work of God the imparting of grace, virtue; the infusion of the soul into the body. cf. *Summa Theol.* I q. 12 a. 13: *anima... consequens esset quod ex sua creatione vel infusione inquinaretur; et sic Deus esset causa peccati qui est auctor creationis et infusionis*; cf. II.1 q. 83 a. 1.

[63] *creatio: emanationem totius entis a causa universali, quae est Deus; et hanc quidem emanationem designamus nomine creationis*; *Summa Theol.* I q. 45 a. 1.

being formed in such a way so that it will finally achieve the form of the parent.

The unmoved mover, then, Scholarios argues proves to be both the efficient and the final cause of the universe (*Contra Plethonem* 27. 24–5). The *kosmos* by definition amounts to a certain existing order (*kosmein*), and if this order were destroyed, there would be no *kosmos* any longer. If without the first principle there cannot be any *kosmos*, it turns out that the imposition of order amounts to the world's coming into being (*Contra Plethonem* 36. 19–38). This order is for the good of the world, and it is imposed by the first principle which cares for the good of the universe (ibid. 36. 20–37. 5). So Plethon's thesis that Aristotle's God is only a moving cause proves to be shortsighted.

If Scholarios follows Porphyry, Simplicius, and Aquinas in his defence of Aristotle's God, his defence of Aristotle's doctrine of the soul as the actuality of the body is heavily indebted to Philoponus. This is not the place to discuss Scholarios' interesting views on Aristotle' specific doctrine in detail, but I would like to make a few remarks in this regard in order to show that Scholarios is indebted to various Platonist sources, and that he is led in his choice of these by his concern to defend Aristotle. As I noted above, Scholarios observes that Aquinas in his commentary on Aristotle's *De anima* drew on Philoponus. I am not in a position to judge such a matter, but it is quite indicative of Scholarios' philosophical erudition that he is aware of the similarity of their views. At any rate, Scholarios was keen to present Aristotle's view as compatible with the Christian doctrine of the immortality of the soul, and he apparently used both Philoponus and Aquinas.

Aristotle maintained that the soul is a substance which actualizes or perfects the human body, so as to be a body properly speaking, namely alive or animate (ensouled). There are, however, two grades of actualization or perfection (ἐντελέχεια), corresponding to the possession of knowledge and the exercise of it. For Aristotle the soul is the perfection of the body in the first sense, as the body is living even when asleep or otherwise unconscious (*De anima* 412^{a}19–28). The soul as the form of the living body (*De anima* 412^{a}20) allows man to perform the various psychic functions naturally, while the loss of that form, when, for instance, the material element is significantly damaged, amounts to a corruption such that the body is no longer a body properly speaking, but only homonymously, in the same sense in which a table is not a table any more when it is significantly damaged. The only exception from this picture of body-based psychic functions is the intellect (*nous*) which Aristotle, at least on one interpretation, considered as immortal (*De anima* 403^{a}5–8, 430^{a}10–25). When Aristotle discusses whether the soul is separable from the body, he also wonders whether the soul is to be paralleled with the sailor on a ship (*De anima* 413^{a}9–10). This was a passage much discussed by Platonists and Peripatetics in late antiquity who were interested in Aristotle's view on the relation between body and soul.

Scholarios follows Philoponus in arguing that, while the soul as entelechy is inseparable from the body in the same way that the activities of the steersman are inseparable from the ship qua steersman, it is separable as a substance like the steersman is separable from the ship qua man (on Aquinas' commentary on *De anima*, see *Opera*, vi. 405. 2–3).[64] So, the implication is, the soul as a substance is separable from the body but is inseparable as the principle of life of the body. But quite apart from that Philoponus and other Platonists maintained that for Aristotle the intellect is separable from the body and what is inseparable from the body is only the vegetative and the irrational soul (e.g. *In de anima* 10. 7–11. 30). This also is Scholarios' view. The rational part of the soul, Scholarios argues, is not bound to the body as the entelechy of it, but rather is supposed to be immortal and somehow divine (*Contra Plethonem* 79. 15–19, 80. 10–13, 83. 4–6).[65]

We see that Scholarios draws on a source which construes Aristotle's view in such a way that it comes to be in accord with the Christian doctrine of the immortal soul, and rejects others like Alexander of Aphrodisias, for instance (*Contra Plethonem* 77. 25–8), who strongly favoured the complete inseparability of the soul from body. But Philoponus would not agree with Scholarios that Plato's view of the soul is less in accord with the Christian account, as Scholarios goes on to argue, so that he can present Aristotle as being closer to Christian doctrine than Plato (*Contra Plethonem* 80. 18–27).

Conclusion

It is often said that Plethon follows Neoplatonists and uses Neoplatonist language, while Scholarios attaches himself to scholasticism.[66] The picture which emerges from the above suggests, I hope, that things are more complicated. The term 'Neoplatonism' is too vague to explain anyone's philosophical affiliations, as within this late phase of Platonism, to which this term refers, there were many currents and thus there was plenty of room for differentiation. Hence to say that Plethon was indebted to the Neoplatonists does not amount to much. Scholarios is also heavily indebted to them, and, as we have seen, employs their terminology. Both were knowledgeable of Plotinus, for instance, and had an admiration for him.[67] And most probably

---

[64] See Philoponus, *in De anima* 224. 15–37, 246. 25–247. 7. I am here indebted to a chapter of Uwe Lang's unpublished D. Phil. thesis, *Studies in the Christology of John Philoponus* (Oxford, 1999).

[65] Εἰ δὲ τὴν ψυχὴν ἐντελέχειαν ὁριζόμενος σώματος ὀργανικοῦ, τὸν νοῦν μέρος μὲν οὐσιῶδες τίθησι τῆς ψυχῆς εἶναι τὸ κράτιστον καὶ μόνον ἀνώλεθρον, ὄργανον δὲ αὐτοῦ μηδὲν εἶναί φησι... (*Contra Plethonem* 80. 10–13).

[66] e. g. Woodhouse (1986: 19 and *passim*).

[67] Scholarios draws a favourable comparison between Aristotle and Plotinus in ethics (*Opera*, viii. 499–502). For Plethon's knowledge of Plotinus see n. 32.

both had read Porphyry, Philoponus, and Simplicius. Yet their different views on crucial philosophical issues led them to prefer one Platonist source rather than another.[68] Hence, as we have seen, Plethon presumably follows Philoponus and Proclus in his criticism of Aristotle's view on the world's constitution, while Scholarios followed Aquinas, Porphyry, and Simplicius. On the other hand, Scholarios follows Philoponus on how to construe Aristotle's view concerning the nature of the human soul, a view which largely reconciles Platonic and Aristotelian conceptions of the soul. Plethon seems to have followed early Christian Platonists and, often via them, anti-Aristotelian Platonists, while Scholarios refers us to Neoplatonists like Porphyry and Simplicius who were students of Aristotle's work, and clearly is inspired by them.

We also have seen that when it comes to reconstructing Plato's ethical doctrines, Plethon very much relies on Stoicism. Plethon's debt to Stoicism also indicates that the view we have of Plethon as a Platonist who follows Neoplatonist sources is so simplistic as to be inaccurate. Furthermore, Scholarios does not merely follow Aquinas. His hostility to Plato's philosophy is quite unlike Thomas' attitude towards Plato. Aquinas used to think of Plato and Aristotle as being in accord or as holding similar positions on many fundamental issues, while Scholarios suppresses such points of accord. It emerges then that both Plethon and Scholarios made very selective use of the ancient sources to support their arguments about ancient philosophical authorities, and to justify their preferences. Their selective use was dictated by their wish to show their preferred philosopher closer to Christianity. And by making such a selective use of ancient sources, they also took position towards their contemporary scholastic philosophy.

The ongoing Plato–Aristotle debate in the fifteenth century made clear to philosophers with a more scholarly eye that criticizing Aristotle or Plato by means of referring to or exploring select ancient sources was quite unfair and that a closer and thorough look at the ancient sources was necessary, if they were to appreciate what the ancients had thought about the relation between Platonic and Aristotelian philosophy. This is what Bessarion did. He probably realized that there were several varieties of Platonism and Aristotelianism and that the label 'Platonist' or 'Aristotelian' did not amount to much, as there were in antiquity Platonists who considered Aristotle's view on a certain issue to be in accord with Plato, and others who claimed quite the opposite; and the same also was the case with Peripatetics.[69] Hence progressively the

---

[68] Scholarios' remark that Plethon ignores Porphyry and Simplicius and prefers Proclus highlights this selective use of Neoplatonist authors (Letter to the Princess of Peloponnese, *Opera*, iv. 153. 23–6). References to Neoplatonist sources become increasingly more varied, as Byzantines seek arguments in support of their views. See for instance Theodore Gazes, Ἀντιρρητικόν, ed. Mohler, iii. 207–35.

[69] I focus on the discussion among Platonists on Aristotle's philosophy and the various positions they take in my D.Phil. thesis, *Plato and Aristotle in Agreement? The Platonists' Discussion of Aristotle's Philosophy from Antiochus to Porphyry* (Oxford, 2001).

need to write a history of ancient philosophy was felt. This is what Bessarion's friend, Sekoundinos, would do, writing a short treatise in Latin to outline the history of ancient philosophical schools.[70]

With Bessarion a debate which had been going on for many years engaging even the interest of the Byzantine royals[71] basically dies out, and this era reaches its end. But there were considerable consequences and repercussions. First, this debate contributed substantially to the widening of the channels of philosophical communication between the Byzantine and the Western world. It is with this debate that for the first time the philosophical frontier opens up. Philosophers in East and West share the same concerns, read each other's works, which can be in Greek but also in Latin, and engage in debate. Italian humanists, whom Plethon originally addressed in his lectures, show a revived interest in ancient philosophy and Platonism in particular. Marsilio Ficino who revives Platonic philosophy refers explicitly to Plethon.[72] Scholarios also had an impact, perhaps much more lasting than Plethon. As a Churchman he did not hesitate to exercise his authority. For instance, he had little difficulty in persuading the royal authorities that Plethon's *Book of Laws* had to be committed to the flames as heretical.

Scholarios was to become the first patriarch under the Turkish rule. From his earlier days he had done what he could to establish Aristotle as the standard philosophical authority of the Orthodox Church.[73] The anathemas of Italos and Michael of Ephesus in eleventh century were by then remote past. Aristotle would indeed become an authority for the Orthodox Church under the Turkish rule. For centuries Aristotelianism will be part of its official ideology with which the intellectuals of the Greek enlightment will have to fight hard. Scholarios is perhaps to be seen as the first mover towards the establishment of such an ideology in the Orthodox Church, a rigid ideology which would treat with suspicion any attempt to revive Plato.[74]

---

[70] *De origine et sectis philosophorum*. The work, which is still unpublished, addresses the Venetian patrician Fantinus Cuppus and was written between 1453 and 1455. It stops with the Hellenistic schools and says nothing about the variety of views among Platonists and Peripatetics. See Monfasani (1976: 213); Mastrodemetris (1970).

[71] I already mentioned Scholarios' epistle to Constantine Palaeologos. John VIII writes to inquire of Plethon about some of his views expressed in his *De differentiis*: ed. L. Benakis, Πλήθωνος, Πρὸς ἠρωτημένα ἄττα ἀπόκρισις', Φιλοσοφία, 4 (1974), 348–59.

[72] See above, n. 19. For other references to Ficino to Plethon see Kristeller (1979: 150–63; 1985: 288). Kristeller draws our attention to the fact that we ignore the precise links between Plethon and Bessarion with Ficino and his contemporaries. So we do not know to what extent the revival of Italian Platonism was influenced by Plethon and Bessarion. Already before Plethon, humanists like Petrarch and Valla showed their preference for Plato and criticized Aristotle. See Hankins (1986: ii 436–40); Kristeller (1979: 153).

[73] It is quite indicative that in the 15th century the MSS of Aristotle reach the figure of about 450, which is almost twice the number of Plato MSS from the 9th to the 16th centuries inclusive; see Wilson (1996: 384).

[74] On the fortune of Plato's philosophy in the era of Greek enlightment see Angelou (1963).

BIBLIOGRAPHY

A. TEXTS

Bessarion, *In calumniatorem Platonis*, ed. L. Mohler, *Kardinal Bessarion als Theologe, Humanist und Staatsmann*, ii (Paderborn, 1927).

——— Πρὸς τὰ Πλήθωνος πρὸς 'Αριστοτέλη περὶ οὐσίας, ed. L. Mohler, *Kardinal Bessarion als Theologe, Humanist und Staatsmann*, iii (Paderborn, 1942), 149–50.

George Gemistos Plethon, Περὶ ὧν 'Αριστοτέλης πρὸς Πλάτωνα διαφέρεται, ed. B. Lagarde, 'Le *De Differentiis* de Plethon d' après l'autographe de la Marcienne', *Byzantion*, 43 (1973), 312–43.

——— Πρὸς τὰς Σχολαρίου περὶ 'Αριστοτέλους ἀντιλήψεις, ed. E. V. Maltese, *Georgius Gemistus Plethon Contra Scholarii pro Aristotele objectiones* (Leipzig, 1988).

——— Νόμων Συγγραφῆς, ed. C. Alexandre, *Traité des Lois* (Paris, 1858; repr. Amsterdam, 1966), 1–269; Περὶ εἱμαρμένης, 64–78; Ζωροαστρείων τε καὶ Πλατωνικῶν δογμάτων συγκεφαλαίωσις, 262–9.

——— Πλήθωνος Πρὸς ἠρωτημένα ἄττα ἀπόκρισις, ed. L. Benakis, Φιλοσοφία, 4 (1974), 348–59.

——— *Correspondence with Bessarion*, ed. L. Mohler, *Kardinal Bessarion als Theologe, Humanist und Staatsmann*, iii (Paderborn, 1942), 455–69.

George Scholarios Gennadios, *Oeuvres complètes de Gennade Scholarios*, ed. L. Petit, M. Jugie, and X. A. Siderides, i–viii (Paris, 1928–36).

George Trapezountios, *Comparationes philosophorum Aristotelis et Platonis* (Venice, 1523; repr. Frankfurt, 1965).

Matthew Kamariotes, Λόγοι δύο πρὸς Πλήθωνα περὶ εἱμαρμένης, ed. A. S. Reimarus (Leiden, 1721).

Michael Apostoles, Πρὸς τὰς ὑπὲρ 'Αριστοτέλους περὶ οὐσίας κατὰ Πλήθωνος Θεοδώρου τοῦ Γαζῆ ἀντιλήψεις, ed. L. Mohler, *Kardinal Bessarion als Theologe, Humanist und Staatsmann*, iii (Paderborn, 1942), 161–9.

Nikephoros Gregoras, *Florenzo o Intorno alla Sapienza*, ed. P. Leone (Naples, 1975).

Theodore Gazes, Πρὸς Πλήθωνα ὑπὲρ 'Αριστοτέλους, ed. L. Mohler, *Kardinal Bessarion als Theologe, Humanist und Staatsmann*, iii (Paderborn, 1942), 153–8; 'Αντιρρητικόν, 207–35; Περὶ ἑκουσίου καὶ ἀκουσίου, 239–46.

Theodore Metochites, *Miscellanea philosophica et historica*, ed. C. G. Müller and T. Kiessling (Leipzig, 1821).

B. SECONDARY LITERATURE

Angelou, A. (1963), Πλάτωνος Τύχαι (Athens).

Boys-Stones, G. (1997), 'Thyrsus—Bearer of the Academy or Enthusiast for Plato? Plutarch's *De stoicorum repugnantiis*', in J. Mossman (ed.), *Plutarch and his Intellectual World* (London), 41–58.

Diller, A. (1956), 'The Autographs of Georgius Gemistos Plethon', *Scriptorium*, 10: 27–41.

Düring, I. (1957), *Aristotle in the Ancient Biographical Tradition* (Göteborg).

Garin, E. (1973), 'Il Platonismo come ideologia della sovversione Europea: La polemica antiplatonica di Georgio Trapezuntio', in *Studia Humanitatis Ernesto Grassi zum 70 Geburstag* (Munich), 113–20.

Gouillard, J. (1967), 'Le Synodikon de l'Orthodoxie: Édition et commentaire', *Travaux et mémoires*, 2: 1–316.

Hankins, J. (1986), *Plato in the Italian Renaissance* (New York, 1986), i–ii.

——(1996), 'Antiplatonism in the Renaissance and the Middle Ages', *Classica et Medievalia*, 47: 360–77.

Jugie, M. (1941), 'Scholarios Georges', in *Dictionnaire de Théologie Catholique*, xiv. 1521–70.

Hoffmann, P. (1987), 'Simplicius' Polemics', in R. Sorabji (ed.), *Philoponus and the Rejection of the Aristotelian Science* (London), 57–83.

Klibansky, R. (1950), *The Continuity of the Platonic Tradition during the Middle Ages* (London), 22–9.

Kristeller, P. O. (1979), *Renaissance Thought and its Sources* (New York).

——(1985), *Studies in Renaissance Thought and Letters*, ii (Rome).

Lloyd, A. C. (1987), 'The Aristotelianism of Eustratios of Nicaea', in J. Wiesner (ed.), *Aristoteles: Werk und Wirkung II* (Berlin), 341–51.

Mastrodemetris, P. (1970), Νικόλαος Σεκουνδινός. Βίος καὶ ἔργα (Athens).

Mercken, H. P. F. (1990), 'The Greek Commentators on Aristotle's Ethics', in R. Sorabji (ed.), *Aristotle Transformed* (London), 411–19.

Mohler, L. (1942), *Kardinal Bessarion als Theologe, Humanist und Staatsmann*, 3 vols. (Paderborn).

Monfasani, J. (1976), *George of Trebizond* (Leiden and New York), 201–29.

Papadopoulos, S. (1974), 'Thomas in Byzanz: Thomas-Rezeption und Thomas-Kritik in Byzanz zwischen 1345 und 1435', *Theologie und Philosophie*, 49: 274–304.

Podskalsky, G. (1974), 'Die Rezeption der thomistischen Theologie bei Gennadios II. Scholarios (ca. 1403–1472)', *Theologie und Philosophie*, 49: 305–23.

——(1977), *Theologie und Philosophie in Byzanz* (Munich).

Ševčenko, I. (1962), *Études sur la polémique entre Théodore Métochite et Nicéphore Choumnos* (Brussels).

Sorabji, R. (ed.) (1990), *Aristotle Transformed* (London).

Tavardon, R. (1977), 'Le Conflit de Georges Gémiste Pléthon et de Scholarios au sujet de l' expression d'Aristote τὸ ὄν λέγεται πολλαχῶς', *Byzantion*, 47: 268–78.

Turner, C. J. G. (1964), 'Pages from the Late Byzantine Philosophy of History', *Byzantinische Zeitschrift*, 57: 346–73.

——(1969), 'The Career of George-Gennadius Scholarius', *Byzantion*, 39: 420–55.

Waszink, J. H. (1962), *Timaeus a Calcidio translatus commentarique instructus* (London and Leiden).

Weisheipl, J. (1974), 'Thomas' Evaluation of Plato and Aristotle', *New Scholasticism*, 48: 100–24.

Wilson, N. G. (1996), 'The Manuscripts of Greek Classics in the Middle Ages and the Renaissance', *Classica et Medievalia*, 47: 379–89.

Woodhouse, C. M. (1986), *Gemistos Plethon: The Last of Hellenes* (Oxford).

Zisis, T. (1988), Γεννάδιος Β΄ Σχολάριος. Βίος, Συγγράμματα, Διδασκαλία (Thessaloniki).

Epilogue: Current Research in Byzantine Philosophy

LINOS BENAKIS

There is no doubt that certain aspects of Byzantine civilization, for instance Byzantine literature and history, have been studied much more intensively than Byzantine philosophy and the sciences (e.g. mathematics, astronomy, medicine). Yet, during the last few decades, a considerable number of books and articles in this area have begun to appear. My aim here is to present an account of the most recent research in Byzantine philosophy, hoping that it thus might be easier to form a judgement as to the level of knowledge we now have about the subject, but also to see the directions our work should take in the future.

Critical Editions of Texts

In 1984 a new series of critical editions of Byzantine philosophical texts was started, as part of the *Corpus Philosophorum Medii Aevi (CPhMA)*, namely the series *Philosophi Byzantini*. It is published by the Academy of Athens, under the auspices of the International Union of Academies; I am serving as its general editor. Ten volumes already have come out with works by Nicholas of Methone, Nikephoros Blemmydes, George Pachymeres, Barlaam of Calabria, George Gemistos Plethon, and others. Each volume contains the Greek text with a critical apparatus, an introduction, a translation into English or French or German or Modern Greek, and indices. I. N. Polemis has recently edited the unpublished work of Theophanes of Nicaea, Ἀπόδειξις ὅτι ἐδύνατο ἐξ ἀϊδίου γεγενῆσθαι τὰ ὄντα καὶ ἀνατροπὴ ταύτης. Further volumes are in preparation. For example, P. Carelos is

An earlier version of this survey has been published in German: L. Benakis, 'Griechische Philosophie im Mittelalter: Stand der Forschung', *Cahiers de l'Institut du Moyen-Age Grec et Latin*, 66 (1996), 51–65.

preparing the critical edition of the well-known work of Nikephoros Blemmydes 'Ἐπιτομὴ λογικῆς, P.-M. Palaiologou the unpublished work of Theodore II Laskaris, Περὶ φυσικῆς κοινωνίας, B. Tambrun-Krasker Plethon's Νόμοι, and I am editing the unpublished treatise of Theodore of Smyrna, Περὶ φύσεως καὶ τῶν φυσικῶν ἀρχῶν ὅσα τοῖς παλαιοῖς διείληπται. Moreover, V. Tiftixoglou is preparing a critical edition of an unpublished work by Bessarion on Plato's *Laws*, a work which was prompted by this Byzantine scholar's desire to amend the Latin translation of the dialogue by George Trapezountios; this volume, as well as the commentary of George Pachymeres on Plato's *Parmenides*, I hope, will make us reconsider the established view that there are no Byzantine commentaries on Plato's works.

Furthermore, in 1994 the first volume of a parallel series, called *Commentaria in Aristotelem Byzantina*, came out. The series mainly includes Byzantine commentaries on Aristotle's works; the first volume is an edition of Arethas' scholia on Aristotle's *Categories* and on Porphyry's *Isagoge*. One of the forthcoming volumes in the series, prepared by E. Pappa, is devoted to George Pachymeres' scholia on Aristotle's *Metaphysics*. I am editing the extensive unpublished comments of Michael Psellos on Aristotle's *Physics*.

In the 1970s Byzantinists in Naples, on the initiative of A. Garzya and with the support of U. Criscuolo, published some volumes with critical editions of works by Michael Psellos, the anonymous *Timarion*, and Nikephoros Gregoras' *Florentios*.

During the same period (1976–82), part of the Greek translation by Demetrios Kydones of Aquinas' *Summa Theologica* appeared in four volumes in the series *Corpus Philosophorum Graecorum Recentiorum*, under the editorship of E. Moutsopoulos.

Finally, it is important to mention the critical editions published by the *Biblioteca Teubneriana*, which include the philosophical works by Photios, Arethas, and Michael Psellos.

Bibliographies

At the end of the modern Greek translation (1977) of B. N. Tatakis' *La Philosophie byzantine* (Paris, 1949), I added a thirty-page bibliography of the major books and articles which were published during the years 1949–76 on Byzantine philosophy, including those on the Church Fathers. This bibliography lists more than 500 titles; it follows a chronological and systematical rather than an alphabetical order.

In 1991, at the 18th International Congress of Byzantine Studies in Moscow, the Greek Committee of Byzantine Studies presented the volume *Bibliographie internationale sur la philosophie Byzantine*, which covers in its 378 pages a list of books and articles published in the period 1949–90 on

Byzantine history, art and archaeology, law, and Byzantine philosophy. In the philosophy section, more than 400 titles from the period 1977–90 were added to the previous bibliography of the years 1949–76.

We hope that we soon will be able to complete a bibliography covering the years 1991–2000, which will also appear in electronic form.

Other bibliographies which also are helpful to students of Byzantine philosophy are those to be found in the journal *Byzantinische Zeitschrift* and those prepared by the Center for Byzantine Studies at Dumbarton Oaks, Washington, DC.

General Surveys

B. N. Tatakis' *La Philosophie byzantine* (Paris, 1949) was the first general introduction to Byzantine philosophy to appear; it came out as part of E. Bréhier's voluminous *Histoire de la philosophie*. Although a lot of work has been done on the subject since then, I believe that we are not yet ready to replace Tatakis' work with a new, more comprehensive history of Byzantine philosophy. But the publication of Tatakis' introduction raised, right from the start, two of the most discussed issues in connection with Byzantine philosophy. (i) Did philosophy, in the strict sense of the word, exist in Byzantium, or was it simply, with very few exceptions, a handmaiden of theology? (ii) When does Byzantine philosophy actually start? In his introduction Tatakis presented Byzantine philosophy as an autonomous discipline, independent of theology, and he was not interested in providing a treatment of the philosophy of the early Byzantine period. However, he did discuss the influence of the Church Fathers on Byzantine thought in a later work of his, namely the long chapter which he wrote on Byzantine philosophy for the *Encyclopédie de la Pléiade*, 'La Philosophie grecque patristique et byzantine' (*Histoire de la Philosophie*, i (Paris, 1969), 936–1005).

G. Podskalsky's book *Theologie und Philosophie in Byzanz: Der Streit um die theologische Methodik in der spatbyzantinischen Geistesgeschichte (14/15. Jh.)* (Munich, 1977), focused mainly on the specific topic of the conflict over theological method in Byzantium during the fourteenth and fifteenth centuries; but its findings are of more general interest, especially in connection with the issue of the relationship between Byzantine philosophy and theology. For Podskalsky claims here that, precisely because theology in the East never became a science with its own epistemology and methods, the borders between theology and philosophy were clearly defined, and philosophy always preserved its autonomy.

H. Hunger's chapter on Byzantine philosophy in the first volume of his handbook *Die hochsprachliche profane Literatur der Byzantiner* (Munich, 1978), 3–62, contains a helpful summary of a great number of Byzantine philosophical writings, without discussing the general issues in detail.

K. Oehler, on the other hand, shows both in his collection of articles *Antike Philosophie und byzantinisches Mittelalter* (Munich, 1969), and in his article 'Die byzantinische Philosophie', in *Contemporary Philosophy: A New Survey*, vi/2. *Philosophy and Science in the Middle Ages* (Dordrecht, 1990), 639–49, that philosophical thinking in Byzantium arrived at original solutions to real philosophical problems, even though it was always developed in close association with theology. The concluding remarks of his article are of particular interest:

Today we know that only through a precise analysis of the development of thought in its procession from Plato to Aristotle and thence to mid- and neo-Platonism and later in Byzantine philosophy, shall we obtain a full picture of the course of Greek philosophy in antiquity and the Middle Ages. We are still a long way from possessing this picture, although we now see this continuity much more clearly than before, and often acquire new sources for an understanding and interpretation of earlier philosophical notions in more recent ones. But it seems that the question remains: To what extent may we consider ancient and medieval Greek philosophy as a coherent whole? We shall get closer to the solution of this problem through contemporary historical and philosophical methods and through sound knowledge and comprehension of the philosophical and theological systems of these two periods.

In his critical appraisal of the publications on Byzantine philosophy from 1968 to 1985 ('Kritischer Forschungs- und Literaturbericht 1968–1985', *Historische Zeitschrift*, 14 (1986)), G. Weiss claims that Tatakis' book deals only partially with the issues, while he observes that Oehler exaggerates when he sees Byzantine philosophy as the direct, living continuation of ancient philosophy. At the same time, though, he agrees that a one-sided consideration of the Greek Middle Ages from a Latin or Western point of view should be avoided.

It is also telling how J. Beckmann's short chapter on Byzantine philosophy (in *Geschichte der Philosophie*, ed. K. Vorlander, ii (1990)) ends:

Our knowledge of Byzantine philosophy, of course, is still limited, chiefly because of the difficulties involved in securing the texts and because some critical editions are unobtainable. Nonetheless, most recent research has shown that the importance of philosophy in Byzantium is not limited to the preservation and the teaching of ancient Greek philosophical thought or to the cultivation and exaltation of mystical theology. No less important is the achievement of Byzantine thought in the field of logic and the metaphysical treatment of philosophical problems.

My own view on the subject was presented in the article 'Die theoretische und praktische Autonomie der Philosophie als Fachdisziplin in Byzanz' (in M. Asztalos *et al.* (eds.), *Knowledge and the Sciences in Medieval Philosophy*, Proceedings of the Eighth International Congress of Medieval Philosophy (SIEPM), i (Helsinki, 1990), 223–6). I argued there that we can better appreciate the complexity of Byzantine philosophy, if we keep in mind that philosophical theorizing in Byzantium was historically the medieval phase of

Greek philosophy, and was distinguished on the one hand by the final phase of ancient philosophy and on the other by the theology of the Church Fathers. I also tried to show that, in contrast with the West where philosophy is the *ancilla theologiae*, and despite the influence of the Patristic tradition on Byzantine thinkers, there is no instance in which we sense that philosophy in Byzantium was the handmaiden of theology.

Therefore I think that it is much clearer nowadays than it was in Tatakis' time, what the term 'Byzantine philosophy' refers to. 'Byzantine philosophy' refers to the autonomous philosophical activity of the Byzantines in the teaching of philosophy and the writing of commentaries on ancient philosophical texts (chiefly concerning logic and physics), as much as in their treatises on more general subjects, for instance on Nature and on Man, which aimed at rebutting ancient doctrines and at advancing new arguments in the light of the new Weltanschauung. For that reason, recent books and articles like the following are very useful in understanding the milieu in which Byzantine philosophy developed: H.-V. Beyer, 'Zum Begriff des Humanismus und zur Frage nach dessen Anwendbarkeit auf Byzanz und andere vergleichbare Kulturen', Βυζαντινά, 15 (1989); S. Vryonis, 'Introductory Remarks on Intellectuals and Humanism', *Skepsis*, 2 (1991); A. Kazhdan and G. Constable, *People and Power in Byzantium: An Introduction to Modern Byzantine Studies* (Washington, DC, 1982).

As to the chronology of Byzantine philosophy, it is my opinion that it extends from the ninth century to the fall of Byzantium in the middle of the fifteenth century, that is, from Photios and Arethas up to Plethon and the other learned thinkers of the Palaeologan period (1261–1453). In other words, I do not think that we can speak of Byzantine philosophy before the ninth century at the earliest; for at that earlier time the philosophy was the philosophy of the Church Fathers who belonged to the eastern provinces of the Roman Empire. Yet, there is no doubt that it is extremely useful to study Byzantine philosophy in close association with the intellectual, theological, philosophical, and scientific thinking of the earlier centuries.

However, K. Niarchos' introduction to Byzantine philosophy takes a quite different approach to Byzantine philosophy, which becomes clear even from its title *Η Ελληνική Φιλοσοφία κατά την Βυζαντινήν της Περίοδον*. For Niarchos treats philosophical activity in Byzantium mainly as a continuation of earlier periods of Greek philosophy, without acknowledging its particular character, namely its Christian character. I think that it is important to stress the continuity between antiquity and Byzantine thought, but I do not believe that Byzantine philosophy is a mere continuation of ancient philosophy; for Byzantine philosophy is the philosophy of a period in which the social, political, cultural, spiritual, and intelllectual circumstances were utterly different from those in antiquity. N. Matsoukas' recent book on Byzantine philosophy (*Ιστορία της Βυζαντινής Φιλοσοφίας*, Thessaloniki, 1994) avoids this problem by discussing the first five centuries of the Christian era as well as the period from the sixth to the ninth centuries in a chapter under the general title 'Landmarks of Byzantine Thought'.

The most recent introductions to Byzantine philosophy can be found: (i) in the second edition of *La philosophie medievale* (Paris, 1995), in which A. de Libera wrote the chapter 'La Philosophie à Byzance'; (ii) in the volume *Philosophie Grecque*, ed. M. Canto-Sperber (Paris, 1997), in which L. Brisson has written two pieces on Byzantine thought, 'L'Aristotelisme dans le monde byzantin' and 'Le Monde byzantin et la philosophie grecque'; and (iii) in L. Couloubaritsis' learned volume *Histoire de la philosophie ancienne et medievale* (Paris, 1998), in which we have for the first time a parallel assessment of the philosophical development during the Middle Ages both in the East and in the West.

Entries in Dictionaries and Encyclopedias

It is quite telling that there have recently been a lot of dictionaries and encyclopedias which also have included a lemma on Byzantine philosophy. For instance, H. Hunger wrote an entry for the *Lexikon des Mittelalters*, vi (Munich, 1993), cc. 2092–100), D. O'Meara for the *Oxford Dictionary of Byzantium*, iii (Oxford, 1991), 1658–61, and I wrote one for the *Routledge Encyclopedia of Philosophy*, ii (London, 1998), 160–5.

Journals

I should not fail to mention the two new journals which include articles on Byzantine philosophy: *Medieval Philosophy and Theology*, ed. N. Kretzmann and S. MacDonald, published biannually by Cambridge University Press; *Bochumer Philosophisches Jahrbuch fur Antike und Mittelalter*, ed. B. Mojsisch, O. Pluta, and R. Rehn.

Of course, more research needs to be done in connection with the philosophical writings of Byzantine thinkers as well as in related areas, like for instance the organization of the higher education in Byzantium, the status of teachers of philosophy, the role of political and ecclesiastical authority, the language used in philosophical texts, the Byzantines' knowledge of Western scholasticism, and the relationship with the religions and cultures of the East. However, judging from the work which has been produced during the last decades, but also from the great number of modern scholars who are now interested in studying this neglected area, I am optimistic that Byzantine philosophy will in the future receive the attention which it rightly deserves.

INDEX LOCORUM

INDEX OF NAMES

I. ANCIENT AND MEDIEVAL

Academics 36–7, 186–7, 193, 195
Adam Balsham 19
Adam of Marsh 68
Aenesidemus 191, 193, 196, 199
Aeschines 194 n.
Aetius 40, 193 n.
Agapetus 55
Agathias 192 n.
Alberic of Paris 19
Albinus (Alcinous) 38 n.
Alexander of Aphrodisias 23 n., 36 n., 37 n.,
    64, 104 n., 106 n., 107 n., 112 n., 115 n.,
    116 n., 120 n., 121 n., 122 n., 128 n., 130 n.,
    131 n., 132 n., 136 n., 157, 164, 179, 198, 270,
    278
Ambrose 17, 68
Ammonius 33, 55, 106 n., 107 n., 108, 112 n.,
    115 n., 116 n., 119 n., 120 n., 121 n., 128 n.,
    154, 160–5, 166 n., 167 n., 168–70, 172 n.,
    173–7, 179, 191–2, 195
Anaxagoras 186, 205 n., 206 n.
Andronikos Kallistos 6, 254, 255 n., 262 n.
Anselm 68
Apollonius Dyscolus 18, 170
Apuleius 101 n., 102 n., 104, 106, 107 n.,
    114 n., 128 n.
Arcesilaus 193 n., 194, 195 n.
Archilochus 193 n.
Archimedes 98 n.
Arethas 3–5, 12, 144–5, 153, 157–8, 237,
    238 n., 284, 287
Aristo of Alexandria 104
Aristo of Chius 193 n.
Aristocles 186 n., 191–2, 195
Aristotelians 10, 255
Aristotle 2–4, 9–13, 18–19, 22–5, 31, 33–4,
    39 n., 45, 51–2, 60, 64–7, 70–1, 79, 88, 93–4,
    98 n., 99–100, 101 n., 102 n., 104 n., 105–6,
    107 n., 108, 112–14, 115 n., 125–32, 136, 144,
    147, 150, 153–4, 157–79, 186 n., 193 n.,
    194 n., 195, 197, 202 n., 206 n., 207, 219–35,
    253–80, 284
Aristoxenus 260 n.
Arius Didymus 35 n.
Asclepius 195 n.
Aspasius 157
Atticus 260 n., 265–7
Augustine 18, 26–7, 68, 70–1, 77, 87, 116 n.,
    194 n., 200, 203, 208, 269, 271–2

Averroes 26, 249
Avicenna 26

Barlaam of Calabria 6, 9, 12, 26, 190, 202 n.,
    204, 220–1, 224–35, 283
Basil the Great 5, 9, 11, 32, 40–7, 141
Bernard of Clairvaux 19
Bessarion 4, 6, 24–5, 200 n., 254–5, 261 n.,
    262 n., 279–80, 284
Boethius 17–18, 23, 25–6, 59, 102 n., 106 n.,
    107 n., 112 n., 114 n., 115 n., 116 n., 118 n.,
    121 n., 122 n., 123 n., 269
Burgundio of Pisa 67–8, 87

Carneades 17, 37, 46
Cassiodorus 115 n., 116 n., 118 n.
Cato the Elder 15
Cerbanus 67
Chalcidius 272 n.
Chrysippus 20, 34–6, 39 n., 197, 203 n., 223
Cicero 16–17, 51, 60, 114 n., 115 n., 116 n.,
    118, 186 n., 187, 194
Clement of Alexandria 2, 9, 99 n., 100 n., 192,
    197, 203 n., 205–6, 264, 271
Constantine the Philosopher 145
Constantine Porphyrogennetos 142
Cosmas of Jerusalem 197
Cosmas the Melode 146, 197 n.
Cratylus 192, 198 n.
Critolaus 17
Cynics 192
Cyril of Alexandria 263, 271

Damascius 41 n., 58, 198, 200 n., 237
David 140–2, 178 n., 191 n., 192, 195
Demetrios Kabasilas 205
Demetrios Kydones 6, 27, 227, 249, 257, 284
Democritus 193 n.
Democritus (the Platonist) 41 n.
Dexippus 46 n.
Dicaearchus 194 n.
Dio of Prusa 57 n.
Diogenes of Babylon 17, 34, 38 n.
Diogenes Laertius 34 n., 184 n., 191, 192 n.,
    193, 195–6, 202 n., 260 n.
Dionysius Thrax 38, 40, 42, 169–70
Diotogenes 55 n.
Donatus 26
Duns Scotus 69–70

Elias 52 n., 99 n., 178 n., 191 n., 192